Hamish Henderson: A Biography

Volume I: *The Making of the Poet*

This book is volume 1 of a two-volume biography,
which will later be published in a single
paperback volume entitled

POETRY BECOMES PEOPLE
A Biography of Hamish Henderson

Hamish with partisan comrades celebrating the fifth anniversary of the
end of the Second World War in Dongo, Italy, May 1950

HAMISH HENDERSON

—— A BIOGRAPHY ——

Volume 1: *The Making of the Poet*

TIMOTHY NEAT

Polygon

First published in Great Britain in 2007 by
Polygon, an imprint of Birlinn Ltd

West Newington House
10 Newington Road
Edinburgh
EH9 1QS

www.birlinn.co.uk

ISBN 10: 1 904598 47 1

ISBN 13: 978 1 904598 47 3

British Library Cataloguing-in-Publication Data
A catalogue record for this book is available on request from the British Library

Typeset by Hewer Text, Edinburgh
Printed and bound in Britain by Athenaeum Press, Gateshead

To Katzel Henderson,

Martyn Bennett
(the music maker),

Howard Jones
(my English teacher)

and

Harry Patch
(veteran of the battle of the Somme who, at the age of 109,
continues to speak out
against the villainy of war
and the medieval madness of
our latest war on 'Terror')

Contents

List of Illustrations

All photographs are from the Henderson family archives unless otherwise stated.

Preface

Be the depth that awaits the hour   HH 1950

'Hamish's phrase "Poetry becomes People" captures the essence of his beliefs and his life's work. Hamish not only created poetry but nurtured poetry, in Scotland and abroad: in doing that he set in train a cultural force that has transformed Scotland and engendered new political realities . . . ' These words were spoken in the first of the eulogies in honour of Hamish Henderson at his funeral in St Mary's Episcopal Cathedral, Edinburgh, on 15 March 2002. That funeral marked 'the end of an auld sang' but as fifteen hundred people rose to sing Hamish's international anthem 'The Freedom – Come a' Ye', and see his coffin borne out into the afternoon sun, feelings of completion were accompanied by a strange sense of expectation. This was a man who was much more than a poet and a singer: Hamish nurtured human lives and set in train many of the cultural and political forces that have transformed modern Scotland. He was 'a lad o' pairts' but perhaps above all a teacher – a man of Franciscan simplicity, Socratic wisdom and Druidic authority:

> Under the earth I go
> On the oak-leaf I stand
> I ride on the filly that never was foaled
> And I carry the dead in my hand
>
> There's method in my magic[1]

I first met Hamish at five to midnight on Monday 2 May 1967. We had both travelled to North Cornwall to document the Mayday 'Obby 'Oss festival in the fishing village of Padstow. I was a final year student making

---

1. 'Under the Earth I Go', Hamish Henderson, *Collected Poems and Songs* (Curly Snake 2000).

a film. He was a distinguished folklorist doing anthropological research. Having packed my camera and equipment away, I went down to the small bar of the Ship Hotel for a drink. As I ordered, I noticed a man seated alone at a table. He gestured that I should sit with him. We talked for two hours, and long before one of the great days of my life drew to a close I knew I had met a man of genius. Next morning I was up early, to get out on the road, but Hamish was there before me – eating his breakfast – with 'my' place reserved opposite him. Over the following thirty-five years Hamish and I were to collaborate on many projects, films, books, cultural and political campaigns, and we remained close friends until the day of his death.

At the time, Hamish was forty-eight, a tall, slightly dishevelled, shambling man who emanated energy and clarity of vision. He was married, had two young daughters and was employed as a folklorist at the University of Edinburgh, but he had already lived many 'lives' – as a soldier, Intelligence Officer and Partisan commander; he was a republican socialist, a Scottish nationalist, one of the founders of the European Peace Movement, a leading figure in the campaign for nuclear disarmament, a seminal figure in the Scottish literary renaissance, a multilingual polymath and veteran anti-apartheid campaigner. He had something of the Pied Piper about him, something of the Ancient Mariner, but his look was forward – towards a future lighted with possibilities. His self-evident love of Scotland and life's pleasures were 'ideas' that Everyman could share.

Hamish had much more than charisma: he left an indelible 'impress' upon almost everyone who met him. In Sicily, when Hamish was twenty-three, Major-General Tam Wimberley described him as 'already a legend within the 51st Highland Division'. In 1949, the English poet David Gascoyne commended Hamish's *Elegies for the Dead in Cyrenaica* in similarly exulted terms: 'it occurs to me that you may not care for the epithet "aristocratic" as applied to the spirit of your poetry; but of course I don't mean anything ruling class by the word, only the sense in which the Carpenter's Son was aristocratic.' Later with down-to-earth humour the Irish folk singer Dominic Behan described Hamish as 'A certain Giant of Celtic Culture', whilst the American musicologist Bud Bronson, writing to thank Hamish for years of 'invaluable advice', could scarcely contain his enthusiasm:

My cup runneth over – and it was your divining-rod, Hamish, that beyond all others in these latter days, found the springs of native song and brought them again to the surface for the refreshment of our generation and generations to come . . . You touched the rock and living waters gushed forth. Posterity's debt to you is incalculable and will not be forgotten . . .

In 1979 Amleto Micozzi informed BBC Scotland that 'in Rome, Hamish has a salvivic power'. In 1988 John Berger described him as perhaps the last of the great communist thinkers: 'Hamish, Gramsci, Marx – I see these three as champions of a crucial and continuing strand in modern European thought'. Certainly Hamish rarely shied from controversy and, when his 'contra-dictory character' was decried, he proudly took the insults offered – as compliments. He delighted in conviviality but retreated from 'society'; he was a man of commanding natural authority but refused every trapping of power; a humanist Christian who despised Christianity's institutional brutalities; a communist purist with Rabelaisian appetites; a Scots patriot who tore into 'Scotchness' with withering savagery; a revolutionary Jacobin who embraced Jacobite tradition; a 'scientific rationalist' who personified the heroic values of old Highland society; a decorated British Army officer, who worked to break England's Unionist hegemony; an outstanding orator who wandered Scotland like a tinker, addressing the poor 'whom the age put aside'. Despite his huge gifts as an art-poet, he spent the best years of his life encouraging others to be 'makars' and his nation to 'sing again'. He had enemies but few denied his talents – or the 'drama' that followed him wherever he went. Thus, the question arises: why has the general public heard so little of this man? Why did Hamish not write an autobiography? Why did he discourage the various biographers who made offers?

Hamish knew he had a life-story well worth the telling. He started a personal archive at the age of eight! By the time he retired from the School of Scottish Studies in 1987 this had become a treasure-house of 'every-thing concerning people', and included a huge correspondence with a worldwide network of friends and colleagues on a vast range of subjects. He also knew that a great deal of 'disinformation' about his life and work had been circulated and that a 'biographical account' was the obvious means of setting the crooked road straight. During the 1980s he did write a series of semi-autobiographical essays for the Scottish literary magazine *Cencrastus*, and in the nineties collaborated with Alec Finlay on the publication of two books, *Alias MacAlias* (a selection of essays) and *The Armstrong Nose* (a collection of letters). But, with regard to his life as a whole, Hamish consciously and deliberately remained silent. The reasons for this silence were both personal and ideological – and they made the writing of this biography a doubly challenging responsibility.[2]

---

2. One clue to the nature of Hamish's 'autobiographical thinking' appears in the introduction to his translation of *The Prison Letters of Antonio Gramsci* (Zwan, 1988), where he quotes Gramsci's friend Piero Gobbi (murdered in Paris at the age of 24): 'More than a tactician and a fighter, Gramsci is a prophet. The only way it is possible to be one nowadays is to be unheard of – except by fate . . .'

Hamish lived life on a Byronic scale: like Shelley, he believed that 'the poet' can shape the world; that national poets have 'prophetic powers'. One of the Gaelic words for 'poet' is *filidh* (from the verb 'to see'), and, as a child brought up in the Perthshire Highlands, Hamish always understood poets and 'seers' to be one and the same – artists who could foresee and direct the future, singers who kept secrets and promoted tribal wellbeing. As a teenager, Hamish thrilled to the creativity surging within him and, entirely naturally, embraced his 'bardic responsibilities' not as onerous labour but as the very stuff of his life. He knew that much of the world's greatest poetry had run in harness with the making of nations, and he was determined to dedicate his life to the service of the Scottish people.

Hamish recognised culture as a Darwinian force in society, and 'folk wisdom' as the bedrock of even the greatest individual achievements. He also knew that all truly original ideas take longer than a single lifetime to find acceptance and become integrated human and political realities. Thus he embraced the idea of the folk-continuum and looked for heroes who embodied modern, proletarian values. One such hero was Antonio Gramsci (the Sardinian communist philosopher, who had died in 1936, after ten years incarceration in Italian prisons) and, between 1949 and 1951, Hamish dedicated himself to translating *The Prison Letters of Antonio Gramsci*. His sense of identification with his subject is palpable: 'It is necessary with bold spirit and good conscience to save civilisation. We must halt the dissolution that corrodes and corrupts the roots of human society, the bare and barren tree can be made green again. Are we not ready?'[3] In 1950, while still immersed in his Gramsci studies, Hamish outlined the framework within which he would advance his Scottish Folk Revival, as the catalyst of national renewal in Scotland:

> . . . Lie alongside me, put your ear to the ground and listen: the
>   earth rocks
> with fruitful adventures
> and listen: the sap rises – sweet springs of song
> like hymns of belief to the buds that will blossom.
>
> The hard way is the only way
> The worst enemy is *acedia*
> The greatest mental weakness the failure to tackle it at the root:
> Stick to your guns:
> If you win your children will justify you.
> If you don't it's just too bad.[4]

---

3. HH translation of Gramsci statement of 1919 (Henderson archive).
4. HH, unpublished poem/jottings (Henderson archive).

'Wholeness' was crucial to Hamish: wholeness in life, wholeness in art, wholeness in his 'divided Scotland', and he believed that it was 'poetry' alone that could encompass this whole. In 1952 the publisher John Lehmann asked Hamish to explain a new sequence of poems he was planning and Hamish sent back a long statement that begins with a quotation from the German poet Heine:

'Freedom, which has hitherto only become man here or there, must pass into the mass itself, into the lower strata of society, and become people.' It seemed to me when I first read those words, that what Heine said of Freedom also applies to Poetry. Poetry becomes everyone and should *be* everyone. But in fact – at any rate in the Western World – it only becomes individuals here and there. Our most important task is *still* to make poetry 'become people' . . .

Hamish was constitutionally unable to separate his art, life and politics, and he knew that if he was to achieve what he was determined to achieve, he must 'go underground' – like Wallace and Joan of Arc, like Burns and Blake – and work with and through the common people. He had long foreseen that the historical 'apostasy of the Scottish elite' made new forms of cultural and political activism absolute necessities. Thus he made 'poetry' his chief tool of change: he would invert received opinion, exult 'the humble lowly', espouse and disseminate new values, much as the Chinese sage Lao-tse had done two thousands years earlier:

How did the great rivers and
Seas gain dominion over the
Hundred lesser streams?
By being lower than they.

Like Yeats, Hamish had no fear of 'the foul rag-and-bone shop of the heart'. He knew that personal honesty, beyond shame or the law, was a prerequisite not just for good poetry but for effective participation in any kind of revolutionary politics – because personal dishonesty preconditions both artists and political leaders to compromise and failure. Such honesty is meat and drink to a biographer.

Hamish had a sublime self-confidence. For him the possibilities of political and cultural defeat did not exist, at least while Scotland stands and mankind survives. As Hugh MacDiarmid recognised, Hamish was a force of nature, a man who somehow 'embodied' the Scots nation. He championed 'the lived moment', which he defined as 'thrusting a rock in the craw / of devouring time'; he glorified in the oral tradition but also ruthlessly set down his inner thoughts, feelings and ambitions in private jottings, poems, songs, letters, aphorisms, anecdotes, essays, lecture notes. The Henderson archive is an enormous, un-catalogued collection of fascinating, largely unpublished material. Quotations from this magnificent compost heap of an archive feature prominently in this book and give it what I hope is an autobiographical vividness. As an artist, Hamish knew the power of the surprising. Lifelong he took pleasure in his ability to shock the complacent but, more importantly, with Druidic cunning he delighted in revealing more by always concealing something. Like any good teacher, Hamish Henderson liked to leave a student, an audience, an opponent, a drinking partner, a biographer, the reader, with something to do, with ideas to develop; the future to make.

Acknowledgements

This biography is the product of a friendship and professional collaboration that began in 1967 when I was a student and ended with Hamish's death on 8 March 2002, thirty-five years later. Its content, however, is hugely dependent on information in the Henderson family archives and I would like to extend unqualified thanks to Hamish's wife, Felicity Henderson (Katzel), for the open access she gave me to this material. I also thank her for the friendship and great generosity she has shown towards me and this project – not just over the last five years but since our first meetings in 1973. My deep thanks also go to Tina and Janet Henderson, Hamish's daughters: I hope they find my efforts worthy of their father's great contribution to the national life of Scotland and the wellbeing of mankind.

The Henderson archive is large but remains an uncatalogued jumble. Because the general public is now largely unfamiliar with Hamish's literary work and ideas I have quoted extensively from this archive in an attempt to give readers direct access 'to the word and to the man': again I thank the Henderson family for giving me permission to do so. Beyond them, many friends and associates have been of great assistance to me: like the oral tradition to which Hamish gave so much of his energy, this book stands on the shoulders of giants. In particular I thank Mairi Sutherland, my editor (she had a big job to do and I am greatly in her debt); Raymond Ross, editor of the magazine *Cencrastus*, and of *Hamish Henderson: Collected Poems and Songs* (Curly Snake, 2000); also Maurice Fleming, former editor of the *Scots Magazine*; Jennie Renton, Lorn Macintyre, John Frew, Ian Robertson Hamilton (who brought the Stone of Destiny back to Scotland), and Neville Moir at Birlinn who has been greatly loyal to the Hamish project and to me. In Italy, my thanks go to Hamish's dear friends, Amleto Micozzi and Pino Mereu, who have given invaluable help and support – also to Carla Sassi, and Simone and Luciana Micozzi. In England my special thanks go to Violet Hawkes and the Hawkes/Armstrong clan of Dry Drayton; to Marian Sugden in

Cambridge, to Paddy Goldring of Ingleton House, and Kate Thomas of
Clapham. Amongst the singers and music makers I extend deep thanks to
Alison MacMorland and Geordie McIntyre, Margaret Bennett, Martin
Bennett, John MacEvoy, Ella Ward, Ewan McVicar, Sheila Stewart,
Sheila Douglas, Jamie MacDonald Reid, Allan MacDonald, Dolina
Maclennan, Ruth Frame. Amongst the poets Hayden Murphy, Donny
O'Rourke, John Brookes, Maurice Craig, David Craig, Duncan Glen, Eck
Finley and Ian Hamilton Finlay, John Herdman, Alisdair Gray, Eddie
Linden, Gerry Mangan, Martin Green, George Gunn, Joy Hendry,
Harold Glasser, Norman MacLean, John Berger, Nicholas Johnson.
Amongst the teachers and politicians Maggie MacKay, Marian Blyth-
man, Janey Buchan, Stuart Boyd, Andy Boyd, David Blakely, Danny
Cooper, Stuart McLennan, Donald Meek, John MacInnes, Willie Gillies,
Michael Law, Fraser MacDonald, Mairi MacArthur, Murdo MacKenzie,
Ishbel MacLean, Rene MacLean, Paul Nolan, Alan Riach, Ian Spring,
Trevor Tolley, Willie Wolfe, Arnott Wilson, Bill and Anne Imrie.
Amongst the archivists Caitlin McAuley, Jane Anderson, Ken Fraser,
Dick Greenhaus, Ian Olson, Ross Roy and Mrs Bayne of Perth. Amongst
the journalists and artists Maeve Ryan, Des Wilson, John MacLeod,
Donald MacKenzie, Will Maclean, Jack Knox, Flora MacNeill, Andrew
Hood, Peter Adamson (photographer of St Andrews), Deirdre McClure,
Jim MacGregor, Anne Hutcheson, Jim Hutcheson (designer, Edinburgh),
Jean Mohr of Geneva, and Andrew Ward (painter, Ullapool). I also offer
special thanks the School of Scottish Studies at the University of Edin-
burgh, which was so important to Hamish during his life and has greatly
assisted me.

My work has been financed by a bursury of £8000 from the Scottish
Arts Council and an advance of £2,700 from Birlinn Books. In addition
my thanks go to David Wilson of the Peat Inn in Fife, and Antonio
Carluccio of London, who over many years have bought my honey,
candles and wild mushrooms, partly just to keep the wolf from my door. I
also thank Ross Carstairs, who has supplied logs, and Christyna McNeill
and Charlie Barron, who have looked after my dog Meg. Finally, deep
thanks to my wife Caroline, our family and grandchildren.

                                                   Timothy Neat

Publisher's Acknowledgements

The author and publishers would also like to thank the following for permission to reprint quoted material:

JOHN CORNFORD: extract from 'Huesca' from *Collected Writings* (Carcanet Press,1986), reprinted by permission of the publisher; KARL DALLAS: extract from letter to Hamish Henderson, 28 November 1997, reprinted by permission of the author; G.S. FRASER: extract from *A Stranger and Afraid – The Autobiography of an Intellectual* (Carcanet Press, 1983), reprinted by permission of the publisher; two extracts from letters to Hamish Henderson, 15 August 1942 and 1 January 1945, reprinted by permission of Mrs Eileen Fraser; DAVID GASCOYNE: extract from letter to Hamish Henderson, April/May 1949, reprinted by permission of Enitharmon Press; AKIRA HAYAMI: extract from letter to Hamish Henderson (1984), reprinted by permission of the author; JOHN LEHMANN: extract from letter to Hamish Henderson, 4 October 1949, reprinted by permission of David Higham Associates; NORMAN MACCAIG: 'Hero' from *Collected Poems* (Chatto & Windus,1985), reprinted by permission of Birlinn Ltd; EWAN MACCOLL: extracts from three personal letters to Hamish Henderson, 16 February 1948, November 1948, and one undated, reprinted by permission of Peggy Seeger; HUGH MACDIARMID: extract from 'Glasgow' from *The Voice of Scotland* (July, 1947); extracts from A' men's institutions and maist men's thochts', 'The Mavis of Pabal', 'A New Scots Poet', 'The Poet as Prophet – The Man for whom Gaeldom is waiting' and 'King Over Himself' from *The Complete Poems of Hugh MacDiarmid, 1920–1976* (Martin Brian & O'Keeffe, 1978); extract from Vote of thanks at the People's Festival Ceilidh (August, 1951), and extract from letter by Hugh MacDiarmid to *National Weekly* (26 June,1952), reprinted by permission of Carcanet Press; SORLEY MACLEAN: extract from 'The Cuillin', and 'The Clan MacLean' from *From Wood to Ridge: Collected Poems in Gaelic and English* (Carcanet Press, 1989), reprinted by permission of the publisher; RUSSELL MILLER:

extract from letter to *New Statesman*, 29 November 1974, reprinted by permission of PFD (www.pfd.co.uk) on behalf of Russell Miller; ALAN RIDDELL: 'Free One' from *Poetry Broadsheet* (January, 1952), reprinted by permission of Ann Barr; JAMES BURNS SINGER: extracts from 'The Best of It' and 'Your Words, My Answers' from *Burns Singer – Selected Poems* (Carcanet Press, 1977), reprinted by permission of the publisher; E. P. THOMPSON: extract from letter to Hamish Henderson, February 1949, reprinted by permission of Dorothy Thompson; W.B. YEATS: extract from *Memoirs: Autobiography – First Draft. Journal*, transcribed and edited by Denis Donoghue (Macmillan, 1972), reprinted by permission of A.P.Watt Ltd on behalf of Gráinne Yeats; DOUGLAS YOUNG: two extracts from letters to Hamish Henderson, 30 January 1949 and March 1949, reprinted by permission of Clara Young.

ONE

The Spittal of Glenshee
and Lendrick School

My blue-blooded and black-hearted family
HH[1]

'Youth and age on the face of Corravine': Hamish Henderson was born on 11
November 1919, exactly one year after the Armistice brought the First World
War to a close. His mother, Janet Henderson, had recently returned from
France, where she had served with the Queen Alexandra Nursing Sisters; she
was thirty-nine and unmarried. Janet registered her son's name as James Scott
Henderson but, from the beginning, called him Hamish. He was born in his
grandmother's house, Ramleh, a small sandstone villa on the outskirts of
Blairgowrie in east Perthshire. Granny Henderson was a highly respectable
Dundonian but she gave unstinting love to her wayward daughter and her
new grandson 'out of the blue'. Beyond the garden gate, however, things were
very different; during the nineteenth century, Scotland's aspirant middle
classes had come to assume illegitimacy as morally intolerable and, within
weeks of Hamish's birth, mother and child moved out to a rented cottage at
the Spittal of Glenshee, where Hamish lived most of his first five years. Here
was an older, more tribal society. Gaelic was still spoken by the 'old people'
and it was they who gave Hamish that ancient phrase, *òige agus aois air
aodann Cùbhraidh Bhein*, 'youth and age on the face of the sweet mountain',
which so eloquently expresses the spiritual bond that exists between a long-
settled rural community and the land that shaped it. From childhood, Hamish
had a natural sense of the human continuum and, as an old man, he would
relate how old ladies, native to the glen, had looked in his pram and
announced: 'you can see he's been here before!' Not surprisingly, towards
the end of his life, Hamish asked that his ashes be taken back to Glenshee,
carried to the summit of Ben Gulabin, and scattered there to the wind.

Glenshee, 'the glen of the fairies', is a long glacial valley gouged out of
the barren uplands of the Grampian plateau. Its woods and salmon-rich

1. HH (Hamish Henderson), unpublished, from notebook unless otherwise specified.

waters encouraged early settlement and for 2,000 years Glenshee has featured large in Celtic legend and literature. Hamish proudly related: 'It was in Glenshee that Diarmid hunted and killed the great boar . . . He measured its back with his naked feet – took a spine in his sole and died of blood poison! Here in this glen – on Gulabin. That's what we were told when we were young.' In Gaelic, Ben Gulabin means the mountain of the whaup, or curlew, and this green-shouldered mountain became a living presence to the young Hamish – greeting him each morning 'through the chitterin' leaves o' life that tapped at my bedroom window'. At the age of four he climbed to the summit; '2,641 feet above sea level: I went with my mother and one of my aunties. The view is spectacular – east down the glen towards the North Sea; south to the Sidlaws, Edinburgh, and Pentland Hills; while west and north range after range of the Grampians silhouette themselves – brushed in by a Chinese hand.' Hamish was always at home with 'romance' and at the age of fourteen he wrote a long poem entitled 'The Mountain', extolling the land, the history and the psyche of the early Caledonian peoples.

> Thine
> Were gentleness and pride,
> Thine was the love of poet bands
> Bringing honour to the Grecian Gael
> In Alban and in all Ireland.
> Thine my love
> . . .
> Look on the ancient wonder of the Sidhe
> Who are dead. For all gods die. But sure
> Their ghosts live, and their power
> Endures for the seeing soul. They give
> Graciousness to the race of the Gael
> And unfastened eyes. My heart
> O child heart. They took in this hand
> Under the Whaup's mountain.
> Here they had ruled endlessly,
> The men of Peace in the blessed glens . . .[2]

Also entitled 'The Gods in Exile' and 'The Gael from Greece', this poem is a panegyric to the land between the Bridge of Cally and the great straths

---

2. This poem, 'The Mountain', is unpublished. It is dated by a letter from James McLaren to Hamish Henderson. It was written shortly after Hamish left Lendrick School at the end of 1933 for Ingeleton House, Clapham (January 1934). McLaren asks his former pupil whether his poem 'The Mountain' is finished yet.

of the Dee and the Don – Caledonia. In particular it praises the Sidhe – the fairies and old peoples of Scotland – whose descendants still, in the early twentieth century, saw the Gaels, who forged Scotland into being, as threatening latecomers. It was they (the people of Glenshee and the lion mountain, Schiehallion) who took Hamish and his mother in, when the world looked askance. His vision, however, is one of Christian brotherhood and, very consciously, embraces all Scotland. After presenting a truncated history of medieval Scotland, the poem draws to a conclusion with 'prophetic words', addressed by Hamish to himself:

> It comes upon me to listen:
> The cry is far from Loch Awe
> And help from the Clan of O' Diubhre
>
> *Who now, in that man's wise,*
> *Will succour Gael from Saxons,*
> *In our time, as once Lugh*
> *Aided his race against reproach?*
>
> Our distress
> Thou knowest, therefore make
> No tardy coming; the islands
> Are dark to this day. With Aonghas
> Their house if he cometh not.
> For the Highlands
> A cold house Mhanuri. Come, come
> In the name of Fionn's race!
> Save us from the honourless,
> Know thine own children,
> As in old time – with thy sword
> Deliver us . . .

'Know thine own children' is a rallying cry but also refers to Hamish's illegitimate status and his understanding that all life must start with the realities of particular bodies, communities and nations. The fact of illegitimacy undoubtedly influenced Hamish's early life but he never lacked personal love and, far from pushing him towards introversion and resentment, his mother's 'shame' propelled him towards a lifelong identification with the suffering of others and gave him an unquenchable capacity to love. He knew he existed only because his mother had stepped beyond 'the pale of the law' and throughout his life he exalted the purely animal, the purely spiritual, the purely human. Propriety would have snuffed him out and – like Scots balladry – he was proud to be the product of 'a rebellious house' and would lifelong glory in it. As a schoolboy Hamish read Fiona MacLeod's *Life of St Columba*, and MacLeod's recognition of the forces that drove the bardic-warrior-saint thrilled him. Being – not power, authority or law – was to become his watch-word. Columba's love of life was his, and he was only eight years old when he wrote his first anti-war poem, 'After the Battle of Trafalgar – A Thanks Giving Service'.

> Ye Hypocrites
> Mon be yer pranks
> Tae murder men
> And then give thanks.
>
> Stop!
> Go no further
> God wont accept your thanks
> For murder.[3]

War cast a long shadow over Hamish's boyhood; his mother had witnessed at first hand the bloody carnage of mechanical warfare, her eldest brother, Dr Patrick Henderson, had been killed in France in 1916 and it was the fact that one of Hamish's great-great-grandfathers had been killed at Trafalgar that triggered this remarkable poem. It was based on a Burns quatrain but is a genuinely original creation, and Hamish's use of the word 'Stop!' is brilliantly effective; Burns had written 'desist for shame!'. The precociousness displayed here was no flash in the pan, and this poem is just one of more than forty songs, rhymes and jokes that Hamish copied out as writing exercises in one of his mother's recipe books, flanked by ingredients for meat pies and ice-cream. They are described as 'recitations' and were learned by heart for presentation at family ceilidhs. Hamish was a 'ceilidh-house' performer long before he returned to Blairgowrie – from the mountains – to start school at the age of five.

The Spittal of Glenshee was a typical small Highland community; it consisted of a few scattered crofts, a farmhouse, a kirk, a large manse, a Victorian hotel – and the Henderson cottage hunkered down by the

---

3. Hamish's 'recitations' were written between 1928 (when he moved with his mother from Scotland to Somerset) and 1930 when he became a boarder at Lendrick School, Bishop's Teignton, Devon. They were writing and memory exercises but also very conscious literary efforts – overseen by his mother.

Glenshee Water. Today, it remains very much as it was eighty years ago, a grey-tiled but-and-ben with pink-painted harling, much photographed by tourists looking for an example of 'Granny's Hielan Hame'. At the front, a sunken garden catches the sun; over a low wall at the back lies a medieval graveyard with a rowan tree, a ruined chapel and a standing stone. As soon as he could read, Hamish was deciphering names, declaiming inscriptions, imagining the lives of the dead. Despite population loss due to war and urbanisation, Glenshee in the twenties retained a vigorous farming community, and the Spittal was a traditional meeting place for hill-walkers, shepherds, gamekeepers and shooting parties. In addition a strange array of stone-breakers, old soldiers and tinkers hawking their wares were regular visitors. July/August was 'the season' and Hamish was proud to have been taught 'auld style dancing by Dancy Reid – one of the last travelling Highland dance teachers'. Mr Ramsay, the owner of the cottage, was also a regular visitor:

One of my earliest memories is of him 'gien me a hurl' along the road and over the humpbacked bridge, in his wheelbarrow. He knew everybody and it was he, more than my mother, who got me interested in the old Perthshire dialect of Gaelic – still very much alive on the lips of the old folk. Ancient place-names rolled off his tongue like rhymes: Creag Dhearg, Creag Bhreac, Glen Lochsie, Dalmunzie, Carn Tarmachain, Tom an t Suidhe . . . In public, Gaelic was used as a secret language that kids were not supposed to understand – but natural curiosity urged me to crack the code and I learned enough to give myself an interest and sympathy which has stayed with me for life. I was brought up in a fully bilingual community full of songs and stories – it was an experience that gave me an organic insight into the nature of language and popular culture and was to shape my whole life . . . I remember my mother telling me, 'not all the songs we sing are in books' and this inspired me – I took easily to singing and song-writing and, as a bairn, I composed numerous songs – all sung to dance tunes – reels – jigs – strathspeys. My mother was a fine singer with a big repertoire – she sang in Scots, in Gaelic – and in French . . . One of her 'party pieces' was 'La Marseillaise' . . .

In 1924 Janet Henderson returned to Ramleh so that Hamish could begin his formal education at Blairgowrie School, which catered for local children from five to fourteen. The 'infants' were taught by Janet Peterkin, a youthful but old-fashioned Highland woman from Morayshire. She was deeply interested in Scots song, history and tradition and quickly recognised 'the Glenshee lad o' pairts' as an 'apprentice' very much out of the ordinary. Janet Peterkin was Hamish's teacher for only three years but kept in touch with him for the rest of her life.

Years later, Hamish described the Blairgowrie of his boyhood as a place of 'shining cobbles still releasing the smell of illicit whisky brought down from the mountains – and hearing, on street corners, tales of rammies between smugglers and the gaugers. Blairgowrie was right there on the Highland Line, and the berryfields above the Ericht and the Isla had attracted tinkers and travellers for hundreds, perhaps thousands of years – and, by the late nineteenth century, the railway system was bringing in new breeds. "Corner boys from Glasgow, kettle-boilers frae Lochee / And miners frae the pits o' Fife, mill-workers frae Dundee . . ."' Hamish is here quoting Belle Stewart's famous song 'The Berry Fields of Blair' and, warming to his folk theme, goes on to describe Blairgowrie as an 'exchange and mart' for folk-song and balladry.

All his life Hamish embraced history, people, places and ideas as being part of a single reality, and this sense of wholeness is very apparent in one of his first 'mature' poems, 'Scottish Childhood' (completed in 1940, it was later retitled 'Ballad of the Twelve Stations of My Youth'[4]).

> I climb with Neil the whinny braes of Lornty,
>   Or walk my lane by drumlie Ericht side.
> Under Glasclune we play the death of Comyn,
>   And fear, wee boys, the Auld Kirk's sin of pride.
>
> Spring quickens. In the Shee Water I'm fishing.
>   High on whaup's mountain time heaps stone on stone.
> The speech and silence of Christ's world is Gaelic,
>   And youth on age, the tree climbs from the bone.

'Neil' was Neil Grant, a friend whom Hamish 'defended' against bullies in the Blairgowrie school yard. His stance proved highly successful and it nurtured in Hamish an impassioned immediacy of response that was to be a hallmark of his behaviour across a lifetime.

In adulthood, Hamish always stressed his Highland and Perthshire origins but his mother's ancestry was Dundonian. She was the youngest daughter of Alexander Henderson (1831–1912), a Dundee silk merchant, and Helen Jobson (1844–1928), daughter of a wine and spirit merchant who was for many years Lord Provost of Dundee. Alexander Henderson

---

4. It was published (for the first time in its entirety) in *Hamish Henderson: Collected Poems and Songs* (Curly Snake 2000) [hereafter abbreviated to *Collected Poems*].

was the second son of a surgeon from Fife who set up a medical practice in Dundee's wealthy eastern suburb of Broughty Ferry. As a young man Alexander had also wanted to pursue a medical career but, after a bout of tuberculosis, moved sideways into the silk trade. For more than forty years Alexander ran a prestigious shop in Dundee High Street but found his chief pleasures elsewhere: he was a hill-walker, a keen golfer and curler, a historian, singer and lifelong member of Dundee's Scottish Music Association. All his six children were encouraged to sing. After retiring to Blairgowrie in 1903 he wrote an occasional diary for the *Dundee Advertiser*, and one column précises his family history:

> My family originates from Caithness. 'Gunn' is the name for Henderson. We are descended from the third son of the Princess of Norway, daughter of the King of Norway . . . Counting back three generations, my great-grandparents on my paternal side were in succession the heads of the Inland Revenue, or Custom House officers, in Dundee. Colonel Henderson, my ancestor, fought in the Battle of Culloden. He was a colonel in the Hungarian Hussars. My great grandmother, Catherine Walker, rode all the way from Aberdeen to Coupar Angus to be married, accompanied by her groom. My grandfather and my father (Mr Patrick Henderson) had each thirteen of a family, seven sons and six daughters. My mother's grandfather was killed at the Battle of Trafalgar . . .

For some reason Alexander omits mention of the man who was, perhaps, his most celebrated ancestor – Sir Lachlan Gunn of Braemore, a six foot seven inch giant, who, in the seventeenth century, gathered an army of kinsmen from Caithness and Sutherland and sailed to Sweden to fight on the Protestant side in the Thirty Years War. As the result of heroism at the Battle of Breitenfelt, Lachlan Gunn was knighted, amidst the slaughter, by King Gustavus Adolphus. Hamish spoke frequently of Sir Lachlan but he was equally proud that it was Elizabeth Livingstone, daughter to Catherine Walker of Aberdeen, who had given his mother many of her best songs. Thus when, in later years, he made his great folk-song discoveries in Aberdeenshire he knew himself 'amang his ain folk'.

Hamish's Jobson ancestry is less well documented but the Jobsons, too, were Dundonians with strong Presbyterian convictions. Granny Henderson's father, Lord Provost David Jobson, lived in some splendour at Falcon Villa, Broughty Ferry, and died there on 12 February 1880. (His death was probably hastened by the recovery from the sea, five days earlier, of his eldest son's dead body. This man, Hamish's great uncle, also named David Jobson, is described on his death certificate as having 'accidentally drowned from the fall of a Railway Train and portion of the Tay Bridge into the River Tay on December 28th 1879'. He was thus one of the seventy-six victims of the Tay Bridge disaster.

David Jobson's will shows him to have been an extremely wealthy man. Generous provision was made for his widow (Mary Fenton) and various local charities: it also decreed that his trustees were to give his children and grandchildren such sums as would set them 'to business or setting them up in business or otherwise advancing them in the world'. This provision made Hamish's mother and grandmother prime candidates for funds. What they received before 1919 is unknown but after Janet gave birth to her illegitimate son they got nothing. Consequently when Hamish writes of 'my blue-blooded and black-hearted family', the black-hearts can be presumed to belong mostly to the Jobsons. He never spoke about them to his wife, or to me, but the Jobsons seem to have personified, for Hamish, the kind of inverted 'morality' that has blighted Scotland's sense of social propriety in the name of 'rectitude'. This Victorian cold-heartedness is encapsulated in a letter sent to Hamish by his 'Aunt Janie' in September 1938. She wrote to congratulate him on having won a State Scholarship to Cambridge.

> I am sending to you Colin's gold studs for evening wear which I feel sure you will appreciate. They may not arrive at once because I have asked Lucy to send them on as soon as she can . . . About Aunt Mary having so much and Aunt Mabel having so little, it makes one feel rebellious but you see Aunt Mary was lucky in marriage, Mr Clarke gave her such a lovely home. It is the same with me, I have more than any of my sisters and have two brothers who can only keep themselves out of debt. This happens all the world over so don't feel too keenly about it as it could never be otherwise. Even if the 'Goods' were divided every month, at the end of each month some people who were prudent would still have something sound and others would have spent every penny.

When Hamish received that letter he had just completed five years in a London orphanage and it cut him to the quick. There is no record of Hamish having any further contact with his Jobson relatives after this. He saw them as embodiments of a deforming class-ridden self-satisfaction that he was to oppose vigorously throughout his life. In old age Hamish would still swell with anger when recounting his mother's reaction to an unctuous Blairgowrie notary who announced their removal from their family home: 'Suddenly, my mother thumped the table with her fist and moved round the table to physically challenge this man who, so calmly and properly, was putting me, and my mother, out on the street!' It is not clear when this incident took place, but between 1925 and 1928 the Hendersons moved house down-market four times. They were 'evicted' from Ramleh in 1925, after that they lived in rented rooms at Collinslea in nearby Emma Street where Janet tended her mother until her death on 17 February 1928. Four months later, after a stay in Cottage B in William Street, Janet and Hamish left Scotland for Somerset, where Janet became housekeeper in a 'big house' that offered free accommodation as part of the deal.

After the death of Granny Henderson, Hamish's mother seems to have jumped at the opportunity of leaving Blairgowrie. In June 1928 Hamish was sent to Dundee to sit a series of examinations that would give him certificates to take into England, and one school report reads: 'James Scott Henderson has passed standard 1 and I, Robert Robb, rector of Blairgowrie School, beg to report as follows: conduct = excellent, attendance = excellent, papers = very good.' Thus armed, Hamish went into an 'exile' that would last almost twenty years – but, like his mother, he embraced the change as an opportunity:

> In 1928 my mother went to Somerset as a cook-housekeeper – to a family with mair silver nor sense. By chance it was a part of England still rich in singers and I soon realised in the orchards and stables of that big house, near Yeovil, that Strathmore and the Perthshire Highlands had no monopoly of good tunes, songs and interesting stories. Quite soon I also had the good fortune to hear Irish traditional singers on their native heath: thus I heard and sang the folk songs of three nations [in five dialects and two languages] long before I had the faintest knowledge what a folk song was. Ten years later, when I met ballad scholars like my fellow Scot M.J.C. Hodgart, at Cambridge, I realised that whilst there was a vast amount I did not know about traditional song I had reason to bless my childhood luck.

The Hendersons' arrival in the West Country coincided with the death of Thomas Hardy and they soon found themselves part of a rural community very like that recently inhabited by Bathsheba Evergreen and Tess of the d'Urbervilles. Mother and son got themselves bikes and started touring the countryside – into Chard, and out to West and East Coker.[5] They also visited Chagford on

Dartmoor and Ottery St Mary, the boyhood home of Samuel Taylor Coleridge, the poet whom Hamish saw as the most Celtic of all English poets.

Janet Henderson boldly encouraged Hamish in both his literary precocity and his passion for Scotland. They began keeping a scrapbook into which they pasted newspaper cuttings 'of everything concerning Scottish song and tradition'. A standing order ensured the arrival of the *Weekly Scotsman,* and parcels of the Perthshire and Angus papers came by the month. This historical scrapbook encouraged Hamish to work on his book of recitations, and many display insight, humour and a consistent sexual self-awareness: 'One day a simple country girl / Stooped down to pick a lettuce / A bumble bee came buzzing round / And whispered – shall us, let us.' Another ditty is entitled 'Dear Old Daddy':

> Everyone's singing of mother
> Praising her up to the sky,
> Mother is this
> And mother is that
> Yes, mother makes wonderful pies
> Mother is one of the angels
> Yes, mother is going strong –
> But we don't want to bore you by singing of mother
> And this is my little song.
>
> Dear old daddy you are the one for me
> Dear old daddy you have the L.S.D.
> Mother's the mother of twenty kids
> And her swanking makes me mad
> But mother could never have been a mother
> If it hadn't been for dad . . .[6]

All his life, Hamish could be thrawn as well as charming. And when he ends his poem 'Seascape' (1940) with the words, 'You really are perfectly impossible' – it is clear that this was one of the 'regular rebukes' his mother flung at him.

---

5. East Coker was the village after which T.S. Eliot was to name one of his *Four Quartets.* When Hamish read the poem in the Tunisian desert in 1943 he notes dryly 'This is a poem that takes a very long time to say *that which is, is not.*'

6. Whether this poem is by HH is unclear. He may merely have copied it into his book of *Recitations.* But there can be no doubt it is a poem that spoke to him.

After a holiday in Ireland, a series of 'Irish gags' appear in the book that seem chosen to test his mother's patience. 'I was just after meeting Flanagan, he was one of the brightest men I ever met. He was wearing a white flower in his coat. Says I, where have you been? Says he, I've been to a wedding. Says I, did you give the bride away? Says Flanagan – I could have done, but I kept my mouth shut!'

Sometime during 1929 Janet Henderson made arrangements for Hamish to become a boarder at Lendrick School, a small mixed preparatory school in Bishop's Teignton, close to Teignmouth on the South Devon coast. The headmaster, James Maclaren, was a tall, imperious Edwardian gentleman whom Hamish describes as 'a bluff and massive Scot with grizzled moustache and mischievous eyes'. Maclaren was a brilliant linguist and a pillar of the local community but he also proudly retained close contact with his native land. His school was called Lendrick because it is an old Perthshire place-name (a hill above Glen Devon, and an estate at Brig o' Turk) and the school 'house' in which Hamish boarded was called Huntly for similar reasons. Accommodation consisted of two large, interconnected buildings, set amidst fine lawns and cedar trees looking out across the tidal estuary of the Teign. In 1930, the school had 45 boys and 20 girls. Hamish adapted easily to life as a boarder, and was soon noted as an exemplary scholar. Discipline was firm but pupils enjoyed wonderful freedoms – wandering the woods, camping out on Dartmoor, visiting Exeter Cathedral – and Maclaren took school parties into Kent's Cavern near Torquay, a magnificent palaeolithic cave.

Whether Hamish was sent to Lendrick because of his mother's domestic situation, because she thought it educationally to his advantage, because he had won a scholarship, or because she had been diagnosed with cancer and knew she was dying, is not known. What we do know is that, when Janet Henderson died, James Maclaren became Hamish's legal guardian and, long before this, Maclaren was taking a 'fatherly' interest in this highly gifted boy, who appears to have raised the intellectual standard of the whole school and began what Maclaren was to describe as the 'Lendrick Renaissance'. Beyond his scholastic abilities and his role as the school 'bard', Hamish was a noted artist and 'theatrical entrepreneur', writing, directing and acting in a string of plays.

While he was at Lendrick, Hamish experienced one of the first of many metaphysical experiences that were to punctuate his long life. He described it to me on several occasions. One day, confined to the sickbay with influenza, he had a premonition that something was wrong; he got up and in his dressing gown went out onto the landing of Huntly House. In the entrance hall below, Mrs Maclaren and some of the masters were gathered in whispered conversation. As Hamish slowly descended the banistered stairwell, the front door opened and another master entered – carrying in his arms 'the dead body of a boy – killed by a Devon Red General Omnibus'. Hamish walked forward to take the hand of the dead boy. Having done so, one of the masters came to him, picked him up and carried him back up the stairs to the sickbay. The last time Hamish described this experience to me, he was very old and he kept repeating – as though it was a mantra: 'A Devon Red General Omnibus – a Devon Red General Omnibus. It was the body of a boy, killed by a Devon Red General Omnibus' and the tears were running down his face. From his early days in Glenshee, Hamish had felt a kinship with the dead, and this incident brought what had been a generalised feeling into permanent focus. From this time on, Hamish believed he had a special responsibility for the dead, a duty to the dying and to the wounded: as a poet he would 'sing them' and from this time on he felt bound to be 'a remembrancer'.

Maclaren was an exceptional teacher and, before leaving Lendrick, Hamish could read Latin and Greek, converse fluently in German and French, write excellent English, draw and sing well, and speak publicly without notes. In the summer of 1933, he was entered for scholarships to Dulwich College and Gordonstoun. Dulwich was Maclaren's alma mater in South London; Gordonstoun a brand new public school in Moray-shire, recently set up by Kurt Hahn, a distinguished German-Jewish educationist. After interviewing Hamish, Hahn informed him: 'I see you as a future Bishop of the Episcopal Church in Scotland and we should be very pleased to offer you a place at Gordonstoun.' The prospect of a return to Scotland was tempting but Hamish took Maclaren's advice to follow his footsteps to Dulwich and Cambridge. Hamish never regretted this decision and, with regard to Scotland, he already knew he must play 'the long game'. By going to Dulwich he was assured a superior education, contact with a broader cross-section of society and open access to the cultural riches of a great metropolis. He relished the thought of immersion in the city of Chaucer and Milton, Blake, Keats and Dickens: he was proud to follow a path trodden by Lord Byron and Robert Bruce.

Hamish's scholarship to Dulwich provided for his education but not for his board. Consequently, Maclaren arranged for him to be placed in the Clapham Boys' Home, an Anglican orphanage, thirty minutes by bus north of the College. The move from rural Devon to Clapham took place at Christmas 1933. Because Janet Henderson's post as housekeeper was 'residential', when her cancer was diagnosed as terminal, she had been moved into a Poor House at 2 Upper Shoreham Road, Kingston-by-Sea,

Sussex, where she died on 9 July 1933. Despite clashes, Hamish's love for his mother was huge and unqualified: he liked to say 'my mother had a heart that would sink a battleship' and he saw her as embodying the 'high spirit' of Scotland. In his 'The Ballad of the Twelve Stations of my Youth', however, she gets just one verse:

> Brighton. Last night to the flicks. And now I'm sitting
> In a dressing gown on the rumpled unmade bed.
> There's a trunk in the room, and plates, and morning sunshine,
> And Mrs. O' Byrne saying my mother's dead.

The brevity is brutal but also strangely calming. Hamish was always on to the next thing. And his sense of being 'a remembrancer', far from making him mawkish, thrust him forwards towards the world of William Blake's 'Bright Day'. He had a Darwinian understanding that 'the reality is a thing that has to be reinvented continually' and he delighted in his own existential being: 'The lived moment / Jammin a rock in the craw of devouring time.' When I asked him where his mother was buried, he said 'in Sussex'. He never visited her grave.

Hamish was thirteen when his mother died, and her death forced to the fore the question of who his father was. Throughout his adult life this question provoked wide speculation – among friends, family and foes – but no clear answer was forthcoming. When I asked him directly he replied 'no one knows who their father is – though science is now helping us along that road'. And that was that.

The mystery of Hamish's paternity is heightened by the fact that the Henderson archive contains a letter that makes it clear that Janet Henderson wrote a series of letters to James Maclaren about Hamish's father – and that Maclaren destroyed these letters. It is not clear why. In September 1939, having volunteered for war service, Hamish wrote to Maclaren asking for these letters (which he had been told about but had not read). On 4 October, Maclaren replied: 'Dear Hamish, I am sorry about your mother's letters but a long time ago I wrote and asked you if you would call and have them but as you never answered that letter I had to destroy them. They were mostly about her early life and about your father and relatives and, of course, well full about only Hamish . . .'

Why did Maclaren destroy these letters? Was he trying to protect his guardee from knowledge that he believed might harm him? Had he made some kind of promise to Janet Henderson? Was he 'paid' by some third party to destroy these letters? Was he trying to stimulate 'the poet' in his young protégé (the mystery of 'origination' being one of world's most creative cultural and religious forces)? There are no obvious answers, and many more questions. Did Janet Henderson ever tell Hamish who his father was? Is it possible that Hamish genuinely never knew who his father was? This seems unlikely: it is much more probable that Hamish not only knew the name of his father but also knew him personally. If this is the case then he deliberately chose to remain silent about the name and life of his father.

All his life Hamish had a fondness for the phrase 'we're a' Jock Tamsin's bairns' and delighted in asserting the anarchic chancefulness of all sexual reproduction. Towards the end of his life, conscious that contradictory stories were circulating about his origins, Hamish seems to have taken an increasing pleasure in mildly encouraging them. His interest was not in where he came from but where Scotland and mankind were heading. At an early age he wrote 'Genealogy = your ancestors swinging by their tails!' before adding 'the word and naught else / in time endures'.

Hamish was thus content to let the issue of his paternity remain a mystery. Yet, despite this, genealogy is a subject of great interest, particularly in Scotland, and any biographer has a responsibility to address the parentage of their subject – even when confusion reigns. Also, numerous facts about Hamish's paternity have come to light since his death, so a brief statement about Hamish's paternity is set out here.

Rumours about Hamish's father began to circulate soon after he returned to Scotland at the end of the Second World War. Over the next thirty years, various contenders came to the fore, including James (Hamish) Stewart Murray, ninth Duke of Atholl, various cousins within the Atholl family, the Duke of Argyll, an Italian Count, the novelists Neil Gunn and Neil Munro, an unnamed Irish officer, and an officer in the Cameron Highlanders wounded in the First World War. By the time of Hamish's death, however, the two men considered most likely to have been his father were James Scott of Glasgow (1874–1934) and John George Stewart Murray (1871–1942), Marquis of Tullibardine and eighth Duke of Atholl. Today, it seems most likely that James Scott of Glasgow was the father of Hamish Henderson.

James Scott is known to have served with the Camerons and is believed to have been wounded, but the crucial evidence that he was Hamish's father comes from a family 'birth certificate' for Hamish, found by his wife Felicity (Katzel) Schmidt Henderson after Hamish's death in 2002. It states that James [Hamish] Scott Henderson was born to Janet Jobson Henderson on 11 November 1919 in Blairgowrie, Perthshire, and that Hamish's father was James Scott, a commercial traveller (born in Glasgow 29 May 1874). Katzel Henderson also found a photograph of a middle-aged man, on the back of which the words 'my father' are written in Hamish's hand. She and her daughters assume this man to be James Scott, and this attribution has now been confirmed by other members of James Scott's family. The existence of these two items seems to indicate that Hamish's father was James Scott of Glasgow, even though Hamish's original and 'official' birth certificate in Registry House (Edinburgh) has a blank space where the name and occupation of the child's father should be registered.

James Scott was the eldest son of another James Scott (a wine merchant born in Glasgow in 1848) and his wife Lizzie Dishington (born at Bridge of Allan, Stirlingshire, in 1853). This 'grandfather' Scott was descended from a long line of James Scotts who farmed in Renfrewshire. The Dishingtons were from Fife and the Lothians and traced their 'distinguished' ancestry back to a sister of Robert the Bruce. James Scott had two brothers, Isaac Scott (1876–1952) and William D. Scott (1878–1952), and one sister, Elizabeth W. Scott (1881–1962). All became notable citizens of Glasgow with strong military connections. Information about their elder brother, James Scott, however, is scanty – he appears to have been 'the black sheep' of the family. He was educated at Glasgow Academy, then studied civil engineering but did not complete his articles (possibly because of the death of his father in a drunken fall on the Isle of Arran on 18 August 1891). Subsequently, James worked on the West Highland Railway, and in northern Nigeria – from whence he returned to marry Camilla Sutherland at Rossie Lodge, Inverness, on 23 August 1905. She came from a notably Presbyterian North Highland family. The wedding was a grand affair, followed by a honeymoon 'in Sweden and on the Continent'. The marriage produced two children but was not a success. Camilla did not go out to Africa with her husband and by 1917 the marriage was over. Their eldest daughter, Camilla Elizabeth Scott, remembered her father returning to Inverness in 1917 in disgrace. He was served meals in a separate room and, after this visit, was never seen by the family again. On several occasions he requested a divorce but this was refused by his wife.

Four years later, James Scott resurfaced in London, where he is understood to have 'married' Adelaide Lois Taverner (a nurse from South Wales who had been working in Bristol) on 22 January 1922. However, no official records of this marriage exist so it is assumed to be a fake marriage or one conducted under the auspices of the Mormon Church of Latter Day Saints (as one strand of family tradition suggests). Eight months later, Adelaide Taverner gave birth to a daughter, Jeanne Elspeth Scott. Two more children followed: Margueritte Dion Scott (known as Peggy) and John Ferguson Scott. Peggy remembers her father as a charming, magnanimous man, always short of money and often drinking too much. She also pointed out that, after his death, his pension went not to her mother but to his wife Camilla, then resident in Edinburgh. In London the Taverner–Scott family lived at 23 Pemberton Gardens and James Scott commuted to work at HM Stationery Office in the City. James Scott died just a year after Janet Henderson, on 4 October 1934, of acute pancreatitis. His death certificate, signed by his brother William, makes no mention of his marital status. His body was interred in the family plot in Cathcart cemetery in Glasgow.

Assuming that James Scott was Hamish's father, his two 'marriages' raise interesting questions about the relationship with Janet Henderson. Was it short, was it sustained, did they too 'marry'? The writer John Herdman of Blair Atholl says that Hamish once told him that his mother had married late in life and that 'her husband treated her very badly'.

James Scott and Janet Henderson would have had plenty of opportunities to meet and establish a relationship during, and immediately after, the First World War. There is, however, no evidence that they lived together in either Blairgowrie or Glenshee where the appearance of 'a man' would have made Janet's exposed position even worse. A strange incident that took place at the family home of James Scott's original wife (Camilla Sutherland Scott) shows the problems that such liaisons generated at the time. Camilla Elizabeth Scott (James Scott's legitimate eldest daughter) has documented that, in the early 1920s, a woman with a small child arrived at her mother's door (Rossie Lodge, Inverness) to plead with her mother that she give James Scott a divorce – so that *she* could marry him and legitimise their child. The place and date of this meeting make it more likely that that this couple was Janet Henderson and Hamish (from Perthshire) than Adelaide Taverner and Jeanne Elspeth (travelling from London) and, if it was them, it adds a poignant note to Hamish's childhood and his mother's hardships.

James Scott was clearly a colourful and charismatic character, but Janet Henderson appears to have accepted him for what he was and, when she moved to England in 1928, she may well have renewed their relationship. Her death certificate contains some clues. It was witnessed by her sister Mabel (on 2 August 1933) and she registers Janet Henderson as '*widow* of James Henderson an architect'. As no architect named James Henderson was registered with either the RIBA or RSIBA at the time, and the likelihood that Janet had married someone with the same name as her illegitimate son is small, it seems probable that 'by habit and repute' Janet had been living, at least occasionally, in some kind of 'married' relationship with James Scott and that it suited them both to be known as Mr and Mrs James Henderson. In such circumstances Hamish would have known of his mother's relationship with James Scott and almost certainly knew him personally.

It seems that Hamish's father was a character driven by unfathomable enthusiasms and impulsions, whose life and actions defy explanation. One can understand therefore why Hamish, as well as James Maclaren, should hesitate to explain or deny anything. Maclaren may have thought it better for Hamish to have a loose medley of subjective memories rather than be weighed down by his mother's attempted explanations by letter. And Hamish appears always to have accepted his father's nature and situation with stoical equanimity. Felicity Henderson remembers that, in the mid 1960s, when their two children were young and they were very short of money, Hamish engaged a genealogical researcher to trace the Scott side of his ancestry – in the hope that the wills of his Glasgow uncles might contain a bequest to his benefit. His hopes were in vain, but copies of the wills of Isaac and William Scott remain in the possession of the Henderson family. Neither contains any mention of James Scott, or James Scott Henderson, and the language of both wills makes it clear that it is 'lawful children' alone who will inherit anything from these Scott estates. Thus, after breaking all contact with the Jobsons in 1938, Hamish made no attempt to contact any of his Scott relations after January 1946 but the information now available about James Scott and Janet Henderson makes the case for James Scott being Hamish's father overwhelming.[7]

---

7. Hamish's relationship with the Marquis of Tullibardine is so strange, legendary and fantastical that it would take another chapter to explore properly. It is, however, discussed briefly in Appendix 1.

TWO

The Home of the Good Shepherd, and Dulwich College

We are lived by forces we cannot understand.
HH

The Clapham Boys' Home, where Hamish lived from January 1934 until the autumn of 1938, was a charitable Anglican foundation run by the Society of the Good Shepherd. The Master was Arthur Russell Baker, an ageing autocratic gentleman committed to good works, good manners, the imperial virtues and a rigorously muscular Christianity. Baker normally referred to his charges as 'boy!'. They addressed him as 'sir' but, amongst themselves, they called him ARB, a nickname that betokened a genuine respect. Accommodation consisted of a conglomeration of red-brick buildings at the corner of Larkhall Rise and Rectory Grove in Clapham, south London. A fine study-library had recently been built within the home and there were plenty of sheds and play areas. The number of boys had fallen from over 100 early in the century to about 45 in the early 1930s and when Hamish was there the name was changed from Clapham Boys' Home to Ingleton House. Discipline was strict but far from oppressive, and most boys looked back on their years at Ingleton with gratitude and satisfaction. Hamish enjoyed his years in Clapham but, as soon as he left, he appears to have decided to expunge his orphanage years from both his conscious memory and the public record. At the time of his death, in 2002, neither his wife nor his children knew anything about them, and the facts about Hamish's life in the Boys' Home only came to light in a letter of condolence from Paddy Goldring, a retired journalist and author, who had been one of Hamish's contemporaries in the home.

Why did Hamish go silent about his years in the Boys' Home? A note, jotted down in 1953, after he had had a meeting with some hard-line communist steel workers in Rutherglen, gives a clue: 'Everything opposed to the revolutionary convention is ruthlessly suppressed from the histories of revolutions by the same obscure forces that erase shame from private memories.' Hamish accepted his illegitimacy with a mixture of pride and shame, but his years in a London orphanage were essentially shameful. Confident of his talents, he was no more interested in explaining his orphaned status than his father's passions. He knew that Ingleton House had helped develop his sense of brotherhood and discipline, but the idea that he might be described as 'a London Barnardo's Boy' was not part of his self-image as a Scot. He would let people take him as they found him.

In 2003 Paddy Goldring described the Ingleton regime as

Spartan and monastic: everyone was up at six for a cold wash, followed by household chores, a short religious service, and breakfast at communal tables. The staff consisted of ARB, his deputy Mr Waite, a cook and a housekeeper. Most senior boys had their own room. Everything was spick and span: the cleaning equipment came, once a year, from Buckingham Palace! There was little contact with girls but sex was never a problem. Mr Waite organised more circumcision inspections than seemed strictly necessary but no overt homosexuality ever came to my notice. Hamish was a scholarship boy and went off to Dulwich by bus, the rest of us went on foot to the Henry Thornton Secondary School. Race was no problem in those days, the 'head boy' in our last year was an Indian named Swami; later, he was one of many Ingleton boys killed in the war. We had regular trips to the pictures, to the theatre and ARB would take us off in groups to Westgate and Margate on the Kent coast for weekends. Sea-swimming was compulsory – tree houses built, rough-and-tumbles organised – keeping yourself to yourself was not encouraged.[1]

Paddy Goldring was editor of the Ingleton House magazine, the *Ingletonian Raconteur*, but Hamish was his assistant and wrote most of the copy. In 1936 the magazine published a seven-page poem, 'Merrie Ingleton – a fragment of an Epic Poem' in 'vers tres libre' by Hamish, plus a five-page comic opera entitled 'The Sole Survivor'. In 1937 there were three major pieces by Hamish. The first, 'Mint Sauce, Lamb's very last Essay of Elia (taken from a Lost MS in the British Museum)' was a Proustian exploration of the delights of eating lamb. The second was a long satire on literary critics and the writers they abuse, entitled 'Broken Fetters'. The third was a five-page Ossianic poem entitled 'A Fellow Traveller' (from the Gaelic):

---

1. Conversation with Timothy Neat (TN), 2003.

. . . But one day, sick at heart, I heard a song.
A slow, sad ballad by the East sea's edge
Telling how, patiently, a hermit sat
In humble mountain cave far to the West
Awaiting who should come – as willed the Gods –
To beg his magic aid to make anew
The glory of the kingdom Angus ruled . . .

. . . a glimmering light shone through the gloom.
With reverend steps the cavern I approached
And whispered: 'Holy seer: thy wait is o'er!
The Gods have willed a pilgrim youth to come
To beg the magic aid to make anew
The glory of the kingdom Angus ruled'
I entered then the cave and knelt to wait
The longed-for charmed answer of the seer . . .[2]

Hamish and Paddy also collaborated on various in-house theatrical productions, the most notable of which was a play, *Dr Clogg's Last Séance*, in which 'living realities were contrasted with the mindless superfluities of Spiritualist nonsense'. The setting was 'a small pub in the East End of London. Around the walls are painted slogans such as "Beer is Best". The barman is behind the counter, polishing glasses and humming to himself.' Vernacular speech and folk-song were integrated into the performance. On the back of one page of dialogue, Hamish drew a sketch of Shakespeare's Prospero and wrote out a quotation from the eighteenth-century poet Christopher Smart: 'For in my nature I quested for beauty; but God, God, has sent me to sea for pearls'.[3] Hamish and Paddy shared a wide range of political and cultural interests and after leaving Ingleton House remained in contact throughout their lives. Not surprisingly, Paddy has 'a walk-on part' in Hamish's 'Ballad of the Twelve Stations of my Youth':

Cramming ourselves with fish and chips we saunter
    Myself and Paddy, down the Wandsworth Road.
'Good beds for men' the shabby chapel offers:
    Sup of salvation in the Lord's abode . . .[4]

---

2. A copy of the *Ingletonian Raconteur* (in which 'A Fellow Traveller' appears) was sent to the Henderson family in 2005 following the death of Paddy Goldring.
3. Christopher Smart (1722–71): 'Jubilato Agno'.
4. Published in the *Collected Poems*.

Paddy also remembered Hamish taking delight 'in what he called his "mystical powers" – he used to take ARB's black pug out for long walks – and he claimed he had special powers over that pug! It had very short legs – they communed together, Leo Hawkes took photographs of them.'

Leo Hawkes was Hamish's second great friend at Ingleton House; his father had been killed in the First World War. Leo had survived an outbreak of rheumatic fever that killed several of the Ingleton boys, but he was left a permanent semi-invalid – with a twisted stomach, a twisted gut and what doctors described as 'less than half a heart'. He missed two years' schooling but he had many natural talents and great courage. Hamish would read to him and take him for gentle walks to Clapham Common. Their friendship was to last for over sixty years and will be returned to later in this biography.

Once Hamish had moved to Ingleton House he deliberately minimised contact with his old teacher and guardian, James Maclaren, who, on 3 July 1934, wrote: 'My Dear "Gunnus" . . . I'd rather expected to hear from you before . . . as a matter of fact old chap, Mrs Maclaren and I felt rather hurt by your long silence – but that is now all forgotten . . . I am delighted you are getting on so well at Dulwich and I hope you keep it up. Evidently Mr MacPherson learnt his German in the south. Personally I do not like "ich liebe dich" . . . Have you come across any good school books we could use at Lendrick?' In November, having received news from Hamish, he writes more encouragingly: 'I am so glad you have moved into Upper VA and equally pleased that you were top for the first fortnight – Keep it up old lad. Scotland forever! We are looking forward to a copy of your poem "The Mountain".' If Hamish accepted his new life within the Boys' Home with equanimity he delighted in Dulwich College, as to the manner born. It was a school with wonderful facilities and exceptional teachers, and he leapt at the matchless educational opportunity he had been given. Looking back in maturity he writes:

Imagine walking into a classroom and finding yourself among Poussin, Claude, Rubens, van Dyke, Murillo, Rembrandt, Hogarth, Reynolds and Gainsborough – not to mention Watteau, Tiepolo, and Canaletto . . . I used to make rhymes about them: 'Where is Watteau? / Lying blotto / In a grotto – with his quine.' I would sit there with Buchan's anthology *The Northern Muse* and read out 'Mars is braw in crammasy' to any painting that would listen: I was lecturing my fellow sixth formers on MacDiarmid and modern Scottish poetry, in South London, when most of the cultured population of Scotland knew neither. I was especially impressed

by 'On a Raised Beach' and 'Water Music'. Poetry laid siege to me
with an antisizygian fury.[5]

The Dulwich College Art collection was originally 'collected' by Stani-
slaus Augustus, King of Poland, to constitute a mini-history of European
art, mythology and religion. It was housed in a revolutionary building
designed by the neo-classical architect Sir John Sloane, and the gallery
served as a 'quiet room' for senior boys. Across the road, the main college
buildings stand in Italianate Victorian splendour amidst cricket pitches,
lawns, quads and mature trees which for four hundred years have
ennobled an area that is now one of London's most desirable suburbs.
Dulwich is just five miles from St Paul's but still retains the rural
splendour that inspired William Blake and Samuel Palmer, and John
Ruskin, who grew up here.

Several of Hamish's contemporaries at Dulwich remember him vividly.
Michael Clarke[6] writes:

> I realise now that I found him slightly too 'large': so clever, so
> fearless, so good a memory, such wide contacts and interests that I
> never felt entirely relaxed, entirely comfortable, in his company. He
> had this amazing Scottish accent, very prominent amid the careful
> non-cockney of the rest of us. He also looked odd: he had thick lips
> and thick spectacles, and he tended to stare at one rather intensely.
> My mother took to him, and I think it was she who elicited from him
> the fact that he was an orphan; he was always friendly, perhaps a
> little anxious for friendship. Hamish and I collaborated with others
> in producing a small magazine called *Caravan*. Hamish was always
> a singer. I met him again in Egypt – there he would deliver his bawdy
> songs as a sort of *sprachgesang* – but, at school, he had a quiet
> singing voice, a sort of falsetto or male alto, but without the force of
> the professional counter-tenor. Of his emotional or sexual inclina-
> tions I knew nothing. He always seemed a rather sexless person.
> Such questions never came to mind – which is strange, because I
> cannot think of any other person of whom I could say that.[7]

Like Paddy Goldring, Michael Clarke gets a mention in Hamish's 'Ballad
of the Twelve Stations of my Youth':

---

5. HH, unpublished notebook jottings.
6. Michael Clarke, a tank commander during the Second World War, made a career
   as a documentary filmmaker.
7. Letter from Michael Clarke to TN, 2003.

> From Acre Lane I catch a bus to Dulwich
> And read *Le Misanthrope* (an act a day)
> Then stroll next door, and say hallo to Michael
> And quiz the Hogarth in our gallery.[8]

Another school friend, Donald Campbell,[9] paints a surprisingly similar picture:

> As I think of Hamish I see him always singing and laughing . . . At Dulwich he was a soft-spoken, courteous young man, with a rich Scottish accent. I was awe-struck by him, tall, angular, bespectacled, with an early academic stoop. He was unique in being a Scot, a State Scholar, having the ability to speak Gaelic, and taking no part in sport – presumably because of his eyesight! . . . I was a classicist but we had a common interest in the readings he organised.[10]

All his life Hamish remained proud to be an Old Alleynian and he saw himself as exactly the kind of 'poor scholar' for whom 'Alleyn's College of God's Gift at Dulwich' had been originally founded. Established in 1615 by Edward Alleyn, the College is an enduring monument to the Elizabethan Renaissance. Alleyn was a Rosicrucian, a well-connected theatrical entrepreneur and philanthropist who, having bought the manor at Dulwich, established a free hospital and then a free school. Over the last two centuries the College's imperial, military and literary reputation has been particularly strong, with Ernest Shackleton, C.S. Forster, Raymond Chandler, P.G. Wodehouse and Captain Gordon Campbell VC being noted Old Boys. Professor R. Ian McCallum, another of Hamish's contemporaries, describes him as a gentle scholarly boy – whom he found one day 'rather morosely wandering on the periphery of the school playing fields; he had come to school in brown shoes instead of the required black, and had been severely told off by a prefect and ribbed by the boys'.

Brown shoes or black, no prefects prevented Hamish from enjoying Dulwich or the school holidays, during which he wandered far in search of poetical experience and adventure. By the age of sixteen he was a seasoned hitch-hiker with a Byronic taste for the open road. His first major hike was to the West Country at Easter 1935. He was supposed to visit the Maclarens at Lendrick but actually wandered through Dorset,

---

8. Published in the *Collected Poems*.
9. Donald Campbell was a linguist, wartime munitions officer and, post-war, Buildings Administrator at the University of Hull.
10. Letter from Donald Campbell to TN, 2003.

Devon and Cornwall, and returned to London without seeing his guardians at all. His first night was spent in a roadside wood, the second in a barn. On the morning of the third day he heard singing coming from a chapel in Brixham and wandered in, whereupon the minister, seeing him at the door, announced 'He whom the Lord has called will lead us now in prayer'. So Hamish did – and received a good lunch in return.

At Whitsun, Hamish took off for Offa's Dyke and the Welsh Marches, where he was thrilled to hear 'spoken', in the Shropshire hills, the ancient folk rhyme that Housman had embraced as poetry: 'Clunton and Clunbury, / Clungunford and Clun, / Are the quietest places / Under the sun.'[11] He read Wilfred Owen, visited Shakespeare's grave and looked for remnants of the great bard in the bars of Stratford. Returning east, he slept out in the Forest of Arden. He was now well over six feet tall but his demeanour was more gentle and benign than it would be again until old age was upon him. At College he had been studying *Macbeth*, identified strongly with the youthful, idealistic King Malcolm and, as soon as the summer term was over, he headed north to explore the East Highlands where Shakespeare had set his 'Scottish play'. He joined the British Cycling Club and set off from Perth to bike up the A9 – past Blair Atholl – to Kingussie and Newtonmore. He slept in youth hostels, B&Bs, and sometimes in the heather. In the Monadhliadh mountains he notes: 'ganging a straight gait ower a tight Hielane cheekbane . . . a drookit rat in my streaming waterproof – still climbing – and now hail as well as rain . . . all I need is a spread of thunder and lightning to make the meal complete.'

As he cycled, Hamish began to conceive a third long poem, more ideological and political than either 'The Mountain' or 'The Fellow Traveller'. East of Grantown-on-Spey, he attended the Lonach Gathering and it inspired him to entitle the poem 'Journey to a Kingdom'. Hamish recognised that Lonach – with its grand procession and territorial courtesies, its camaraderie, its pipes, drums and dancing – embodied the continuance of truly ancient Highland tradition. Here was living history that all Scots should know themselves heirs to. And, on returning to London, he began serious work on a poem that was to obsess him, on and off, for four years.

In the spring of 1936 Hamish visited Dublin. Knowing that W.B.Yeats often visited Oliver St John Gogarty at the Shelbourne Hotel, he decided to hang about and, late one night, introduced himself to the great poet and joined the small band that strolled with him down O'Connell Street. In 1974 Hamish told me the only thing he remembered clearly was 'Yeats coming to a tree and pausing – he was at that time a distinguished senator

---

11. A.E. Housman (1859–1936): 'In Valleys of Springs and Rivers', *A Shropshire Lad*.

of the Free State – pausing to pish against a tree! It was only a small thing, but it meant a great deal to me.' And he roared with laughter.

Three months later Hamish was in Germany. Arthur MacPherson, his German master at Dulwich, had helped him organise a study-trip to Berlin. Hamish was now deeply in love with German literature, particularly with Hölderlin, and desperate to see the city that had so recently enthralled Auden and Isherwood.[12] He joined a huge crowd outside the Tiergarten to watch Hitler drive by in an open car: 'hearing that crowd, seeing the girls swoon in adoration, witnessing those strident, vulgar salutes, I felt Europe coiling for war – and I felt that here was something I must oppose with every fibre in my being'.

At the start of the autumn half-term break Hamish took the night-sleeper to Aberdeen to attend a Bothy Nicht at the Imperial Hotel, organised by the Aberdeen Scottish Literature and Song Association. He hugely enjoyed himself and met two men who were to play important roles in his life. The first was the Aberdeenshire farmer John Strachan, a splendid bothy-ballad singer and raconteur, who, fifteen years later, was to become one of Hamish's most valuable ballad informants. The second was Alexander Keith, author of *Last Leaves*,[13] an acclaimed book about traditional song in Scotland. Hamish, who already knew the book well, told Keith that he believed the title to be misleading: far from being 'last leaves', the songs they had heard that evening were, he said, 'clear evidence that the auld Scots tradition is still alive and not dead, and, must be kept going!' Keith was delighted and encouraged the young enthusiast to return,[14] as soon as possible, to study the great Greig–Duncan collection in the archives of Aberdeen University.[15]

---

12. The visit gets one, rather dull, stanza in his 'Ballad of the Twelve Stations of my Youth': 'With Frau Popo I tour baroque museums / And throw largess – mit Meisterhand gemalt – / Then leave behind the puffy Prussian statues / And stroll with Gieschen through the Grunevald.'

13. Gavin Greig and Alexander Keith: *Last Leaves of Traditional Ballads and Ballad Airs* (Aberdeen: The Buchan Club 1925).

14. In 1938 Hamish was back in Aberdeen, poring over the thousands of songs, in high excitement. Many came from the eighteenth century, some were truly ancient, but the fact that they had all been 'collected live, from living singers, within living memory' was what most thrilled the budding folklorist. Here was living proof that 'Scots song was not dead but green and still alive on the tongues of the people: out of sight, perhaps, but vitally alive in bothies, in kitchens, in pubs – even in drawing rooms. I had heard it as a boy and I knew I would find it again. And there it was – vivid on the page and resonant in the voice of both farmer and farm servant.'

15. Gavin Greig (1856–1914), champion of Buchan tradition, whose great folk-song collection was made with the Rev J.B. Duncan (1848–1917).

Throughout this time Hamish was keeping diaries and notebooks. Unfortunately only one, documenting January to March 1937, appears to have survived, but it is a real treasure. It was written up, late at night, in Ingleton House but it is Dulwich College that dominates the content. It begins at Christmas 1936, in the home:

> A day of sheer superfluity. Christmas Day passed off gorgeously – with games of all sorts in the evening. The next day we went off to see the colossal Christmas Pantomime at the Streatham Hill Theatre – *Humpty Dumpty* – not so much a pantomime as a series of brilliant variety turns. You can't hang much on the bare Egg Story. Leonard Henry was most amusing as King Half-a-crown – and a good comedian is half the show ... Also 'Green Pastures' – a wonderful delineation of the Negro's conception of God – but I must concentrate on the future ...

The following diary extracts provide us with a vivid picture of Hamish's intellectual and creative life at this time.

> 15th Jan. 1937: More *Iphigenia* in the morning. In Latin we made a swift onslaught on Virgil. Read Flecker's letters in the dinner hour; am very interested in tracing the concept of Hassan. Discussed internationalism in the afternoon with a blatantly Cockney new Geography master; then Corinthians with dear old Mr Fenn.
> 16th Jan: Gave in French and German Prose. Resumed *Don Karlos* with Mr Russon – a long colourful play of Spain under Philip II. In the afternoon went again to see *Der Alte und der Junge König*; various fine moments – the King and the money-lenders, Prince Bairentz mistaking the King for a serving man, Frederick addressing the bloody shade of Katk, appearing to him in the cell – this a moment of wondrous fascination to me, Frederick's words were a tragic poem.
> 17th Jan: I was again on the washing-up this morning which is addedly disagreeable because I generally read the first lesson immediately afterwards and one's fingers, occasionally, become crinkly. Isaiah 44. Read Greek. A very typical Sunday with Mr Hevellyn's sermon – on covetousness – a chubby bespectacled little man who reminded me of Father Brown.[16] ...

---

16. Hamish was a great admirer of G.K. Chesterton and at Lendrick School he read most of the Father Brown books and Chesterton's *St Francis of Assisi*.

24th Jan: Sunday: Experienced novel sensation in the morning – was so intoxicated by my own rendering of Genesis I, as the morning's lesson, that the book nearly fell from my shaking hands. Talked on the *Raconteur*'s future with Paddy Goldring after the service – wrote part of my melodrama in the afternoon.

31st Jan: Last night I fainted just after getting out of my bath, so I took things as easily as possible today; wrote three articles for the *Alleynian*. Excellent sermon from Mr Ellingham on why we are obliged to attend chapel – very witty and sincere withall.

1st Feb: Accomplished a pretty considerable feat of will-power – set the alarm for six and got up. And had finished a full length essay on the philosophy of the Third Act of *Don Karlos* by breakfast, with the mind deliciously refreshed. Read the Jeistliche Leider of Novalis in the afternoon – what marvellous peace and sureness. Would I had It! A large chunk of Cicero in the evening.

6th Feb: Oppenheimer, the gentle, brilliant and good-natured Jew who gained a scholarship to Cambridge recently, presented a petition from the entire form to Eric today – that *he* will talk in French in future in his French periods just as Mac does in German. It was an intolerable piece of well-meaning impudence but Eric took it with beautiful, assenting good-humour – and, from then on, we spoke French . . .

9th Feb: [Shrove Tuesday] The chief grievance today was that there were no pancakes for lunch. A dreadful state of affairs, which I remedied soon enough when I got home in the evening![17]

After a while, gaps begin to appear in the diary and after his first blank page, Hamish writes, 'Here for the first time I am carrying out my policy of ruthlessness – though it grieves my heart to see a space after so many close-written pages.' He knew he must pass exams and win scholarships if he was to achieve the ends he had set himself. His commitment to the needs of the moment was ruthless and nothing would divert him from laying the foundations on which his vision of the future would be constructed.

Once the examination season was over, Hamish was ready for another European adventure and in July 1937 he set off for Paris, albeit in a slightly disturbed state of mind. He had become aware of a weakness within his own nature: his memory for poetry and song was so phenomenal that it threatened his development as a creative poet.

---

17. This enthusiasm for ritual is typical of Hamish: all his life he loved to adhere to the observance of ceremony.

Thousands of lines had now locked themselves so firmly inside his head that he began to feel hooked to every genius but his own. In particular he found himself 'possessed' by the percussive drama of MacDiarmid's magnificent early Scots lyrics. Looking back years later, he writes: 'Try hard as I might I was unable to rid myself of a horrible compulsive urge to parody; it is a kind of literary self-abuse . . .' In the long term, however, Hamish was one of the few twentieth-century Scottish poets not overwhelmed by MacDiarmid, and this may well have been a consequence of the completeness of his youthful immersion. Hamish's enthusiasm for MacDiarmid was further nurtured by Mr MacPherson,[18] whom he describes as having given him the key to unlock his understanding of the MacDiarmid phenomenon: 'MacPherson compared MacDiarmid to Goethe's Faust and argued that MacDiarmid's predicament and genius were indivisible and triumphant. I remember him quoting Goethe's words, "The good human being, in the midst of dark turmoil / Knows in himself the right way to go". Destiny, suffering and great art – are indivisible forces.' It was a moment of genuine insight and the insight remained with him long after he had got to know MacDiarmid well. Hamish was remarkably self-aware and, having recognised that his bardic capacity for 'total recall' was threatening his creative output, he began quite consciously, at the age of sixteen, to compartmentalise his creative work into sections: oral work, written art literature, ideological enquiry – and folk collecting.

Arriving in Paris at the Gare du Nord, Hamish was met by a thunderstorm, and within a few hours had struck up a liaison with a young Frenchman, whom he introduces in a notebook (written many years later) with these words: ' "Allay for the lack of rouge and lipstick" . . . That line comes from a poem I wrote – about an absurdly beautiful seventeen-year-old male prostitute I met in Paris 1937. This boy had arrived in the capital shortly before – from Nancy, believe it or not – to look for custom amongst the homosexual foreigners in Paris for the Exposition. He liked the look of me and – seeing I had no money, he showed a Cyrano de Bergerac generosity by shagging along with me, for nothing! And, for two weeks, we had the pleasure of a mini-two-in-a-bed relationship. Eventually we ended up singing folksongs in the YMCA in the rue de Treviso.' Hamish's fearless sexual amorality was part poetic licence and part revolutionary stance: he would exalt libertarian standards – standards that were the exact opposite of those that had so willfully and destructively been used against his mother. When he returned to London he notes

---

18. Mr MacPherson was a brilliant right-wing Germanophile of Perthshire origin who nurtured Hamish's interest in German literature.

'Every night I should offer up thanks to the Serapis that I escaped the terrible degenerate dithering respectability of a crazed Scotch Calvinism at the age of eight.'

Hamish was never to become part of any 'gay scene' and his occasional homosexual 'outbursts' were invariably short, sharp and shocking, to himself as much as to others. However, he refused to be ashamed by what 'life' sometimes delivered and, in both youth and age, he gloried in life's unscripted pleasures. His Paris was the world of William Blake's 'Proverbs of Heaven and Hell': 'the cut worm forgives the plough'. And, in Paris, he produced several poems that divide neatly into the sacred and profane. In October 1937, two were published in the *Alleynian*: one is an elegiac, Wordsworthian salute to French civilisation and the Cathedral of Notre Dame, entitled 'The Isle de St Louis – on a September evening', the other an 'Epigram – on being handsomely "done" by an all too plausible confidence trickster in Paris'.

The most significant work of art Hamish encountered in Paris was Picasso's *Guernica*, a centrepiece in the brilliantly modern Spanish Pavilion at the World Exhibition. Hamish spent several hours in front of it. However, it was in the British Pavilion that Hamish met a second man with whom he was to strike up an important short-term relationship. This man was Sir Walter Elliot, Secretary of State for Scotland. Sir Walter was in Paris to get ideas for the British Empire Exhibition being planned for Glasgow the following year, and for which he was responsible. Hamish got himself invited to lunch, and the conversation soon turned from smoked salmon to Scottish literature, the politics of MacDiarmid and Yeats, to fascism, communism – and 'next year, in Glasgow!'. Before they parted, Hamish tried to persuade Elliot to view Picasso's masterpiece in the Spanish Pavilion but the Minister declined. All the same, Hamish had been greatly impressed by the old Tory's courtesy and was never to forget his insistence that 'whatever is done in Scotland's name should be done well'. Consequently, in the summer of 1938, Hamish headed north to view Sir Walter's British Empire Exhibition in Glasgow. He toured it with pleasure but little satisfaction: an Art Deco demonstration of the White Man's burden was not what he believed modern Scotland should be offering the world. He had no wish to glorify the British Empire; his plan was to break it. He wanted Scotland to lead the way towards the democratisation of the whole British Empire: freedom, not subjection; peace, not war; equality, not dominion were the things he was interested in.

However, he was not in Scotland to see his nation make an exhibition of its lesser-self; he had come to make his 'Journey to a Kingdom' and to write poetry. For that reason he had got off the train at Carlisle so that he could 'physically experience' crossing and re-crossing the Border, on foot.

'About two miles into Scotland I met an old bloke who looked as if he'd been installed there to impress tourists – a magnificent looking patriarch, roman-nosed and white-bearded, wearing a broad bonnet; his horse cropped at the side of the road . . .' In Glasgow, Hamish stayed with the family of one of the boarders at Dulwich and together they viewed Glasgow Cathedral, the Clyde waterfront and the slums of the Gorbals. Hamish then continued his journey alone, along Loch Lomondside.

> Ben Lomond from the North West, descending;
> Like an Epstein or Henry Moore –
> Deuteronomy, perhaps, with a small
> Smooth featureless lump of a head cocked at an angle,
> And a great sweep of brawny arm
> Over brilliant multicoloured moors
> As scrunchable as honey-comb.[19]

In Glencoe, he met an old man who told him 'at third hand' the facts of the massacre in 1690. In Fort William he called on old Episcopal friends who had helped his mother when she was suffering ostracism, and with whom they had holidayed in the mid 1920s. He then hitchhiked towards the Kyle of Lochalsh where, weary and sore after a midge-scoured night in the heather, he awaited the ferry for Kyleakin:

> a green van had pride of place on the quay. Yes, he would give me a lift to Portree, but I'd have to wait half an hour or so on the other side of the narrows. 'That's fine' – and I hopped in out of the light rain that was spraying the jetty. As the big mother ferry churned songless over the strip of sea-loch the sluices of rain broke, and in the driver's cubbyhole of this ferried van I felt I was in the hold of Noah's Ark – when the land was breaking up and dissolving in one vast rain-beaten-wilderness . . . Would I be able to get another lift on to Uig? Or sleep, after drenched fever, a gutter sodden 'corpse in the heather'. Dr Johnson came in at the wrong end of the island, so might I.

Completely exhausted, Hamish fell asleep long before his driver returned and didn't wake up until the van arrived in Portree. He then crossed to Uig, where he stayed in the Youth Hostel, ceilidhed with the local doctor, and sang himself drinks in the bar of the Uig Hotel. Before long he fell-in

---

19. Unpublished stanza from Hamish's long poem 'Journey to a Kingdom', worked on intermittently between 1935 and 1940.

with an old crofter named Willie Campbell, who lived alone and was fond of a dram. They had a great time together and, during the following winter, Hamish wrote the old fellow several letters from Cambridge. He received no answer, so he wrote to Mr MacLeod, proprietor of the Uig Hotel, who on 23 May 1939 responded:

Dear Mr Henderson, I remember you perfectly well and I'm glad that you are hoping for another holiday in Skye this summer. About Willie Campbell, I don't advise you to stay with him although, I believe, when there's an overflow from the Youth Hostel he takes them in. Of course I have never been to his house but a man like him – staying alone – I can't think of his house being comfortable. However I will make a point of seeing him and ask him if he got your letter . . .

MacLeod was well-meaning, but the 'censorial values' evident in that letter were exactly those that Hamish was now determined to oppose; whereas Willie Campbell, in his poverty and isolation, was exactly the kind of man he wanted to celebrate as 'the salt of the earth'. And when, two decades later, Hamish wrote an article exploring the qualities of Highland culture, for the *Spectator* magazine, the dark kitchen-bedroom of Willie Campbell of Uig loomed up like a vision. The article was titled 'Come Gie's a Sang':

Unlike the peasantry of most other European nations, the Scots country folk do not decorate and paint their homes much. The interior of an old-style Highland cottage is austere, the predominant colours black and white, or else seedily dingy. People have sometimes mistakenly put this down to Calvinism; however, the same thing is true of the Catholic areas of Scotland, and indeed of the Irish domestic landscape. It looks as if in Scotland and in Ireland all of the urge of the people towards artistic self-expression has flowed into the oral folk-arts, into song and story. These we have, and galore.[20]

Hamish had now decided that his 'Journey to a Kingdom' must begin in Glasgow – amidst the poverty of the Great Depression. For Hamish, unemployment, poverty and disease had reduced industrial Clydeside to a symbol of everything that was socially and politically wrong with modern Scotland. As the Ossianic bards had sung Auld Scotland into being, so Hamish decided he would sing a new Scotland into being – out of the black despair of the Gorbals, he would draw 'a singing light'.

---

20. *Spectator*, 25 May 1954, later published in *Alias MacAlias: Writings on Song, Folk and Literature* (Polygon 1992).

Alone and alonie
I climb Balmano Street. The haggard houses
Spew out their wizened withered aged children
On to the dirty stone. They puke and sprawl
And play, while in the fetid passage-ways
Coated with venomed slime, our hairy marys
Lick poison out from bloody blackened nails.
So howl, ye ships from Clyde![21]

Hamish knew that the Arthurian dream of a benign resurrectional kingship was a nonsense in the twentieth century, but he believed that the Ossianic force of Scotland's song-tradition was of permanent value, and (despite his socialist republicanism) he had begun to believe that poetry was perhaps the only means by which the Scottish people could, once again, become 'kings over themselves'. And, if they did that, he foresaw that both the Ossianic and Arthurian prophecies might be fulfilled.

The poem opens with deliberately visceral brutality. Hamish seems to expose not just 'capitalist exploitation' but the attitudes nurtured by slum-living. He writes 'he who makes his bed / On velvet coal-dust must cut out his eyes / And impale them on a pin' and it is only after he has set down the Hell he wishes to transform that he moves north into the clean mountain air of future possibilities. Here, he explores the prophecies of the Brahan Seer, the legacy of the Highland Clearances, the impact of years of foreign wars and mass emigration. Having established these parameters to his poem, he looks at selected individuals and the current realities of 'the land we live in'. As he does this, the poem changes gear and, cinematically, introduces a group of Highland protagonists, each brought to the screen by the flaring of a match or a flash of revelation.

While he was brooding on Scotland's history and destiny, Hamish also fumed at contemporary injustice burgeoning abroad. He knew that time was against him and that his plans for Scotland would have to wait until after Hitler's vision of Teutonic dominion had been neutralised or destroyed.

Man's misery is little to this fellow.
Blood's river is water to the safely sailing.
No Swift need tell us that the oak's heart's hollow.

---

21. From 'Journey to a Kingdom', published version, in the *Collected Poems*.

Hollow and rotten like the crumbling apple.
Hollow as a skull, hollow as history
On God's blackboard – hollow as death's mystery.

. . . It is ill living now in doomed Troy.[22]

Then he turns aside to address the problem of his own growing 'English-ness'. His Dulwich friends might speak of his strong Scottish accent but Hamish knew that most Scots now heard his voice as English, and he was conscious that with 'his place' at Cambridge guaranteed, he might become, or be thought to be, a stranger in his own country. He was aware that England had seduced many Scots before him and he outlines this continuing problem in a section of the poem in which self-analysis leads to a re-strengthening of his political resolve:

This is the exile's trouble – the treachery of other grown familiar,
The inevitable erosion of early habit
And the early speech grown halting and clumsy.
And again we are reminded – when other is courteous,
Honeyed and wooing us to shame and betrayal,
      The little smile for own foibles
      The smiling excuse for identity
      The excusing joke of our own nationhood and name.[23]

The bulk of 'Journey to a Kingdom' was completed during the summer of 1938 – though Hamish knew the poem lacked unity and, in 1940, he renewed his attempt to draw its many threads together. However, he was always to remain dissatisfied with the poem (as a whole) and it has not been published. Hamish shied from the magnificient 'conceit' implicit in the poem but its importance – to his life and work – cannot be over-emphasised.

     A path through the black-cored moorland
     Is my way home . . .
     Now the west knows
     I am come. Now night has lowered its barrier . . .

---

22. Unpublished section from 'Journey to a Kingdom'.
23. This section of 'Journey to a Kingdom' was later modified and published as an independent poem, entitled 'This is the Exile's Trouble', which appears in the *Collected Poems*.

He knew 'Journey to a Kingdom' was the last of his 'childhood' and, like a young Shakespeare, puts a mirror up to what he believes the future demands of him. Thus, the poem ends: 'Thick darkness is over the people – but wait / But wait . . .' Conceited or not, Hamish means what he writes and, even before becoming an undergraduate, he takes unto himself the mantle of deliverer.

Hamish's work for the Dulwich College *Alleynian* was an experience of long-term consequence. He was an assistant editor from 1936 to 1937 and an editor from 1937 to 1938 and he systematically used the magazine to hone his literary talents and to imprint his vision and values on the life of the College. He wrote editorials, articles and poems, but also presented his work under aliases, including Z. Marcus, Agrippa, Felix, Tusshe, Polonius, Baralipton and Omega. Hamish was determined to make things happen and proudly advertised his role in the transformations he sought to initiate. For example, in the *Alleynian* editorial for December 1937, he writes: 'the appearance of *Caravan* [Hamish's own literary magazine] was a very salutary experience for the *Alleynian*, and contributed, in part at least, to the splendid literary renaissance at Dulwich in the last year'. In another editorial he castigates readers who do not realise 'the organization that lies behind the scenes' and he points out that the *Alleynian* has 'a policy, a plan of campaign, a set of guiding principles . . .', which were of course his own principles.

As a sixth-former Hamish was one of the stars of the Literary and Debating Society: 'Robert Burns is the Prince of Poets! Poets are not weaklings but men of action – who want their thoughts in permanent, beautiful form! Aesthetic poetry is a form of escapism – there was nothing weak about Classical Art!' He also acted in, directed and stage-managed numerous contemporary plays – including *Ascent of F6*, *The Rising of the Moon*, *Campbell of Kilmhor* and *Hassan*. Four entirely new College societies came into being under his wing: the Shakespeare Reading Society, the Modern Sixth Drama Society, the 'Independent Club' (created with his friend Peter Paston Brown, which aimed 'to do *all* not done elsewhere'), and the Dulwich College Puppet Society (inspired by a performance of *Faust*, at Dulwich, by the German Puppet-Maestro, Paul Brann).

Hamish hugely enjoyed his London years and when, in July 1938, he rose to sing the Dulwich College Song for the last time he did so, not in doubt at its imperialistic tenor, but with hedonistic gusto – and carried off a stack of prizes, mostly for languages, but also the Lady Evan Spicer Prize for Art, a Downing College 'Exhibition' and one of the elite UK State Scholarships that would enable him to enjoy Cambridge in some style.

THREE

The Dry Drayton Rectory and Cambridge University

*A man unto himself
a world untold*
HH

At Cambridge, Hamish read Modern Languages (German and French) but the reason he chose to study at Downing College was because it had recently become a powerhouse of radical new developments in English literary criticism. The man at the engine of this movement for change was F.R. Leavis, a modernist who had decided to re-evaluate the history and theory of English literature: the Latinate grandeur of Milton and the sentimentality of romanticism were out; the 'unified sensibility' of the metaphysical poets was in – as were Ezra Pound, D.H. Lawrence, and modern master T.S. Eliot. Leavis also took the Scots literary tradition seriously and in the mid thirties had invited John Speirs, a brilliant young academic from Aberdeen, to join him and apply his methods to Scots literature. Hamish had studied the work of both men at Dulwich and was delighted to be asked to join Leavis at High Table within weeks of taking rooms in Downing. The two men quickly struck up an inspired relationship: Leavis encouraged Hamish to add modernist rigour to his Celtic romanticism; Hamish stated his determination to look back beyond Dunbar, Chaucer and Cadman to the very origins of European literature – and remain a Scottish writer. Invited into the Leavis house, Hamish immediately struck a rapport with Leavis' wife, Queenie, and his university career took off at the double.

Among the Old Alleynians who went up to Cambridge with Hamish were two close friends Michael Clarke and Donald Campbell, but he was determined to spread his wings and soon joined a brilliant student circle that included Raymond Williams, Maurice J. Craig, George Scurfield, Michael Orram, Stephen Coates and D.J. Enright. The man most like himself was Maurice Craig, a Northern Irishman, who recalled in 2003:

We were all 'fellow-travellers'; lunching together in Cambridge University Socialist Club (which was nominally socialist but actually communist). Hamish was, as I remember, half a head taller than we were (I am still 6′1″ or so) and large in proportion. He was very loud-voiced, very insistently Scottish, and constantly singing. I can remember, 'The Road to the Isles' and 'Saw ye the cotton-spinners, saw ye them gaun awa / Saw ye the cotton-spinners marching doon the Broomielaw?' . . . It was I that wrote the first stanza of the song he developed into his 'Ballad of the Taxi Driver's Cap'. We sang it to 'The Lincolnshire Poacher'. It was a good-humoured salute to Stalin and Hamish expanded it into a popular army song.[1]

Because of his size, Hamish was soon 'body-hunted by the sculling fraternity' and persuaded to become a member of the Downing Eight: briefly, he enjoyed 'skimming the Cam like a dipper'. His real enthusiasm, however, was for the Cambridge Union and the theatre group known as the Cambridge Mummers. Donald Campbell remembers Hamish 'acting, working as a stage-manager, organising play readings and writing at least one play for the Mummers. Its name was "The Humpy Cromm", and set at Speaker's Corner in London.' No original script appears to survive but, in 1980, Hamish 'recovered' the whole play from notes and memory. Its subject is IRA terrorism, English Imperialism, the clash between communism and fascism, and the play gives voice to a radical Irish nationalism rarely heard in England at this time. Political dialectic and cockney slapstick, philosophy and song are flung at the complacent, bourgeois, theatre-going intelligentsia of Cambridge. Hamish poses the question: 'How can we cut the barbarism out of modern society without killing the poetry in man?' 'The Humpy Cromm' gave Hamish a chance to shock the public, and the combative self-confidence evident in Hamish as a dramatist was very much part of his student persona. For example, after a minor argument with his friend Jamie Cable he writes:

Dear Jamie, I never like being angry, just as I never like being slighted, and that is why I will make a gentler end to our friendship by apologizing. It is not regret but courtesy, only, which prompts me to this; courtesy, you will remember, is one of those primitive Highland virtues that I retain. I do not apologize personally, because an 'unbidden guest' who 'only comes to listen to your wireless'

---

1. Letter from Maurice Craig to TN, 2003.

would in any case be *de trop* . . . It annoys me all the more that you can condemn the rumbustious Rabelaisian vulgarities of an Irish street ballad, because it comes out of the 'gutter'. Villon came out of the 'gutter' – he was a boozer, a whoremaster, a thief and a murderer, but he was a great poet. Sean O'Casey's characters breed and brag over the 'gutter' but they are blood-brothers of Falstaff and Bardolph, of Pistol and Nym . . . Burns, who drank himself sick with his Jolly Beggars, is one of the great poets of the world . . .

The truth is that art and civilization are not synonymous and it is farcical to protest that they are. The Congolese fetish-makers were artists, but they were not in the restricted and proper sense of the word, civilized. I have not the faintest wish to disparage those great artists who were civilized – Phidias, Sophocles, Aristophanes, Rapheal, Racine, Milton, Wren, Jane Austen; but I want to take up my cromak in defence of those who were not: the builders of the Gothic cathedrals, Villon, Shakespeare, Rembrandt, Emily Brontë, Rousseau, Whitman, Turner, Wagner, as well as the authors of the *Iliad*, the Scottish Border ballads, *The Mabinogion* and the folk-songs of all countries . . . and I continue to protest, unashamedly, that in a Dublin tenement or a Hebridean 'blackhouse' I find a richer and sweeter human spirit than in the town house . . . When art turns in on itself, when it exists for Art's sake, it is bad art, art gone rotten, and is hardly worth the name art at all . . . The folk culture of America lives – like that of the Celtic Countries, the most vital in the world.[2]

Throughout his two years as a Cambridge undergraduate Hamish was a genuinely 'angry young man' but his wish to honour tradition was very much part of his radicalism. He continued to go to church regularly and attended different College chapels – according to who was preaching the sermon. One Sunday afternoon he walked out to the village of Dry Drayton, five miles north-west of Cambridge, to attend Evensong. Whether he walked to Dry Drayton because the preacher there was a cultured Irishman of Scots extraction, or because he was known to be a committed socialist and pacifist, or because Dry Drayton lies at the end of 'Scotland Road' is not clear – but it was a walk that changed his life. After Evensong, Hamish found himself invited back to the rectory 'for supper – as though I was one of the family'. The rector was Canon Allan Armstrong, a Church of Ireland priest who had been driven out by the IRA. After some years in the United States he had been offered the living at Dry Drayton. It came with a large Georgian rectory, sheds and

---

2. Henderson archive.

outhouses, great trees and seven acres of meadows. Thus he, and his large family, moved in 'to keep open house in the old Irish style'. And, with its thirty rooms, ill-sprung beds, sun porch and rough-cut lawns, the rectory quickly became 'a home from home' to a rotating community of relatives, footloose bohemians and refugees of every description. And it suited Hamish down to the ground. Within weeks he had his 'own room' and, for the next twenty years, Dry Drayton provided him with his one permanent address in the world. Here was the 'Human House' of which William Morris had written; and in that sun-drenched, paint-peeling, roof-leaking rectory Hamish found a second 'Glenshee' – shabby, genteel and sublime. From Dry Drayton he went out to fight fascism, and to Dry Drayton he would return until he was too old to travel.

Canon Allan Armstrong and Hamish became close friends. They played chess late into the night, talked politics, drank, sang and 'got to grips with the world'. Hamish was thrilled by the old man's humanism and his deeply Celtic Christian belief. They laughed at the woolly-headed nonsense that passed for Christianity with too much of the Anglican hierarchy; Armstrong was always eager to hear Hamish's latest poem and encouraged him to make limericks:

> It was the old Bishop of Birmingham
> Who wrote 'Legends and my view concerning 'em'.
> He's dispensed with the need
> Of an Anglican creed
> And as for the Gospels – he's burning 'em![3]

The rectory was almost self-sufficient in food, and at weekends Hamish would help Violet, the Armstrongs' youngest daughter, in the garden and stables. They got on very well: 'One day I rode out with Violet into a great field where, at the far end, we saw that a herd of horses had gathered. I suggested we race towards them: as we did so, the herd charged towards us! We rode on, close together, at full speed – we two against the hordes of Asia! At twenty yards the herd opened – like the Red Sea – and we sailed through on the wind. At the far end of the field we wheeled round – to watch the herd wheeling round at the other end! Then we, and they, set off again, and repeated the charge! Happy times we had at Dry Drayton.' Of course, not everyone at Dry Drayton was a liberal, let alone a socialist, and Hamish was well aware of the aggressive Irish Ascendancy attitudes that occasionally flared up at the rectory. However, his criticisms of the

---

3. HH, unpublished, from notebook.

Armstrongs were always laced with love, as is displayed in his poem 'High Hedges', written in 1940:

'Look at this rug. It's from Kesh in Fermanagh.
My mother used to say it was older than the Union.
When you ride down the road looking so grand on your horses,
I shall come to the gate and watch.'

. . .

She speaks from a world I am helping to deforest,
where our job is to level and to clear, for the building
of our human house on the level, in the sunlight.
We have boasted our Universe ghostless and godless.

So what? – I'll not slacken in the necessary labour
with handsaw and axe, with trowel and with mortar,
but must freely acknowledge Christ to live among gods
while that white cottage can boast its high hedges.[4]

In debate at the Cambridge Union, however, Hamish spoke with a no-holds-barred ferocity that marked him 'a man to watch'. He argued against Chamberlain's appeasement policies, against Nazism and fascism, and in favour of the Spanish Republic, Scottish republicanism, socialism and peace. He believed that only strong and united action by 'the people' could deflect Europe from another World War even more grotesque and destructive than the last. His speeches caught the attention of Quakers recruiting peace activists as messengers and escorts in Germany. He agreed to join their operation and in July 1939 attended a briefing in Regent Street, London, with the distinguished art historian Dr Niklaus Pevsner. All instructions had to be held in the head. It was an arrangement that suited Hamish: 'the oral tradition in action!'.

Hamish went out to Germany at the end of July 1939. While still engaged on his mission he received the following letter from S.M. Robinson, the British Consul General, Hamburg, dated 14 August: 'In view of the present strained relations between His Majesty's Government and Germany I suggest that you should urgently consider the desirability of removing your residence from Germany for the present.' Hamish stayed on for another fortnight. One of his jobs was to convey a young Jewish girl called Lotte across Germany (probably to the Swiss border),

---

4. Published in the *Collected Poems*.

another to bring a half-Jewish teenager, Karl Heinz Gerson, to England –
and they got out by the skin of their teeth, three days before Hitler's
invasion of Poland. On the evening of 28 August while their train waited
on the German side of the border for guards to check papers, things got
very tense, so Hamish asked an elderly Dutchman to teach him and Karl
Heinz the Dutch national anthem. By the time the train was allowed to
move out over the Rhine, they knew it well enough to sing, and with
gathering exhilaration 'we sang that song! We sang until we knew we
were beyond the mid point of the river and into the Netherlands.' After
delivering Karl Heinz to a Quaker hostel in Ledbury, Herefordshire,
Hamish wrote a long article entitled 'Germany in Tormentis'; signing it as
by 'a Cambridge undergraduate who has just returned from the Reich'.
Whether it was published is unknown but it remains a vivid and
important first-hand account of Germany on the eve of war.

On 3 September 1939 Hamish hitch-hiked from Ledbury to London;
en route he heard the news that war had been declared. He slept the night
in Kensington Gardens and, on waking, wrote 'Bonjour, Misère':

> We had twenty years – twenty years for
> Building and learning.
> Those twenty years come back no more.
> An incendiary dawn is prelude to this soft morning
> First morning of the new war.[5]

Over the next two years Hamish kept a fatherly eye on Karl Heinz –
writing him letters and sending presents. Unfortunately, Heine developed
into an obstreperous young man with aggressively pro-German sympa-
thies. Indeed, his 'guardians' in Ledbury found him so difficult that after
the Blitz he was moved to London to stay with relatives. In 1942, other
relatives in New York paid his passage to America where, three years
later, having been drafted into the United States army, he was killed on
manoeuvres. In 1946, when Hamish finally learned the facts of Karl
Heinz's tragic end, he went to Germany to meet the family. Ironically,
Karl Heinz's younger brother and both parents had survived the war.
After his visit, Frau Gerson wrote:

> My dear Hamish – You don't know how happy I was that you, at
> least, returned safely from this dreadful war. We had almost given
> up hope of ever hearing from you again. The boy's letter, for which I

---

5. Published in the *Collected Poems*.

thank you with all my heart, tells us how lovingly you looked after him. How can we ever thank you. You are right. Love is the only weapon to conquer all the devils of this world. May God strengthen us in this love. It is often hard for us to believe in the good when scoundrels rule the world, but he who said, 'My Kingdom is not of this world' was capable of such a love – which passeth understanding . . . My husband thanks you for the cigarettes. He was very disappointed to have missed you. Peter was very touched to get the birthday telegram, the delicious sweets, and the twenty marks. He said with a smile, 'This is most unScottish!' With witty remarks like that he often eases our stress. What good wishes can I send you for the coming winter . . . Above all, the necessary peace, and time, for your writing . . . I enclose a poem for your collection that was sent to us by a young friend, on the Polish front, before he was killed in action . . . With regards and gratitude – Dora Gerson. PS. Dear HH, if ever I was sorry to miss the visit of a friend, it was yours . . . Your visit here was like a ray of sunshine for us in these desolate times. Herr Gerson.

On 4 September 1939 Hamish tried to enrol with the Cameron Highlanders (the regiment in which James Scott had served in the First World War). Because of his poor eyesight he was told to await call-up. Consequently, with the Hilary term at Downing still a month away, he decided to look up his old friend Leo Hawkes, from Ingleton House. Leo was living in a one-room bed-sit and had a job as a clerk paying 17/6 a week – so they decided to go out for a night on the town. However, Hamish's trousers, after a month in Germany, were ragged and dirty and he asked if he could borrow a pair of Leo's. Despite the fact that 'they flew at half-mast', Hamish took a fancy to them and, a day or two later, asked if he could keep them to take back to Cambridge. 'But I've only got two pairs,' said Leo. 'And I've got none,' said Hamish. Leo remained adamant until Hamish suddenly got an idea: 'Look, Leo,' he said 'I promise you this, if you give me the trousers I'll introduce you to the Armstrongs – you need a holiday. I'll arrange for you to stay at the rectory and I'll introduce you to Violet – she's a beautiful young woman . . .' Leo soon perked up and agreed, and Hamish returned north 'in breeches fit for the Prodigal Son'!

A couple of weeks later on a fine September evening Leo stepped off the train at Cambridge Station and set off for Dry Drayton. Because of his weak heart he got no further than Madingley that evening but, when he finally arrived, Violet Armstrong came sweeping down the hall stairway to greet him and remembers the moment 'as though it were yesterday':

He came in, I showed him his room, we went out into the garden, we had lunch and he never left us. Leo seemed destined to be mine. My mother was very keen on a curate called Geoffrey with money and a secure living, whereas Leo had nothing. 'Life Expectancy – NIL', that's what the doctors would write on his medical certificates. But Leo had such spirit. You see, at the Home, ARB never spared him; Leo had to do what all the other boys did. There was no moping with Leo. We got married. We had three children. Leo built us a house and he was with us for fifty years. He was never well, our life was a continuing miracle, and when Leo died Hamish came and read from the New Testament. Leo was a great father to the boys and Hamish was like an uncle to each one.[6]

Among the many European refugees who stayed at Dry Drayton during the war years was a fourteen-year-old Jewish boy called Werner Peritz. In March 1940 he learned that his parents had managed to get into Holland and were about to sail for New York, via Southampton. When Hamish heard that Werner's request to meet his parents on the *Volendam* had been turned down 'on account of regulations', he determined to act. Werner would see his parents! Thus, with Werner and Violet's younger brother, Charles, Hamish hitch-hiked down to Southampton. Refused entry to the docks, Hamish made contact with the *Volendam*'s pilot and persuaded him of the great good only he could do. And so it was agreed that Werner would go out in the pilot's launch and have two hours on board the *Volendam* as it sailed down the Solent. After the war, Werner Peritz rejoined his parents in New York, where he still lives.

Unlike Auden, Hamish believed that poetry could and should make things happen. For him life was poetry, and poetry life, and he determined to use the Cambridge Union as a platform from which his poetry and his opinions would be heard – not just across the city but across Britain. When Stephen Spender appeared as a guest debater, Hamish took the opportunity of both speaking his mind and ridiculing a man whom he considered an over-rated poet and a dilettante:

Sir, I am a Scot – and, there is one thing which Scottish poets should avoid – according to the redoubtable Hugh McDiarmid – and that is the harmful influence of the Auden/Spender School. It is pernicious! It is . . . It is . . . But I thought it would be fitting to compose a

---

6. Violet Armstrong, conversation with TN.

Hamish's mother, Janet Henderson, c. 1908

Janet Henderson (on the left)
with two of her sisters,
Broughty Ferry, c. 1898

Hamish's mother and
grandmother, Helen Jobson
Henderson, Blairgowrie, c. 1910

James Scott (centre, presumed father of Hamish), with his family c. 1894. Standing are his brothers, William (left) and Isaac; seated are their mother, Lizzie Dishington Scott, and sister Lizzie.

James Scott with his wife Camilla Sutherland Scott (on the left of James); to his right is his sister, Lizzie; seated to his left is his mother, Lizzie Dishington Scott, c. 1912 Inverness

Hamish's uncle, Patrick Henderson, a doctor in the British Army, killed in France, 1916

John Stewart Murray, Marquis of Tullibardine (8th Duke of Atholl) off Gallipoli, 1916. Legends circulate that 'Bardie' was Hamish's father, but current evidence suggests that this is unlikely

Hamish and his mother enjoying a little *porta beula* (mouth music), 1921

Hamish, Somerset, c. 1929

Hamish on holiday in Brighton, c. 1929

Hamish on holiday from Lendrick School with his mother at Brighton, c. 1931

Life at the Ingleton House Orphanage, Clapham (Hamish's home 1934–8). Top: shoe inspection. Middle: theatrical games. Bottom: sea bathing (Hamish in the towel turban)

Hamish as a Dulwich College schoolboy, and on holiday, 1935–37

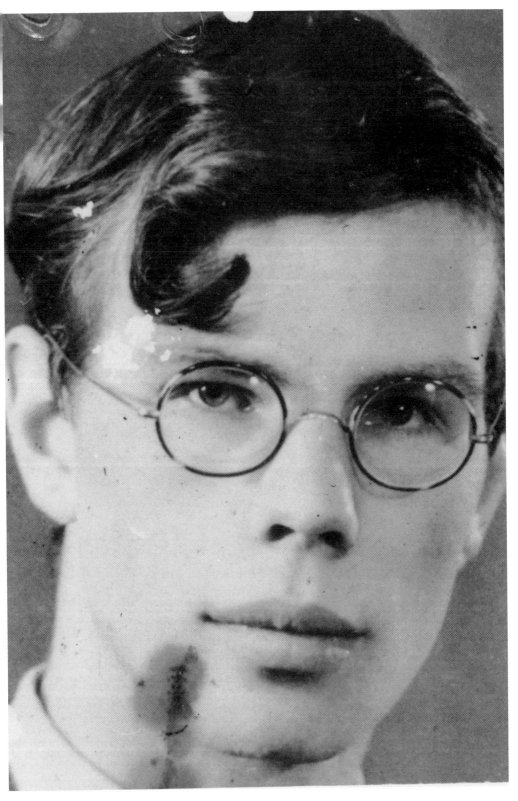
Hamish as an undergraduate at Cambridge, 1938

Hamish taking tea with the Armstrongs at the Dry Drayton Rectory, summer 1939

Downing College Rowing Eight, 1939: Hamish is seated far left

Violet Armstrong with her father, Canon Allan Armstrong of Dry Drayton, c. 1939

Leo Wallace Hawkes, Hamish's friend, who married Violet Armstrong after the war

Dry Drayton Rectory, 2003

Dry Drayton Rectory lawn: refugees, socialists, students and kittens on a summer's evening

Violet Armstrong with refugee Werner Peritz, whom Hamish reunited with his parents

Hamish on leave at Dry Drayton, 1941

'Hamish' playing the goat in the grounds of Dry Drayton, 1940

Hamish in uniform as a private in the Pioneer Corps – with Violet Armstrong, early 1941

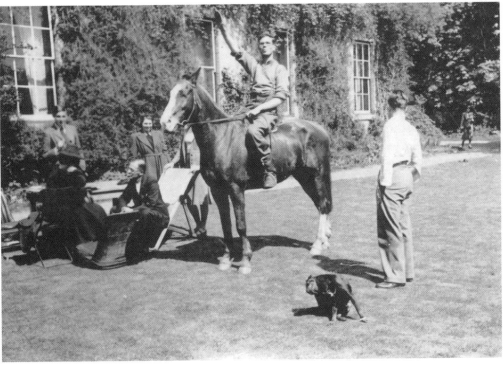

Hamish 'practising for the invasion of Sicily', 1941

A visionary image of the bard Ossian by 'R. R. 1937'. This portrait (strikingly like the young Hamish) was used by Glasgow University Ossianic Society as the front cover of its magazine in 1949, when Hamish was heavily involved in its activities (HH archives)

greeting to Mr Spender – in Shakespearean hexameters and on Sunday evening I attempted to produce a few. But – but – I was so frustrated by the effect that – I had to lie down . . .

. . . See, see, the am'rous nymph who sweet and slender
Heaps roses on the laurelled brow of Spender –
She charms him to her well-upholstered grot,
And every Autumn Journal is forgot . . .[7]

In another Union debate, on the desirability of marriage, Hamish took an equally controversial libertarian stance:

Asking your pardon, sir – I approach this subject not from the standpoint of the Marxist dialectitian – but from the standpoint of the complete Rabelaisian man – the man for whom beauty is only skin-deep – the man for whom Moral *Dis*armament is the imperative doctrine. Love, sir, as you know, is a very dangerous staff to handle – especially if you insist on going to extremes like marriage!

Despite his publicly avowed Rabelaisian enthusiasms, Hamish still believed himself 'hobbled by the monstrous denial of life, which in my adolescence was fobbed off on me as right living' and, as he sought to live 'freely', as opposed to living 'rightly', he found a Herculean ally in the Scots author, Norman Douglas. Douglas had lived many years on the Isle of Capri and used its deeply pagan and hedonistic culture as inspiration for his fictional 'Island of Nepenthe'. Hamish identified closely with Douglas and, in Union debates, quoted great chunks from Douglas' highly controversial novel *South Wind*. He felt Douglas' Mediterranean world speaking directly to him, celebrating

the inalienable right of man and beast to enact that which will confound death, and replenish the land with youth, and joy, and teeming life. The right which priestly castes of every age had striven to repress, which triumphs over every obstacle and sanctifies, by its fruit, the wildest impulse of man. The right to love . . .

. . . He was changing . . . there was so much to learn, to know, to see . . . He descended noiselessly into the cool and dark chasm – like looking into another world, he thought, a poet's world . . . The cave

---

7. HH, unpublished, from notebook.

had been consecrated to older and worthier rights – to some mysterious, primeval, fecund Mother Earth . . . There is something grand in this old animistic conception . . . The spendthrift abundance of nature – not excluding our own.[8]

Hamish was soon involved in a public spat with the young English poet Nicholas Moore. Moore was intimidated by Hamish's 'louring Scots presence'; they corresponded but did not get on. However, Hamish stimulated Moore to write one of his best Cambridge poems:

> You look like history. All the bright caravans
> That ended in no more than a madman's whisper,
> The cavalcade of honour that led to death,
> Is history you have loved and suffered beneath.
>
> You look like fable, myth, and the fairy tale,
> But you are real as the boy was in the stable.
> What agony is to suffer will still be true,
> Though the future open out like a flower in you.[9]

Hamish was ever keen to play the Scottish card and on 11 November 1939 (his twentieth birthday), he announced a forthcoming debate in the *Cambridge Review*:

On Tuesday evening the Union will decide whether it approves of Scottish Nationalism . . . In the eighteenth century Scotland and the wild Highlanders were – for comfortable Hanoverian England – very much what Captain Moonlight and the Sinn Feiners were for the full-bottomed era of Victoria. They were discordant and barbarous elements who insisted on disturbing the sober Anglo-Saxon Mammon, and had to be put down by breeks-wearing and Coercion Acts. Meanwhile, in Scotland, the blood of the old culture was slowly drained away at the price of bourgeois prosperity; and now Scotland is a distressed area with a fertile superiority complex and the makings, so it is said, of a first class revolutionary movement. With this there is, intimately linked, a movement for regaining Scotland's independence and the reconstruction of the state. Scots will please turn up for the debate – for the honour of Alba.

---

8. Norman Douglas, *South Wind* (Martin Secker 1917).
9. Nicholas Moore, 'Poem' (For Priscilla), *A Wish in Season – Poems by Nicholas Moore* (The Fortune Press 1941).

A fortnight later, Hamish organised a special St Andrew's Night Ceilidh, at which he gave the keynote address on 'The Ubiquitous Nature of the Scot'. And, in October 1940, he presented a 'farewell lecture' organised in his honour by the University Socialist Club. Hamish spoke on 'Scotland, Socialism, Nationalism and Ideals'. He believed it likely to be his Cambridge swansong and he determined to go out with a bang:

> Sir – I rise to state that this week is critical – for Socialism and for me. The trouble with Socialism in this country is that we haven't got a Lenin to blast the dainty tripping toes of the Party Liners out of their comfortable ruts . . . Ya frowsy herd of emasculated Yes Men! The nearest we have is a bloke by the name of MacDiarmid, a poet who lives in the Shetland Isles. What we have here is University Bourgeois Communism – an infantile paralysis of the brain! What we don't want is high flown language. What we want is the facts . . . Sir, I have been called a person without ideals. Unkind people without principles, without morals, have called me this . . . But it is really unjust to say I am without ideals . . . One ideal which has stood me in good stead for a lifetime, which first uplifted me at my mother's knee and which still ennobles and inspires me – is the ideal of the Socialist state – that ideal, for me, is bound up with the cause of Scottish Workers Republicanism. I invite you now to subscribe or I will assume you to be no Englishmen . . .
>
> I have not told you yet why this week is critical – you shall hear it. *It is my voice* – which I have never hesitated to raise in defence of liberty, justice, and Scottish Workers Republicanism: *my voice*, which more than any other single factor served to sweep away Chamberlain and his infamous broliarchy from power: *my voice*, which has struck rows of quivering conservatives green and petrified. *My voice* – has gone . . . You will understand . . . Put it down to November – season of mists and general beastliness, in the noble words of Keats . . . My dwelling will soon be in nothing and the void will soon be my sanctuary – in short – I AM BEING CALLED UP. Under the mask of light badinage this is the ghostly death's-head of the doomed man. This is my last appearance in any Cambridge debating hall. But – waste no tears on me – my ideal will not fail me. The torch of Scottish Workers Republicanism will still burn in an alien ground.

When Hamish states that it was *his* voice 'which more than any other single factor served to sweep away Chamberlain and his infamous broliarchy from power' we have to ask what he meant. Is he joking, being rhetorical, indulging in Celtic boasting? Or might he, possibly, be telling what he believes is the truth? Did Hamish, in league with like-minded radicals across Britain – by demonstrating, by intellectual argument, by the fermentation of revolutionary thought, by writing poems, singing songs and by sheer will – transform British attitudes to the 'Phony War' and demonstrate Chamberlain to be a national liability? If they did, their achievement has certainly not been recognised in the history books but the 'small voice' can trigger profound political changes, and Hamish's claim may be less preposterous than it seems.

Since the beginning of the war Hamish had been writing and collecting a body of about forty manuscript poems entitled 'Songs of Sabotage and Sedition'. These songs were created with the specific aim of undermining the Chamberlain government and the muddled-headed, capitalist elite that upheld it. The songs were made to be circulated 'underground' and are proof of the widespread anti-establishment undercurrents flowing through Britain throughout the Phony War period. Today, most Britons like to assume that, unlike the French, the British were, from start to finish, united, clear and determined in their commitment to destroy Nazi tyranny. Far from it. There was in fact plenty of apathy, defeatism and pro-German sentiment in Britain. For example, in Glasgow in 1938, Hamish had been appalled to see graffiti describing Scotland's need for a man 'like Hitler'. During the winter of 1939–40, half the British Cabinet argued to undo 'the war we have so impetuously declared', and Hamish's 'Songs of Sabotage and Sedition' gave expression to a popular anger across working-class Britain that the war was being pursued largely in the interests of a ruling-class establishment:

> Frightfully decent people all
> Coming away from Portugal.
> Nobody knows, when Britain cracks,
> Where they'll pay their super-tax![10]

On 17 November 1939, Hamish attended a meeting of the Cambridge University Conservative Association at which Admiral Sir Herbert Richmond KCB, Master of Downing College, spoke on 'Naval Strategy'. Hamish rose to state that it was Britain that had laid the foundations for this 'latest round of European top-dogism' and that, while England draped itself in veils of 'morality and democratic intention', *it* had been the cause of wars, all round the world, for generations. He denounced the

---

10. From an unpublished booklet in Hamish's hand, entitled 'Songs of Sabotage and Sedition'.

admiral's talk as 'window-dressing to a sham!' The Master of Downing was not pleased; a group of young Conservatives moved to shut the 'Scots Commie' up, and he was ushered from the hall. They could not, however, prevent him from singing and writing poetry; 'Certitude' is an example of the kind of attacks he was now launching:

Certitude

We are bound to win the war –
Some of us –
We know what we're fighting for –
Some of us.
So let us prosecute our aims
However many folk it maims
Consol'd that though of life bereft
There's sure to be somebody left –
Some of us! . . .[11]

Hamish was already involved in setting up the Cambridge Students' People's Convention, 'to steer government policy towards a Socialist future', with the specific aim 'of containing the war before it expands into a worldwide conflict only resolveable by the total defeat of one side'. At meetings organised between 29 November and 1 December 1939, Hamish drafted a letter to the University of Cambridge. It was issued by the People's Vigilance Committee and called for support for the People's Convention, which was to meet on 12 January 1940: 'The convention will discuss the formation of a new government which would carry out the policy set forth in the Manifesto. Already in South Wales the representatives of a quarter of a million people have met in a Convention . . . All over the country people are meeting in an endeavour to find a solution to the terrible problems that confront them. It would be a tragedy if, at a time like this, the Universities were to cut themselves off from the people.' The letter then outlined their six main objectives:

1) Defence of the People's Living Standards
2) Defence of the People's Democratic and Trades Union Rights
3) Adequate Air Raid precautions and facilities
4) Friendship with the Soviet Union
5) A People's Government – representative of the Whole People
6) A People's Peace that gets rid of the causes of War.

---

11. *Ibid.*

University staff involved in this People's Convention included Professors Edward J. Dent, Ludwig Wittgenstein and Sir Peter Chalmers-Mitchell; among the student leaders were John Maynard Smith and Raymond Williams. Like Oxford, Cambridge University still sent two MPs to Westminster, and the People's Convention quickly became a vanguard of a Britain-wide peace movement that sent real fear into the bowels of the British establishment. The Cambridge students joined in marches and demonstrations across the country, Hamish organising the transportation of carriage-loads of Cambridge socialists to anti-Chamberlain protests in London. Government strategists began to see 'outbreaks of violence' as 'holes in dykes' that might break the national will. Following the Soviet invasion of Finland in April 1940 Hamish was involved in a Union debate that ended in street fighting. The university journal described it as 'the Battle of Market Street' and Hamish was given the front page to pen a report:

Just after I arrived someone climbed to a vantage point and said: 'Beware of Communists in your midst!' I grasped my cromak tighter. A moment or two later I was recognised again. 'He's a Communist!' said one gentleman, 'I've heard him speak in the Union!' A number of bravoes encircled me. 'Get his stick,' I heard, and one of them tried to wrench my cromak from me . . . and another, likewise noticing my stick, 'that's a Communist with the knuckle-duster!' Irritated by these insults to my cromak, I gave two unionists a good-humoured bash with it – pushed and buffeted my way into the building and sat down to the meeting . . . Afterwards we walked up the passage to Sydney Street singing 'The Smoke of Battle' to the tune of 'The Lincolnshire Poacher' . . . A small crowd was waiting expectantly. We did not have to wait long for the attack . . . The next moment Maurice Craig was in the middle of them and I was laying about one with my cromak. Michael Clarke turned and charged to our assistance and a moment later was lying supine with a blood-spattered jaw, voyaging amongst the spheres . . . With a few sweeps of my cromak I kept his assailants off and made a ring around us . . . And so we made our way, a trifle erratically, to Toni's for coffee. One more stage in the Class battle had passed.

On 7 May 1940 the University Socialist Club *Bulletin* carried an editorial, almost certainly written by Hamish, addressing issues raised by the Norwegian Campaign:

A New Gallipoli: Despite a stream of propaganda to the effect that all was going well in Norway, 'limited withdrawals' have turned into an evacuation and it is now clear that this particular attempt to spread the war has ended in fiasco. Chamberlain, not Hitler, has 'missed the bus', and the casualty list may be assumed to be long, even though the government refuses to publish it . . . By now it should be clear to those who doubted it before, that this is no 'phony war', in which minor annoyances such as blackouts would be our main troubles; this is a war which, if not stopped, will spread, will engulf the world, killing millions in the trenches and Anderson Steel shelters, and tens of millions by want, starvation and disease. The warmongers, including Churchill, of Gallipolli fame, have launched another such adventure, and are entirely displeased with the result; the war has spread to the North; soon it will spread to the South – unless . . . Yes, 'unless', for it can be stopped. The working class is already, after only 8 months of this second great Imperialist war, becoming restive, questioning, doubtful, many have already taken their stand against it, including the Scottish miners, 80,000 strong; the fight against the war is gathering momentum; we must not be left behind.

The rhetoric here is like that used by John Maclean to draw huge crowds in Glasgow at the end of the First World War – when the British Government, fearing Red Rebellion, ordered tanks and troops onto the streets. With German forces now smashing their way through Belgium into France, the British Government needed to avoid civil disturbance at home at all costs – and the Cambridge Students' People's Convention was soon cheering in triumph as the Chamberlain government collapsed in confusion. Churchill's appointment did not bring peace but, for the first time, the British war effort began to address realities.

Whilst Hamish always took his politics seriously, he also took them with pleasure, and throughout the Phony War period he made regular visits to London, where he soon became part of 'the Soho Set'. This was a group of radical artist bohemians that included Quentin Crisp, Paul Potts and the young Glaswegian painters Colquhoun and MacBryde, and it was with them that Hamish celebrated Hogmanay 1939: 'Three friends and me – arm in arm – ranting and roving through London's New Year quiet! "Marvellous" said the Slade student as he wound his arm around mine; Colquhoun gave him a warning against "wild hielantmen" and "the heilant polismen are the worst of the lot!" ' Looking back, in the early 1980s, Hamish saw this first year of the war as a time of great freedom and well-being:

The loose-limbed gait of the young Quentin Crisp was a familiar sight in the pubs and clubs of Soho then: stepping out in his flowing gaudy garb which would, in two decades, become the hippy norm,

and fashionable! Is it only sentimental hindsight which makes me
think of pre-Blitz Bloomsbury and Soho as an idyllic urban Arcady?
I remember scribbling in a notebook, one lazy afternoon – 'Jours du
York Minster – Nuits de Soho Square'.

The York Minster was a pub, popular with the Soho/Fitzrovia circle and it
was there that Hamish met the Indian writer Mulk Raj Anand. 'I nick-
named him Muck-rake-Anand, and we got on well!' Later, Anand became
a confidant of many of the Third World's international leaders and lived to
be a centenarian. Hamish also began a lifelong friendship with Tambi-
muttu, the Ceylonese poet who created *Poetry London*; however, the man
with whom he established his most important London relationship was
Paul Potts, a benign and colourful character who fell head-over-heels in
love with the young Scots poet. In spring 1940 Hamish invited Potts to the
University Socialist Club to lecture on Mayakovsky, a leading poet of the
Russian revolution and founder of the Russian Futurism Movement. It was
a lively event and Hamish later recalled how, against the tide of student
socialist opinion, he and Potts argued vigorously that 'Roy Campbell was a
bloody good poet and that Campbell's political position, vis-a-vis the
Spanish Civil War was, in literary terms, a complete red herring!' The first
written evidence of the strangely dependent relationship Potts established
with Hamish is a poem by Potts, entitled 'The Poet and the Harvester',
published in the summer issue of *Cambridge Front* 1940:

> . . . Then a man like you has come along
> Who has no wealth to give away
> But a can opener for the mind.
> You make me want to cease, to be a brother to an ox.
> You make me want to read,
> To see the beauties of the field,
> To walk the earth.
> Poet you, not my father, made me become a man.

Potts joined Hamish on various anti-Chamberlain demonstrations and,
after one London march, Hamish notes that they 'wandered up to Hyde
Park Corner to sell copies of Potts' broadsheet – "A Poet's Testament"
(alias Lenin is our Mate) – to people listening to the speakers on their soap-
boxes. Such selling turned out to be illegal "within the gates". Both of us
were arrested and taken off to a police station for a dressing down.
Released after half an hour, we returned to the Park and *gave* the rest
of the broadsheets away – that being legal . . .' In a notebook Hamish
describes Potts as ' "The People's Poet" – the poet who heard his poems in

the streets / and only wrote them down'. He admired Potts but he was never to return the profound, personal love Potts felt for him. However, during the first two years of the war they shared a wonderful platonic relationship, delighting in the raucous popular culture of London. And when, twenty years later, Potts wrote his poetical biography *Dante called you Beatrice*, his love of Hamish haunts every page:

Love is my poetry, I have no other . . . She looked as beautiful as I thought she would before I met her. Men seldom thought so, women always . . . Her hands were as marvellous as St Francis of Assisi's must have been . . . She had the simplicity of a Highland Chief's daughter mixed up with the arrogance of a Borgia cardinal. She had a face a bit like Shelley's and the body of a Chinese empress. Determined as a fault, she was as gentle as a prayer in Gaelic . . . She always thought of Canada as a colony of Scotland. She had an urge to self destruction and a taste in pretty boys. She tried to cure all the ills of the thirties on her own. She gave a huge sum of money to the Communist Party . . . she was a victim of that kind of communism which killed by guilt young sensitive cultured rich people.[12]

In July 1940, Potts introduced Hamish to Dylan Thomas. Thomas was already a famous poet, Hamish a university student, but their brief relationship turned out to be a genuinely two-sided event, described at length in *Alias MacAlias*, in a chapter entitled 'That Dolphin Torn, That Gong-Tormented Face: Dylan in Bloomsbury'.

By August 1940, having got his BA (grade II, division I) and with his call-up imminent, Hamish determined to return to the Highlands and to try to complete 'Journey to a Kingdom'. The start of this journey is documented in 'Ballad of the Twelve Stations of my Youth':

I hitch-hike north from foolish virgin Cambridge,
And in a lorry sleep by Berwick sea
Till shivering dawn – a day more and I'm thonder,
A wolf in Badenoch among rock and scree.

It's tarzan work till sundown in the saw-mill
But Billy, me and Cameron slog along;
Foregather in the Balavil for our Ceilidh
And drink malt whisky, swapping song for song.

12. Paul Potts, *Dante called you Beatrice* (Eyre and Spottiswoods 1960). The canon of it was first published in *London Magazine* by John Lehmann.

The saw-mill was near Laggan in Inverness-shire. Hamish got himself a job, and a brief Highland idyll opened around him. The weather was marvellous, he was speaking Gaelic, testing his skills as a field folklorist, writing poetry and singing songs. The Balavil was a pub, named after the ancient Gaelic/Indo-European word for a tribal meeting place under a great tree, and through the saw-men, foresters and local crofters, Hamish gained direct entrée into a Highland bothy-culture that delighted him. He felt himself part of a living folk-process: 'songs, stories and jokes were passed from bunk to bunk, bar to bar, down the road and over the hill'. With his vast repertoire of songs, Hamish was soon recognised as a 'local star' and found himself tapped for every kind of Scots song but, not wanting to be tarred with the brush of the kailyard, he also began singing German songs, translating as he went along. They too were popular; indeed Hamish's German was so good that the police were tipped off. And late one night on the way back to his bothy, he told me, 'I was stopped by a policeman – on a bicycle – without light! I was questioned and asked to show my identity card. In the dark of the gloaming, he struggled to read the address, until he saw the word Cambridge! And he exclaimed, "Ah, Carrbridge! You're from Carrbridge! They said you were a German! I have an auntie up in Carrbridge! What a lot of nonsense!" So, then we walked back to the bothy thegither – singing and laughing! You see, I mentioned – he didn't have a light!'

A day or two later, in the Laggan shop, Hamish bought a small book, *Seventeen Poems for Sixpence*, by Sorley MacLean and Robert Garioch – half in Gaelic and half in Scots. The work of these poets was then 'unknown' but it struck Hamish with revelatory force and, throughout the war, that booklet went everywhere with him. By chance, MacLean, Garioch and Hamish were all to see action in North Africa, though they did not meet. MacLean was badly wounded at Alamein, Robert Garioch captured by the Germans in Tunisia. Hamish returned unscathed. After the war, Hamish quickly sought out both poets and, over the years, each was to profoundly influence the life and work of the others.

In October 1940 Hamish headed south-west into Argyll, to hike down the Kintyre peninsula to Campbeltown. He got a lift in a lorry at West Loch Tarbert and enjoyed wonderful views of the Paps of Jura, the island of Gigha, the isle of Cara, the distant flat of the Oa on Islay until – with the great head of the Mull before him – he told his driver 'this is the place'.

> I decided to get out at Machrihanish – because the name so appealed to me . . . I got my bivvy planted and got in – and was composing poetry when it started to rain – and soon the rain was slapping-in and gradually the position became untenable: I thought – Oh God, I'd be

better far to walk through the night than to lie here and get my death of cauld, as the saying goes. So, I got up and set off and, in the distance, saw a light. It was a shepherd's house and the shepherd was Jimmy McShannon. He invited me in and we sang – practically all night – these wonderful Kintyre songs like 'Flory Loynachan', 'Donal Clean', and 'Machrihanish Bright and Bonnie'. Ah – it was marvellous – I felt the rain had done me a good turn and that morning I set off for the Mull in high spirits.[13]

Two days later, while walking north, Hamish noticed people keeping their distance and looking at him with suspicion. When two men outside a 'big hoose' roared off in a car he realised he had been taken for a German again. He notes 'I came to a graveyard . . . I was just looking at stones and the graves, with my bivvy and my rucksack strapped to my back, when I heard this scuffly sound coming up the road – and there was the Home Guard of Kintyre! Coming for me – with rifles – ready to do or die. There was little to do but surrender, so I marched out onto the road with my hands up.' Hamish was then arrested by lieutenant Angus MacVicar,[14] and held at Achnamara House until the police took over. This was followed by a night in the Campbeltown Police cells.

Before leaving Kintyre, Hamish posted the manuscript of 'Journey to a Kingdom' to his friend Raymond Williams in Cambridge. At the last moment, he added a few extra lines that in many ways sum up a poem that is at once immature and visionary:

> Through wash of rubble
> this Time defeats me. And the headland's spike
> is crumbling stump. I turn to
> a burnt-out croft behind a ragged dyke.
> From time past a whisper of battle.
> O child, child, hurry.
> For life our mortal blow quickly we'll strike.[15]

Hamish travelled to Cambridge via London, where he stayed with his Aunt Mabel in her roof-top flat at 42 Ashley Gardens, Kensington. The Blitz was gathering momentum and they spent the night, together,

13. HH, unpublished notebook and recorded interview for *Tocher*. no. 43.
14. Angus MacVicar (1908–2001), crime writer and juvenile science fiction writer.
15. From 'Journey to a Kingdom', published as the second half of a short poem entitled 'When we were Children' in the *Collected Poems*.

watching the spectacle of 'London burning'. The flat was close to Westminster Cathedral, and Mabel had appointed herself an 'unofficial fire-bomb watcher; she used to direct the fire-fighters, by telephone!' In April 1941, Hamish was again with her as they witnessed one of the heaviest assaults of the whole war. During the night he wrote 'Dark Streets to Go Through', a poem dedicated to Lotte – the little German girl whom he hoped he had saved from the kind of Hell he now saw exploding before him.

Dark streets to go through, in nights debauched of quiet,
Dark streets blazing like an *auto da fe*, till cease
Well after dawn the bombers' roar and riot.
And the city, in daylight's drawn and haggard relief
Shifts on its side to sleep for half an hour,
And then goes to work, not bothering to count the dead.
Dopes, morons, mortal cousins, fools, heroes, of heroes flower –
From my heart I say it, not minding what others said.

Yet this 'terrible beauty' must not blind us; men who have lost the
    power
To think without anger are not a pretty sight.
Planes tilting over the quaking black ant-heap of houses
Will have much to answer for
(much surely to answer for)
Besides hell through a long-drawn April night.
Making our task less easy.
Still, a task we must carry through.
In spite of murderous men
                    In the fable
God is murdered, but is born again too.[16]

This essentially unknown poem is a tribute to the people and city of London. It carries echoes of the beauties Wordsworth had seen from Westminster Bridge, and this 'terrible beauty'[17] links the present war to future possibilities. Hamish recognises that Western civilisation is facing a crucial moment in its history, not unlike that which Ireland had faced in 1916, and when he writes 'Making our task less easy', he raises profound questions and thoughts. The battle now joined would be long, hard and bloody, and he foresaw that the brutality, the blindness, the retribution

16. Published in the *Collected Poems*.
17. Yeats: 'Easter 1916'.

engendered would corrupt mankind for centuries to come. He knew that the Reformation (in Scotland) had once been the kind of all-consuming issue now facing Europe. That Reformation had triumphed and brought great benefits and glories to Scotland but also planted poisons and pernicious constraints still circulating in the body and psychology of the Scottish people four hundred years later; and he knew that the great campaign against Nazi tyranny, even if it ended in total victory, would leave Britain doused with similar poisons. In this poem, in praise of London's will to resist, Hamish foresees that the heroism born in the streets will in future years make the work of the peace-makers more difficult – because the satisfactions and moral self-righteousness of the victors will hook them to the 'necessary good' of new wars in the 'good name' of democracy and 'civilisation'. He knew that the generation sickened by the bombing of Guernica was already conditioning itself to sanction the bombing of whole cities and nations, and that the idea of 'destroying the whole world' would soon be just another political option for free peoples to debate. Even so, Hamish ends his poem on a positive note: this war must be fought and will be won and after that the eternal task returned to, 'God is murdered but born again too'.

When Hamish wrote that poem he had already been in uniform for six months. On 11 November 1940 he celebrated his twenty-first birthday in a requisitioned Cotton Mill in Oldham, Lancashire. Within days he was 'square-bashing', as a private in the Pioneer Corps. A new chapter in his life had opened and he completed his 'Ballad of the Twelve Stations of My Youth' with two down-beat verses. They look back and look forward – but they end with the melancholy slam of the barrack's door.

> From Spain return the Clyde-red brave Brigaders.
>   I clench my fist to greet the red flag furled.
> Our hold has slipped – now Hitler's voice is rasping
>   From small square boxes over all the world.
>
> There's fog. I climb the cobbled streets of Oldham
>   With other conscripts, and report to one
> Who writes with labour, and no satisfaction
>   That I've turned up. – From now my boyhood's done.[18]

---

18. Published in the *Collected Poems*.

FOUR

The Pioneer Corps and the African Sun

I am tired of reading poems which have an atmosphere of 'Here is Art'. I want poems with the atmosphere 'Here is Life', and this is Hamish Henderson living it.

HH 1941

At the Earls Mill Barracks in Oldham, Hamish did six weeks' basic training before being sent south to Sussex to work on the anti-invasion defences. He was given weapons training but the Pioneer Corps was not a fighting unit – it specialised in construction work, guard duties and humanitarian support. In fact the corps was something of a dumping ground for older recruits, men with physical disabilities or low intelligence, refugees, foreign nationals, and men of suspect political allegiance. Hamish qualified on several counts and took to his new life like a duck to water. He liked his fellow pioneers; many came from deprived and exotic backgrounds and brought with them exactly the kind of knowledge, experience and songs that he was hungry for. Many of the refugees 'had more than a few ideas to rub together' and Hamish describes himself as having 'plenty of opportunity to practise half-a-dozen European languages'.

The winter of 1940–41 was exceptionally cold, and the manhandling of scaffolding, barbed wire and concrete on the Channel beaches was hard and often unpleasant work. Morale played a major part in the efficiency of the various work-gangs and Hamish (inventor of the concept of 'Moral Disarmament'[1]) soon proved himself a master morale raiser: 'I found myself unofficial court jester and Entertainments Secretary to the Pevensey Bay Pioneer Section! I organised the Christmas parties and we put on

---

1. Moral Re-Armament was a movement founded in 1938 by Frank Buchman, an American evangelist and admirer of Adolf Hitler. Hamish was totally opposed to it and wrote a poem called 'The Blubbing Buchmanite' which includes the lines 'You creeping Jesus, damn your eyes! / It's canting cunts like you who sap /The worker's spirit. Shut your trap!'

a madcap play entitled, *Gudger for my Elephants*.' He encouraged the men to sing their own folk-songs, to make up new songs, and to learn his. The best known of Hamish's Pioneer songs is 'The Ballad of Section Three' – a worksong that proved a great hit in both the Mess and the pubs. It is sung to the tune, 'O We're Rusty Bums':

> O, I'll sing you a song, and a damn good song,
>   Of the good old Section Three.
> We carry the pipes, we carry the clamps,
>   And put 'em together do we.
> We jerrymander the bloody things up
>   And we sling them into the sea.
> Then covered in muck we bum on the truck
>   And bugger off home for tea.
>
> Chorus: O we're rusty bums, and jolly good chums,
>   We live like Royal Turks,
> And when we're in luck we bum on the truck
>   And pity the guy that works.[2]

Any number of bawdy verses – describing the characters and antics of the officers and men in the Pioneer Corps – could then be appended before a final salute to 'the Fighting Pioneers!':

> So here's a health to a bloody fine chap
>   Whom all of us know by now.
> Before Dunkirk he did not shirk
>   As even the Guards allow.
> And it's on the cards that he'll lick the Guards
>   At war or women or beer.
> So give a rouse – and it's on the house –
>   For the Fighting Pioneer!

As the threat of immediate invasion receded in the spring of 1941, Hamish was transferred from Section 3 to Section 5, promoted to Lance Corporal and made a quartermaster (warrant officer class 2). He was in charge of pay, clothing, feeding and sanitary arrangements. He describes himself as 'Ma and Da of the company!' and notes: 'Learn to control yourself, be well-balanced, train own mind and temper. Angry when necessary. Blind eye.' He enjoyed the idea of the 'the Nelson touch'.

---

2. Published in the *Collected Poems*.

For Hamish, every action and experience was 'an idea' to be placed within a larger imaginative and historical context. And he was happy to risk stretching the rules according to need. One bitingly cold morning he documents, 'good work had been done, the men's hands were numb, the pace of work was falling off – I noticed the eyes of the men being drawn more and more to a pub a couple of hundred yards away over the shingle. All pubs were out of bounds to troops on duty. I decided to cut the Gordian knot and announced, "If any man feels the need of a drink, or a warm up, in that pub – over there – for the next thirty minutes he's free to go – and if anyone asks you, what you're doing – you can tell them, that what you're doing, you're doing on my orders!"'

When Hamish got leave, he went north to Glasgow. His visit coincided with the Clydebank Blitz, and the following morning he walked the length of the Dumbarton Road and began to compose a poem on the irony of a war in which Britain's industrial poor were, from Devonport to Battersea, taking the brunt of casualties and appeared to have so little to gain. It is entitled 'Brutality Begins at Home':

> Misshapen mortals who snuffle in slums
> Behold! For I bring of cold comfort the crumbs.
> Your bug-bitten dwellings were ruins before
> You were born, yet alone this particular war.
> Your moth-eaten sticks and sweat-mouldy clothes
> (both items which ev'ry good Christian loathes)
> Are not worth the bother you're taking to rescue 'em
> Now that the Peabody Building is only a vacuum.
>
> Still, as 'mid the wreck of Grandma you search
> Shed a tear for the vanishing rents of the Church
> And reflect that the Archbishop, safe in his smuggery
> Is very much grieved that you've been bombed to buggery . . .[3]

Returning to Sussex, Hamish set down a rhetorical question: 'Why do I long for Scotland as Hölderlin for Greece?' He knew the answer well enough and very soon ideas for a fourth major poem about Scotland began to crystallise in his mind. However, living in barracks and working twelve-hour days made writing serious poetry difficult, and the poem he planned was never to develop beyond the concept stage – but his concept was interesting. He saw his poem spiralling out, across time and space,

---

3. From an unpublished manuscript booklet written by HH entitled 'Songs of Sabotage and Sedition'.

from the ancient cathedral city of Winchester in West Sussex to the equally ancient Pictish town of Nairn in Morayshire. He wanted to draw connections and contrasts between these two very separate, but similar, communities. Winchester was a Romano-British centre where the young King Alfred (poet, scholar, soldier, Christian and patriot) later set up court and founded the English nation. And, as Alfred had broken the Danish yoke and liberated the English language and genius, so Hamish, in his time, presumed to break the bands of England's control of Scotland and release again the genius of the Scots people. He foresaw that Nairn, in the heart of old Pictland, could become the ideal launching pad for a new and independent Scotland.[4] He would use the same tools as the young Alfred – scholarship, poetry, organisation, physical courage, Christian vision and civilised virtue. He outlined a new interpretation of Scotland's history with 'Bruce, Wallace, the Wolf of Badenoch, and Jimmy Brennan casting their shadows on modern Scotland. Feudalism was always foreign to the spirit of Scotland . . .' Hamish foresaw the poem as a call-to-arms, a literary statement that would become a self-fulfilling political prophecy.

Whilst on leave, Hamish's political nationalism had been rekindled following meetings with an old Blairgowrie school friend, Adam Malcolm. Adam had originally befriended Hamish when he first returned to Blair, from Glenshee, at the age of five. By the time Hamish moved to England in 1928 they had become good friends and remained in contact. Malcolm was another 'lad o'pairts' and in 1938 had won a scholarship to study English at the University of Edinburgh. By 1941 he was a radical member of the Scottish National Party and, during their reunion, the two men decided to develop a framework of 'political cells' across Scotland – with the long-term aim of establishing a sovereign Socialist Scotland. Malcolm was the organiser, Hamish would be the bard and 'mastermind'. Later that year, having joined the Royal Army Corps, Malcolm wrote to Hamish from Glasgow, to tell him he had set up a 'sub-party' called the Youth Council of Scotland, devoted to 'propaganda, study and ramble'.

On 29 September 1942, Malcolm wrote to inform Hamish (now in Egypt) about major problems within the nationalist movement: 'I fear the SNP has had its death blow – for a split has taken place, but – a new virile party is in being'. This split occurred after Douglas Young was elected leader of the Scottish National Party on the understanding that he and his followers would have nothing to do with 'England's War'. It was a principled and courageous stand but, in the midst of the life-and-death

---

4. HH, unpublished notebook.

struggle with German Nazism, politically foolish and 'morally' highly
debatable. Young's success forced the charismatic nationalist John Mac-
Cormick[5] out of the party, whilst Young himself would soon suffer public
odium and two prison sentences. In 1943, writing to Malcolm from
Tunisia, four months after the Allied victory at Alamein, Hamish makes
his own position very clear:

> As far as my politics goes, I'm a revolutionary! At the present moment it
> gives me great satisfaction to be actually combating the most reac-
> tionary force in the world today – all the more deadly because it
> masquerades as revolution. As far as Scottish Nationalism is con-
> cerned, I think the men of our Highland Div. are doing more to solve
> Scotland's problems (social-economic-political) than Douglas [Young]
> languishing in clink . . . I don't fancy the Slovak type of freedom in a
> New Order. But it's probably right that one or two martyrs should do us
> a favour – by suffering for not seeing the matter whole.

Hamish's demand that anyone dealing with the question of Scottish
nationalism must see the matter whole is typical of him as a political
animal (and as a poet) and clearly distances him from Douglas Young's
self-parading intellectuality and the divisionism endemic in public life in
Scotland. This quarrelsome Scotch divisiveness, which Hamish labelled
'the apostasy of the elite', would be the bane of Hamish's life but in 1943,
lifted by the heroism of the 51st Highland Division and the achievement
of the Eighth Army, he was happy to counter Young's sectarian bitterness
with Blakean joy and his letter to Malcolm continues in verse:

> The juvenile insolence of pride and beauty
> is beauty
> And I'm proud we are very insolent juveniles.

> I called myself and call myself a Scottish nationalist but I have tried
> to make it clear that a good nationalist must first be a good
> internationalist . . . I have no use for the debased cosmopolite;
> he is never the worker anyway . . . and one cannot be a good
> Communist without first being a good man . . . It doesn't interest
> me so much now to know to what depths human beings can sink; in
> my own thought I plumb these depths quite often. But what touches

---

5. John MacCormick (1904–61), lawyer and founder in 1928 of the National Party
   of Scotland, the predecessor of the SNP.

me and enheartens me is to come suddenly on the Himalaya of the soul – the heights to which human beings can rise. Increasingly I find in good and not evil the ultimate interest. My attention has shifted from the denying spirit of Mephistopheles, to the affirming spirit, of Faust, or to Joyce's Molly Bloom if you like. 'Yes I will. Yes.' This is perhaps what Aldous Huxley means when he says the time is ripe for a revolution in the mind, for the whole human race to make a conscious effort and to grow up – if it doesn't want to destroy itself with a surfeit of undigested Progress.

The *joie de vivre* so evident in that letter is indelibly 'Hamish'. His impulse was always towards the positive. He had a compulsively evangelical nature that constantly spilled over in 'teachings' – sometimes purely secular, sometimes clearly Christian-Celtic.

The transforming power of song was something Hamish had delighted in since childhood, and he increasingly saw music and song as the redemptive, purely human force with which he might change Scotland and the world. He had about him the 'urgency' of the true poet; his response to injustice was immediate, his response to human goodness an outbreak of euphoria. That self-dramatising, troubadour quality that G.K. Chesterton describes as the essence of the genius of the young St Francis was something that Hamish also had. He delighted in the synchronicities of chance: the idea of 'luck' was something to which he was always responsive. In his composite song-poem 'Sitzkrieg Fantasy' (1941), Hamish acknowledges 'luck, faith and reason' as 'the holy three' that have shaped history across millennia – and he hopes they will conjoin in his time around him.

> The sons of Mithras have *luck*, but so have
>   The sons of Lugh
> *And holy Lenin sings on Orion*
>   *Till all is blue.*
>
> And Lenin had *luck* – luck, faith and reason,
>   The holy three,
> When he opened wide an historical door with
>   History's key . . .[6]

---

6. From 'Sitzkreig Fantasy' (a Gallimaufry) published in the *Collected Poems*.

In the autumn of 1941 Hamish applied for a commission in military intelligence. His success as an NCO, his language skills, phenomenal memory and psychological insight all made him a strong candidate, and he was immediately accepted for training. Any doubts about his Scottish nationalism, his socialism, or his bolshie pacifism were now set aside as, across the nation, national need and 'ability' began to replace class as the prerequisite of career advancement in the armed services. Hamish was natural 'officer material' and both his Scottishness and his Cambridge connections were to prove big advantages in the Intelligence Corps.

On completing his Intelligence training (mostly done at Bishop's Stortford and Winchester), Hamish was commissioned as a second lieutenant. His document of transfer reads 'Army number 13071358. Name Henderson, Hamish Jobson Scott. Date of joining the colours 17/11/40. Date of transfer to IC 02/01/42. Service with the colours 1 year 57 day. Rank on transfer Lance Corporal. Military conduct Very Good. Testimonial Excellent type.' He also noted a list of the things he required of himself:

> Maintain ideals and get facts
> Remain a Scot
> 'Be truthful to the language of our love'
> Don't let the bastards get you down
> Work to a system
> Don't smile when it is shameful
> Don't let the bastards get you down
> (Remember Death of a Hero)
> Batter down the bloody barriers
> Don't compromise Danton
> No weakness.
> 'I am a contemplative man.'

At about this time Hamish got hold of *Poems from the Forces*, a collection of 'new' war poetry, edited by Keidrych Rhys. The introduction by Rhys, and the preface by Colonel, the Rt Hon. Walter Elliot MC (Hamish's old luncheon partner from the World Exhibition in Paris) are probably the most interesting things in the whole book. Elliot makes the point that the poetry published is not by 'the poets at war' but by 'poets going to war' and their sensibilities have been moulded in the pre-war period. To the rhetorical question, what are their views? He answers: 'mainly a refusal to accept death, and therefore a refusal to accept life'. He states that 'the real war poets' will be those who accept 'the reality of fighting' and who recognise that 'death is not the worst of evils' – and that only after this 'reality' has been accepted will 'the idea of survival take on the quality of a resurrection'. Elliot suggests that the real war poets, in the struggle to come, will 'quite literally take their lives in their hands – accept war with their bodies . . . and not for the first time in poetry, their bodies will teach their souls undreamt of things'. It is brutal stuff but brilliantly anticipated the attitudes that would underlie the achievements of three of the best poets of the Second World War – Captain Keith Douglas, Private Sorley Maclean and Captain Hamish Henderson. There can be no doubt that Hamish, at least, took Elliot's words seriously and, when he sailed down the Clyde in January 1942 to join a large convoy bound for Cape Town and Bombay, Hamish took his 'Rhys' with him. His ship was the P&O liner *Viceroy of India* and in rare comfort, with time on his hands, Hamish set to work tidying up a great backlog of poems and songs so that he would be free to become a serious war poet. He also began a discursive diary. His on-board responsibilities were minimal but his work as a censor gave him 'a Pottsian access to the poetry of the people' that he found hugely stimulating:

for a scavenging writer like myself these letters are a treasure trove. Most of the writers are cheerful even if they don't feel so. Husbands writing to their wives do their best to make light of the appalling separation, to make fun of old memories and to leave no assurance of lasting love unsaid. 'Chin-up' comes often, 'Hulloo you stale piece of overcooked pudding,' begins one Lancashire lad . . .' They give a young unmarried man like myself a real insight into the depth and simplicity of married love – are an antidote to the maladjusted troubles of sex . . . I find something to write about in every room and attic of the human house.

I was told by my colleagues that some letters protested with indignation at the contrast between the officers' 'luxury life' and the troops' 'pig sty' existence. And the contrasts during the first days of the trip were cruel. The menus in the officers' mess seemed preposterous and unreal after the rationed strictness of wartime England. Long menus in which meats and roasts and fish and bacon and eggs and butter and fruits blurred before our eyes. The men got barely sufficient and most supplemented their meals with tins of fruit and blocks of chocolate from their canteen. No wonder 90% were sea-sick . . . Altogether life for us on the *Viceroy* was like a pleasure cruise in peace time . . .

One evening, sipping an iced orangeade and reading William Power's
Literature and Oatmeal[7] in the ship's lounge, Hamish introduced himself
to a Welsh pilot officer who came in carrying the Penguin Welsh Short
Stories in his hand: 'He was like a young Druid novice with a sense of
humour . . . I asked, "Do you speak Welsh?" "Oh, yes, I have the
language." I told him I had the Gaelic, and our conversation turned
to the Highlands and to Ireland.' Next morning, Hamish went on deck
and saw land for the first time in three weeks.

> . . . we watched the coast draw near and become Africa. The scrub-
> covered hills became obscene and hairy, the shacks on the lowland
> reaches beach-combed their way towards the hillsides. From a phallic
> hill, signals flashed to the entering vessels – as our ship moved at last
> into the harbour in the great naval base of Freetown. Then we saw the
> town itself, the walled white bungalows of the Europeans, the bulk of
> Christian churches, the miscellaneous splodge of the native quarter.
> And the boats all around us – cargo vessels, cruisers, our accom-
> panying destroyer and its mate, all the tubs that ride our British
> element. But more interesting than these, which I have seen in
> Glasgow and Portsmouth, were small craft that appeared suddenly
> around us as soon as we were stationary. These were the tree-bark
> canoes of African exhibitionists and they presently gave us entertain-
> ment. First came the variety artistes who shouted 'Okey Doke,
> madame' and dived into the water, the undas of their feet a pinky
> brown like the belly of toads or snakes. Pennies were sufficient bait, at
> first, then they began to shout for 'Glasgow tanners' – and responsive
> tanners came circling down into the water. The language they spoke –
> the local brand of Coast pidgin – was a curious blend of Los Angeles
> English and soldiers' slang. The best study of it could be made when
> then the star-turn came on the scene. This was a burly fellow with
> rather Mongolian features who turned out to be a born comedian –
> his forte the burlesquing of army habits and songs.

In Freetown Hamish transferred to HMS *Nay* ready to be transported
along the African coast to Nigeria. Arriving on board, he was presented
with a *billet doux* which stated that there were ninety officers aboard –
with accommodation for twenty. When he also learned that meals would
be run in three shifts – with the most senior officers being called at six for

---

7. William Power, *Literature and Oatmeal: What Literature has Meant to Scotland*
   (London 1935).

breakfast at seven, and the less senior officers following at hourly intervals – Hamish notes: 'I fell in love with the Navy'. And, to his delight, the leaflet concluded 'If you find us a trifle Nelsonic, remember that we mean well. We ask you to accept the situation, for which we are not to blame, in the Army spirit.' Hamish revelled in the élan and sublime confidence evident in the navy and noted 'the more I saw of the navy the more I considered it not only the senior service but also the infinitely preferable service'.

In his wallet he carried a photograph of a naked woman that he'd bought in Soho. It was for him an image of life, and a talisman. The woman dances, on barren earth – out of which flowers grow as if from nowhere. Hamish kept the photo with him throughout the war and, afterwards, when it was clear that this silver nitrate beauty (with her splendid bush of pubic hair) had survived, to celebrate the Allied victory he wrote on the back of the photograph: 'If divine providence hasn't saved this nation / infernal luck has.'

From HMS *Nay* Hamish transferred to a high-powered Commando boat for an exciting charge along the West African coast towards Lagos. Several of the crew had taken part in the controversial Commando raids on the Lofoten and Channel Islands, and he gleaned from them interesting facts about the half-cock nature of both exploits. As usual he enjoyed his journey and the company he found:

We were three in a cabin, with bunks for two, so we took turns sleeping on the floor, by a four-hour rota. My companions, luckily, were not the average *Viceroy* officers bound for India. One was a shrewd and fly little Cockney Jew, with frizzy hair going back in waves and bristly black moustache. He had all the Cockney's flare for sizing up a mug, and all the Cockney's acrid and thin-lipped sense of humour. I had a bit of a feud with him the first day or two over the arrangement of the cabin, but once he realized there was no green in my eyes (where he was concerned) and I was not the kind of lad to knuckle under, we signed a mutual non-aggression pact and developed a healthy respect for one another. He even kept quiet during my singing of Gaelic songs, and in return gave me sob-sister fruity croonings of the St Louis Blues, Miss Otis Regrets, Frankie and Johnnie, and an Artillery Man's Song . . .

Viewing Lagos from the sea, Hamish makes an interesting cultural point about the conglomeration of architectural styles: 'The waterside residences of the European population are spacious and attractive. The Lagos Yacht Club lends undeniable tone to an architecture mixing Citizen Kane's Xanadu and the monstrous castle in Aldous Huxley's latest book

– a Byzantine Church, a Gothic Cathedral, a mosque, a Shell-Mex erection – all bear witness to the conflict of European influence on this Negro city. But oddly a certain unexpected harmony and dignity manifests itself . . . Africa has pawed many things new but Africa has not yet made them her own . . .'

From Lagos, Hamish flew north over southern Nigeria by plane, the land that James Scott had walked, ridden and been seduced by forty years earlier. In a jerky hand he jotted down ideas for a poem: 'Africa and Hitler / Donation of Central Africa to Germany / As one of the hardest terms of the Peace Treaty / Draconian doom for Hitler.'

Arriving in Cairo, Hamish notes: 'Send poems to Keidrych Rhys. Who am I? Was a private in the Pioneer Corps / Now 2nd Lt in Intelligence Corps / am 22 with a Scots/Gaelic slant / Coming out of the early Pound . . . 42 poems, plus 8 written at sea.' Whether Hamish sent all fifty poems to Rhys is not clear but he obviously hoped to be published in Rhys' next book. (Today at least half of these poems are lost or totally unknown.)[8] He was soon touring the city and, after visiting Ramleh, the European suburb after which the house in which he had been born had been named, he wrote this 'first report' to the Armstrongs at Dry Drayton:

Fetch out the magnifying glass, for I'm going to pack this page as tight as I can. – What's Cairo like? The oddest thing about it is that it so closely corresponds to one's romantic notions of it. I've always had rather a penchant for marmalukes and seraglios, and its all here

8. Unpublished notebook: 1) Journey to a Kingdom 2) Speech for a Sensualist 3) The Ocean's Pride 4) Seascape 5) When the teased idiot 6) Holy Lenin (Sitzkrieg Fantasy) 7) Marching Song for Scottish Workers 8) Strathspey 9) Song for an Irish Red 10) Patmos (translation) 11) A Word for those that Hate me 12) The New O'Casey Play 13) Poem for Eric (L/cpl Eric Hollywood) 14) Severitas in Rebus 15) Because, Because the Mystery 16) The Mind of Man is a Monster 17) A Tongue Loosed by Liquor 18) Fu saw the 42nd 19) Ballad of the 12 Stations of my Youth 20) Rust Bum Ballad of Section 3 21) Backslang Ballad of the Tosharoon 22) Ballad of Scabbytrash 23) Ballad of the Disorderly Corporal 24) Ballad of the Bounding Buchmanite 25) Friend, now Separated 26) I had to Get This off my Chest 27) The Deil is a Black Man 28) There are Still Dark Streets to go Through 29) Inverey 30) Note to a Friend in Cambridge 31) This is the Exile's Trouble 32) Hate Song against a Sergeant 33) Sgt Major Prick Talking 34) Death is Great – after Rilke 35) Thorny Pride 36) Mr Balgownie 37) Mr Duburie Talking (in Hyde Park) 38) I am Fearful of Something 39) Poem to Paul Potts (with John Clare quote) 40) Ballad of Sergeant Simkin Lee 41) To the Germans 42) The Diplomat. The eight new poems were: Confusion to Ingle, Love to Miss T., Is Miss T. in Love?, My Love to Goat, My Love to Parrot, All my Love to Sgt. MacGregor, All my Love to G.B.S., All my Love to Wells.

– beggars and Bedouins, mosques and muezzins, feazzas and fellahs, and old aunty Yashmak and all. And the pyramids, like the leaning Tower of Pisa, are just too like their picture to be true. And garrys (old fashioned carts, drawn by skin and bone horses, in which you feel like Queen Victoria driving through a foreign capital); and importunate shoe-shine boys yelling 'Officer Polish', and sticking to you like leeches; defying you to boot them away; bazaars stacked with bracelets made in Baghdad and Birmingham; garish night-clubs reminding one of prewar Paris; ah this and much more . . . I haven't found an Irish rectory yet but Cairo holds more improbable things – and I'm living in holes. I've made quite a number of new friends including a young Highland laird, MacLeod of Fuinary, and a genial Lancashire man who speaks Welsh and – *mirabile dicta* – even plays the pipes. So you see the atmosphere is not too stuffy. There are one or two kindred spirits. I have already started learning Arabic – there are quite a number of Gaelic sounding gutturals in it, so I'm well away . . .

Out in the desert, Rommel had recently launched a major offensive but it was without fear and in strange mood of contained excitement that Hamish began preparing himself for the coming battles. In an interview with the Scots filmmaker Les Wilson, in the early 1990s, he describes how he decided to carry a Gaelic New Testament in the left breast-pocket of his tunic: 'There was a certain amount of folklore attached to it – the person who gave it to me assured me that it was good for stopping bullets! And it was good reading; let's face it – you could brush-up your Gaelic with it. In the other pocket I kept my will, inside my Anthony Eden Passport. I'd had that passport with me in Germany before the war and I kept it with me because I felt, in a certain sense, it projected into the future something of the good luck of the past: with that passport I'd got into and out of Germany before the war, and I'd do so again, come hell or high water.' This will reads: 'To be acted on if anything should happen to me. 1) All my manuscripts and books to be given to John Speirs, 2) News that I am missing to be sent to a) Miss Mabel Henderson, b) Mrs. Olive Armstrong, c) Miss Edith Cleverly, d) W.L. Cuttle. Signed H.J.S. Henderson – Lieut. Sorry to cause you any trouble.'[9]

---

9. In Cairo, Hamish had made contact with John Speirs, the Leavisite literary critic, who was then teaching in Cairo. They established a close friendship and Hamish asked John to become his 'literary executor'. He was also close to John's wife, Ruth Speirs (then engaged in translating the work of Rainer Maria Rilke).

FIVE

A German Interrogator
in Cairo and Alexandria

Let my words knit what now we lack
The demon and the heritage
And fancy strapped to logic's rock
A chastened wantonness, a bit
That sets on song a discipline,
A sensuous austerity.

HH[1]

When Hamish arrived in Egypt at the beginning of February 1942 the Allied military position, worldwide, was at its nadir. On the eastern front everything pointed to an overwhelming Axis victory – as soon as winter unlocked its grip on an apparently broken Soviet Union. In the Far East the Japanese were everywhere victorious. At sea the submarine menace was at its height and the Battle of the Atlantic was still running in Germany's favour. In North Africa, Rommel's Afrika Korps had recently spearheaded a 'surprise' counterattack that had driven the Allies out of Tunisia and back to the Egyptian border. In Berlin, Hitler was finalising his 'Masterplan' to destroy Soviet Communism and the British Empire in the Middle East, with a gigantic pincer movement down through the Caucasus and up through Sinai. Fortunately, Rommel's forces had overstretched themselves and decided to dig in before launching a 'final assault' into the Delta. This enabled the Allies to establish a stable defensive line – running south from Gazala to Bir Hacheim. Defeat, however, was very much in the air, and the British commanders were preparing plans for a further retreat, across the Suez Canal, into Palestine. Meantime, out in the desert, the Italian commander Marshall Graziani (from whom Hamish, three years later, would accept the surrender of Italy) was so confident of imminent victory that he had ordered that the white stallion on which he would enter Cairo – in triumph – should be brought to the front.

---

1. From the Prologue, *Elegies for the Dead in Cyrenaica* (John Lehmann 1948).

On entering both GHQ and CSDIC (the Combined Services Detailed Interrogation Centre) in Cairo, Hamish was appalled by the conceit and genteel defeatism everywhere apparent: 'When I first entered the perimeter of our doggone camp I was almost knocked back by the atmosphere of electric animosity that was frigging the air – old maid venom – and I sensed then, quite truly, a way of life contrary to my own . . . The efficiency of armies will now be reckoned in inverse ratio to the amount of bullshit in them. That's why the Navy and the Air Force are so good, and why we've been so bloody awful.' He made notes about 'academic sadists and blether about the Hun' and raged against 'pure baloney passed off as preparation for battle'. Hamish did his bit to leaven the loaf, by launching a joke: 'What's the difference between Number 10 Downing Street, a prostitute, a eunuch and GHQ Cairo?' Answer: 'Number 10 is knockerless. The prostitute is knickerless. The eunuch is knackerless. And GHQ Cairo is All Balls!'

Hamish's first formal duties involved the interrogation of German troops captured during the recent (unsuccessful) battles, and this contact with reality stimulated him on many levels. For example, the diary of one soldier carried clear evidence of the commitment, not of the Nazi hierarchy, but of the ordinary German soldier. Hamish made detailed notes about a platoon that had fought 'embattled for 32 days without water', before being relieved. 'Listen to that, leaders, bishops and cabinet ministers, listen to that generals and trade union leaders, listen to that my lord Von Sittart – beg your pardon, Lord Sittart[2] – listen to that and laugh till your farrowed paunches quiver – that a young German soldier can come back from 32 days without water before Tobruk and write that he is "fighting for the Kingdom of God on earth".' There is also clear evidence that, within weeks of arriving in the desert, Hamish had begun planning his *Elegies for the Dead in Cyrenaica* and that pity for the German dead was one of his prime starting points. He writes: 'Reading diaries, one realizes the imaginative worth, the rich potential genius that the German people could contribute to Europe. What an extraordinary people it is. An abstract intellect flowering into music, a sensitive genius twisted under the martyrdom of its history.'

Once the battlefront had stabilised, prisoner numbers began to dry up and Hamish found himself involved in battle planning, radio interception, interpretation of messages, military observation and deception, mapping, interpretation of aerial photographs, and both artillery and aerial targeting. Very early on, whilst studying aerial reconnaissance photographs, he made at least one important tactical observation about transportation and supply: 'In the British army – vehicle to vehicle transfer. In the German army this is the exception: supplies are put on the ground.'

---

2. Lord Sittart wrote a column for *The Times*.

For his first six months in Egypt, Hamish was stationed at the main CSDIC 'Interrogation Cage' just outside Cairo but he was always delighted 'to get out' and he made a number of visits to the front – on the Egyptian-Libyan border.

In March, Hamish translated the entire diary of a German Sergeant Mechanic involved in the German siege of Tobruk, where a mass of Allied troops had been trapped.[3] Hamish entitled it, 'Sitzkrieg in Libya' and it ran to over 20,000 words. He presented seven copies to 'General Signals Intelligence of the Eighth Army and associated propaganda/intelligence groups' and kept one copy for himself. He believed his translation to have literary merit and planned to use information from the diary in a book, 'German Interrogator', that he would write once the war was over. His translation was made so that Allied commanders would have a greater knowledge of the enemy they were fighting; for example, Hamish points out how this 'ordinary' soldier 'scoffs at the misrepresentation of the African war in the German newspapers and how jaundice is rampant amongst the German troops'. He quotes the soldier as stating: 'It would certainly be fine if this plague spot of Cyrenaica could be wiped off the map.'

Hamish was also surprised and thrilled to find that many of his German prisoners carried poems; much of the verse was traditional and predictable, but in the diary of Corporal Heinrich Mattens, of the 225 Shulz regiment, he found an original poem that impressed him deeply. He translated it, and prefaced it with a quotation from E.M. Forster: 'Some sort of form is inevitable. It is the surface crust of the internal harmony.'

Today the swallows have come here, far over the mountains and
    seas – we took
It as a happy omen, for they came from the north.

They came their way to us when war had sent us southwards; now
    they find us by
roads where palms wave on the beaches.

They saw the fields of home, and the villages occupied with harvest,
    they saw the
forests in the brown blossom of autumn, and in the twitter of their
    song they tell it.

---

3. The siege of Australian, British and Polish divisions at Tobruk lasted from 31 March to 27 November 1941.

And one of the dead men in the platoon goes back restlessly to his
  rest in the song.
The twittering flight is around us. My listening ear has caught its
  meaning . . .
Now we go forward on the road to Tripoli, to Tobruk and Sollum
  – 14th October 1941.

Mattens was killed shortly after this last entry and, today, his poem
presumably only exists in Hamish's translation, and it gives this unknown
corporal (from Bad Jageberg, Holstein, Kelting Str. 77) a grain of
immortality: not least because his observations of these swallows, mi-
grating south, helped inspire the conclusion to Hamish's First Elegy (for
the Dead in Cyrenaica).

> There were our own, there were the others.
> Therefore, minding the great word of Glencoe's
> son, that we should not disfigure ourselves
> with villainy of hatred; and seeing that all
> have gone down like curs into anonymous silence,
> I will bear witness for I knew the others.
> Seeing that littoral and interior are alike indifferent
> and the birds are drawn again to our welcoming north
> why should I not sing *them*, the dead, the innocent?[4]

As an interrogator Hamish had daily access to men *in extremis* – of a kind
usually only gained by doctors, psychiatrists and policemen. Like them he
was looking for information but, unlike them, he was also seeking to
digest the totality of the life-experience of men who happened to be *his*
prisoners: through them he hoped to create poetry that would serve the
wellbeing of all mankind. He felt privileged to have open access to the
surreal depths of minds at once hugely disturbed and strangely controlled.
One young German told him 'Let me stand my God in the broken land
and pity me not. The child drops like sand, the marglass will stand':
another so thrilled Hamish with his description of life in the desert that he
noted 'Tobruk and Sollum mean more to me now than Troy town and the
names of the Iliad. When will I see these fabulous ruins of which my
German clients so obligingly talk.' Some remained cocooned in their Nazi
dreams: 'Franz Schwanwecker: "Germany is the centre of the world and
the world cannot exist without Germany. Germany is the Kingdom of

---

4. *Elegies for the Dead in Cyrenaica* (John Lehmann 1948); also published in the
  Collected Poems.

God" . . . This morning, a New Zealand pipe band playing "The Birks of Aberfeldy" passed the camp just as I went into an interrogation and, feeling in an expansive mood, I started the proceedings by asking the prisoner whether he had heard our Scottish dudelsack, and whether he had liked it. "Scottish dudelsack?" he said in surprise. "We thought it was a procession of Indian flutes." This was the most sensitive blow directed at me since I heard, in Gottingen in August 1939, that "Scotland was that part of England where Chamberlain goes fishing".'

As ever, Hamish was hugely enjoying himself. Fellow officers soon learned of his appetite for literary detritus and began throwing him tit-bits of their own. 'Sawny, the Punjab officer here, has been giving me the low-down on Jinnah and Pakistan – but when he starts nayboring me to death with Indian astrology I tell him, with decision, he's weighing himself down with a heavy load of bollocks!' Hamish's German was soon better than that of many of his prisoners – he had an outstanding ear for regional accents, an exceptional knowledge of German culture and history, he had imagination and psychological insight – and hundreds of songs! And, not surprisingly, he used his vast repertoire to seduce, bully and persuade his prisoners into compliance and cooperation. Many 'changed sides' before their first interrogation was finished. Hamish was quickly recognised as a uniquely effective interrogator and was asked to tutor new interrogators being flown-in ahead of the great battles being planned.

However, despite his intense commitment to his duties, Hamish remained deeply involved in literary developments. For example, on 4 April 1942 he received a long letter from his Cambridge friend Jamie Cable, about his 'discovery' of a new poet, W.R. Rodgers. Hamish wrote back on 6 April:

> Spender calls W.R. Rodgers a 'hairy man from the Irish bogs' as far as his poetic appearance goes. I think this phrase most inept. Rodgers is an accomplished and sharp-eared poet who far from being a poetical gallowglass, has absorbed Hopkins and civilised him. He has absorbed Rilke and as much effortless Auden as you please! 'New every morning now the clerk docks off / Yesterday's desk date, jerks back the needle / On duty's desk.' I want to refute Spender. Rodgers is a very good poet indeed. His lines stick in my memory . . . His 'Directions to a Rebel' I have read and pondered. 'The Fountains' is exquisite and has made me realize why I am here in the Middle East and not in any of my private or public worlds . . .

> You will be more free
> At the thoughtless centre of slaughter
> Than you would be

Standing chained to the telephone end
While the world catches fire.[5]

. . . Sometimes Rodgers' diction is too strained . . . his literary language would do well to dip down to common Irish folk speech again for a lyrical impulse – even though there is the danger of itself ingrowing – this is an old melody for a new makar . . . There is too great a complexity of verbal brilliance; so that the self-conscious virtuosity of language, the alliterative arabesques, the onomatopoeic Hopkinsian inventions obscure the feeling of the poem 'Summer Holidays'. The driver of the hatch-back sustains the greasy journey, but the reader is left dazzled and dazed. But I am still overcome with admiration at the power of our Irish poet . . .[6]

On 30 April, having ironically noted 'The Japs have got to Lashio. Are we getting ready in advance for a successful Dunkirk across the Indus?', Hamish went down with dysentery and spent four days in hospital. In a feverish state, his mind teemed with ideas and he wrote a good deal of poetry – notably his hallucinatory 'Hospital Afternoon'. On 26 May the Axis launched a major breakout east from the Gazala–Bir Hacheim line and by 30 June the German frontline had reached El Alamein – and 'the gates of Alexandria'. Here, with only a handful of tanks still in battle-order, Rommel ordered his troops to pause and regroup. Despite this, Hamish, to his great surprise and delight, was offered ten days 're-cuperation leave' in Alexandria. It was a city with a five-thousand-year history, and it was to have a powerful long-term influence on his life and poetry. He writes:

1st June: Looking at the fellaheen from the windows of a train going to Alexandria. I can understand why people love Egypt. Fellaheen in the unwalled fields of the Delta / The culture of these fields / Corralled by a desert / Is human civilisation . . . Immuned by the wire of my camp where Intelligence functions jerkily like an old film . . . there are two circles of wire – one for the PWs and one for the IOs . . . Here in Egypt I'm an awkward symbol of the British Raj.

---

5. W.R. Rodgers, 'Directions to a Rebel'.
6. Perhaps it was Rodgers' line 'There was a halo of hills round me from the start' that set the seal on Hamish's regard for this under-estimated poet, but it was not until Seamus Heaney turned his critical gaze on Rodgers, in 2001, that anyone was to write as perceptively about him as Hamish did in Cairo, in 1942.

2nd June: Arrived too late last night to see anything (blackout very strict in Alexandria and no moon). I stood on the balcony of my room in the Windsor Hotel – 70 piastres a day full board, not bad – and listened to the sea, and sniffed its clean wind. This morning I stood on the same balcony, and saw across the blue of the Eastern harbour the dazzling white of the fort of Kait Bay, where stood the Pharos. In this great harbour of the world rested the fleet of the Ptolomies and the fleet of Caesar. I'd like to strike across this water and, amidst the bastions of an Arab faot see the remnants of the Pharos and the Mathematical Wonders that so impressed the Greek world . . .

On his first morning in Alexandria, Hamish met Robert Liddell, 'a young Kiltish Catholic convert who writes masterly light verse'. Liddell gave Hamish E.M. Forster's *Alexandria: A History and Guide* and together they discussed Cavafy's great poem 'The God leaves Anthony'. Hamish notes: 'I would like, when my life swerves downwards, to write such a poem: like a man prepared, a brave man . . .'

With battles raging out in the desert and many Egyptians expecting an imminent German victory, respect for British soldiers was extremely superficial. However, Hamish set out to enjoy the mêlée of the streets where crowds of boys offered him 'obscene postcards and the visual delights at French exhibitions'. On his second morning in the hotel he notes paying his 'private devotions to the Seraphis . . . Then set off to visit Pompey's Pillar.' Here he came face to face with the sacred filth of the living; here was the flotsam and jetsam of life, here – bloody-minded and chaotic – was death. Standing amidst the human ash out of which Pompey's Pillar had been erected two thousand years earlier, Hamish contemplated the eternal conflict between death and life, a theme that was many years later to seed his magnificent songs, 'Auld Reekie's Roses' and 'The Flytin' o' Life and Daith'.

Hamish describes Alexandria as 'not just the city of Fatimite Caliphs, of warring Sunni and Shia but also – the city of Downes Powell!' Powell, a doyen of London's theatreland, was introduced to Hamish at the Union Club and regaled him with fantastic tales about the ghost in the theatre at Notting Hill Gate and the secrets of the resonance of the human voice.

On 5 June, Hamish swam at the Alexandria Swimming Club with Byatt Pire who discussed 'with complete Midhurst naiveté the curious, the unreasonable and completely Gippo attitude of the native population of Alexandria – which gets badly bombed by the Axis – the brittle ramshackle houses get blown to buggery in all directions – and "they" think we're responsible for it!' In the afternoon he saw a performance of *George and Margaret*, in the evening he enjoyed cabaret at the Carlton where 'the

three stunning Bianchi sisters were entertained by Chesnay and myself'.
Leaving the Windsor Hotel on 9 June, Hamish travelled back to Cairo in
a railway compartment with a Gilrayesque Egyptian man-mountain: 'An
enormous man, everything about him large – face, legs, hands, belly – a
prodigious man beside whom G.K. Chesterton would look like wee
MacGregor . . . He was Ishak Helmy, a great figure in the Egyptian
sporting world – a sometime Channel swimmer and a popular, good-
natured giant.' Next day Hamish was back at work in the Cage: 'A day
and night riot of it – while the bleeding battle rages, we also storm and
rage.' But Alexandria was not forgotten and it was soon to become the
subject of his Third Elegy, 'Leaving the City':

Morning after. Get moving. Cheerio. Be seeing you
when this party's over. Right, driver, get weaving.

The truck pulls out
along the corniche. We dismiss with the terseness
of a newsreel the casino and the column,
the scrofulous sellers of obscenity,
the garries, the girls and the preposterous skyline.

Leave them. And out past the stinking tanneries,
the maritime Greek cafes, the wogs and the nets
drying among seaweed. Through the periphery of the city
itching under flagrant sunshine. Faster. We are nearing
the stretch leading to the salt-lake Mareotis.
Sand now, and dust-choked fig-trees. This is the road
where convoys are ordered to act in case of ambush.
A straight run through now to the coastal sector.
One sudden thought wounds: it's a half-hour or over
since we saw the last skirt. And for a moment we regret
the women, and the harbour with a curve so perfect
it seems it was drawn with the mouseion's protractor.
. . .
Do not regret
That we have still in history to suffer
or comrade that we are the agents
of a dialectic that can destroy us
but like a man prepared, like a brave man
bid farewell to the city, and quickly
move forward on the road leading west by the salt-lake.
Like a man for long prepared, like a brave man,

like to the man who was worthy of such a city
be glad that the case admits no other solution,
acknowledge with pride the clear imperative of action
and bid farewell to her, to Alexandria, whom you are losing . . .[7]

Between 1938 and 1942 a brilliant but rather spoilt collection of
cosmopolitan intellectuals, artists, writers, diplomats and spies had
'retreated' to Egypt – from Greece, south-east Europe and all over the
Middle East – where, stimulated and protected by the huge Allied
military presence, they turned Cairo, for a few years, into one of the
cultural capitals of the world. Literature, broadcasting and journalism
were the most vital areas of activity, and numerous new English-
language publications sprang into being. Prime among these were
Citadel, Personal Landscapes, Orientations and *Oasis.* Hamish was
keen to make contact but was also from the beginning deeply dis-
trustful of most of the Cairo literati – as is made clear in his notes,
written up after his first meetings with George Sutherland Fraser (G.S.
Fraser), a young Scots poet and critic, serving with the British Army
Information Service.

> Fraser asked me what I thought of his poetry. I told him I considered
> his tight-rope act under the parasol most admirable – every con-
> scious tremor of the muscles gauged to a nicety – but I was still
> listening for the sound of the Niagara below. 'Is there a Niagara
> below?' he said, turning to Campion. 'I couldn't say definitely,'
> replied Campion . . . There is about as much lyricism in George
> Fraser's songs as in a *Times* leading article. Poetry must free itself
> from this degrading case of being a kind of supplement to a treatise
> on psychoanalysis . . . Later I went with Fraser to spend the evening
> with Reggie Smith, editor of the local broad-bottomed review
> *Citadel* . . . Fraser drank with ostentation a surprising amount
> during the course of the evening – towards the end he was quite
> drunk and in a maudlin state of self-pity . . .

Hamish had found a follower, and for the next twenty years Fraser's
work bears the imprint of Hamish's character and vision. Hamish
features in several of Fraser's Cairo poems, for example 'To a Scottish
Poet', and his 'Monologue for a Cairo Evening' captures the theatrical,
evangelical Hamish vividly:

---

7. *Elegies for the Dead in Cyrenaica* (John Lehmann 1948).

> . . . who
> Among the projectors on this floating island
> Is such an honest Gulliver as you,
>
> Old friend, who being simple and merciless
> And kind and subtle, can enjoy a show
> Where every part's pat in your repertory:
> Crude Caliban to priggish Prospero!
>
> To you I dedicate this inconclusive
> Conclusion to an unmethodical
> Method of being the mass and the observer:
> To you, the critical, this curtain call . . .[8]

Fraser was hugely impressed by the poetical force of Hamish's political vision – his idea that he was going to 'change Scotland'. And it seems Hamish assumed that Fraser (like Adam Malcolm) would join him in the struggle. As things turned out, Fraser reneged on whatever promises he might have made in the heat of those Cairo nights but, in 1942, Fraser's regard for Hamish was evident, and in his autobiography *A Stranger and Afraid* (written in the early 1960s), Fraser introduces Hamish, after discussing the febrile, inconsequentiality of the Cairo literary scene:

> It was refreshing from time to time to meet a man of action . . . I looked up from my desk in Parade's offices one day to find a very tall, gawky, bony young Lt. in battledress looking down at me. I could place him at once as a Highlander, by something fierce and gentle in his whole bearing. His voice confirmed my guess, soft and lilting, with long vowels and snaky sibilants. 'Would you by any chance be Mis-s-ter George Fras-s-er?' I looked up at a strange face, with a short nose, a broad forehead and high cheekbones, fierce dark shortsighted eyes enlarged by strong glasses, and a wide, loose, sensitive adolescent mouth under an absurd small moustache . . . One large hand dived into a haversack to produce a little pamphlet, which it thrust onto the desk before me. 'These are some verses of yours and I'm very pleased to meet you.'
> . . . He took me out for a drink and began to tell me all about himself . . . He was obviously a born soldier; and ideally fitted for

---

8. G.S. Fraser, 'Monologue for a Cairo Evening', in *Poems of G.S. Fraser*, ed. Ian Fletcher and John Lucas (Leicester University Press 1981).

Intelligence in that he had a spontaneous sympathy for the Germans and their romantic attitude to history – just as obviously, he was out of sympathy with the English, with their tepid self-control, mild dislikes, liberal hesitations, and their passion for compromise. When Hamish loved or hated, he liked to be thorough.

. . . When we sat down over our drinks, Hamish at once began to discuss philosophy. . . Hegelian – as developed by Marx. . . with the rather Germanic mind that overlaid his Celtic temperament . . . The war had exalted and transformed him . . . Yet I sensed a contra-diction in his attitude. He was not only a Marxist but a Scottish Nationalist, and in Scottish history his sympathy was not with the winning faction, the Lowland Whigs, but with the Highlanders, who rode into battle, but they were defeated . . . He saw Marxian Socialism as the means by which the Highlands of Scotland and the Celtic enclaves of Europe generally, from Scotland and Wales to Brittany and Spanish Galicia, could regain their old cultural autonomy . . . Scotland was going through a cultural revival – but that was not enough. The politically central power always imposed its own culture on the outlying provinces . . . Hamish, a Marxist in the Modern World, became, when he considered Scottish history, a Jacobite and a Tory. He was so eager about the old feuds, which he felt stirring again beneath the surface of our time, that it was hard not to catch his enthusiasm. An age of battles! What a splendid prospect. . . So he rallied me and, in the middle of our most obstinate arguments, suddenly broke into a lilting Gaelic song. . . I give myself credit for recognising at once the poet in him (and publishing him, in Orientations) at a time when, to many of the people to whom I introduced him, he seemed merely a strange and noisy swaggerer.[9]

Hamish read *Orientations*, No. 3 (May 1942) from cover to cover. It contained a splendid article by R.A. White, entitled 'Literature of the War' and he noted '*true*' beside the following sentence. 'Writers whether in the Services or not, must be able to grasp the experience of war above general thought and assist the broadening of imagination necessary *to dominate* the course of events . . .' Hamish was a makar – not an aesthete, and on another page he scribbled abuse at the Cairo pundits:

They expect poets to be Audenry and Spenderish – Spender com-pulsory and Auden optional. When I gave them poetry that was

---

9. G.S. Fraser, *A Stranger and Afraid – The Autobiography of an Intellectual* (Carcanet New Press 1983).

neither Audenry nor Spenderish but coarse, sensual, numinous and song-like, acknowledging as influences Lorca, Heine, Clare, Dunbar and Burns and drawing much vigour from my association with Scots and Irish working class people, they squealed and scooted. Such poetry was really *not* Macneice . . . Muck you I thought, and said thank God and Mary for this foul-mouth ram-stam Goggarty of a Reggie, thank God for my bedraggled verminous Aberdeen Fraser – who'll sing the chorus for my songs – and thank the whole Trinity for Paul Potts who's a bangster billy to beat them all . . .

The unreality of the lives being lived by the Cairo intelligentsia struck Hamish as irredeemably bourgeois – they were the literary representatives of a spoilt class, living their elegant, civilised lives on the backs of 'comrades' about to die in their thousands in the desert, on the backs of the labouring masses of an Empire dedicated to maintaining *their* superior status. As a socialist and an artist he was against them: like the painter Paul Nash, who had so marvellously documented the First World War, he would let them know the truth stinking behind the arras: 'I am no longer an artist. I am a messenger who will bring back word from the men who are fighting to those who want the war to go on for ever. Feeble, inarticulate will be my message, but it will have a bitter truth and may it burn their lousy souls.'

The most satisfying personal relationship Hamish established in Cairo was with John and Ruth Speirs. Hamish was full of praise for Speirs' work on the Scots tradition, and the Speirs recognised Hamish as a Byronic new figure on the literary scene. They enjoyed debate, and Hamish was soon challenging Speirs' 'inadequate critique of MacDiarmid and his gross under-estimation of the importance of the folk tradition to the wider literary tradition'. Hamish recited great chunks of MacDiarmid and pointed out the crucial importance of his 'folk sources'. He sang ballads, arguing their merits as independent literature, and encouraged Speirs to continue his radical review of the whole range of Scots culture. In turn both Ruth and John encouraged Hamish to be boldly ambitious in his 'Elegies' project. Speirs, who was still in close contact with Leavis and Eliot, also reinforced Hamish's instinct that whilst this 'big poem' should be Scottish it must also be modernist and international.

Over the years, however, the Eliot/Leavis/Speirs influence on *Elegies for the Dead in Cyrenaica* has been over-emphasised. They did play a part in the poem's inception but it was Eliot's criticism, rather than his poetry, that provided Hamish with the richest fuel. As a schoolboy, Hamish had read 'Reflections on *Vers Libre*' and 'Tradition and Individual Talent', and he had been genuinely excited by Eliot's commendation of the 'absence of pattern, absence of rhyme, absence of metre', but it was

Eliot's re-evaluation of the role of 'tradition' that struck the deepest chords. For example, when Eliot writes 'only in closely knit and homogeneous societies, where many men are at work on the same problems, such a society as those that produced the Greek chorus, the Elizabethan lyric, and the Troubadour canzone, will the development of such forms ever be carried to perfection', Hamish felt himself personally addressed. In Scotland these traditions were still living realities: the links between ancient tradition and modern literature were facts of life and part of a living cultural phenomenon; the 'unified sensibility' that Eliot advocated as the base-necessity of all major poetry was still extant in the communities in which he had grown up. That Eliot and Speirs should applaud a tradition that he was naturally part of – and which he had so long been determined to serve – was manna indeed. Drinking with Speirs in Cairo, Hamish saw clearly that the desert could be his Wasteland: Scotland was a wasteland for him to farm.

Speirs showed Hamish a copy of Eliot's wartime booklet, *London Calling* (Harper 1942). Eliot had become pessimistic about both the human and the literary future and he questions whether 'mechanised war' can produce any poetry of the highest standing – but he goes on to state that, if it should do so, 'it could only happen to a very young man'. And, in his poem 'A Note on War Poetry', Eliot asks this future poet:

> In the path of an action merely typical
> To create the universal, originate a symbol
> Out of the impact . . .
>
> . . . The individual
> Experience is too large, or too small. Our emotions
> Are only 'incidents'
>
> In the effort to keep day and night together.
> It seems just possible that a poem might happen
> To a very young man: but a poem is not poetry –
> That is life . . .
>
> War is not life: it is a situation[10]

Eliot had also written 'Every nation, every race, has not only its own creative, but its own critical turn of mind . . .'. These thoughts, so close to his own, gave Hamish confidence. They embraced him as a

---

10. T.S. Eliot, 'A Note on War Poetry', *London Calling* (Harper 1942).

carrier of a living Highland tradition, and as Hamish began to establish the architecture of his Elegies he determined to speak primarily for the Scotland he loved: originality and form would look after themselves. Late into the night, Hamish would recite his poems to the Speirs; they encouraged him to see his fabulous memory, not as a block to creativity, but as an ancestral blessing. And it is not surprising that, when Hamish's Elegies were published in 1948, the Prologue was dedicated to John Speirs.

Hamish's relationship with Ruth Speirs was equally propitious and more surprising. She was a petite, vivacious young woman engrossed in translating the poetry of Rainer Maria Rilke when in walked Hamish – a man who loved Rilke like a brother and spoke German like a native. They got on famously, and Hamish overflowed with enthusiasm for her translation project. He helped Ruth complete her translations with a rare mixture of linguistic accuracy and poetic empathy. She was 'bowled over' by this stranger out of the desert, and in the summer of 1942, Hamish noted in his diary:

> Ruth said to me, with gross flattery, the other day, 'You're only twenty-three and you know and do so much already. What will you be like when you're fifty-three?' Unfortunately, though I have Rolfe's talent for feeling quite convincingly omniscient, my life these last few years has been necessarily too political and military to reach beyond to things of real human interest.[11] Time I could have spent learning more languages, getting deeper knowledge of those I know already, getting acquainted with different social customs and cultures, thoroughly identifying myself with the culture of my country (such as it remains – instead of condemning and speechmaking against its decay), time that I could have spent as a student acquiring a deeper apprehension of life for my poetry, has actually been spent putting up anti-tank defences along England's invasion coasts and asking German prisoners about the muzzle velocity of the 7.5 cm anti-tank gun . . .

By August 1942, military preparations for what would become the battle of El Alamein were gathering pace, and the pressure of work within the Cairo Cage became intense. No information about either planning or interrogations appears in Hamish's diaries at this time but his work as a censor was not 'off-limits' and he continued to note some of the Rabelaisian gems crossing his desk. He quotes one young private, hoping for leave with his wife: 'Be sure and get a lot of fresh air from now on, love

---

11. Frederick Rolfe, Baron Corvo, who inspired A.J.A. Symond's classic of literary detection, *The Quest for Corvo*.

– for when I turn up you'll see nothing but the ceiling for a week.'
Comment from censor: 'go to it and keep at it . . .' On 24 July, he received
a typically warm 'house-letter' from the Armstrongs:

> 'Are you coming home for your birthday?' Love from Mina Arm-
> strong. 'I hope you're fighting fit and will soon win the war', Alan
> Armstrong. 'How are you doing toots? Don't forget to come home for
> Christmas as there's a nice fat chicken', Violet Armstrong. 'All the best,
> keep your chin up', love Theodore. 'Hope you're getting big and
> tough', Betty. 'Howdy Hamo! Howya doin'. Somebody needs a kick
> in the gents out there. I hope you will administer it!', all the best Leo.
> 'There's no news at all except that Leo has another animal out in the
> stable – a pig I think – not Leo – the animal. Well, Hamish, we're
> expecting great things from you – Here's sand in your ears!' Carter . . .'

With those words of encouragement fresh in his mind, Hamish went
down with a bout of fever, and ended up in hospital for a second time. As
usual, enforced horizontality inspired an outburst of poetry – including a
surrealistic vision of the ward, entitled 'Back from the Island of Sulloon'
and a stream-of-consciousness series of jottings. He also ran Charlie
Chaplin and Laurel and Hardy films through his head, noting the tragedy
that underpins so much of the best comedy. And, in a rare moment of
depression, he addressed the idea of suicide: 'On the whole I bear up not
badly, even this sin against the Holy Ghost is not drubbing me down too
abjectly – only once in this war have I felt a nightmarish desire to
immolate myself before the senselessness of slaughter, and that was when
I first rode a motorbike, in convoy, wearing a bleary-eyed gas-mask.'

Restored to health, Hamish took himself off to a Cairo cinema to view
Citizen Kane for a second time: 'It is a film of great promise, but as far as
I'm concerned *The Grapes of Wrath* is the greatest film yet – see that film
and read Cedric Belfrage's book *Let My People Go* and you hear America
singing.' By late August, however, such night visits were few and far
between. Montgomery was reconditioning the Eighth Army, and the war
in North Africa was about to enter its decisive phase. Having established
contact with a number of officers in the 51st Highland Division, and
knowing battle was imminent, Hamish now requested that he leave the
Cage and join the Highlanders as a field Intelligence Officer. His request
was refused. However, in early September he was sent out to join the 1st
South African Division, guarding the south end of the Alamein line; it,
too, was a first-rate fighting division and Hamish was glad, at last, to
align himself with men in the frontline. As 'a poet at war', he must – he
would – share the experience of the fighting men.

SIX

From El Alamein to Constantine

In this Intelligence racket, as in the Propaganda racket, you get colour-blind to the truth – told by yourself anyway . . .

HH

The battle of Alamein began on 23 October 1942 and ended a fortnight later in an overwhelming Allied victory. Intelligence played an important part in the Allied success: Axis Intelligence worked badly, British Intelligence worked well. For example, in mid August, Major 'Bill' Williams (Head of Eighth Army Intelligence) was able to inform Montgomery that he had the 'Ultra decrypt' of Rommel's battleplan for the Axis assault on the Delta. Consequently, on 30 August, when the Afrika Korps launched its 'surprise attack' at Alam Halfa (a right-hook at the south end of the Alamein line) the Eighth Army was waiting and employed new tactics that came as a shock to the over-confident German commander: Allied tanks fought from protected, dug-in positions – and were not 'loosed' to fight a 'sporting match' with a mechanically superior enemy. Major Williams later summed things up by stating 'Montgomery won Alam Halfa by accepting the intelligence with which he was furnished.' Williams thereafter became one of 'Monty's' elite and permanent advisers – from Egypt to final victory in Berlin. The great battleplan for El Alamein was very much Montgomery's, but many of the concepts, the preparatory deceptions and the 'geography of the battle's execution' were decided as the result of information provided by the Intelligence Corps: and, within that small, high-powered unit, Hamish was to play a significant role.

Between June and late August 1942, the desert battlefront had remained essentially static, and Hamish spent most of his time at the Eighth Army's Intelligence HQ just outside Cairo. On 10 August he wrote to his old English teacher, Eric Parsley:

The wind here is furnace breath and the sands blowing about still; however if the Afrika Korps thinks it's going to throw a swastika flag over the sphinx it's got another think coming. In a tent in the Western desert a few days ago I found an old friend, and remembered Matlock just a year ago . . . You can get to like the damned desert – it hands out a crack in the eye impartially to both sides . . . Life out here has one big advantage – there is a war going on in the desert, and you feel there's some point in you wearing uniform.

On 30 August, within hours of Rommel's attempted breakthrough on the southern flank, Hamish notes: 'Balloon goes up at Alam Halfa!' On 2 September he entered the fray: 'Tour of Battlefield, after Alam Halfa, with James Mark – see Mark IVs (long barrelled) looking like shot-up buck elephants. Mark IIIs in various stages of dilapidation and an 88 looking like a petrified erection. Doss down for the night on the side of the Ragil depression – after a good stew cooked on petrol flares. Wakened up before dawn by a tank clattering by – luckily not part of the 15th Division . . . Put number of tanks destroyed at 50–60.' (Hamish marked each German tank he found with a chalk cross and later concluded that the comparative losses at Alam Halfa were '140 Axis tanks to 37 Allied tanks'.)

Success at Alam Halfa prepared the way for Montgomery's great offensive at Alamein. His tactic now was to keep Rommel occupied at the south end of the Alamein line whilst secretly planning that the main battle would take place at the north end. Hamish notes that 'build-up, training, and deception were rigorously pursued'. After 'a day's practice with Bakelite grenades and Mills grenades', on 25 September, he was formally attached to the 1st South African Division as Intelligence Officer (IO). He describes it as 'a first-rate fighting unit – well-ready – for war fighting in a frontal attack against prepared positions'. With the South Africans, Hamish was responsible for 'deception, camouflage and the collating of information about enemy positions'. In addition, anticipating the imminent arrival of large numbers of Axis prisoners, Hamish briefed the Division's officers on 'the interrogation of prisoners, making it clear that "Voices" are valueless unless the actual words are reported – any hint of "Chinese whispers" is anathema to successful Intelligence.' He also advanced plans for 'a new kind of interrogation – for use on the battlefield'. He believed that field interrogation tactics could give commanders engaged in the fighting possibly crucial intelligence much more quickly than anything CSDIC could provide 'via the cage system'.

On his second day with the 1st South African Division Hamish was given a copy of Arthur Koestler's *Darkness at Noon* by Dr van der Merwe, a man whom he describes as a small, anti-English Boer. He offered Hamish the book with these words: 'I was never out of South

Africa till I came with the Union Forces to Egypt. But I've had my difficulties to face and decisions to make and this book recalled them all to me. I can't say I enjoyed it, because it gave me too much excitement and pain for that, but I thought it one of the most important books I've ever read.' It was an incident 'outside time' and began what was to become Hamish's intense sixty-year relationship with the people and problems of South Africa.

Despite, at one moment, describing Montgomery as 'a snotty little shit', Hamish – like the bulk of the Eighth Army – was thrilled by the arrival, on 13 August 1942, of a general who immediately appeared to know exactly what had to be done. Montgomery had been brought up within an Anglo-Irish Episcopal tradition and was proudly part of 'the oral, military tradition'. He thought on his feet and spoke as he thought.

Within days of Montgomery's arrival, Hamish had written a ballad in his honour: 'The Ballad of the Big Nobs'. It was a song for the common soldiery – witty, ironic and bawdy – but it recognised the military transformation that the new general was effecting and itself became part of 'the legend' that was to make the man. From the start, Hamish saw that Monty had the makings of a 'folk hero' and he began a collection of the new general's sayings: 'I believe the first duty of an officer is to create what I call atmosphere. I do not like the general attitude I find here – it is an atmosphere of doubt. All that must cease at once. Here we will stand and fight. There will be no further withdrawal. I have ordered that all plans and instructions dealing with withdrawal are to be burnt – and at once. We will stand and fight here. If we can't stay here alive, then let us stay here dead.' Those famous words come from Monty's speech to senior officers on his arrival, but Hamish gathered many less-known fragments. 'I've got a good job waiting for me at home, so I'm not going to be long over this one . . . I am the general. Nothing that Rommel can do will embarrass me. The other generals who were here before me failed, because they weren't the right kind of general. I am the chap . . . I am going to speak for half an hour. During that time there will be no smoking or coughing. Then there will be a ten minute interval, during which there will be smoking and coughing . . .' And when Monty announced he was going to 'hit Rommel for six – out of Africa', Hamish roared with laughter. The general's rhetoric had reached a level of 'theatrical absurdity – that was artistry of a high order!' Within a few months, the Little General had become, like Charlie Chaplin, 'a star' – a man for whom hundreds of thousands of men were prepared to lay down their lives.

Everyone involved in the Battle of El Alamein knew the coming battle would be a hinge of world history, and Hamish was determined that it would provide the fulcrum of his *Elegies for the Dead in Cyrenaica*. He believed that the battle would be as important to Western civilisation (and to Scotland) as the Siege of Troy had been to Ancient Greece and he knew he had a Homeric opportunity. Originally, he entitled this battle elegy 'The Highlanders at Alamein', but as he worked on it he subtly changed certain aspects of the poem and retitled it 'Interlude – Opening of an Offensive'. Here is the final version.

a) the waiting

Armour has foregathered, snuffling
through tourbillions of fine dust.
The crews don't speak much.They've had
last brew-up before battle. The tawny
deadland lies in a silence
not yet smashed by salvoes.
No sound reaches us
from the African constellations.
The low ridge too is quiet.
But no fear we're sleeping,
no need to remind us
that the nervous fingers of the searchlights
are nearly meeting and time is flickering
and this I think in a few minutes
while the whole power crouches for the spring.
X-20 in thirty seconds. Then begin

b) the barrage

Let loose (rounds)
the exultant bounding hell-harrowing of sound.
Break the batteries. Confound
the damnable domination. Slake
the crashing breakers-hurled rubble of the guns.
Dithering darkness, we'll wake you! Hell's bell's
blind you. Be broken, bleed
deathshead blackness!
               The thongs of the livid
firelights lick you
                    jagg'd splinters rend you
                              underground
we'll bomb you, doom you, tomb you into grave's mound.

c) the jocks

They move forward into no man's land, a vibrant sounding
     board.
                As they advance
the guns push further murderous music.
Is this all they will hear, this raucous apocalypse?
The spheres knocking in the night of Heaven?
The drummeling of overwhelming niagara?
No! For I can hear it! Or is it? . . . tell
me that I can hear it! Now – listen!

            Yes, hill and shieling
sea-loch and island, hear it, the yell
of your war-pipes, scaling sound's mountains
guns thunder drowning in their soaring swell!
– The barrage gulfs them: they're gulfed in the clumbering guns,
gulfed in gloom, gloom. Dumb in the blunderbuss black –
lost – gone in the anonymous cataract of noise.
Now again! The shrill war-song: it flaunts
aggression to the sullen desert. It mounts. Its scream
tops the valkyrie, tops the colossal
            Artillery.

Meaning that many
German Fascists will not be going home
meaning that many
will die, doomed in their false dream

We'll mak siccar!
Against the bashing cudgel
against the contemptuous triumphs of the big battalions
mak siccar against the monkish adepts
of total war against the oppressed oppressors
mak siccar against the leaching lies
against the worked out systems of sick perversions
mak siccar
            against the executioner
against the tyrannous myth and the real terror
mak siccar[1]

---

1. *Elegies for the Dead in Cyrenaica* (John Lehmann 1948), also published in the
  Collected Poems.

Hamish's Alamein is clearly described from a Scottish perspective; in particular it documents the contribution made to the battle by the 51st Highland Division. Hamish was particularly keen to salute this Division (the Second 51st Highland Division) because its predecessor had been sacrificed, to save the rest of the British Expeditionary Force, at Dunkirk in June 1940. Thus, a new 51st Highland Division had had to be created, almost from scratch, and Hamish saw the heroism and success of this new division at El Alamein as 'a moment of resurrection', and a symbol of national renewal. It was a battle as worthy of bardic remembrance as any victory (or defeat) in the whole history of Scotland, and Hamish makes this historical point very clearly by the manner in which the phrase 'mak siccar' is repeated six times and the even stranger phrase 'X-20 in thirty seconds' stands out.

In 2002, in his book *Alamein,* the military historian John Latimer describes the opening of the Battle of Alamein with these words:

> in an instant, at 21.40 hours, flashes from hundreds of guns were seen sparkling in a long line across the desert . . . After about fifteen minutes the roar of continuous firing, suddenly, died away – there was a breathless stillness . . . While above the Eighth Army's hidden array two searchlights pointed long, still fingers into the sky. Five minutes passed . . . At 22.00 hours the two beams swung inward, intersected and stopped, forming a pointed arch dimly seen in the moonlit vault, like a remote symbol of crossed swords. At that instant the British guns opened a barrage of unimaginable intensity, eclipsing their first performance, and to the urgent drumming of the guns the infantrymen stepped out . . .

The idea that this great battle for the future of civilisation should begin with an image of crossed swords might have appealed to a Whitehall planner, but for the men of the Highland Division and for many others gathered beneath them, those great crossed beams of light – dividing the clear night sky before them – were not crossed swords but the Cross of St Andrew. It was the flag of Scotland – the Saltire – that the searchlight operators had conjured into being, over Alamein. As the Highlanders walked towards their deaths and towards a victory that would lighten the lives of generations unborn, it was this cross – in the moonlit sky – that was the last thing many of them would see on earth. On their backs, small St Andrews flags had been painted (to guide the man behind through the minefields). Hamish introduces his image of the 'nervous fingers of the searchlights' just before the poem announces the first great barrage at 21.40 hours, and he defines this moment as 'X-20'. This neatly describes the time (twenty to ten) but also, anticipates the fact that, in 20 minutes, an X will appear in the sky.[2]

On that night, 23 October 1942, Hamish was not with the Highland Division; he was some miles south with the South Africans but in a good position to see the searchlight Saltire and – in imagination – he strode into battle with his kinsmen.

In reality he went forward with the South African sappers as they cleared the minefields of the southern sector and they completed all their battlefield objectives on schedule. Further north, however, the main battle went on for over a week before the Allies, at last, began to make decisive breaks into the Rommel/Kesselring defences, and the famous 'Supercharge' began.

On 4 November Hamish sustained his only real injury of the war. He notes: '8.00 am, out of the blue, a Stuka raid . . . We dive into a slit trench. My back hurt. Kettle shouts: "Fuck the fucking fuckers!"' No one was badly injured but Hamish damaged ligaments and vertebrae, and his back was to remain a recurrent problem for the rest of his life. The same day he noted that the 'Germans began stealing the Itis transport and beating it westwards.' As this retreat turned into a rout, Hamish was ordered 'to join 10th Corps – Monty's newly created elite Armoured Corps [formed to counter and destroy Rommel's Africa Korps] under the command of Lumsden who is leading the "Supercharge" breakthrough as the German/Italian line at Alamein begins to collapse'.

On 9 November, Hamish describes 'trailing' 10th Corps through the heavy rain and floods which had 'on the 6th/7th saved much of Rommel's army'. On 12 November he entered Sollum, one day after the Allied frontline had re-entered Tobruk. On 13 November he was in Capuzzo, where a German prisoner informed him that 'at Fuka an order had come from Rommel, ordering everyone to fight to the last, but the retreat had

---

2. Whoever conceived the idea of this great cross is likely to have had some knowledge of Scottish history, and the power of art. No military man involved at Alamein has claimed the idea. The probability that the idea was Hamish's is, I believe, extremely strong. Two years earlier his poem 'X Still=O' begins 'the searchlight fingers stroke the sky' and ends 'X still equals nought' (a reference to what he saw as Scotland's political impotence in the face of the coming slaughter).

continued'. He also notes looting by British Forces: 'Binoculars, watches and gold . . . Nip looting in the bud – no unauthorized person to have access to PWs – No PWs' property to be left in the open to be fingered by a lot of ghouls sitting in their bunkers. Take action against *anyone* who prejudices the success of interrogations, or the safety of intelligence documents . . . Nothing can so antagonise a prisoner amenable to interrogation as the wanton theft of his private property . . .' Hamish believed looting to be the thin edge of wedge of a corruption that could do huge damage to the Eighth Army. He knew the problem was acute within some sections of the Intelligence Services and the Military Police, so, to educate, entertain and ridicule he created a song he entitled the 'Ballad of Gibson Pasha'. The song begins with the line 'My name is Gibson Pasha. I'm a wily PMC' and ends with this powerful verse.

> If ever you've been naughty (for example, thieved and raped)
> You'd better pay hush money, for I've got your dossier taped.
> And a warning in conclusion – if you try and queer my pitch
> I'll bleed you till you're just as poor as Gibson Pasha's rich.[3]

Keen to get away from the problems of post-battle greed and *tristes*, Hamish got himself driven into Tobruk (by Jeep) to view a city 'that had been the hinge of two years of desert warfare' and whose dereliction reminded him of Dundee. Thus he wrote what he describes as a 'A MacGonagallesque Ode on our Re-entry into Tobruk'.

> While proceeding, as ordered, to Tmimi
>   I turned aside to take a look
> And see what cruel war had done
>   To bonnie Tobruk.
> But now I'm here and have a shuffty, all
>   I can say for this accursed (unprepossessing) spot
> Is that today, on the evening of 16th November 1942, the
>   The Eighth Army is in it, and the bloody Jerry is not . . .[4]

The following day, an official war photographer took a photograph of Hamish standing by his Jeep, watching a sand-storm – of biblical proportions – rolling in across the desert. During the night he had visions. Meantime, news of the on-going Allied victories was being celebrated all

---

3. From 'Ballad of Gibson Pasha', in *the Collected Poems*.
4. This poem was later published in a slightly different form in *Alias MacAlias: Writings on Song, Folk and Literature* (Polygon 1992).

over Britain, and the Dry Drayton Armstrongs were delighted to send a round robin out 'to their man in the desert'.

> Dear Hamo – We hope you're still trying to win the war and get home for your birthday . . . We had Harvest Festival on the 1st Sunday in October. D. Davis preached and we had a full church and a good choir – all we needed to complete it was your 'umble self' . . . This is your birthday, 11/11/19 . . . We have had some Dutch RAF boys coming out here to ride the ponies, eat apples etc. They're coming back to spend their leave here . . . We are to ring the Church Bells on Sunday in view of your victory, so we will think of you all when they peel again . . . Stanley Holmes, Leo's friend, is missing over Germany . . . All the best dear Hamo, with love Violet . . .

On 19 November Hamish took 'his' Jeep into Acroma. 'In the naval workshops I interrogate two Jerries by an electric hand light salvaged from Kreigsmarina dump – an emergency light from a submarine (like a miniature lighthouse). One communicative bloke gives me my latest scoop . . .' This 'scoop' stimulated the interest of the Intelligence top-brass and next day Hamish records:

> Who should give me a glad hullo this morning but Weidy, come up with a carnival of vehicles and a comic opera of Intelligence officers – to take over from me! I must say I felt a bit sore about that – at this stage in developments . . . Weidy suggests I join 51st HD . . . but Tasker says Cairo HQ . . . Anyway, thought I, fuck this! I wrote a poem. We ended the evening drinking Chianti, eating fried onions and bully and inveighing in full-throated chorus against CSDIC.

It is not clear what poem Hamish wrote at Tmimi but there are two candidates. One is entitled 'Kitsch – written in a moment of depression' and begins: 'I wish I could emulate Oates' confident step / Recover the cool of the confident eye: / For all my outward panache, recover the inner grace . . .' The other is a denunciation of the brutality that war brings out in men (on all sides).

> For the sadist and the slayer
> The flogger and the slave
> For them we'll say no prayer
> For them we'll dig no grave.

> If all lay swollen rotten
>   Black on the German plain –
> The pure sky they'd forgotten
>   Its tears of joy would rain.[5]

On 21 November Hamish was informed he would *not* be transferred to 51st Highland Division. In high dudgeon he went off to see 'Murphy' at Army HQ, who informed him: 'They want you back at CSDIC – so back I'm afraid you'll have to go.' Thus, it was with real regret that, on 26 November, Hamish flew from Tobruk back to Cairo: he had greatly enjoyed his two months on the frontline; he felt he had made a real contribution to the Desert War and had no wish to be corralled in the 'Cage' again but orders were orders. In the plane, as usual, he made notes. Such flights gave Hamish time and perspectives that raised important thoughts, some of which are given futuristic expression in his Tenth Elegy:

> *One must die because one knows them, die*
> *of their smile's ineffable blossom, die*
> *of their light hands*
>
> But dust blowing round them
> has stopped up their ears
>   o for ever
> not sleeping but dead.
>
> The airliner's passengers,
> crossing without effort the confines
> of wired-off Libya, remember
> little, regret less. If they idly
> inspect from their windows the ennui
> of limestone desert
>   – and beneath them
> their skimming shadow –
>   they'll be certain
> they've seen it, they've seen all
> . . .
> Yet that coastline
> could yield much: there were recces and sorties,

---

5. HH, unpublished, from notebook.

drumfire and sieges. The outposts
lay here: there ran the supply route.
Forgotten.
By that bend of Halfaya
the convoys used to stick, raw meat for the Jabos.

And here, the bay's horseshoe
how nobly it clanged through laconic communiqués![6]
. . .

Arriving by bus in Cairo, 'quintessence of filth, altar of excrement', Hamish went straight to Shepeards Hotel for a drink in his desert gaiters and tie-less battledress, observing the officers 'in their fantastic regalia – which never saw war'. In the evening he went to All Saints Cathedral and noted: 'these English carols make even the memories of Talbots and Etheringtons sanctified, and soften for an hour the wrath of Lenin'.

Hamish's much battered 'first' desert notebook concludes here. Inside the back cover is a map of the Eastern Mediterranean, North Africa and the Middle East – on which he has doodled notes and a thumbnail caricature. Such sketches are scattered throughout his early notebooks: in Scotland, he usually sketches himself as the aged Ossian; in the desert, as an Arab; in Ethiopia, as a Negro, and here in the Middle East he appears as a bearded Moses with the word 'genius' beside the head.

In Cairo, overflowing with creative energy, Hamish wrote songs, collected songs, worked on 'The Highlanders at Alamein' and completed his 'Report of the Battle of El Alamein', for CSDIC. The final paragraph reads:

Summing up the battle, we can say the enemy was taken by surprise by our first attack, that he consistently miscalculated where we would strike next, that he wore out his mobile striking force by engaging it piecemeal at first and, when it was concentrated, by using it up on purely local objectives, and that when the final blow came, again in an unexpected direction, he had already committed his reserves.

After that, Hamish flew south for three days' leave in the ancient cities of Thebes and Karnak, which he wandered in a Rilkean reverie: 'This civilisation was filled, so great was its complacency on this earth, with profound death-longing – it longed, dreamed, lusted, went awhoring after death . . . If we of the modern West devoted a tenth of the time to life that

6. 'Tenth Elegy', *Elegies for the Dead in Cyrenaica* (John Lehmann 1948).

Karnak devoted to death, we'd bring a tangible hope, even to the inhabitants of the Nile Valley.'

Whilst in Luxor, Hamish began to write 'Karnak', a poem that would become the eighth of the ten elegies that comprise *Elegies for the Dead in Cyrenaica*. It is the longest and most 'intellectual' of the poems, examining (among other things) what Hamish describes as 'the umbilical cord of history' linking Ancient Egypt, Islam and the Arab world with Western Christendom and the politics of modern Europe. It is a philosophical and prophetic poem that strikes powerful contemporary chords in relation to the recent history of Iraq. Hamish completed his first full draft of this poem in February 1943 and, conscious of its complexity, wrote beside it: 'I disapprove of notes to poems on aesthetic grounds, but for some of my poems they're necessary – and, anyway, I like writing them.'

Back in Cairo, Hamish immersed himself in work at CSDIC HQ. Occasionally, it took on a James Bondian flavour. For example, on 17 December he was instructed 'to proceed by train to Alexandria today, taking charge of documents that will be handed to you at CSDIC. These documents are not to leave your hand, and are to be handed over on arrival to an officer from the staff of C-in-C Med., who will meet you at Sidi Gaber Station by car . . . deliver documents to the Duty Officer in the operations Room of the Offices of C-in-C Med., Lorenz Buildings, Sidi Bishr. You will return to base p.m. Friday 18th December.' At HQ he found himself in regular contact with his chief Bill Williams. Williams had been an Oxford don in civilian life, and Hamish delighted in his literary acerbity. He notes: 'Bill Williams' review of the battle of El Hamma which led to the German withdrawal from Mareth is as usual excellent. What a pleasure it will be for future historians to find that such appreciations were nearly all first-rate pieces of allusive, rich, flexible and satiric English'. Montgomery, in his *Memoirs*, praised Williams with enthusiasm:

> As the campaign developed I learnt the value of Intelligence. Bill Williams was the main source of inspiration; intellectually he was superior to myself or to anyone on my staff, but he never gave one that impression. He saw the enemy position whole and true; he could sift a mass of detailed information and deduce the right answer . . . He could tell me in ten minutes exactly what I wanted to know . . . He was 'accepted' and trusted right through the Eighth Army . . . [7]

7. *Memoirs of Field-Marshall the Viscount Montgomery of Alamein, K.G.* (Collins 1958).

Christmas celebrations in Cairo in 1942 were full-blooded, and Hamish took charge of the CSDIC party. He put on a play that poked fun at authority and named nicknames – including the Toad in Uniform, the Commie, Black Dwarf of Maadi, Heller the Horror, Little 'Orrible, Little Nasty, Black Mamba, Der Sitzriese – and he himself appeared in a Nazi uniform. However, it was Hamish's new song, 'The Ballad of King Faruk and Queen Farida', that stole the show – everywhere! It had been written as a skit on the corruption of the Egyptian Royal House (and the British Colonial administration that supported it) and had been immediately taken up by the Allied soldiery with ribald enthusiasm. It lampooned King Faruk and Queen Farida and was sung to a version of the Egyptian National Anthem (based on a splendid composition by Verdi). Thus, wherever loyal Egyptian citizens rose to salute their monarch, well-oiled Allied soldiers were likely to bellow out Hamish's 'alternative anthem', as a magnificent, revolutionary bacchanal! Well sung, 'King Faruk' is an anarchic, sexually cathartic rabble-rouser and it proved a phenomenal, long-term success. In the 1960s, for example, when President Gamel Abdul Nasser was asked, in a filmed interview, what had first drawn him into Egyptian Nationalist politics, he answered, unequivocally, it was hearing British soldiers singing the 'Ballad of King Faruk and Queen Farida'. In creating this song, Hamish can be seen to have risen from what G.S. Fraser had described as his 'prompter's stool' to put his head around the curtain of the world stage. Five verses are set out below (another eight are much more risqué!).

O we're all black bastards, but we do love our King.
Every night at the flicks you can hear us fuckin' sing
    Quais ketir, King Faruk,
    Quais Ketir, King Faruk,
O *you can't fuck Farida if you don't pay Faruk.*

O we're just fuckin' wogs, but we *do* love him so,
And we'll all do without just to keep him on the go –
    From Sollum to Solluch
    Tel el Kebir to Tobruk,
O you can't fuck Farida if you don't pay Faruk.

O we're just damned niggers that a bugger brought to birth,
But when we have a bint we want our money's worth.
    You may have a tarboosh,
    A gamel, a gamoos,

But you can't have Farida if you don't have filoos.

O it's no use to say, if you want to have it in,
'Be a sport, King Faruk,' he would only fuckin' grin,
    You may beg on your knees,
    He would just say 'Mafeesh.'
O you wont get Farida if you don't give baksheesh.

. . . And this song that you've heard is the song the Gippos sing,
And they'd sing just the same if they'd Rommel for a king.
    Quais ketir, Rommel dear,
    Quais ketir, Rommel dear,
O we're so glad you won the battle, and we're so bucked up you're
here! . . .[8]

When this song was first published in *Ballads of World War II – in Five Languages* (Glasgow, 1947), Hamish added this note: 'Tune, Salem ei Malik (Egyptian National Anthem). Chiefly the authentic version as sung (1942) in the First South African Division, Seventh Armoured Division, Ninth Australian Division, Second New Zealand Division and Fifty-First Highland Division.' Thus Hamish probably composed this ballad while with the South African Division, in September–October 1942. Its popularity within the Eighth Army was huge, and the manner in which it gathered momentum throughout the Second World War is demonstrated by the following story, told by Stuart Boyd, an ex-paratrooper, at his home near Dornoch in Sutherland in 2002:

> I never met Hamish Henderson and I have never seen any of his songs in print but I know a stack of them – and they kept me alive for eight months, on the Eastern Front where I was taken as a prisoner after Arnheim. I can still sing 'The Ballad of King Faruk and Queen Farida', every verse! I learned it in the cinemas in Cairo . . . As the war drew towards its end we joined what was called the 'Long March' and – it was Hamish's songs that kept us going. We always sang as we marched: I was one of the leaders, 'Quais ketir, King Faruk, Quais Ketir, King Faruk . . .!'

During Hamish's second spell in Cairo (December 1942–February 1943) he made several visits to El Eazher, 'the mind of Islam', the Muslim university. He was given a brief introduction to the language and history

---

8. Published in *Hamish Henderson's Ballads of World War II* (Lili Marlene Club, Glasgow 1947).

of Arab civilisation. One of the mullahs offered him a handsome volume on the Muslim faith – which he declined: 'it's the first *baksheesh* I've been offered (on a large scale) in Egypt. Islam means surrender, submission, with its root in Salem – peace . . . My most rewarding literary find, however, remains the poetry of Mahmoud Teymour – lucid, perceptive latinity.' And, having learned that the name El Alamein means 'the two cairns', he wrote an 'Epitaph for Alamein':

> We biggit here / their twa cairns
> Bane on bane
> To keep yoursel / and bairn's bairns
> Frae makin mane.[9]

By early March 1943 Hamish was back in the desert (in Tunisia), at last, formally attached to the 51st Highland Division. Immediately, and for the first time, he got involved in close quarters combat. On 17 March 1943, he suffered another bout of dysentery. After four days he was up and about but not before horizontality had produced another glut of poetry:

> Curious that I am able to write best either when on a journey (in which I myself have no operative part, and in which I am not too tightly bound to companions) or in hospital during convalescence. The chief reasons I suppose – a lack of responsibility – with, in the first place a mental alertness due to the stimulus of motion, and, in the second, a quickened sense of relief and well-being.

While in hospital he wrote or rewrote the following unknown poems, 'Eleba', 'Frontier Country', 'The Germans', 'In Bishops Teignton', 'Scheik' and 'Volupte'. Also, he set down the lines with which he would open his *Elegies for the Dead in Cyrenaica*. 'There are many dead in the brutish desert who lie uneasy / among the scrub in this slavish landscape of stunted ill-will.' The word 'slavish' is then crossed out and replaced with 'arid' – and it is with those two lines that the 'First Elegy – end of a campaign' starts. On 24 March he wrote to Dry Drayton:

> things are hotting up here and there's been some pretty tough fighting. Rommel has been chasing himself round in circles trying to ward off the final blow – jabbing at the Yanks, jabbing at us, and jabbing at the day of doom we've kept piping hot for him since

---

9. HH, unpublished, from notebook.

Alamein. In short, as [Bill Williams] put it the other day, 'the wounded tiger is behaving like a scalded cat!'. So the battle continues . . . It seems I'm to be the only 'vacant chair' at family reunions that sound as regular as Saints' Days. If absence makes the heart grow fonder the Armstrong clan should be weeping tender tears for me now! Any more news about my wandering library? Or is this the sort of law case that drags on for years and years, world without end, Amen? It was at the start of Alamein (Oct. 4th) that I wrote to you the list of books. I've travelled several thousands of miles since then in different directions, and I'll bet they're still arguing it out in the courts as to whether I'm in Africa or not. Anyway after this sparring match with Rommel, I'll look forward to an event with Ma Edwards some sunny day . . .[10]

Back in the desert, Hamish maintained a regular correspondence with John Speirs in Cairo about the war and his latest poetry. In the late spring of 1943 he writes: 'My "Elegy for the German Dead" has been turned down by the Cairo censor – so I hear – from the editors of *Orientations*, because such morbid writings have a depressing effect on troops! What a laugh. However, it may be more expedient in every way to publish it after the war.'

Hamish felt this exclusion from *Orientations* (and other Cairo magazines) strongly, and in retrospect one can see it as the prime reason why Hamish's reputation as a poet of the Second World War is recognised in the breach rather than the observance. Academics, going to what they regard as the 'primary sources', don't find much Henderson in 'the literature'. Thus, his vast contribution to the poetry of the Second World War is often assumed to have been small and hardly worth mentioning. The *Orientations* rebuff, however, may have had one positive result. Hamish's natural sympathy for 'his' German prisoners had, perhaps, begun to distort his moral and literary judgement – and the censors' action brought him back on

---

10. The reference to 'Ma Edwards' is to Hamish's (second-year) landlady in Cambridge, with whom he had 'left' his library and various personal items. When, on Hamish's instruction, Leo Hawkes and Charlie Armstrong had gone to collect them, Mrs Edwards informed them that her sister had got rid of them. Leo and Charles made attempts to retrieve 'the books at least'. When nothing was returned, Hamish asked Leo to take the matter to court. The police, however, refused to pursue such a trivial matter and there things rested until Hamish returned to England in October 1945 when 'the first thing I did was to visit Mr. and Mrs. Edwards!' When the door was shut in his face, Hamish wrote Mr Edwards a letter (14 October 1945), after which about one third of Hamish's Dulwich prizes were returned.

track. Certainly, it is noticeable, from this time forward, that Hamish's sympathy for the enemy is more than balanced by empathy and love for the Allied soldiery. And 'The Elegies', which might have become an eccentric lament for the German dead – or mere propaganda for his beloved Highlanders – become a sublimely equal-handed treatment of men and nations at war, a work of art beyond 'censorship' of any kind. However, Hamish's sense of having been unjustly treated stimulated him to challenge the literary criteria of his judges with vivid insight:

> Why the English poet doesn't take over from Tommy[11] his inimitable burlesque 'goddam' gameness Jeeza only knows. You find something of it in the N. Winty reportage but not enough. If ever I have the time, I'll give you some of the Eighth Army balladry – 'King Faruk and Queen Farida', 'Wadi Makhlia', 'This Damnable Desert of Egypt', 'El Alamein', 'Rommel and the 51st' and some more – to show how a well-functioning army, conscious of its own vigour and efficiency, can produce its own camp literature, of often surprising merit – and demonic and direct enough to lift *Orientations* with a hefty swing.[12]

By May 1943, well aware that Italy was the Eighth Army's next big target, Hamish was busily brushing up his Italian. There was no shortage of teachers: 'The trouble with the Itis is not to get them to talk but to stop . . . Some, that had been in the desert for three years were saying: "*Abbiamo coglioni cosi!*" – "bollocks as big as this!"' Such nuggets encouraged him to note other 'oral eroticisms' he had gathered, on the road since Alamein: outstanding among these was a rhyme by his Cockney Jewish driver, Private Kettle: 'Oysters is amorous, lamfrey's is lecherous, and whelks goes straight to the balls – but shrimps! Shhhrrriimps! Them's the fuckin' awfillest things of all!' Hamish then adds, 'Songs to learn – Shrimps, Bosun, Ringaringaroo, Red Plush Beaches, One Eye Riley', and it was with boyish glee that he wrote to Dry Drayton on 7 May:

> The news we're celebrating today (which is worth any extra liquor you can smuggle into the rectory) will already be as stale as Stalingrad by the time it reaches you, but I'm going to repeat it all the same. Tunis has been entered by our armoured cars, and Bizerta has fallen on the same day. This is the end of the Axis in Africa. The Germans and Fascists are now definitely *de trop*. From

---

11. Tommy: a British soldier who has seen action.
12. Letter written by HH, probably to John Speirs.

Alamein to Northern Tunisia we've kept them running, and now they've got where they just can't run any further. Too bad. More chewable carpets needed: Führers for the use of . . . There's been a helluva lot of correspondence in the papers about the boys from the Middle East getting a break and coming back, and I hope it works out that way, but somehow I think we'll see a bit more action before we're homeward bound. The clearing of Africa has been a long job, but we've another to do yet. . . N. Tunisia is the most attractive part of Africa I've come across, and the little walled town of Monastir is the most desirable place in it. Elegant Arabs with flowers at the ear sell lemonade to British and Yank troops, and the local French population is delightful, speaking a Gallic and not Levantine dialect of the tongue.

When Eisenhower's American Army, advancing from the west, and Montgomery's Eighth Army, coming in from the east, met in Tunisia, the war in North Africa was all but over. For years Hamish had had an instinctive distrust of the American approach to life and politics, but the one area in which he gave them credit was their commitment to an international future defined by the Declaration of the United Nations, signed on 1 January 1942. Subsequently, he hoped that the United Nations would create the legal framework within which peace would be instituted on the post-war world. However, by the summer of 1943 it was clear to Hamish from the manner in which the United States was 'greeting Vichy collaborationists as long lost brothers' that little had really changed. He notes:

a grave danger for the United Nations – a Germany which shakes off Nazism and not the HerrenKlub, an Italy that shakes off Mussolini and not Volpi . . . By its own acts the German people must prove that it has nothing in common with Hitler. Sentiment is worth nothing when it is a matter of life and death. When on the coming day of judgment the terrible accusation is spoken 'Germany has burned my home, killed my child and tortured my wife to death,' then humanity must be allowed to rise and say, 'German hands helped to destroy the criminals.'

Hamish believed it vitally important that the German and Italian peoples (and their many allies in Eastern Europe) should be actively involved in the cleansing (ideally, the self-cleansing) of their nations, and he quotes Josef Goebbels to show how a romantic sense of 'self-martyrdom' was a permanent factor in the German problem: 'We are spared nothing. History is quite without grace or mercy. Wherever we look, we see mountains of problems confronting us. Everywhere the path ascends at a steep and dangerous angle, and nowhere is there a shady spot where we may stay or rest.' The combination of sentimentality and conceit that Goebbels embodied was also evident in the behaviour of many German prisoners. After reprimanding an Afrika Korps tough-guy (formerly a French Legionnaire), for speaking condescendingly about 'the youth' of the Eighth Army's 'Desert Rats', Hamish notes his reply as poetry.

> Sharp-toothed desert rats I'll grant
>   you sir
> but they're not a patch on the likes
>   of me.
> How can they be, seeing they're
>   youngsters mostly –
> I was in the Legion.[13]

The heroism, self-delusion and brutality in that statement can be contrasted with a strange, 'humanitarian' incident that Hamish got himself involved in at this time. It sprang from a battle of wills between General Freyberg VC, commander of the New Zealanders, and German soldiers of the 90th Battalion fighting under the command of von Sporeck. After days of hard fighting, most of the Germans had been captured, but one unit was determined to fight on, despite hopeless circumstances. Freyberg issued an ultimatum to the Germans to surrender. They refused. Freyberg then asked Hamish, as interpreter, to make a formal request to the German prisoners in custody that one of them act as 'ambassador' and personally carry the surrender terms to the besieged Germans. All refused. Hamish then suggested that he (with Martin Taubmann, an Austrian auxillary working with Allied Intelligence) should be allowed to take the prisoners to the top of a small hill, where they would hold a short religious service. Freyberg gave permission and the prisoners were taken up to this knoll overlooking the desert battlefield. Hamish spoke first and then 'Taub gave an *informal* address after this manner – in German: "We have a human problem – one man only is needed – anyone of you, willing to go to the others, can perform this human duty . . ." They retire a jury to deliberate and then return, and the spokesman makes the decision known – Obergefreiter Stahl has volunteered to go, alone . . . His name may be remembered.' Hamish underplays his role in this strange 'Sermon on the Mount' but it was his idea, and his actions prevented the deaths of many brave men in what would have been a useless slaughter.

With the final surrender of the Axis forces in North Africa, Hamish was

---

13. HH, unpublished, from notebook.

made responsible for organising the writing, publication and distribution of leaflets and posters aimed at facilitating the surrender of the remaining pockets of enemy resistance: '*Français de Tunisie – Ceçi est Destiné aux Soldats Allemands – Faites qu'ils le Reçoivent! Nur Einen Ausweg!*' Most were very simple: 'To British And American Outposts: Any German Soldier Presenting This Safe Conduct Is To Be Disarmed And Taken Prisoner.' Then, almost by chance, Hamish was given the job of interrogating the Italian commander, General Mannerini. 'Two Yank officers turned up at Gabes just before I left for Tripoli – with General Mannerini. One commented, "You started this desert show so you might as well finish it. We'll stand around on the hills and cheer."' Hamish conducted his interviews in French, because his Italian was not yet completely fluent. 'When I asked Mannerini about the Americans he said: "ils ne sont pas encore des soldats!" – Well – cor strike me dead!' Hamish does not document his interrogations but does describe acquisition of a fly-switch which had belonged to Mannerini. It was huge! 'A flamboyant member of the tribe that Cairo knows in its millions! This fly-switch creates a sensation in Tunisia. The population (Arab, Jewish and French) ask with incredulous wonder what it is. What hope for pan-Islamic unity if this is the speed news travels in the Arab world?'[14]

Since early April 1943 Hamish had, recurrently, joined the team planning 'Operation Husky'; the codename for the Allied invasion of Italy through Sicily. It was a top-secret project. His particular responsibilities related to 'psychological' questions and he gave talks on 'Italian morale and the likely response to the Allied invasion'. His lecture notes begin:

> Hard to generalise from the opinion of the wounded and captured but one fact does emerge – reaction of the Italians will not be lukewarm or passive. After an attack, their response will either be that outburst of mercurial bravery we know from before, or an equally wholehearted welcome of the Allies, coupled possibly with anti-German insurrections . . . Our propaganda offensive should play on A) the corruption of the Fascist bosses (Gerarchi) – Fascism has brought only war to Italy etc. B) Traditional Italian friendship for Britain (Risorgimento etc.). C) Treat the Italian people as duped by the Germans and their mercenary leaders. D) Emphasise the principles of the Atlantic Charter.

---

14. This fly-switch proved such 'a glorious conversation piece' that Hamish decided it was far too valuable to leave in Africa. He took it to Sicily and up into the Tuscan hills where his partisan comrades surveyed 'Mannerini's pride' with the pleasure of stallions!

The idea to invade Italy was Churchill's. He wanted to get at the 'underbelly of the dog'. Planning was initially the responsibility of Field Marshall Alexander but later passed to Eisenhower as the new Allied Supreme Commander. Monty remained in charge of the Eighth Army and when he saw Alexander's plans for the invasion he was far from impressed. On 24 April 1943 he sent a highly critical message to Alexander's HQ advancing new plans of his own – and the very first of Monty's counterpoints appears to have come from Hamish's recent Intelligence briefing. Montgomery argues: 'Planning to date has been on the assumption that resistance will be slight and Sicily will be captured easily. Never was there a greater error. Germans and Italians are fighting well in Tunisia and will repeat the process in Sicily . . . If we work on the assumption of little resistance . . . We will merely have a disaster. We must plan for real resistance . . . And a real dog-fight to follow the initial assault.' Montgomery's revised plan was fully accepted by Alexander, and when Monty met Eisenhower in Constantine, Algeria, on 2 May he delivered the same message. 'Enemy resistance will be very great; it will be a hard and bitter fight; we must be prepared for a real killing match . . .' Hamish travelled with Montgomery's team to Algeria, and was in attendance as Operation Husky was hammered into its final shape. Not surprisingly, Hamish's notebooks make no mention of particular meetings but he describes the city of Constantine with great satisfaction:

> The first thing one notices on arriving in Algeria is that the racial texture of the population has changed. These Berbers are not brown like Arabs or Bedouins, or orange-brown like the Tunisians – they are pale faces – blond almost. And in dress too, the appearance they present is quite different – tall white bulbous turbans, the loose woollen overcoats that flap in the winds of this hill country make you realize that there is a sharp distinction between highland and lowland musulmans. And this, like the Cyrenaican Gebel, is Highland country. Constantine has a superb setting on its rocky hills, straddling an abyss and commanding a great sweep of upland culminating in the peaks of the west.

Hamish now knew that the 51st Highland Division would, as it had throughout the desert campaign, play a major role in the battle for Sicily. Believing that an unfair burden of 'expectation' was being placed on *his* division, he decided to make it clear that he believed the Highland Division had been 'over-publicised in the media since Alamein . . . the fault of English reporters – weakness for kilts and coronachs'. He conveyed his opinions to Allied Forces HQ and, within days, Alan

Humphrys, the Reuters correspondent, informed Hamish that '"I'm going to be with the Highland Division for the Husky show – and that the official policy of AFHQ is that the HD has received too much publicity and that it should be soft-pedalled." Thank Christ for that!'

Hamish was glad to be leaving Africa and excited by the thought of returning 'to Europe' as part of 'the army of Scotland'. He had learned much in Africa but, in sailing for Italy, he felt he would be sailing home. 'I thought before I came to Africa that I was broad-minded, that I was cosmopolitan, that I had a world view. Nothing more stupid. I was hopelessly European . . . African endpiece? A camel convoy with a red light swinging from the tail of the last camel.' The desert was not where he wanted to be and as he turned his back on the Sahara he wrote a valedictory poem, 'So Long'; it provides a 'full stop' to a great military campaign and his part in it.

> To the war in Africa that's over – goodnight.
>
> To thousands of assorted vehicles, in every stage of
> decomposition
> littering the desert from here to Tunis – goodnight.
>
> To thousands of guns and armoured fighting vehicles
> brewed up, blackened and charred
> from Alamein to here, from here to Tunis – goodnight.
>
> To thousands of crosses of every shape and pattern,
> alone or in little huddles, under which the
> unlucky bastards lie –
> goodnight.
>
> Horse-shoe curve of the bay
> clean razor-edge of the escarpment,
> tonight it's the sunset only that's blooding you.
>
> Halfaya and Sollum; I think that at long last
> we can promise you a little quiet.
> So long, I hope I wont be seeing you.
>
> To the sodding desert – you know what you
> can do with yourself.
>
> To the African deadland – God help you –
> and goodnight.[15]

---

15. 'So Long', published in the *Collected Poems*.

SEVEN

Sicily

Farewell to the known and exhausted
Welcome to the unknown and illimitable.[1]

The Allied invasion of Sicily began two hours before dawn on 10 July 1943. Landing with 154 Brigade of the 51st (Highland) Division on 'Amber Beach' at Rada di Portopalo, Hamish noted:

> there were very few Germans and the only Sicilians to be seen were at pains to identify themselves as civilians . . . Leading elements of the Brigade were soon in Pachino . . . My first job, as IO, was to interrogate four German deserters. They assured me there were no Germans south of the plain of Catania. I decided to see for myself, and after borrowing a motor bike from a Military Policeman rode north in the gathering light, with a tremendous feeling of exhilaration: we were out of Africa and back in Europe . . . The *contadini* working in the fields hardly gave me a glance and when I waved to them, one or two waved back! After several miles I reluctantly turned the bike round and rode back the way I had come; fairly soon I encountered sections of a Black Watch company, recognisable at once by the red hackles in their bonnets . . . I informed the first senior NCO I came across that they could afford to take it a bit more easy: there were no enemy troops for miles ahead.

One of Hamish's Sicily notebooks was later lost in Italy but what was to become, for Hamish, a thrilling campaign is still documented in remarkable detail.

---

1. Inscription from the Celtic cross at Fiona MacLeod's grave on Mount Etna, which Hamish visited while in Sicily; Fiona MacLeod was the pen name of William Sharp (1855–1905), a Scottish mystical writer prominent in the Celtic revival, who died in Sicily – and whose *Life of St Columba* had greatly excited Hamish as a schoolboy.

On the evening of 6th July 1943 I had embarked at Sfax, on the
south east coast of Tunisia, on LST No 8 which was to carry us back
to Europe. On deck the following morning, I counted some sixty
vessels visible to me, riding in the Sfax searoads. This was only a
smallish percentage of our convoy, which was only a small part of
the whole invasion fleet. The atmosphere aboard was calm; rather
like a Mediterranean Cruise. Our deck was crammed with vehicles;
you could hardly move edge ways . . . Up till then the weather had
been calm but on the 9th July a juicy roll developed. I surveyed the
convoy from the upper deck, and read up once again the enemy
order of battle, as we knew it at the time; I idly committed to
memory the units of 206 Coastal Division (due to enter the bag the
following day). During the night – the last night before D-Day – the
roll got worse and the whole ship shuddered. I stayed awake, and
two lines of poetry started circulating in my head.

>   To Sicily, to Sicily
>   Over the dark moving waters . . .

And shortly I had the first stanza of what would become a quad-
ripartite poem that I finally christened, when I finished it on the
Sangro Front six months later, 'Ballad of the Simeto'.

>   Armament, vehicles and bodies
>   make heavy cargo that is checked and away
>   to Sicily, to Sicily
>   Over the dark moving waters . . .[2]

The Allied landings were widespread and largely unopposed: by 14 July,
2,400 ships had disembarked hundreds of thousands of troops, vast
amounts of heavy armour, weaponry and supplies, with minimal losses.
Historical accounts, and the cinema, have subordinated the Allied invasion of Sicily to the great D-Day landings in Normandy a year later – but
'Sicily' was a highly significant military event and, within six weeks, Italy
had been knocked out of the war. This success, however, was not easily
won and Hamish's motor-bike ride into Europe was quickly followed by
a prolonged series of bloody battles in which the Highland Division
played a highly aggressive central role. For the first eight days, Hamish
was too busy to make diary entries but in a letter to John Speirs, dated 11
August 1943, he gives a dramatic, retrospective account of events.

What are things like here? Well, for the first day or two it was
almost impossible to believe it was real . . . Where were the

---

2. Published in *the Collected Poems*.

Germans? Well, the desired had happened, we'd caught them on the hop. Since then, as you'll have read, they fought like blond devils before their line, on the plain of Catania, was broken.

To be on European soil again was a thrilling delight. I felt like Tullibardine when the ship of the Prionnsa Ban sighted the Hebrides – with tears streaming, he pointed to the rocky, rain-driven trash of the skerries and said 'Sir, ye're hame'. Sicily is poor parched ground in all conscience but I had been homesick for Europe and I was home . . . And the Sicilians – I've seen nothing like the welcome they gave us since the fall of Tunis. They accept us now as though we'd arrived with the expedition of Garibaldi. Anything you may have read about this in the papers is not bullshit – it's actually true – the local population making the V sign and clapping like hell – whenever a lone motor-cyclist enters their doom-tummelt clachans.

The Jerries have been browned-off, which is a gratifying sight at any time: even the elite troops of the paratroops – when this division wiped the road with them further south – were fed-up to the teeth with this war. Yet they fight – by Christ they fight, and with a ferocious science: this springs not from their political fanaticism but from the tradition and discipline of the German army. However, Communist and Anti-Nazi dissenters are getting more frequent among prisoners. I prime them with literature and ideas and whatever else their guardian angels might *conduct* them to receive in these troubled times. A young officer we captured the other day ended the story of his capture by saying 'then I was taken prisoner by troops of the Highland Div.' . . . On the strength of that I got MacDonald to pipe him my new pipe tune, 'The Highlanders of Sicily'.

Ti hey durry ha durry hum da
    Ti hee durram durry dum dumda.
Ti hey durry ha durry hum da
    Ta hurry dum da durm deeree.
    Ti hey durum hee
    Ti hi durum ha
Ti hi durum hurry dum deerr
  – Tate hidurum hurry dum deeree –
    Te hie hiderum dee
    Te hie diderum da.[3]

---

3. HH, unpublished, from notebook.

The sense of 'Jacobite Romance' that Hamish felt on sighting the coast of Sicily takes on 'flesh' in a colourful incident that only came to light after his death in 2002. Brian McNeill, Head of Scottish Music at the Royal Scottish Academy of Music and Drama in Glasgow, had gone to Edinburgh to attend Hamish's funeral. On his way home, he called in to see his father in Falkirk. The old man asked him where he'd been 'dressed up like that!' Brian told him he had been to the funeral of Hamish Henderson. At the mention of Hamish's name, the old man's face lit up:

> I kenned Hamish very well. I mind him at the invasion of Sicily. As we came ashore, doon he came aff the sand-dunes – on this big white stallion! . . . He'd been intae a fairm and requisitioned this horse – a big white stallion – and he wis gettin' it to rise up on its hind legs, like in an oil painting! And the boys were all cheerin'. Hamish, welcoming the Highland Division – on this a white horse, wi' his bonnet akimbo – splashing through the waves – I see it like yesterday.

Another more dramatic incident is described by Hamish himself in a magazine article published forty years after the event.[4] It concerns his capture of two German paratroopers:

> Three battalions of the German First Paratroop Division were sent from the Avignon area in the South of France and landed, as reinforcements, in Sicily on 12th and 13th of July . . . and after some very fierce fighting, mainly against No 2 battalion of these paratroops, the Camerons sorted them out near Francofonte on 16th July; they were pretty soon encircled and completely cut-off. The commander of this 2nd battalion was one Captain Albrecht Guenther, and – against the rules of war – this officer ordered his men to discard their uniforms, and collect civilian clothes from the terrified citizens of Francofonte. This they did at gun point, and a number did manage to get through to the German lines . . . On the morning of the 17th July I was proceeding in a jeep up a road near Buccheri when I noticed two characters in ragged civvies standing close to the side of the road. They did not look much like Sicilians – one shortish, one a lanky galloot – and I decide to have a word with them . . . As I approached the taller of the two, he involuntarily drew himself up and came to attention in the German fashion, clapping his hands on his hips. '*Sind Sie Deutscher?*' I asked, and he replied '*Jawohl*'. I asked him his name, rank and number, which he

---

4. *Cencrastus*, vol.53.

gave – as indeed he was bound to give under the terms of the Geneva Convention; then I asked him what his unit was – this he was not bound to give – but he at once identified it as No 2 battalion 1st Fallsschirmjaeger (paratroop) regiment . . . So far so good. Then I turned my attention to the other German; he at first refused to say anything but then revealed he was Captain Guenther, OC of the battalion who had held us up (but not for long) two days previously! So here I had two valuable prisoners, and was alone with the driver of my jeep, in the middle of a vast expanse of mountainous Italy . . . there was nothing for it but to risk it; I put Guenther in the front seat next to the driver, and his batman/orderly (for that's who he was) in the back seat on the right; I sat, myself, as far back as possible on the left, and covered them both, but mainly the officer, with my pistol . . . At HQ I delivered the Jerries to General Intelligence – remarking that I was pretty sure that Guenther would at some time try to escape. I was just about to get into my jeep to return to 51 Div. when a photographer from the Army Film and Photographic Unit turned up – wanting to take a picture of the two of us, and over the years it has appeared in book after book, and film after film, about the Italian campaign.

When I reported back to 51st Div. HQ I was told to proceed immediately to the HQ of 152 Brigade (which had had to deal with Guenther's paratroops from Avignon) and try to placate Brigadier Gordon MacMillan of MacMillan, who was threatening to shoot another batch of paratroops (in civvies) captured that morning. To mollify him – and I could see that there was a genuine danger that he would carry out his threat – I explained that all captured German personnel were needed for interrogation at Army HQ, and that he might be denying valuable operational information to Monty. So, to make the point and mollify the irascible clan chief still further, I paraded the Germans in front of him, and tore strips off them! Telling them that under International Law we would be quite justified in executing them summarily, and that they were darned lucky to fall in to the hands of this particular civilised Highland gentleman . . . The brigadier complimented me on my command of vituperative German, and offered me a glass of vino . . . And there is a sequel to this story – sixteen months later I was to encounter Captain Guenther again – in the Apennines, north of Florence! He did escape – as I predicted he might. He made his way through Italy to the South of France and back to Germany. And, in December 1944, interrogating paratroop prisoners in the area of Montecalderaro, I learned their commander was the same Albrecht Guenther whom I had captured in Sicily! He had rejoined his regiment and was, once again, sending his troops into savage, almost suicidal assaults against us.

Hamish was mentioned in dispatches for his part in this action, and his account is interestingly taken up by Hugh Pond in his book *Sicily*:

> 28-year-old Lieutenant (acting Captain) Albrecht Guenther, captured behind the lines in civilian clothes, was taken to 8th Army Headquarters and interviewed by Major General de Guingand, where he was warned that under International Law he could be taken out and shot as a spy. Quite calmly the young man replied: 'That is quite understood. But as a parachutist who has fought in Holland, France and Russia, it does not alarm me. I took the risk and I failed – I deserve it – Heil Hitler!' De Guingand ordered him to be taken to a prison camp, and released the story to the BBC, in the hope that it might lead to better treatment for some of the Allied prisoners.[5]

During the second week of the campaign, after the battlefront had moved forward, Hamish was asked to go out into the local communities to persuade them to accept the Allies as liberators, to expose Nazi collaborators, and to start building 'a new democratic Italy from the toe up!' And after 18 July his diary contains an outline of his day-by-day activities for the rest of the campaign. His notes are factual but also designed to trigger future memories (for inclusion in his book *German Interrogator*).

> 18th July: A Wachtmeister from 6tp HG Arty spills the beans in a big way – get his stuff away to Div. by D.R. Splendid view of Etna and the whole plain of Catania.
> 20th July: An attack by the Highland Division goes in on the Dittaino front – Sferro and Gerbini – reports of savage fighting. The Goering boys are putting up a helluva resistance . . . New identification – Kampf Battalion ORIA. Anti-Nazi Berlin student tells all he can about it. Recalcitrant Catholic from 256 AA Bty.
> 25th July: Hear Jerry news at breakfast; no less than 16 *Glockenshlage* for sinking in the Med! Boy are they doing fine! Afternoon: get order of battle on HD front taped with Guest. (The order of battle that has just emanated from Army seems curiously haywire . . .)
> 26th July: Musso packs in! Good show! Horse-ride around neighbourhood – great to feel a horse under me again . . . Plenty of Fascist secretaries are decorating the cages these days.

5. Hugh Pond, *Sicily* (Kimber 1962).

This sudden resignation by Mussolini, and the Sicilian response, is described at length in Hamish's letter to John Speirs:

> . . . The fall of Mussolini was greeted with acclamation. In one town a lawyer got up in the Piazza and cried 'This is the first free speech in Italy for twenty years. Down with Fascism! Down with Fascism! Long Live Democracy!' I wish I could hear this without a nasty memory of the American record in North Africa. What marvellous material we have here – grisly to think that we may make a complete balls up of it. Dio Mio! What an opportunity – I hope that after the fighting troops have gone – someone has the job of using it . . . 'United Nations' is either a more cynical catch phrase than anything the First World War threw up – or it is a potential reality. It is either and both of these things – it is also entirely what we choose to make it . . .
>
> Not long ago I got a letter from one of my friends, the Cambridge communist [Michael Clarke], who is now an officer in the Indian Army. It's interesting to note that all the members of our restless house are now complaisant servants of the Imperial British state – all except me. That's because, by plenty of wrong roads, I've arrived at the Scottish National Army. There is a strong rumour in the division that when this lot is over, our general will make the pipes sound against Saxons and write his operation order for the march on London. For the moment, however, our bayonettes are reserved for German and Italian Fascists. The English can wait . . . But let me close this letter by giving you a respite from these barbarities. How are you? Is your Byron done yet? I hope you quote for comparison this epigram of Burns. 'Far ran thy line in Galloway / Through many a famous sire / So ran the ancient Roman way / So ended in a mire.' I am now speaking four languages every day – English, Gaelic, Italian and German – adding a fifth, French, occasionally, and, for good measure here – the Doric.

Hamish's statement about the Scottish National Army was not a fiction of his imagination. Pond's book *Sicily* contains a section that reflects very closely Hamish's vision of a post-war independent Scotland. Pond describes the 51st Highland Division as pretty much a law unto itself, 'from its tall, gangling commander "Lang Tam" Wimberley down to the humblest Jock private . . . One often had a feeling that they were fighting a Holy Crusade, and at the end of the war they would return to Scotland, take Edinburgh by storm, put a Scottish King on the throne, and form an independent country! . . . Wimberley was an untiring, see for himself commander; he did not believe in "bumph", and the closer he was to the fighting, the better he liked it.'[6] Hamish continues:

> 8th Aug: Am summoned to our General to translate some letters which he has found on a scrounge-around. General Wimberley is the right General for our Jocks – and that is certainly the tribute he would like best himself . . . He seems to have a becoming respect for a) my reputation and b) my legend in the division. He is very keen on our (Intelligence) establishment and – on having a buckshee interrogator . . .
>
> 14th Aug: I hike over to the Black Watch and scrounge a truck off them for the day . . . Drive through Belpasso, Nicolosi and Tre-castagni to Zafferana Etnea – in the main Piazza of which Main Div. has established itself. Get myself a nice suite of rooms. The population of Via Grande is in good form, saying there's been an Armistice. A trifle premature this!
>
> 17th Aug: Six Jerries arrive – write report and take it to Div. – the Campaign is officially over. I arrange with Archie Angus to give a series of talks on the Germans to the battalions. My chief aim will be to give each of the individual battalions an account of the actions in which they took part, as seen from the other side. Thus, with the Black Watch I'll concentrate on Spesso, with the Argylls on Gerbini, with the Camerons on Francofonte, and so on.

These 'debriefing' lectures were of great psychological benefit to the men of the 51st Highland Division and, historically, well ahead of their time. They took place within days of the cessation of hostilities. Hamish knew exactly what he was talking about: as the division's Intelligence Officer, he had drawn up the orders of battle, watched the conflict unfold, and interrogated hundreds of enemy prisoners. Throughout the fighting, he had been in constant contact with the officers and men of both sides, and with the civilian population. He had a knowledge of Mediterranean civilisation and a clear understanding of the wider international struggle their battles in Sicily were part of. By presenting each battalion with an objective and detailed account of the actions in which it had been engaged Hamish did something seminal in the history of warfare. This was living history – by a soldier for soldiers – here was the oral tradition in action, here was a modern panegyric being delivered by the 'tribal bard' within hours of the battle ceasing. Hamish reviewed hard facts, spoke of home and spoke sacred names. He gave honour to battle-scarred men in a

---

6. Hugh Pond, *Sicily* (Kimber 1962).

manner that allowed them to digest grotesque experience and go forward, cleansed and fortified. The man who, in Cairo, had sung King Faruk to shame, now spoke of Scotland's pride in them – the battalions of the 51st Highland Division – and they cheered him to the echo.

> Strong-winged
> our homing memory held us
> on an unerring course . . .
>   Aye, in spite of
> the houses lying cold, and the hatred that engendered
> the vileness that you know, we'll keep our assignation
> with the Grecian Gael. (And those others.) Then foregather
> in a gorge of the cloudy jebel
> older than Agamemnon . . .[7]

Hamish's image of the gorge 'older than Agamemnon' echoes the Latin poet Horace's great ode to 'the unsung': 'many brave men lived before Agamemnon's time; but they are all unmourned and unknown, covered by the long night – because they lacked their sacred poet'.[8] Hamish was determined that the new heroes of the Highland Division would be honoured and remembered in Scotland till 'the rocks melt wi' the sun!'. During the thirty-seven days of the Sicilian campaign, 1,436 men of the 51st Highland Division had been killed or badly wounded and, when it was over, one of Hamish's friends, Lt Ian Eadie, a talented artist from Dundee, serving with the Gordons, was asked to design a memorial to their dead, on the heights above Tircizi. Hamish describes it as being 'in the form of a cairn, with a Celtic cross inset. Very good and simple. Inscription: "To the memory of the officers and men of the 51st Highland Division who gave their lives for their country during the Campaign in Sicily 10th July–16th August 1943. *Maraidh a ainn gu bràth*. This monument erected by their comrades, overlooks the battle-fields of Gerbini and Spesso." ' Hamish then adds 'I would like to put this on a similar war memorial at home. "God took from them the day of their homecoming".' The Tircizi Memorial was constructed by the Royal Engineers and finally unveiled on 4 November 1943. The ceremony was low-key because the bulk of the Highland Division was by then fighting on the Italian mainland.

Once the battle for Sicily had been won, Hamish moved into 'creative overdrive' and quickly produced several important poems and one of his

---

7. From HH, 'Fifth Elegy', *Elegies for the Dead in Cyrenaica* (John Lehmann 1948).
8. Horace, *Carmina* IV, 9, 25.

great songs, 'Banks o' Sicily'. It was conceived – and largely completed – within half an hour on 16 August 1943. Fifty years later Hamish described the moment in an article in *Cencrastus* vol. 53:

I was being driven in a jeep from Zafferana Etnea to the little town of Linguaglossa (tongue in two lingoes!), when I heard, coming from a small piazza on the outskirts of the town, the unmistakable sound of a massed pipe band. I hadn't heard a massed pipe band since Libya – since the great parade for Churchill in Tripoli, in fact . . .' I moved forward with some difficulty through a dense crowd of enthusiastic Sicilians, shouting things like 'Viva la Scozia!' 'Viva i Scozzesi!', till I got to the top of the approach road to the piazza, and saw there a magnificent and heart-warming sight. It was the massed pipe band of 153 Brigade – two Gordon battalions and one Black Watch battalion – and they were playing the beautiful retreat air 'Magersfontein'. Presiding over the occasion was the immense bulk of Etna, with a plume of smoke drifting lazily from its crater.

In the silence after the retreat air finished, I stood wondering what the Pipe Major was going to get his boys to play for March, Strathspey and Reel. When they struck up again, the March turned out to be one of my favourite pipe tunes – 'Farewell to the Creeks', a tune composed during World War 1 by Pipe Major James Robertson of Banff. And while I listened to it, words began to form in my head – particularly one recurrent line 'Puir bluidy swaddies are weary' . . . And they were too! . . . I knew that shortly they were going home, presumably to take part in another D-Day in north west Europe. By the time I had elbowed my way through the crowd back to the jeep, I had the beginnings of a song half-completed; that night it had its first airing in a Gordon Officer's Mess, and I was soon scribbling the words out in pencil for all ranks. And it took off with amazing speed – and, in the event, preceded me back to Scotland . . .

> The pipie is dozie, the pipie is fey,
> He winna come roon, for his vino the day.
> The sky ow'r Messina is unco an' grey,
>   An' a' the bricht chaulmers are eerie.
>
> Then fare weel ye banks o' Sicily,
> Fare ye weel ye valley and shaw.
> There's nae Jock will mourn the kyles o' ye,
>   Puir bliddy swaddies are wearie.

Fare weel, ye banks o' Sicily,
Fare ye weel, ye valley and shaw.
There's nae hame can smoor the wiles o' ye,
    Puir bliddy swaddies are wearie.

Then doon the stair and line the waterside,
Wait yer turn, the ferry's awa'.
Then doon the stair and line the waterside,
    A' the bricht chaulmers are eerie.

The drummie is polisht, the drummie is braw,
He cannae be seen for his webbin' ava.
He's beezed himsel' up for a photy an a'
    Tae leave wi' his Lola, his dearie.

Sae fare weel, ye dives of Sicily
(Fare ye weel, ye shieling an' ha'),
We'll a' mind sheebeens and bothies
    Whaur kind signorinas were cheerie.

Sae fare weel, ye banks o' Sicily
(Fare ye weel, ye sheiling an' ha');
We'll a' mind shebeens an' bothies
    Whaur Jock made a date wi' his dearie.

Then tune the pipes and drub the tenor drum
(Leave your kit this side o' the wa').
Then tune the pipes and drub the tenor drum
    A' the bricht chaulmers are eerie.[9]

Originally entitled 'The 51st Highland Division's Farewell to Sicily', this song is now generally known as 'Banks o' Sicily'. Cold on the page the words may look ordinary enough but – well sung – this can be an electrifying song. It was immediately taken up by the Highland Division and is, today, internationally recognised as part of the great canon of Scots balladry. It is also a song that has had significant influence on various strands of modern popular music, including the work of Ewan MacColl, Pete Seeger and Bob Dylan.

    During his three and half years of frontline service Hamish rarely

---

9. Published in *Ballads of World War II* (Lili Marlene Club, Glasgow 1947) and later in the *Collected Poems*.

enjoyed what might be described as 'the officer life' but, for three weeks, at the end of the Sicilian campaign, he did. And he describes it with gusto in a letter (written some months later) to his old Dulwich friend, Michael Clarke.

> The time I had in Sicily was great – after the end of the campaign I occupied a villa on an eminence south of Messina which commanded an incomparable view of the straits and the mountains over the Reggio de Calabria. In this villa I gave myself up to literature, pipes and the lusts of the flesh. Both Fritz [a Tyrolean deserter from the Italian Army] and Peppino [a young southern Italian] developed into not bad cooks and from time to time I invited my friends among the officers to the best Italian meals they had ever tasted. There was one risotto especially which reduced Capt. Douglas of the Gordons to slobbering dithyrawls. Then, in wicker chairs on the balcony, sipping my artfully procured Vermouth, we after listened to Sicilian folksongs sung by Nando with his guitar, or wearying for the music of Zion we called for one of our own pipers to play a *pibroch* . . . One of the Indian officers with whom I developed a close friendship sang me several songs in Sanskrit which, in the idiom of poetic convention and the genius of the music reminded me strongly of some of the ancient Ossianic songs in High Gaelic – such as the 'Banner of the Fingalians' . . . Recollection of that period still fills me with serene content.

While enjoying his cliff-top idyll, Hamish also worked hard on what would become the second long poem of his adulthood, 'The Ballad of the Simeto'. Unlike *Elegies for the Dead in Cyrenaica*, which is a consciously literary, symphonic and orderly poem, 'The Simeto' is an essentially oral poem carrying echoes of Homeric tradition and Orphic song. It is a highly ambitious, song-poem that attempts to give expression to the totality of the 51st Highland Division's campaign in Sicily in the context of a European history going back twenty thousand years.

> Armament, vehicles and bodies
> make heavy cargo that is checked and away
> > *to Sicily, to Sicily*
> > *over the dark moving waters.*

> The battalions came back
> > to Sousse and Tunis
> through the barrens, and the indifferent
> > squatting villages.

Red flower in the cap
    of Arab fiesta!
and five-fold domes
    on the mosque of swords!

We snuffled and coughed
    through tourbillions of dust
and were homesick and wae
    for the streams of Europe.
      . . .
Och, our playboy Jocks
    cleaned machine-guns and swore
in their pantegruelian
    language of bothies,

and they sang their unkillable
    blustering songs,
ignoring the moon's
    contemptuous malice.

All the apprehensions, all the resolves and the terrors
and all the longings are up and away
      to Sicily, to Sicily
    over the dark moving waters.

      II
Take me to see the vines
    take me to see the vines of Sicily
for my eyes out of the desert
    are moths singed on a candle.

Let me watch the lighthouse
    rise out of the shore-mist. Let me seek
on uplands the grey-silver
    elegy of olives.

Eating ripe blue figs
    in the lee of a dyke
I'll mind the quiet of the reef
    near the lonely cape-island

> and by swerve of the pass
>   climb the scooped beds of torrents:
> see grey churches like keeps
>   on the terraced mountains.[10]

The ballad continues for two more long sections: Part III records the battles
as the Highland Division fought its way across the plain of Catania; Part IV
celebrates victory but then looks ahead to renewed, remorseless fighting on
the mainland of Italy. Since it was written, 'The Ballad of the Simeto' has
rarely been sung but Hamish set down the following vocables – 'Hum da
dum da diddle / da diddle da diddle dum / Hum da dum da diddle da / hai da
durum deevee', and they cry out for melodic development.

  While still luxuriating on the terraces of his Sicilian eyrie, Hamish got
hold of *The Oxford Book of Modern Verse 1892–1935* edited by W.B.
Yeats. He underlined Yeats' statement that the modern poet must express
'something steel-like within the will, something passionate and cold', and
the 'evident purpose' of the Irish visionary re-aroused in Hamish all his
old resentment against the 'Stephen Spenderish world' of contemporary
English poetry. It was not him and he would not have it. He writes:

> The really damaging weakness of these latter day Yogis is the fact
> that whilst they are fasting and meditating, others have got to work
> to keep them alive – their 'Spirituality' is simply the by-product of
> money and military security . . . The cult of detachment always has
> to be practised in a warm climate . . . I think it is the duty of every
> man to live as normal a life as he can for himself, and as happy a life
> within the bounds of his own personal mission. Are saints, martyrs
> and messiahs to be excused their first duty because of the highness of
> their mission? I am yet to be convinced that saints, martyrs and
> messiahs – or the common ruck of their too numerous community –
> do a good to humanity in anyway proportionate to the ill they do
> themselves . . . All revolutions are set in motion by the right centre.

Hamish was now deeply in love with Italy and he began to envision a
post-war, post-fascist renaissance – a new twentieth-century Risorgimento. He had noticed how many of the Scots troops felt at home in Italy, and
he began to see Italian renewal as the first step towards a new Enlightenment that would, once again, illumine Europe – and Scotland – in the
wake of war. And instinctively he believed he could play a part in the
process. To this end, he prepared a major lecture on the origins, nature

---

10. 'The Ballad of Simeto', published in the *Collected Poems*.

and psychology of fascism as the dung-heap that a new generation must turn to a tilth. To whom this lecture was delivered is unclear: presumably it was to British Army officers and troops about to enter mainland Italy. By this time he knew a sizeable proportion of the Eighth Army shared his vision of a more socialist future and, with the Mediterranean now open to Allied convoys, a surprising amount of socialist and 'revolutionary' literature was circulating within the Allied armies. In early September, Hamish received a bundle of the *New Statesman and Nation* and writes:

> Thank God someone knows what we ought to be fighting for, even if we don't! Actually, it raises my morale more to get hold of a little topical mental food from Kingsley Martin[11] than to see a hundred of the *Herrenfolk* debussing at the Cage . . . Kingsley Martin asks for a political analysis as ruthless as the military appreciation that a Commander in Chief demands before a battle – and he is right to do so . . . In the *New Statesman* of the 5th June, Laski[12] has an article called '1848 and Ourselves' which brings out, with drastic concision, the parallel with that previous period of opportunity.

> 'They failed because on the left their divisions were stronger than the unity that bound them together. They failed because they did not adapt their programmes to the problems they faced. They failed because the principles they sought to promote had meaning only to a directing elite and could be confounded with their antithesis . . . Their legislative assemblies never realised that the purpose of discussion, at least in a revolutionary time, is not the glory of eloquence, but the actuality of decisions. Their politicians did not know that if they must destroy – it is not less urgent for a revolution to fulfil . . .'

Hamish then adds his own response:

> Popular solidarity is the price of popular victory . . . Above all they did not learn that in a revolution, only those who have the élan which drives to innovation can hope, if they are of the left, to succeed; for it is in innovation that the masses find courage and proof that they have the capacity to govern. Delay to experiment, in a revolutionary time, is always the bulwark of reaction; for when

---

11. Kingsley Martin (1899–1969), then editor of the *New Statesman*.
12. Harold Laski (1893–1950), political theorist, influential in shaping Labour policy in the forties and fifties.

men are not pressed to hope they are driven to fear. The power of property has always been in its ability to re-establish its claims by postponing the hopes which threaten its dominion . . . Kingsley Martin's writing confirms my own duty and makes it sharp for me. Defeat of Fascism does not stop short at the defeat of the Italian and German armies. It will mean an intensified campaign when I return to the shores of Britain . . .

Immersed in the camaraderie of the 51st Highland Division, Hamish's determination to effect radical political change in Scotland became an all-consuming passion. But he remained a realist and, knowing that the new Scotland must be nurtured, not bludgeoned, into being, realised that he must 'ca canny' and carry the military – always close to Scotland's heart – with him. Thus he began reviewing Scots history, building personal alliances and sowing poetry and song within the Highland Division – for everyone's short-term pleasure and for the long-term glory of a revitalised Scotland. He made a collection of what he believed were the most 'telling' of Highland toasts. '*Tìr nam beann, nan gleann, 's nan gaisgeach. Slàinte is buaidh gu brath le gillean an airm seo* – Land of the hills, the glens, and the heroes. Good health and victory for ever – to the lads of this division.'

> Well may Scotsmen, while life lasts remember
> The brave ones who fell among the numberless hosts.
> They tried to defend her, in memory uphold her,
> May their names never die – that's a Highlandman's Toast.
>
> Our forefathers halted the proud Roman legions –
> They fought to a stand-still that famed foreign host.
> They battered the Viking and Saxon besiegers
> May their names never die, that's a Highlandman's Toast.[13]

In private notes he also girded up his own loins, asking 'the gods' that they give him 'the energy and the demon of Rabelais, George Buchanan and Sir Thomas Urquhart – to dominate and make my own civilisation – Gaelic, German, English, French, Italian . . .' He reread *The Scotch Paraphrases*,[14] copying down those that linked the biblical Zion with his vision of a new Zion in Scotland. He was in a magnificently heightened state of mind – sometimes euphoric, sometimes serene – and, in high happiness, he wrote to Violet Armstrong:

---

13. HH, unpublished, from notebook.
14. *The Scotch Paraphrases* was an eighteenth-century book of praise.

Dear Violet . . . around here the country is lovely; the mountain ranges edge down to the fertile level country with wheat-fields, vineyards and orange orchards, and the farms are full of splendid Arab horses – a fact I've not been slow to take advantage of. I think I'll bring one home as a present for the rectory . . . But the life here is not all guitars and spaghetti I can tell you . . .

The fact that the 51st Highland Division had now been ordered to return to Britain with Montgomery, to prepare for the invasion of north-west Europe, put Hamish in a quandary. Should he go back with them, or seek to stay with the Eighth Army in Italy? The final decision was not his to make but Hamish was remarkably adept at getting his own way and he discussed his options with Major General Wimberley. His notes reveal his thinking: 'Attractive though the prospect of going home is, I won't disguise the fact that in other ways I should be strangely sorry. For one thing I should be sorry to leave the 8th Army, and the people with whom I've worked in it, with whom I've made the whole 2,500 mile odyssey. For another, I should be sorry to leave Italy, for which I've conceived an enthusiasm (needless to say, not military) – but for the language and culture that I'm now studying.' Wimberley took the view that Hamish should return to Britain with him, and the division, but this decision was rescinded. Higher authority, apparently in London, decided that Lt Henderson would stay in Italy, and that was that. Six months later, Hamish sent the following explanation of events to Michael Clarke (then stationed in Palestine):

I didn't get home with the division, although the general wanted to take me, and the Army was enlightened enough to support him. The silly sulky sods further back though, that never heard a shot fired in anger and never heard the pipes, except in 'Lives of a Bengal Lancer', were cute enough to dish me, after giving a preliminary verbal consent. The full swinery of this Jesuitical piece of counter-revolutionary Anglo-Saxon swindling would need a letter to itself. However as I'm now on the Anzio Beachhead with quite a lot of work to do, I can't spare it that . . .

This suggests that it was Military Intelligence that insisted Hamish stay in Italy, not because he was an excellent Italian-speaking Intelligence Officer but because they wanted to sever his links with the Highland Division. They may have feared that Hamish's revolutionary influence might create a genuinely Scottish Army that, once the war was over, could become a real threat to the United Kingdom (rather as Hugh Pond has suggested).

Hamish was obviously angered but also strangely satisfied. He knew that Scotland must wait, whereas the unique educational, cultural and political opportunities now opening before him in Italy would never come again.

The 51st Highland Division was to fight nobly in 1944/45 in France, Belgium, Holland and Germany but the transcendent sense of 'destiny' that had accompanied it from Alamein to Tunis, to Sicily and to Vasto slowly evaporated. The division had been decimated, its Highland component was much reduced, many men were close to mental exhaustion, and returning to Britain without their 'singer and philosopher' was an unfathomable blow. In particular, it seems that the loss of Hamish was a personal blow to Tam Wimberley, an old-fashioned and eccentric commander who knew the nature of the men he commanded. In losing their bard, he knew the Highlanders felt they lost something that was 'deeply themselves' and he himself was to miss his *filidh,* like a brother killed.

The Eighth Army's invasion of mainland Italy began on 3 September 1943. Knowing he was soon to lose close contact with the Highland Division, Hamish decided to acquire a new 'family' – of Italian freebooters – and for the rest of the war a slowly changing retinue of Italian assistants lived at his side. The first two were deserters from the Italian army: Fritz (from the Tyrol), who acted as a bodyguard and linguistic assistant, and Peppino, who was his batman-mechanic.

In Sicily, Hamish had found that lack of a vehicle had severely curtailed his work as a frontline interrogator. Consequently, before embarking for the mainland, he requested a means of independent transportation. When the army denied his request he took the law in his own hands and 'requisitioned' an unguarded American Jeep, and Peppino drove it straight on to the landing craft that took them to Italy on 7 September 1943. On landing, Peppino repainted the bodywork, Hamish invented a number-plate (M 5237223) and Fritz, having bought a bottle of red wine, christened *their* Jeep 'Black Maria'. After that, in a cloud of Calabrian dust, like a band of chevaliers, the Scotsman, the Italian and the German Tyrolean disappeared into a maelstrom of two years of war-fighting – and nation-building.

EIGHT

From the Sangro River to the Eternal City

Then Alex said: 'Oor troops maun land
A few miles Sooth o' Rome;
The Banffies are my strongest point
They sure can send it home.'

HH[1]

Montgomery announced the invasion of Italy on 2 September 1943, with this pre-battle message to his troops: '1. Having captured Sicily as our first slice of the Italian home country, the time has now come to carry the battle on to the mainland of Italy. 2. To the Eighth Army has been given the great honour of being the first troops of the Allied Armies to land on the mainland of continental Europe. We will prove ourselves worthy of this honour . . .' The invasion, next day, coincided with the announcement that an armistice had been signed between the Allied High Command and the leaders of anti-Mussolini forces in Italy. Overnight, most of the Italian units defending southern Italy melted away, some 'changing sides'. The Germans felt betrayed and for the next two years treated the whole of Italy as an occupied country – to be used as a battlefield, with few holds barred. Consequently, when the Americans made their major landings further north at Salerno on 9 September, the Germans were well prepared and launched a bloody counterattack that came close to driving the US forces into the sea. To relieve the pressure, the Eighth Army moved quickly north through Calabria to attack the Germans' southern flank, and a nationwide battlefront opened up across Italy.

Hamish had joined the fray on 7 September. Two days later he was formally attached to the 4th Indian Division and describes how 'in a few days I had enough Urdu to give orders to the Gurkha orderlies – who speak mainly Gurkhalil'.

---

1. From 'Ballad of the Banffies', in the *Collected Poems*.

Driving to Foggia via Lucera on 25 November, he had a chance meeting with his old friend Martin Taubmann. Taubmann was carrying a painting he had looted from the house in which he had lodged the previous night. Hamish remonstrated with him, but to no avail. That evening Hamish organised a meeting with local people to discuss the problem of looting by Allied forces and noted what he describes as 'a good crack' by one of the Italians: 'we expected when the Germans were here that they would take things and not pay for them; but we didn't realise that when you came there would also be Germans who would take things and not pay for them.' A year later, when Hamish learned that Taubmann had been given a full British Army commission, he wrote him a letter full of ironic contempt:

> My heartfelt congratulations on your commission. But, of course, in your case the army could hardly help recognising *de jure* what had prevailed *de facto*. I imagine you have had time to deepen your friendship with the Foggia family of whom you were telling me. The picture you were lucky enough to acquire has stayed in my mind since I left the Army Cage: it's altogether one of the most stinking things I remember from these months in Italy . . . Have you read 'Darkness at Noon' by Arthur Koestler? – in my opinion one of the greatest achievements of Modern literature.

On 29 November, while introducing two Canadian officers to the basic principles of prisoner interrogation, Hamish elicited some important intelligence: 'I interrogate Ludwig at length about the Belgian coast – Ostendo section . . . Write up report on "Ludwig, the Atlantic Wall Boy".' Fortification of Europe's North Sea and Atlantic Coast was a crucial part of Hitler's plan to create an invincible 'Fortress Europe', and Hamish's information was sent straight back to the D-Day planners. On completing his report a Russian-speaking officer named Tennell asked Hamish if Peppino might drive him to Naples for a meeting. Hamish agreed if he could join them on the 'outing', and off they set. Within hours of arriving in Naples, Hamish had got himself introduced to 'several of the leading lights of "artistic society" on the Isle of Capri' and, after an evening's carousing, spent the night at the villa of Prince Parenti. Hamish was delighted to be invited to visit the island and the 'strange world of Norman Douglas' but he did not like Parenti and made a note not to visit him at his Capri villa.

Next day, back with the 4th Indian Division, Hamish suddenly realised that he had lost his Sicilian diary, 'which may have been distributed to the PW – nice irony!' It was never found. Hamish was deeply upset, lost his temper and blamed Fritz. Hamish in a temper was cold-bloodedly ferocious and extremely intimidating. He knew this, and a few days later apologised to Fritz and, together, they reconstructed the lost diary from memory and other notes.

On 2 December, after a period of heavy fighting, Hamish entered Vasto on the Adriatic coast with 5 Corps, and the following day 'identified and interrogated 169 PWs, including 4 officers'. This is probably the largest number of prisoners he dealt with in a single day and he celebrated with 'cognac at Tennell's villa'. When prisoners came in *en masse*, interrogations lasted a few minutes but important prisoners would be interrogated for hours. Hamish's average workload appears to have been in the region of ten prisoners a day. Thus, during his three and a half years of active service, he interrogated at least 10,000 German prisoners of war.

On 10 February 1944, Hamish reports: 'I have moved C Mess into a palace – the Marquis's palace to be exact – Palazzo Chaze. The sappers are impressed. On the snow-sodden streets of this town an icy wind circulates: I shall acquire, by any means, a greatcoat tomorrow. Write up report for I . . . Change boots and socks. Read 13 Corinthians.' (Hamish did acquire his greatcoat and it was to serve him well for ten years: it cloaked Marshall Graziani at the surrender of Italy in May 1945 and kept Hugh MacDiarmid warm on the back of Hamish's motorbike in 1947.) On 15 February he wrote to Warwick Marshall (editor of *8th Army News*)

Dear Warwick – I was glad to see Guest when he came up on his front-line tour, you should come up and see me sometime as well . . . An offensive patrol of ours recently killed seven Germans. The Indians are amazing. They endure the cold better than many whites and the civvy population (full of prejudice at first against the 'neir') almost always takes to them quickly. One old Iti referred to them as 'all very well educated'. He said, when they entered the village they made straight for the church, and the priest followed them in consternation – fearing they were about to loot his altar cloth. Instead, he found them praying. It turned out they were both Catholics, educated at a mission school in the Punjab . . . and the Iti's, with a poor-white grudge, gradually come to admit that the brown troops are not nearly such predatory vandals as the British . . . If you want any more stories, like the above, keep sending me copies of the *News*. Keep the present standard of the paper up. It's a great morale raiser. I mean it.

8th Army News had a political edge that few modern armies would tolerate, and Hamish records that as early as the spring of 1943 'post-war issues are sounded with radical enthusiasm'. For soldiers fed on 'censored guff from London', it was a breath of fresh air, and Hamish offered Marshall articles on the Yugoslav traitors (Mihailovic and Nedic), the Royal Court in Cairo (Faruk), Tito, the Italian leader Badoglio etc. When he heard that Eisenhower had written to complain about the seditious nature of certain articles in *8th Army News* and that Monty had replied by return 'I like the paper – and I'll have *no one* interfere with my army!' Hamish felt 'our champion was doing woti otta!'.

As time passed, Hamish found himself being drawn ever deeper into Italian life and he set himself the task of trying to encompass, poetically, the 'whole reality' of Italy's people, history and culture. He talked in the bars, went into the churches and devoured any book on Italy he could get hands on. One day Peppino brought him a stack of guidebooks, one containing vivid extracts by Byron, Shelley and Henry James – describing Italy – and their 'voices' soon start appearing in his notebooks. Ensconced in a battle-post above the hill-village of Frentano, he feels himself like Byron before Marathon: 'Frentano, which looks with uneasy familiarity at Orsogna, is still fightingly in enemy hands . . . At first, I hermit in a cold cavern on a hilltop – which serves reccying officers as an Observation Post of enemy lines: then we move into our most comfy and snug quarters yet, with a solace of braziers.' He then quotes Shelley – 'Buildings are less ephemeral than men, and unless there come a tyranny of dunces, and universal darkness buries all, men centuries hence will still be finding in the Italian scene creative happiness, inexhaustible inspiration . . .' Henry James' perceptions were in tune with his own: 'The Venetian's easy surrender to the senses is the sign of an unconscious philosophy of life – the philosophy of a people who have lived long and much, who have discovered no short cuts to happiness, and no effective circumvention of effort.' (These thoughts may have provided Hamish with inspiration for the memorable lines at the end of his 'Fourth Elegy': 'Endure, endure. There is as yet no solution / and no short cut, no escape and no remedy / but our human iron.') And Hamish appended to James' quotation a remarkable statement of his own: 'Out of this war, out of the suffering of Scotland across the ages, we can build our cairn – a civilisation as beautiful, as different, as Venice and Barra . . .' His words conjure a marvellous pan-European vision of civilisation – in which Venice and Barra become the twin poles of a continent's past and future greatness.

With winter stalemating the battlefront, Hamish suddenly got the offer of ten days' leave and he decided, after a discussion with Fritz and Peppino, that it was time they enjoyed the great city of Naples. Conscious that both they and 'Black Maria' might be arrested in what was very much 'the American Zone', Hamish organised himself a Special Jeep Pass before, in high spirits, they set off westward through the snow-covered mountains. At two o'clock on the afternoon of 20 February 1943, they came down out of the clouds to see the Bay of Naples spread out before them. Hamish asked Peppino to halt the Jeep; 'so that we could take in, for a moment, the view as far as the triangular mountain – a miracle – after the snow and mist of the Abruzzi, intensified in the central Apennines – we had come out into the plain in brilliant winter sunshine. The snow on Vesuvius glistening!'

In Naples Hamish bumped into John Coates, an old friend from Downing College who was serving with the Commandos: 'John has a flat here: arrange to put up with him for my leave, incredible luck . . . Naples is almost spoilt by the Cairene misery and economic hopelessness of the people – it's fine fertile soil for my red propaganda though . . .' John Coates, like Hamish, was a diarist and their separate accounts of this week in Naples make interesting parallel reading. Coates writes:

20th February 1944 – in comes Hamish Henderson of Downing, whom I didn't recognise at first. CSDIC at 8 Army. Original and entertaining remarks. Parked him at flat with Peppino (his batman-driver, picked up in Sicily, part of a team with Fritz, an Italian Austrian) down below. Over tea he told me about his successes as a political commissar, rounding up local Fascists etc . . .

On 23 February Hamish strolled in spring sunshine 'enjoying chocolate and dulce in several of the city's cafes' – before being driven by Peppino to Pompei:

The carriages of Pompeian patricians must have produced a fine hard-arsed race in no time. After Egypt (and particularly Luxor), Pompei has a vulgar and, curiously enough, a transitory effect on one and the climate is all against Pharonish permanence. The Pompeians also painted their dirty postcards on the wall which argues a very 'tired business man' civilisation. I prefer the glorious unflagging erection of Min, the unchallenged phallic champion of the ages. But the Villa of Menander, Villa de Misteri, and (for me) the houses of the fountains – large and small – right the balance a bit. Evening: glut myself in unprepossessing sin in Casenova. A Fascist!

Next day Coates records: 'HH and I wake late. More and more food seems to arrive – thanks to Peppino (who has scrounged more coffee from the Americans)'. By lunchtime, however, Hamish was alone and about to fulfil his long-held wish to visit the sacred, pagan island of Capri.

At Santa Lucia, where I ask for the civvy 'ferribo', I meet a Lewis-man and exchange a word with him in the Gaelic. (He's a sailor.) Hear again the intermezzo from Cavelleria Rusticana at a waterside cafe where I take a Vermouth. At 13.30 the ferribo leaves for Capri: fine weather with a minor swell only. The to be expected Yanks clutter the civvy boat as well as their own military launch . . . On Capri enquire after Parenti but hear that he left this morning for Naples. *Forse è meglio cosi.* The little man with the big Alsatian takes me for a stroll to see the Faingliani and the Piccola Marina. There was enough sun to rouse all the colour and make me (in a stroll of forty minutes) quite drunk with Capri . . .

Next day the wind rose and Hamish had difficulty getting back to Naples:

The wind's knout sends waves scudding in the harbour – I almost lose my balmoral, and do lose one destroyer pulling off back to Naples – but arrange, with the Elgin skipper of a fleet-tender (which has, as crew, personnel from Peterhead and Shetland), to cross at ten, which I do. A brisk sea: I maintain equilibrium by being in the dead centre of the boat and fixing my eyes on receding Capri. That island is maybe the one place in all my travels that I shall certainly come back to. Ciao, Capri!

Back in Naples, Hamish renewed contact with John Coates who, on 3 March, notes: 'Transit Mess. HH comes to tea. We discuss tomorrow's strike. HH told us what the fighting men thought; that he would not shoot on workers if it ever came to the point . . .' This strike is not mentioned in any of Hamish's writings and it raises interesting questions. Did the two men discuss this strike in a disinterested fashion, or was Hamish in some way involved? The likelihood is that, as usual, his interest extended beyond the academic: he now spoke excellent Italian and was deeply angry at what he saw as the criminal behaviour of the US administration in Italy. Since the Armistice of September 1943 Hamish had consistently given support to representatives of the Italian Socialist and Communist Parties, and a letter to Michael Clarke (written a week or two later from the Anzio Beachhead) makes his disgust at American political policy in Italy crystal clear. 'Naples is a depressing sight – hunger, misery, confusion, corruption, high prices, unemployment, liberation! . . . Nobody contemplating the Doodles in Naples can doubt that Italy, in the C20th, is suffering the scourge of another barbarian invasion . . .' Thus, even if Hamish had no direct contact with the Neapolitan strikers of March 1944 he was with them 'in spirit and in song' and it is likely that his long formal association with the Communist Party of Italy got off to a dramatic start with his support of the Neapolitan dockers, at this time.

On 9 March John Coates' diary records: 'HH to Anzio. Peppino stays with me . . .' Thus, as Hamish went forward to join a battle in which the Allies were to suffer well over 100,000 casualties he 'gave' his faithful servant and Jeep-driver to his old university friend. As an army deserter and a known anti-fascist, Peppino lived in a permanent no-man's land, and if he were to have been captured on the Beachhead he would almost certainly have been shot.

The Allied Landings at Anzio had begun on 22 January 1944. The Americans went ashore at Nettuno and the British at Anzio, once again almost unopposed. Rome was only a hard day's march from the invasion beaches but, to the chagrin of many of the invading troops, and Churchill's righteous anger, the American commander waited to accumulate massive forces before risking an advance. Thus, a golden moment that might have changed the whole course of the war in Italy was lost: a campaign that might have been over in days, and which would have made the terrible battles for Monte Cassino unnecessary, was now to last six months.[2] As things turned out, several heavily armoured German divisions quickly surrounded the Beachhead, and the Allies found themselves locked in what would become static warfare with a battle-hardened and ruthless enemy. For five months, every inch of the Beachhead was within range of German artillery; and German fighter-bombers were able to mount frequent attacks from local airfields. Consequently a form of trench warfare, very similar to that which had killed so many on the Western Front in the First World War, became an enduring reality. Hamish was to spend four months in this killing zone. As usual his prime responsibility was as a German interrogator but he was also involved in battle-planning and propaganda. Anzio itself was a pleasing spot; it had been one of the major seaports of Ancient Rome and birthplace to two of the most notorious emperors, Caligula and Nero. With its gravelly beaches, pine-clad hills, criss-cross of roads, railway lines and large industrial buildings, Anzio was also a perfect battle zone.

Hamish's Beachhead diary begins in Naples as he queued for the ferry to Anzio. Perched in his Jeep, he writes:

---

2. When Hamish finally got to Rome in June, anti-fascist partisans informed him that, at the time of the Anzio Landings, 'Rome was only guarded by a syphilitic battalion licking its wounds and the city – there to be taken – like a late-night whore!'

It reminds me so exactly of the last days before the Sicilian invasion that it seems almost like a time lag. My new driver-batman [Grey] was at Francoforte in Sicily with the 5th Camerons and is one of the surviving three from a platoon at Wadi Akarit. Only twenty-two. But he's the right lad for an assignment the like of this, which seems on the way to be brief and bloody . . . After seeing the bloody porkery the Yanks and the British have allowed Naples to get into, I don't go to the Anzio Beachhead with the good heart with which I came to Naples. But I go with resolution all the same because the defeat of reaction in Europe is still in the preliminary – but maybe the hardest – phase: the smashing of the military power of Germany. I have spoken and argued so often that the annihilation of the German military machine is the only real and realistic war aim that I am not afraid to go into the frizzling cauldron of Anzio (and wherever else) in order to do my utmost to accomplish it . . . Fritz and Peppino, faithful servants of a wayward master, I'm leaving behind in Naples. Both are Italians and it's not fair to expose them to the obvious dangers of Nazi blood-lust – if they were captured. But I shall return to Naples and pick them up – Fritz is wonderful. He has forgiven me so much folly and has stuck by me with such unprovoked devotion. He's the nearest thing to a family I've picked up yet.

10th March: At 06.30 hrs, after a wash and shave, put on my top coat and look through field glasses at Anzio and Nettuno, and the wood between them. A smoke-screen is laid as the first ships enter the harbour, but it has cleared away by the time we pull in to unload. All pretty peaceful and reminiscent of Sicily, except for one solitary shell which makes a dusty puff of smoke over Nettuno. A whistling Pete (170 mm) locates HQ 6 Corps, and am introduced to a wheen o' Yank colonels who say things are brighter than they have been since the first days of the landing.

12th March: It's pissing with rain in endless sewers – but finally go off to HQ 6 Corps and talk over Order of Battle with boys there. Find 5 Div. well dug-in in sylvan surroundings recently evacuated by 56th Div. Finally, a glint of sun through the wet branches, and round the bend of the glade the sea! Talk over with M. [Michael Clutterbuck] and Jepson the deep corruption of CSDIC which will one day be exposed – if any justice in the world is done.

Following these discussions about CSDIC, Hamish requested a meeting with Colonel MacMillan (whom he had dissuaded from executing the German paratroops caught in civvies on Sicily) to inform him about the abuse of prisoners and general corruption within the Intelligence Corps. Only a torn fragment of the notes Hamish made before meeting MacMillan exists, but it is clear that he wanted MacMillan to know that unnecessary brutalities were being used during Beachhead interrogations. However, his opening remarks were very comradely: 'The atmosphere here is exhilarating and takes me back twenty months to my first days in the desert with the South African Division – the same Alamein feeling of competence and backs to the wall, the same Stuka raids before breakfast. Even the sand blowing round the tent of a CCS gives the desert illusion . . . The darker side is here too – I interrogated inside the CCS this morning, and I can assure you it was not pretty . . .' This was the third and last occasion on which Hamish raised the question of CSDIC corruption; perhaps the situation improved, but it is more likely that he was informed that, if he continued to complain, he would be removed from the battlefield. This he did not want. He knew it was far more important that he continue his frontline battle against Nazi tyranny than luxuriate in 'self-righteousness'; also, what more could he do than make his views and information known to senior officers?

Besieged on the Beachhead, the morale of many of the troops was far from good and Hamish instinctively acted to improve it. He encouraged 'night-time sing-songs' and quickly put together a Beachhead poem, 'Anzio', which proved quite a hit when published in the *Beachhead News*.

> When the MGs stop their clatter
> And the cannons stop their roar
> And you're back in dear old Blighty
> In your favourite pub once more
> When the small talk is over
> And the war-tales start to flow
> You can stop the lot, the lot, by telling
> Of the fight at Anzio.
>
> Let them bum about the desert
> Let 'em brag about Dunkirk
> Let them drag about the Jungles
> Where the Japanese did lurk.
> Let them talk about their campaign
> And their medals till they're red:
> You put the lot to silence
> When you mention the Beachhead.[3]
>
> . . .

---

3. This poem was not republished after its appearance in *Beachhead News*.

'Anzio' is a very British army ballad that echoes songs dating back to the War of the Spanish Succession, and in it Hamish speaks for the ordinary English soldier. Having given his salute to English troops at Anzio, however, Hamish now turned with real enthusiasm to salute the Beachhead Jocks in his 'Ballad of the Banffies'. The Gordons are its heroes and this is a poem that needs to be *sung*; its tune is 'The Gallant Forty Twa'.

> Ye can talk aboot your Moray loons,
>   Sae handsome and sae braw;
> The Royal Scottish Fusiliers,
>   A scruffy lot and a'
> The Cameronians frae the South,
>   They sure are mighty fine,
> But in the Battle of Anzio
>   'Twas the Banffies held the line.
>
> The crofters' sons o' Banffshire,
>   The cooper frae the glen,
> The weaver frae Strathisla,
>   Aye, and shepherd frae the ben;
> The fisher lads alang the coast,
>   They a' made up their min'
> Tae fecht and save their country
>   In Nineteen Thirty Nine.
>
>   . . .
>
> Ye can talk aboot your Scots Guards
>   Sae handsome and sae strong,
> But unlike oor wee Banffies
>   They canna haud on for long.
> In years to come, when Italy
>   Is free, an' the Balkans too
> Your bairns will read in history
>   How the Banffies pulled us through . . .
>
> *Where'er ye be, by land or sea*
>   *Or hirplin' in the road*
> *If ye can meet a Banff, ye'll find*
>   *He sure can bum his load.*[4]

---

4. 'Ballad of the Banffies', in the *Collected Poems*.

Hamish's presence appears to have delivered a genuine fillip to the men of the various Scots battalions at Anzio. On 15 March he visited the 6th Brigade Gordon Highlanders and exchanged reminiscences with Drummond Smith. This visit inspired him to create what was to become known as the Beachhead Pipe Band. It toured the Anzio battlefield, visited the Beachhead hospitals and would become famous when it played a leading role in the celebrations following the liberation of Rome in June 1944. At the outset, Hamish struggled to gain the support of senior officers: Richmond, of the 2nd Camerons, for example, told him all his pipers were being used for portering. But Riach of Seaforth and McConnachie of the RSF offered full cooperation. Returning to the Gordons, Hamish notes with pleasure, 'Cpl Smith plays for me "Leaving Glen Urquhart" and "Farewell to the Creeks": have not heard either since HD left . . . Howell Rees gives me the latest guff – not very encouraging about Cassino. Stalemate looks like descending on the Beachhead – in fact on Italy. Roll on the 2nd Front.'

Hamish's first Pipe Band rehearsal took place on the morning of 21 March and consisted of 'just three Cameronian pipers having a blaw' but, later, having enlisted the support of Brigadier Lorne MacLaine Campbell VC he proudly writes, 'the combined pipe bands of the four Scottish Brigades – brought together by myself – do their first practice . . . It's a great sound, and a fine setting. Afterwards have tea with Howell who says it's a great morale-raiser.' That evening Hamish felt inspired to let Michael Clarke, now in Jerusalem, know what was going on.

You'll be asking what this bloody Beachhead is like. Well it's not as fucking awful as you might think. If the Boche could shell us to shivers and bomb us to buggery he'd certainly do it – luckily he can't. Nobody kids himself he isn't in a tough spot here, but it has its compensations – there are enough Scots here now to make the thing tolerable. This afternoon I organised the first performance of the massed pipes of our Scottish bands, which were playing a retreat just up from the beach. It was a brilliant sunny afternoon; while they played, some Jocks were bathing in the Tyrrhenian Sea, and others were putting a mortar through its paces by firing it into the sea over their heads. One or two Yanks went by, gazing at this scene incredulously – over the woods brisk AA indicated the resumption of enemy air activity . . . The first essential in the fight against Fascism is still the complete smashing of German military power, and the annihilation of the Prussian military machine as a cadre for future armies. This is for me the sole reality at the moment, and the idea of accomplishing it has kept me going from Egypt to this.

Neither my love for Germany – nor the sight of Naples as it is in a state of liberation – can deflect me from this purpose. If I failed to go forward into any theatre of action or combat zone (pardon the Yankism – I'm with 2 US Corps now) where any Jocks are fighting, I would be untrue to Scotland and myself, and be no better than a fucking English bourgeois communist . . .

Shortly after this, Hamish received a letter from Nicholas Moore, who had recently launched a magazine called *New Poetry* and wanted contributions. By return, Hamish sent off his 'Ballad of the Simeto'. Moore was impressed and immediately published it in *New Poetry* No. II. However, nine months were to pass before Hamish received his complimentary copy and, when he did, he was encamped in the Apennines north of Florence. He writes that he was never to forget the thrill he got 'up there in the mountains, when that bundle of magazines was delivered. I opened one, and found my work along side that of Conrad Aiken and Wallace Stevens and other poets whom I had long admired from afar. Even a paid up member of the oral tradition responds to seeing his work in print on occasions like that!' Not all contact with the homefront, however, was so productive: a self-satisfied anglo-centric letter from his old *bête noir*, Jamie Cable, roused real anger:

when I read in your airgraph about the Gael being a more efficient ally 'than many who have attached themselves to our tail' I think of many countrymen of mine strewing the route from Alamein to Anzio and feel like telling you what I think in this letter. Scotland, a small country, has done a lot in this campaign, but she doesn't do it for the *beaux yeux* of James Cable and his complement from the UK. We're hacking sense out of a war that had little sense in it, but no thanks to Amgot or the State Department. At Alamein we thought of Stalingrad – at Anzio we think of the Soviets killed in the battles for Rumania – and we look forward to the Second Front for Russia's sake, not our own . . . Pardon my frankness – it's Beachhead lingo and I can't help it.

On 7 April Hamish had a nasty reaction to two anti-typhoid injections. Confined to his dug-out for two days, he read George Blake's *The Path of Glory*, describing it as 'a sickly, shoddily written book about a Scots battalion at Gallipoli in the last war . . . However, the passages about Gallipoli itself are quite well done, and make depressing Beachhead reading.' As with all his bouts of sickness Hamish also found himself writing serious poetry and, before returning to duty, he completed what is his major Beachhead poem, 'Anzio April'. Here are three of seven verses:

> Headlines at home. The gangrel season varies,
> And Spring has gained a beach-head with our blood.
> I've half a mind to kiss the blooming Jerries
> And then just beat it while the going's good.
> I'll bed down where deserters live on berries . . .
> I'll play at possum in yon cork-oak wood . . .
> > Machine-guns prate, but dannert flowers, this Spring.
> > *Over the grave all creatures dance and sing.*
>
> > . . .
>
> The watching Jerries sight a convoy's funnels;
> It's coming into range now, Anzio-bound.
> Their railway gun emerges from a tunnel's
> Commodious depth, and plonks a single round
> A hundred yards beyond one mucker's gunwales.
> I bet they'd feel much safer under ground!
> > This fight one's better off inside the ring.
> > *Over the grave all creatures dance and sing.*
>
> > . . .
>
> Red Neil, whom last I saw at lifting tatties
> Pulls-through his rifle, whistles Tulach Gorm.
> . . . Two drops of rain. We know whose warning *that* is.
> A plum-hued cloud presents in proper form
> (The old court-holy-water diplomat) his
> Most courteous declaration of the storm.
> > The dance is on. Strike up a Highland fling!
> > *Over the grave all creatures dance and sing*
> > *(And numbskull death his little tabor beats).*[5]

On 8 April Hamish marched the pipe band to the American hospital, 'to raise our brothers' morale with a bit of piping. The Yank Col is persuaded by me to take the salute which he does very nervously . . . But does he wait for it! No, sir. He just can't wait for the pipe major to come up. So, he salutes and gives them permission to play the regimental marches all on his own! The show goes off very well with no end of applause from the patients: all, according to their padre, that can walk or crawl, getting out of their beds to see what's up . . .'

---

5. From 'Anzio April', published in the *Collected Poems*.

That evening, Hamish interrogated an 18-year-old Viennese deserter at 18 Brigade Headquarters during a major artillery bombardment which, he states, encouraged the terrified youngster 'to deliver up plenty, plenty locations for the guns to get cracking on, and anti-tank gen as well. Next morning, with the benefit of air photos we get going . . .' Desertion on the Beachhead, however, was not just a German problem: as 'Anzio April' suggests, a number of British troops took to the woods and Hamish was involved in preparing a series of 'wanted' posters aimed at luring them back into the ranks.

On 2 May, Hamish joined in work aimed at further securing his sleeping quarters against increasingly regular artillery bombardments:

a lot of today taken up with myself stripped to the waist and calling a spade a bloody shovel. My shelter, a dark horse among the others, now looks very much as if it's going to turn out the best of the lot. Cpl Stuart in the afternoon collects a few stakes for me and together we get cracking on sinking-in the timber. Four sleepers reinforced with sand bags under corrugated iron is about as effective protection as you could wish for . . . [That night] AP bombs fall on either side of the house – on the side of the bed one lacerates a tree and shrapnels the walls; on the side of the table another severs one of the guy ropes and causes the sandbag to slump to the ground. This is one of the narrowest squeaks ever. Finish my shelter today. It would stand (I think/hope) a direct hit from an 88. No one can assert that, having done it, I haven't done it properly. Another Gordon (MacLachlan, but not the Gaelic speaker) is buried in the fast growing cemetery – to the 'Flowers of the Forest'.

By 1 June, the Allies, at last, were in a position to make a major break-out and, while interrogating a German paratrooper named Peters, Hamish got information which he immediately circulated to Headquarters: 'Peters was for a while doing guard duties for General Lelzer, GOC Rome Area and knows details of the defence line before Rome – which hinges on the road junction Rome-Ostia and Rome-Piccola Marina and consists of concrete strong-points along the outer circumference of the city'. Next morning he notes: 'Main Div. moves 14 miles away to Torre, up the railway bed which is a real pox horror. The musty grey dust, a blanket-covered corpse, two ghastly horses, stinking to high heaven, and the moth-eaten junk of battle litter the way . . .'

But the breakthrough had been made, and Hitler himself ordered the evacuation of Rome. On 4 June Hamish rose late, having spent the whole night grilling prisoners, to hear 'from G31 that recce troops of the Yanks entered Rome at 10.30 hrs this morning. Announce this fact to PW in Cage amid scenes of jubilation . . . the Italian campaign gets going at last! Over to Main Div. to discuss plans for the future. I intend to get into Rome with the pipe band – but don't say so. Peter [Clutterbuck] fears it won't be possible. I play the trump card . . .' What this trump card was is unclear but Hamish had written a new pipe tune, 'The Roads that Lead to Rome', and a song to go with it, 'The Beachhead Band's March on Rome', both created to commemorate Scotland's part in the Liberation of the most famous city in world history.

Hamish informed the Scottish brigade commanders that the entry into Rome must not be a purely American triumph. He insisted that the British and Scottish contributions be recognised; he argued that the Beachhead Pipe Band should play a major role in the celebrations and that it could put an indelibly Scottish signature on the Liberation – like nothing else. Thus, early on the morning of 5 June, Hamish secured a bus (for the band) and, in his Jeep, rushed from the Royal Scottish Fusiliers to the Seaforths, to the Scottish Horse where 'from Dingwall, I finally, got permission to enter the Eternal City – with pipes and drums . . . Then into Rome via the Albano Road: a great crush of Yanks on the home stretch. The Romans give us a welcome that eclipses Tunis, flowers, shouts and welcome to "Scozzezi" – we seem to many to be the first British troops in Rome. Evening in Piazza Venezia and down Corso Umberto.'

Hamish found the band a *pensione* but at six next morning he was off in his Jeep to 'collect rations for the men'. The band then assembled in the Piazza Venezia and at 11.00 sharp began the first of dozens of open-air 'concerts' delivered all over Rome during the following ten days. Suddenly, Hamish got news that caused him to silence the band and make a public announcement: 'During the night Allied Forces landed in Normandy. Rome is free, *and* the Second Front is open!' Pipe Major MacConnochie then led the band off towards the Coliseum where Hamish notes:

we secure what must be one of the historic photos of the war: the band playing down Mussolini's Via dell'Impero with the most grandiose monument to Imperial Rome behind it. Rome is certainly a wonderful city, *und wie!* Return to lunch in the Pensione Nationale, and I do a publicity tour of the city's newspapers to boost the band . . . Performance at 1800 hrs. Fritz and Grey try to keep off the crowd, almost an impossibility. To the Piazza Colonna. "*Viva la Scozia!*" Bed down in the Pensione Nationale.

The Highlanders had made themselves one of the enduring images of the Liberation.

> 7th June: PLAY IN FRONT OF ST PETER'S: We proceed down the corso Via dell' Impero to St Peter's and the band has the greatest success of its career to date in the Piazza – filmed by Movietone, playing 'Anzio' and 'The Roads that Lead to Rome'. Meet Michael Clutterbuck and Sgt Soira in an ecstasy over it all. The Pope alleged to be watching the scene from a window. An Irish priest greets us, and another asks us, during the playing of 'Anzio', 'is this a Catholic song?' Am introduced to the British Minister in Rome, who . . . has been cooped up in the Vatican these last three years. Afternoon, we play once more from the Coliseum to the Piazzo Venezia, then down the Corso Umberto, filmed all the way . . . 'Alamein' and 'The Creeks'. Evening – great throng turns out to hear us. I incur the wrath of Brigadier Matthews (of 59 Area) who wants to know what pipers are doing in Rome! Great evening. Content: with songs from signorinas.

> 8th June: 'Twice today we play Foro di Traiano, which makes the best piping site we have had yet. A setting like Balclutha, full of desolate dignity which the disciplined Picts match . . . Spend part of the afternoon looking for new digs for the band – give the OK to the Pensione Eletta in the Piazza de Gesu . . . The Drummie [Drum Major] of the Seaforth is on parade tonight with the band. Acting on information supplied by him, I go off to see Gen. Gregson Ellis at HQ 5 Div. – and arrange a super massed pipe band parade . . . boy, it's a great spectacle – and, at 18.00 hrs on the 11th June, with 48 pipers and a good score of drummers we give the Via dell'Impero, on the fourth anniversary of Mussolini's declaration of war against us – something to remember. Gregson Ellis takes the salute half-way along, while frantic MPs and myself try to keep the crowds back. Have dinner with the Silva family tonight and, in addition – have my jeep stolen!

This massed band comprised five Scottish units (Camerons, Royal Scottish Fusiliers, Scots, Gordons, Scottish Horse) and one Irish (the Enniskillens). Hamish now arranged that BBC Radio and Radio Rome would make a programme about the band and its role in the Liberation. Godfrey Talbot fronted for the BBC, and Liana Silva spoke for Radio Rome. Hamish devised the script, acted as translator and kept a note of the commentary. The programme began with a quotation from Liana: '*I cuori degli spettatori vinti, vibrano di viva commozione'* – 'The hearts of the spectators have been won and are vibrating with living emotion.' Godfrey Talbot first introduced piper Frank Stewart of Dufftown, and then Hamish himself: Hamish began by speaking in Gaelic, giving a consciously Celtic slant to this great Roman occasion, then continued: 'I'm very glad to be in Rome, though at one time I never thought we'd be in it at all. It's a wonderful city – it makes the island of Lewis seem very far away. But I don't think I could ever stay in Rome – when I saw the beauty of it – the exile's poem came into my mind. "But still the blood is strong, the heart is Highland / And we in dreams behold the Hebrides." '

Hamish then asked Liana Silva how she liked the Scots. Hamish's friend Amleto Micozzi translates her statement as: 'The Romans receive with enthusiasm the music of these soldiers arrived from far-off Scotland – men strong and severe like their rocks – who know with admirable art how to speak to the artistic and warlike spirit of Rome – melting the two peoples together in the same ideal.'

It was a beautiful and historic broadcast, and via Movietone News the image and sound of the Pipe Band – conceived in blood on the Anzio Beachhead – went round the world. It was a *coup de théâtre*, and Hamish orchestrated the moment as an artistic event, exulting not in war, or in victory, but in the possibilities of peace and new cultural beginnings. At home in Scotland, as the Highlanders marched on flickering cinema screens across the nation, Rome's joy also became theirs, because Hamish's fantastic *tableau vivant* also did something else, something more tribal: his first duty was to transform Italy's fascist shame into human joy, but his second was to assert and rekindle Scotland's historic destiny. With these parades of Scotland's music through the streets of Rome, Hamish's pipe band was paying homage to the nameless tens of thousands of Celtic tribesmen and women who had been brought and bought into slavery in Rome, over many centuries. The conjunction of heroic virtue and self-sacrifice, of art and felt-destiny, are a very Celtic and very dangerous combination, but Hamish believed such realities better addressed than denied or repressed. And, on the Beachhead, he had written a poem that touches this timeless human reality, head-on: 'Song for an Irish Red Killed in Sicily'.

> Comrades onward
> The raging sunward
> The fleeing moonward.
> Our rifles thunder
> The stars asunder
> *Till the axe falls.*

Down we'll tumble
The wormwood lumber
The clutterclumber
    Their straw and wicker
    'll frisk and flicker
        Till the axe falls.
For us no moaning
No wakes and keening
No whines and screaming.
    We'll mind the heroes
    That fell before us
        Till the axe falls.[6]

After ten days the pipe band stood down and the men had a few days' leave before returning to their units. Meanwhile Hamish found himself being drawn into the cultural life of Rome as a much admired, larger-than-life hero. Liana Silva was first his guide but soon became his muse, and conspiratorial confidante. She was young and beautiful, an artist, a broadcaster and a radical political activist, only too delighted to introduce Hamish to a Roman intelligentsia brimming with the hope of a new age. On 20 June Hamish notes:

> For a while I've promised Liana to pay a visit to her artist friends of the Via Margutta, and today (with Sgt Haymann) I keep the promise. The first artist we visit is Angelo Savelli, an unassuming little man who shows me his latest paintings. A Christ. The Son of man in very human torment, an agony grotesque and not heroic (like all human suffering outside that of fanatics and ecstatics: Christ seems to me to be neither). Also two studies of obsession (one male, one female) . . . Savelli offers me a sketch, I choose the fantasy on war and destruction . . . Next – to Pericles Fazzini, sculptor, who shows me his portrait of Ungaretti (the poet, whose work was later presented to me by Liana and Elvira) . . . Then on to see Montanarini, the most flamboyant and Oscarish of these artists – also, I should judge the least important. . . . Then with Liana and Savelli we climb from Via Margutta to the bounds of the Villa Borghese through the high steps of Trenita dei Monte.

After that, Hamish, Liana, Savelli, Sgt Haymann and others spent the evening in the See of Trionfale – dining in the street, reading poetry,

---

6. 'Song for an Irish Red Killed in Sicily', in the *Collected Poems*.

singing and talking of 'a new risorgimento rising from the ashes of Fascism'. Liana made several sketches of Hamish, including a line portrait in pencil, which shows him as a beautiful, sleepy, poetical, wickedly smiling satyr, with skin like alabaster. She was in love, and for days they strolled and talked in the streets of the Rome that Fellini would soon document in his film *Open City*. They were wonderfully happy and Liana's friend, Angelo Savelli, seems to have immediately recognised that Hamish had brought something unfathomable into the life of Rome: poetry and hope.

Savelli had been born in Pizzo, Calabria, in 1911: after training as a painter he settled in Rome and, when he met Hamish, had a considerable reputation as 'a realist interested in religious and allegorical subjects'. In the late forties he moved to Venice where, in 1964, he won the prize for Graphic Art at the Venice Biennnale. Although Savelli's wartime friendship with Hamish was brief, it was renewed in 1949 and 1950, and the sketch shown on the endpapers of this book was treasured by Hamish for the rest of his life; it is discussed in Appendix 2.

The day of 20 June 1944 was important for a second reason because it was on that day that Hamish decided to replace his stolen Jeep, and the next night, in Cavour Square, he announces: 'we have luck. A jeep without arm and key – but – we push it for several streets, and then leave it in a garage of Firemen. Then back to AFPU to borrow a jeep to tow it home – but – no luck. We pinch the rotor arm from another jeep and go back, with plenty of rations for the firemen, to the garage. Put in the rotor arm; with a bit of a struggle it starts, and we drive home. Erase the number on it – work all night (getting up the signorina) – go to bed at dawn with another jeep in my possession. *Gott mit me!*'

The following afternoon, Hamish persuaded a British Military Policeman called Clark from 1st Division to paint a new number on the new Jeep (the same as that on Black Maria) and, for good measure, he added a sign saying '50 mph'. On his last night in Rome he had supper with Liana – 'next morning spent choosing one of Liana's sketches, which she gives me with a dedication'. Then, in a convoy with Grey's truck leading, he drove down Route 7 towards Naples. Peppino put his foot on the accelerator, and Hamish experienced another moment of sheer euphoria.

After the strain of the Beachhead, Rome and Liana had re-energised him but in the temple of delight he also shied from Rome's dominion. He knew that this was a place with values very different from his own. In old age, when he introduced his *Collected Poems* with the lines 'Ladys / this is the legend of my life, though Latyne it be nane', he meant it. And, leaving Rome on Midsummer Day 1944, his eternal wariness of 'power' is made clear in this extract from a letter to John Speirs:

This city is fascinating. In many ways it reminds me of Karnak; there's the same impression of pre-occupation with death, with being weighed down with a profound death-longing. The peculiar mixture of sexuality and death in a 'holy city' – Thebes or Rome – is at once attractive and terribly repellent. No spirit could be more opposed to that of the passionate logical, restless Greeks (and Gaels) than the spirit of Catholic Rome.

NINE

The Partisan Commander

Look around the mountains, in the mud and rain –
You'll find the scattered crosses – (there's some which have no
> *name).*
> > *Heartbreak and toil and suffering gone,*
> > *The boys beneath them slumber on.*
> *Those are the D-Day Dodgers who'll stay in Italy.*

HH[1]

After four days' debriefing at CSDIC in Naples, Hamish was given a week's leave. He had not had a day off duty for five months and, on 27 June 1944, set sail – back to Capri – in high spirits.

> Peppino lands me at Santa Lucia just in time to take off for the island: once again hum to myself 'The Siege of Delhi' as we cross the stretch to my island . . . I went down to Ende Guarini's villa and announced my presence. Later that evening I was looking out through the window at a scene almost Japanese in its simplicity: the silhouette of a pine, the serene azure of the bay of Naples, one white sail against the water and, as a background, wicked old Vesuvius (or is it Fujiyama?) looking as if it had never heard of lava . . . Feel in the mood to write poetry but doubt I'll have the time to do so . . . The vulgarity and extravagance of the Yanks on Capri makes me turn with more decision than ever to the austerity and discipline of Russia. Ironic this, that Capri, the proverbial paradise of the escapers should, by reducing escape to absurdity and nausea, keep me from suffering the influence of Scirocco or Nepentle . . . Reunion in the Settanni with Paulo D' Elia, Castello, Calabria and the rest. Drink.

---

1. The last verse of HH's ballad 'The D-Day Dodgers'.

Next morning, Hamish had a leisurely bath in the Villa Eudysandra: 'the first genuine warm bath (in a bath) that I've had since we left our first location in Anzio at the beginning of March. It's warm, drowsy, delightful. Afternoon, take a walk through Certosa, and then down to the Officers' Boating Club. Borrow bathing trunks and have a great bathe: the heat outside makes the water like a Turkish bath.' By the following day Hamish was an integrated member of the island's literary 'intelligentsia' and thereafter he enjoyed Capri like a native.

On 2 July Hamish climbed to the heights of the Faso where he introduced himself to one of Capri's most famous residents, Carmelina: 'now a wizened old crone of 68 but once carrier-off of all the Tarentella dancing prizes. She describes to me the Capri of 40 years ago, shows her souvenirs and parades her knowledge of most European tongues'. She was 'a mine of Capri folklore', and when he returned next day she was at the door to greet him, 'dressed in the traditional costume – and was soon singing songs from the Capri past. *Quando tu nascesti, fiore di bellezza.* She is in many ways just like an old Highland woman – very like Catherine M Grant.'

Next morning he was invited into 'Munthe's private home – never yet visited by an American – one bit of Capri soil unsullied! So much of interest gathered here that the effect is almost stultifying: an unmatched Egyptian bust – the perfectly calm serenity which maintains millennial repose twice as naturally as the Greeks . . .' Later, signor Mosquitti took him by boat to see the White Grotto and the Grotto Meravigliosa: 'Here we see the little white Madonna left piously by German sailors in the rock under the Arco Naturale, and the grotto itself – which has been stripped of its stalagmites by Yank souvenir hunters. What an excess of vandalism. Resolve to leave by the 4.00 ferry for Sorrento – to get hold of a piper!' American excess had finally snapped Hamish's holiday restraint. From Sorrento, he hitch-hiked to Pompeii and then on to Battipaglia where the Scottish Horse were encamped. There Hamish laid out his 'master plan' before senior officers. He requested that he be allowed to take a piper back to Capri.

Thus, on the afternoon of 8 July 1944, Lt Henderson crossed to Capri in battle-dress and balmoral, before marching – behind Ramsay playing the pipes in full Highland Dress – up to the gates of the US garrison. There, Hamish requested a meeting with the commanding officer, while Ramsay marched and counter-marched before a gathering crowd. When the US major appeared, Hamish informed him that, as a Scottish officer in the Eighth Army, he was requesting, on behalf of the Scottish nation, and in the name of civilisation, that the despoliation of Capri by US trophy hunters should cease forthwith. He pointedly drew the major's attention to the damage being done to the Grotto Meravigliosa by the removal of hundreds of stalactites and stalagmites. He stated that he believed the war they were fighting – they were both fighting – was for the maintenance of civilised values and the preservation of artistic and natural treasures; it was a duty they should uphold – even in the face of the enemy – even on the isle Capri! He spoke in English, then turning to the Caprese translated what he had said into Italian for the crowd. They cheered. The major then invited both Hamish and Ramsay inside the garrison, where, with bad grace, he agreed to take note of the complaint. Outside, Hamish again addressed the crowd before marching with Ramsay – and a tail of excited children – down to D'Elia's villa, where they were invited onto the terrace, and a day of celebration opened around them.

On 11 July, Hamish, Peppino and Fritz headed north in the Jeep 'making an average of 60 mph along the Via Appia. We wander off the road and buy vino in one little village that had probably seen no Allied troops . . . Get on road to Frascati (by Castel Gandolfo, summer residence of the Pope) and stop to look at Lago di Albano in its saucer with Rocca di Papa over it. Arrive Cinecitta.' Hamish was clearly excited. This was the country of J.G. Fraser's *Golden Bough*, and a new chapter in his life was opening. He had been assigned new responsibilities as a liaison officer and would in future work increasingly closely with the partisan battalions now springing up all over central Italy: he was about to become a 'semi-independent guerrilla fighter and partisan commander'. And as his Jeep roared up the Appian Way – that most famous of ancient roads – he must have thought of James Leslie Mitchell's brilliant novel *Spartacus* (he had read it as a schoolboy at Dulwich) and known that he, Fritz and Peppino were travelling in the very footsteps of Spartacus' great Slave Army. It had survived ten years in the field against the might of the Roman Empire. As a historian and as a poet, Hamish knew that for men like them, and him, there was no turning back.

Despite the Armistice of September 1943, the military/political situation in Italy throughout 1944 remained extremely confused. Mussolini's renewed alliance with Hitler had precipitated a civil war that saw large numbers of Italian irregulars fighting alongside the regular troops of the German and Allied armies. This resulted in brutalities and atrocities that scar Italy to this day. Many anti-fascists became socialist and communist *partigiani* fighting to create a 'new society'. Hamish became an 'informal liaison officer' with the partisan battalions in Liguria and Tuscany, and he tried hard to integrate them into the Allied military machine. It was no easy task. The majority of Allied commanders preferred to delegate authority to the mafiosa rather than to the politically suspect partisans. But Hamish delighted in his new responsibilities and remained particularly proud of his relationship with Aligi Barducci, the commander of the four brigades of the Partisan Division of the Arno: Sinaglia, Lanciotto, Caiani and Fanciullacci.

Barducci's battle-name was Potente, and Hamish recognised him as a modern hero whose character and vision helped set in train one of the most extraordinary and memorable years of Hamish's life.

On 30 July 1944 Hamish worked with Potente on the construction of a declaration published in the clandestine newspaper *l'Azione Communist*. He then sent it, with the following message, to Eighth Army HQ: 'The Committee of the National Liberation for Tuscany – with all its political, administrative and military services – remains at the complete disposal of the Allied Command and desires to establish a liaison with a view to effective collaboration . . .'[2]

Meanwhile, Hamish's work as a German interrogator continued. On 16 July he notes: 'Interrogate a Free Austrian this morning: free in spirit if never in fact, for he has, up till now (how usual) been a keen and efficient soldier for the German Reich (instructor at Malpasso). He gives me a wonderful phrase for the Elegies – '*Kadavergehorsam*' – that word hits off perfectly why thousands of young Germans continue to die for a lost cause.' Next day Hamish bumped into piper Robertson of the Gordons, who told him that he had just read a report about 'our Gaelic broadcast from the Beach-head and that news of the pipe band's appearance in Rome had attracted great interest at home'. On the 17th, Hamish was back in Rome and notes that he had spoken at length to 'Elvi and Liana about Italy and the need for a new Risorgimento – and to my Calalinan brigades of the fatal day. Liana attracts me terrifically. I think I'll tackle Liana . . .'

Hamish was now consciously striving to stimulate and orchestrate a post-war renaissance in Italy. The reference to 'my Calalinan Brigades' is presumably a reference to the communist partisans in Rome with whom he had made contact in June. Next day he continues:

> A Communist friend shows me, in the Pantheon, the tomb of Umberto Primo (Pater Patriae): it has a dignity. The interior of the Pantheon; the flawless dome – with a bird across its open

---

2. The declaration states: 'Marshall Kesselring [German commander in Italy]. Having robbed us of our wealth, of our industries, after deporting and killing thousands of our brothers; having deprived us of water, gas, electricity, transport, auto-ambulances, and every other public service; having destroyed our factories, our mills, our public buildings; having condemned us thus to the torments of an existence lower than the brute beasts, you now have the utter shamelessness to assert that you and your Nazis have conducted yourselves correctly towards us, and to accuse Alexander and the British soldiers who have done everything possible to respect our city [Florence] – of being the cause of our misfortunes!'

apex . . . Discuss the differences between the Latin and Greek mentalities. The Greek the colder, the more logical (a stick descending to a point and writing in sand) and the Latin warmer, completer (the stone in water that raises circular ripples): also the Latin more tranquil, the Greek passionate and, like the Celtic, more fanatical ('my fantastic heart', 'ingenium perfervidium Scotorum'). Also the Greek landscape – the hard bright dry hills, and the Greek type, the fisherman 'muscular, sinewy' – the Latin, a contadino even in hill country, tough but less wiry. Evening: to see "Blyth Spirit" by Noel Coward. Emlyn Williams good but always bletherin in Welsh parts: pleasant to see a play well acted again.

On 20 July Hamish made a reconnaissance of the Viareggio and Torre del Lago areas in the company of a Pole called Buschke. Reporting back to CSDIC, he was cheered to hear 'Hartze bring first news of the attempt to do the Fuehrer in. Good work. Here's to the next one! Now it may start.' Next day he adds, 'Info coming from Germany about the recent events suggests that a military coup was attempted, and might well have succeeded. But I think in the long run it's just as well it didn't: in any case, the priority for the lethal chamber is still reserved for the big Jerry generals themselves. The more of the bastards that shoot themselves in internecine warfare now the better.'

Hamish was regularly in the Tuscan frontline, and the dangers to Fritz and Peppino were so great that he was forced to terminate their service with him. He wrote each a glowing reference and got himself a new driver named Ivan. The name 'Bandiera Rossa' (Red Banner) – 'the great battle song' of the Italian Left – was now emblazoned across the bonnet of Hamish's replacement Jeep. He was proud to display his allegiance to the partisan cause and, as he toured the hill villages of Umbria, the sight (and sound) of the tall, balmoraled Scot became part of a folklore that lingers to this day. Here was a British officer who spoke their language, sang their songs, suffered like them and represented their needs. His stance was dangerous but his status within the partisan movement ensured his protection in the countryside while his partisan contacts made him a valuable asset to British military planners. He was a voice and an ear in areas outside conventional military control. Learning from three Allied prisoners of war, who had crossed through the German lines, that the north bank of the Arno was only lightly held, he notes: 'Why not attack? Answer (I suppose) is that Florence must be spared the horrors of all-out war. Means the partisans will have a job to do.' Years later, in *Cencrastus*, No. 54, he reports the battle for Florence in some detail, and his regard for the young hero Potente is obvious:

On the night of 3rd/4th of August the Germans blew up the bridges over the river Arno, including the Ponte Santa Trinita – frequently described as the most beautiful bridge in Europe. The only bridge they left was the Ponte Vecchi, the picturesque bridge with shops over it, beloved of tourists, but they ravaged both ends of it, and the houses on its approaches were completely destroyed. Furthermore the German demolition experts placed hundreds of mines and booby traps in the wreckage, effectively denying use of the bridge to our forces. . . . The Germans, retreating across the Arno, left behind a number of well-trained snipers who, cooperating with Italian Fascist snipers (*franchi tiratori*), accounted for quite a number of our troops and Potente's partisans . . . On the 6th of August 8th Army HQ sent a message that it had decided to utilise all 1600 Partisans of the Garibaldi Division of the Arno in the forthcoming operation for the liberation of Florence . . . From the time the Garibaldini had come down from the mountains, Potente had lived for the moment when the partisans, under his command, would be authorised to cross the Arno, and to take on the hated Nazi-Fascists in the Tuscan capital. On the 6th of August the order came. I remember it as though it were yesterday, the handsome blond Partisan general, in his red shirt and khaki breeks, poring over a sheet map of Florence, and issuing orders to his red-necker-chiefed subordinates (and to the Canadians who were, also, under his command). The major attack would be launched in three or four days . . .

Cencrastus volume 54 then continues the story, as of 9 August:

the Germans seem to have got wind of the forthcoming attack and, that evening, a ferocious mortar bombardment raked the areas where the Partisans were concentrated (San Frediano and Santo Spirito). Potente, and a British officer (Captain Wilmot) who was assigned to him, were wounded by the same shell. Potente suffered a terrible stomach wound and another wound to his thigh, and bled to death from these wounds. When British ambulance men arrived they went first to the British officer, but he refused attention until Potente had been attended to – a chivalrous gesture remembered to this day by the surviving Garibaldini who were present. Immediately after Potente's death, the brigade commanders decided to re-christen the division the 'Brigata Potente dell' Arno'. And, Potente's passionately expressed wish – that the brigata should not be dissolved, as was intended by 8th Army HQ, was to a certain extent fulfilled – for

I succeeded in persuading our Div. Commander to allow me to organise a small stream-lined corps of our own, recruited from volunteers among the partisans.[3]

Hamish does not mention his own involvement in the action preceding Potente's death, but all afternoon he had worked with Potente, planning the offensive that would take – but not destroy – the city. The mortar bombardment that killed Potente started just minutes after Hamish had left his side and he turned back to watch the explosions that he later learned had killed this brilliant young commander. Hamish believed Potente to be a great man and when he entered Florence he did so in Potente's name, recording the scene with vivid emotion:

Florence under the partisans. Potente – green-white-red – tricolour armbands and flaming red necker-chiefs. Franchi Tiratori make us dodge into a side street off Prince Eugene . . . '*Avete visto, Fiorentino, la civilta tedesca*' scrawled on wall (You now know, citizens of Florence, the German civilisation). Partisans round up Franchi Tiratori – black-shirted, black-gartered Italian SS men – shot out of hand. Partisans of Lanciotto crouching in doorway – mate wounded. Lovers strolling in Piazza della Signoria . . . My new driver is Napoli, for whom the Jerries offered a reward: '1000 Lira for Banditi Napoli'. He was in a partisan squadron and went under the battle name 'Fulmine' or Thunderbolt.

Hamish then notes that one of his Division 1 prisoners had been the first to reveal information that the Germans had made a major withdrawal from the north and east of Florence and that the whole city was now 'open'. However, instead of launching a major assault in that direction, Allied commanders decided to grab their opportunity and disband all the partisan brigades involved in the liberation of Tuscany as politically dangerous organisations. Hamish was disappointed but could do nothing about it. However, when partisan leaders decided to make their disbandment a dramatic and memorable event he joined in with a will. And, on 7 September, Hamish describes the last afternoon of what had been a four-day Florentine pageant.

3. They were to act, principally as guides, in the Borgo San Lorenzo area and accompany Allied troops on the advance towards the 'Gothic Line'.

In the Fortezza da Basso there is today a great occasion – the apotheosis and downfall of the Division Potente de Arno. In the square of the fortress, the aduneta – the brigadier, the division and 'Guistizia e Liberta' are drawn up with their flags, and before all – a flag with the shirt of Potente on top of it. On the balcony of the building is displayed the Divisonal flag, with Garibaldi's head on a white background, – and on the tri-colour was pinned a portrait of Potente. The GOC 13 Corps gave a speech and afterwards Aldo added his say. The wounded of the Division were on chairs beside the reviewing stand. Then (after the Corps Commander's departure) the great 'bandiera rossa' with its red flag was brought out, and the partisans marched through Florence singing the most stirring of revolutionary songs, while the population gave the clenched fist salute. I marched with them (what a blow in the balls to convention), aggregate, for one day to the Brigata Buozzi. Then (arrived back at the fortress) I enlist men for our private corps – had little difficulty (with Lazio's help)[4] in enrolling the needed 25 . . .

Thus, Hamish began to build what was, in essence, a small 'private' partisan army – working in a loose liaison with the British Army, and sixty-six men were soon involved in the Borgo San Lorenzo area alone. They were known as La Guardia Rosa, and Hamish's list of their 'covernames' makes their anti-fascist enthusiasms clear: 'Uragano, Fulmine, Lupo (snuffed out Fascists in a house – "I can smell them!"), Sangue, Diluvio – from the squadron of Potente (Temibile), Donatello [Donatello Donatini, commander of the 6th Brigata d' assalto 'l Lavacchio, Borgo San Lorenzo], Bionconcini . . . ' In addition, Hamish notes the fame of 'Corbara – who had killed a German Consul but been betrayed by 2 comrades'. Corbara was an Emilian partisan in whose honour Hamish would write a major ballad in 1947.

On 13 September Hamish moved forward into the hills above Borgo San Lorenzo, where he was to stay for ten weeks and which became his partisan HQ. 'The cage is a house that looks a bit depressing (blitzed shithouse!) from outside but whose possibilities become increasingly obvious inside. The 5 paratroops help clear up the house no end . . . Later in the day, a young Christian deviationist comes in – he has been a good soldier this laddie, and makes you despair of the Germans: so decent and perceptive and yet how many 'stur Ivans'[5] has he mown down in the

---

4. Lazio, however, was the one partisan who, having commited himself to Hamish 'disappeared' in what Hamish felt was a 'Judas moment'.
5. Russian soldiers fighting the Nazis on the Easter Front.

interests of the Nazis he despises.' Having accumulating evidence that German morale was on the point of collapse, Hamish advanced the idea that a sustained Allied attack would see the German hold on Italy disintegrate before winter set in. If this suggestion of a major Allied offensive reached Allied Headquarters it wasn't taken up, and both sides began hunkering down for a winter's stalemate. The following day Hamish was in reflective mood:

> Among the battered roofs of Borgo San Lorenzo church bells ring a mockery, and our solitary Jerry sleeps in the cage, wrapped tight in his bivvy . . . Now we are approaching the end, some of the horror of war is finding for me a safety valve. What a barbarous bloody swinery. To kill Fascism what a massacre of the simple of the earth. Especially among the ordinary Jerry swaddies – der deutsche Michael who, only now, is realizing properly how hated in Europe he is, and goes on doing his duty like an automaton . . .
>
> We arrive in Castaglia, and the verdict is, briefly, 'you can have it!' I go into the church which the Jerries seem to have used for quarters, before the Indians used it for mules – and hear the organ play 'Lili Marlene'.

This was an important incident because it seems to have inspired Hamish to start work on 'The D Day Dodgers', the most famous song of the Italian campaign, which is sung to a slight modification of the tune of 'Lili Marlene'.

On 23 September a large group of partisans turned up, and Hamish describes them as 'all very satisfied with life, and wanting to be sent on into the front line. Send them up to 2/B with a truck that brings down prisoners. A heck of a lot of miscellaneous captives through the cage in the last 24 hrs. I'll be grateful for a rest from speaking the German language shortly . . .' Next day the news was less good:

> unexpectedly, the partisans arrive back from 2 Bde [Brigade]; Teddy Deakin being absent at TAC, they have not been received with the enthusiasm they had hoped. I guarantee to put them on the right quarter and they kip down with me for the night . . .
> 25 Sept: during the night a gale of wind and rain twice brings down the western end of the tent. The first time, I've just time to call Ivan and we hoist the bloody thing into position again: the second time, I lie with wet canvas flapping around my face and just creep deeper into the blankets . . . The gunners are howling for targets so I get Chegwin down from his dinner and we identify the ridge – on the rear slope of

which there are positions. I have a fearful cold and can hardly make
my voice heard – a serious drawback for an interrogator . . .

During five days of wind and rain, 'horizontal in my wind-thumped tent',
Hamish worked to complete the 'Ballad of the D-Day Dodgers' which –
with terse lucidity and ironic humour – sums up the story and tragedy of
the whole Italian campaign. It is a genuine soldier's ballad – a collective
creation – given form and artistic force by the hand of a master:

We're the D-Day Dodgers, out in Italy –
Always on the vino, always on the spree.
    8th Army scroungers and their tanks
    We live in Rome – among the Yanks.
We are the D-Day Dodgers, way out in Italy.

We landed at Salerno, a holiday with pay;
The Jerries brought the bands out to greet us on the way . . .
    Showed us the sights and gave us tea.
    We all sang songs – the beer was free,
To welcome D-Day Dodgers to sunny Italy.

Naples and Cassino were taken in our stride,
We didn't go to fight there – we went there for the ride.
    Anzio and Sangro were just names,
    We only went to look for dames –
The artful D-Dodgers, way out in Italy.

On the way to Florence we had a lovely time.
We ran a bus to Rimini right through the Gothic Line.
    Soon to Bologna we will go
    And after that we'll cross the Po.
We'll still be D-Day Dodging, way out in Italy.

Once we heard a rumour that we were going home,
Back to dear Old Blighty never more to roam.
    Then someone said: 'In France you'll fight!'
    We said: 'No fear – we'll just sit tight!'
(The windy D-Day Dodgers to stay in Italy).

Dear Lady Astor, you think you know a lot,
Standing on a platform and talking tommy-rot.
    You, England's sweetheart and its pride,

We think your mouth's too bleeding wide
That's from your D-Day Dodgers – in far off Italy.

Look around the mountains, in the mud and rain –
You'll find the scattered crosses – (there's some which have no name).
    Heartbreak and toil and suffering gone,
    The boys beneath them slumber on.
Those are the D-Day Dodgers who'll stay in Italy[6]

'The D-Day Dodgers' was written at a time when rapid advances were being made on both the Eastern (Soviet) Front and on the Western (D-Day) Front, but when the Italian Front was bogged down in inhospitable terrain that favoured the Germans. The 'problems' of the war in Italy had recently been raised in the British Parliament by Lady Astor, and Hamish uses her as the linchpin of a story told in ballad form. Many have suggested she was unjustly lampooned. Neither Hamish, nor the bulk of the Eighth Army, cared a damn! They were fighting a war, they would sing their song, and niceties would look after themselves. The clearest factual explanation of how Lady Astor got her pivotal role in 'The D-Day Dodgers' is contained in a letter by Russell Miller, published in the *New Statesman*, 29 November 1974.

> Sir, Lady Astor never made a statement calling the 8th Army 'D-Day Dodgers', I was a schoolboy at the time but remember reading her explanation as to how the myth grew . . . Lady Astor received a letter from a group of 8th Army soldiers signed, bitterly, 'D-Day Dodgers'. They were, I believe, complaining that they were a forgotten army. Thinking that the title was a humorous one, rather like the 1914 soldiers calling themselves 'Old Contemptibles', she replied: 'Dear D-Day Dodgers . . .' The recipients then felt she had insulted them and widely publicised their feelings . . .

Thus, rightly or wrongly, Lady Astor became part of the folklore of the 8th Army in Italy – a kind of 'Wicked Queen' whom Hamish saw as fair game for ridicule. With regard to the ballad's 'origination', it appears to have emerged as a conglomeration of 'bar room verses' which Hamish – after 'hearing' the organ in Castaglia church – turned into a poignant and timeless ballad. That the last verse, which is purely Hamish's, should be written while he was soaking-wet and storm-bound in the Apennines gives it an additional resonance. It was first published in Hamish's

---

6. Published in *Ballads of World War II* (Lili Marlene Club, Glasgow 1947).

Ballads of World War II in 1947; since then it has been recorded dozens of times by singers in various countries. Over the years Hamish was to receive many letters about the origins and merits of this ballad but one meant more than the others. It came from Professor Akira Hayami of the Department of Economics at Keio University, Japan, in 1984: 'Dear Mr Henderson . . . I am writing about "The D-Day Dodgers" which you versed on "Lili Marlene" . . . I have published some essays on the story of "Lili Marlene" . . . I have thought the poem of the original "Lili Marlene" was not worth being called poetry at all – but when I happened to know "D-Day Dodgers", I realised that this was art . . . How can I obtain the original edition?'

After a two-day lull the rains returned on 2 October. Hamish notes in his diary:

> We wake up to hear the rain making more row on the tent roof, and I curse the malice of the hour. We pack up and fold the tent in conditions of the most exquisite discomfort . . . Then up the cross-country hillroad to Palazzuolo where I attempt to find a billet and eventually secure (without any opposition) a very pleasant garret which is a trifle dark but has a fireplace. The impression is that of a room painted by a minor French painter of 1900 – daylight coming in through a gash in the roof and a gin bottle (Booth's first dry) to my elbow . . .

The Borgo San Lorenzo area was now a hive of communist partisan activity, and the local American administration began moves to neutralise it. Hamish notes: 'Guecio, the AMG governor, has dissolved the committee of Liberation and prohibited political activity – but these lads are so used to clandestine activity that it doesn't worry them . . .'

On 20 October, Hamish got 'a letter from *l'amica* Liana which exhorts me to "tornare presto". I think I've won the heart of Liana. Nice leaves I'll have in the Eternal City in the romping days to come . . .' His happiness was soon punctured, however, by news from Palazzuolo that the Americans had overseen the dissolution of one of his most active partisan groups, run by a ferocious young man called Bobby. 'They say that Bob wept when he heard that the 3 Bde was to be split up and not allowed to continue to fight. What a slimy political racket which debars from battle the keenest Tedescophobes in Italy . . . We expect 10 PW from the Heights but they don't come down. They have been recaptured by the Germans – together with our platoon!' The following evening 'Archie Mac' brought a macaroni 'carry-out' and, with Luigi Castigliano, Hamish enjoyed 'one of the pleasantest evenings for a long time, singing the partisan songs and discussing literature'. Luigi was a classics student from Milan who, while undergoing training as an officer in Mussolini's army in southern Italy, had deserted and become a 'camp-follower' with the Eighth Army. It is unclear when and where he met Hamish but he now became another of Hamish's 'assistants', also his student, his protégé and his closest intellectual friend of the Italian campaign. Hamish notes in his diary:

> Luigi has the mentality of a sensitive and amoral Cambridge student – literature is for him a sensual pleasure, and his only ambition is to remain a university student for his lifetime. To his remarks 'getting away from material things – to the worship of form and beauty' I oppose my new conception of the Gaelic ideal: the accepting of material things as solid good, the realization that *Ding an sich*[7] must be spurned by a logic Gallic, Gaelic and Greek. Out of things visible only – comes the knowledge of things invisible . . . But curiously enough, I'd regard one of the reasons why I've been fighting (or camp-following the fighters), as the charging up of a certain number of privileged people in this amoral attitude. Because, ultimately, they are the only reliable trustees of a certain non-affected truth.

This remark about 'charging up a certain number of privileged people' so that they will carry forward Hamish's 'Greco-Gaelic philosophy' shows him expanding his methodology as a 'prompter behind the sets'.

On 22 October Hamish received a copy of *New Writing and Daylight*: a handsome hardback book forwarded by John Lehmann – editor of the book, and of *Penguin New Writing*. It contained 'Fragment of an Elegy' (Hamish's First Elegy) and having signed the book Hamish dedicated it to Luigi with a quotation from Rilke 'about things visible and invisible'. He then asked Bobby to take it as a gift to Liugi in his observation post. John Lehmann was a leading figure in the London literary world, whom Hamish had met occasionally in 1939/41 and who now maintained a regular literary correspondence. The letters make it clear that Lehmann too had come under Hamish's spell. For example, in the article with which Lehmann concludes *New Writing and Daylight*, he quotes Hamish: 'we are lived by powers we do not understand' and the last sentence in the article reads as though it might have been written by Hamish: 'Even those who are convinced that no people can escape the pattern of its fate, should not shut their minds to the possibility that from among the doomed destroyers of

---

7. *Ding an sich*: thing-in-itself (a reference to Kant).

themselves, the clearest vision of the path that was missed, the truth that could save, might arise.' Lehmann was a poet and a good critic. He asked Hamish to send him all his Elegies as they were written. And in 1946 it was he who requested permission to publish *Elegies for the Dead in Cyrenaica*.

Despite the disbandment of Bobby's brigade, partisan and communist activity in the Burgo San Lorenzo area continued, and Hamish mused on the process by which the Left might make a real effect on world politics. He foresaw that real change would come when Europe's 'humanitarian left' had so successfully infiltrated its 'human ideals' into the bedrock of culture and society that the processes of governance would look after themselves. Consequently, while mechanisms of government may be markedly different in different places and nations, Hamish believed that similar 'socialist' values – and a similar vision of the Common Good would eventually underpin the political organisation of all 'civilised' states. This is remarkably like Gramsci's concept of 'a transforming cultural hegemony', which Hamish was to discover and applaud a few years later. However, it is clear that in the autumn of 1944 he was already advancing his own ideals and belief that 'poetry' embraces all.

On 31 October Hamish notes that Allied Commanders in Italy had accepted 'the bitter truth – we just haven't made it; the Boche has scored the tactical success that must be near his heart, and will keep us yammering on the hills for another winter. When you consider what material superiority we enjoy and what wretched dregs of humanity are in the line against us – it makes an ex-member of the 51st Division wild.'

Next day a new partisan turned up, called Naso, whom Hamish describes as 'a sympathetic type – a formidable little tough: retiring to rest each night, with a handkerchief tied round his head and knotted under his chin, he looks like a witch.' The new arrival provoked an argument between Napoli and Bobby about the necessity of discipline and brutality in war, fighting and politics. Cromwell, Robespierre and Danton all featured, and Hamish concludes his notes: 'Faithful's thesis is correct: an army, or society, to be efficient, is virtuous.' Against this, Hamish saw Naso as a classic representative of the continuum in Italian life – that cultural wholeness – that crosses generations and class divisions, conjoins folk art and high art and gives Italian society its dynamism and the Italian people their remarkably unified cultural sensibility. And, twenty years later, in a letter to the *Scotsman* (written on 2 April 1964 as part of one of his 'literary flytings' with Hugh MacDiarmid), Hamish offered Naso an 'invisible' salute across time and space:

Mr MacDiarmid contends that none of the great figures of world literature have also been popular poets. This is not true. Leaving aside the special case of Burns, whose world-wide popularity maintains itself in spite of the cult and not because of it, I can provide from my own experience two cogent illustrations of the position Dante holds in the position of his countrymen. In October 1944 I asked a young Tuscan partisan – an electrician from Florence – why he had joined the Garibaldini, and had elected to share all the dangers and hardships of life in the mountains: his answer was in the words of Dante:

> *Libertà va cercando, ch'è cara,*
> *Come sa chi per lei vita rifiuta.*

'Freedom he is seeking, which is so precious – as they know who give up their lives for it.' A few weeks later, when another partisan was 'missing, presumed killed', one of his mates compared his fate to that of Buonconte, whose body was never found, after the battle of Campaldino in 1289. Somewhat surprised by his recondite allusion, I asked for further information about the earlier casualty, and the red-necker-chiefed tommy-gun-toting boyo floored me completely by quoting from memory some fifteen lines of the 5th Canto of the Purgatorio.

In November Hamish organised the movement of his Cage, up Route 65, north-east towards Bologna: 'the road winds treacherous with slithery mud, between encampments and bivveys perched on the hillside over it – going down to Sillaro the serration of peaks on the skyline is beautiful. We pass into the hurried disorder of the forward zone – live and dead mules beside each other in the fields and the first whiff of the stench of death. Houses hit by arty and sprawling where it hit them: – has Kesselring made it? Were we meant to come into these hills?'

11 November 1944. MY BIRTHDAY – and where the Hell? The answer is – the northern slopes of the Etruscan Appenines, as the German War Communiques call it. Snow in the air, clean, crisp and fresh. But now no snow on the slopes over against us – and the climate a tingling briskness like the shores of Fife in early May. I send off my Income Tax form. About midday, the Germans salute my birthday with six shells . . .

16th Nov: . . . Nice gentle interrogation with no raised voice. The Germans are overcome at the comradely way they are treated in captivity: one says he was wounded in Russia but never got such

treatment as he's got here. I spend another evening talking with
Luigi – about Caldan and the campaign of Moro, about Lorca and
the extent to which his poetry is political; talk about Luigi and the
extent to which his attitude to life is nihilistic.

On 27 November Hamish records the arrival of 'the NAAFI – with two
bottles of gin! Drink with Salari and Mereu [partisans serving with the
Loyals]. We embark on a day of talking, arguing and singing. Salari has a
low opinion of the fighting spirit of our troops at the moment. I point out
their psychology – they know that Italy is not a decisive front, and that the
war is already as good as won, and they, naturally, want to avoid the last
minute bullet. In fact the desire to avoid the last minute bullet has been
quite a feature of the Italian campaign.'

The battlefront was now static, and Michael Clutterbuck invited
Hamish for dinner in the Officers Mess where they met an ex-member
of the Seventh Armoured Division, reminisced about the Cauldron and
'drank the real thing': whisky. Hamish made sure several crates were set
aside for a St Andrew's Day celebration.

As the day draws to a close and no piper shows up I begin to fear for
our St Andrew's Night . . . But – just at the right psychological
moment – in comes the piper! This is piper Smith and we pipe our
way into B Mess. At first all the mutt-faced Southrons sit impervious
to the pipe music but Camp and I dance a Highland fling (myself in
ammo boots!) to get things going – and the company thereupon
repairs down stairs to dance reels (foursome and eightsome) and
miscellaneous Highland dances till my calves ache.

On 3 December Hamish notes:

The only people in the cage are more *sfollati* [refugees] – and a
priest. Invite the three oldest *sfollati* into my house to sit by the fire –
one old thing (female) 89 says '*Non si scommodi*' (please, don't put
yourself out). Something it is to have a thousand years of culture
behind you . . . it seems to me that the Itis are a little too civilised to
fight and win a war, which (we are still in the twentieth century) is a
definite disadvantage. Whether they can make a revolution is
another thing I'm interested in – circumstances are exceedingly
favourable but I have a wheeen doots on the subject . . .

In that aside, 'we are still in the twentieth century', Hamish recognises
that human progress is a slow evolutionary process constantly under-

mined by man's instinct for violence and self-aggrandisement: instincts that 'power politics' endlessly manipulate to the disadvantage of many of the most deeply civilised peoples.

On 5 December Luigi Castigliano returned to camp after a week in Florence during which he had been formally inducted into the British Army – as a Second Lieutenant. It was a small triumph for Hamish. Under his tutelage, Luigi had become not just an excellent interrogator and a fervent Scotophile but a British army officer! And, perhaps even more important, the bourgeois Italian classics student was blossoming into a Celtic scholar with strong socialist leanings who stimulated Hamish's own imagination.

Hamish also suddenly renewed contact with his old Paratrooper adversary, Captain Guenther – from Sicily. Having escaped British custody in Italy, Guenther had returned to Germany as a war-hero. And it was with a horrified sense of 'theatrical irony' that Hamish learned that the Paratroops commander now slitting the throats of 'his' partisans with blood-thirsty abandon was the same man whom he had captured in Sicily seventeen months earlier. Here was the madness and tragedy of war – here was a situation straight out of *Coriolanus*, or *Henry IV*.[8]

For Hamish the last weeks of 1944 were a dispiriting time. While 'bullying' one of his prisoners, he asked what this youngster regarded as 'holy'. He got the reply '*meine Wahrfeit*' (my truth). The answer sickened him. He was not prepared to accept 'my truth' from a callow, indoctrinated youth any more than from Hitler himself. When he learned that Allied Command had decided to move decisively against the Greek socialist and communist insurgents, who had done so much to liberate Greece from Nazi and fascist control, he notes: 'the Yalta agreements with Stalin are no excuse for the Western Powers imposing brutal dictatorships in Southern Europe . . . Spend the evening telling guys I will desert if they . . . send me to Greece. This bloody situation is the most degrading thing we've struck in the war: the most shady and downright dishonest too.' On Christmas Eve he set down a collection of thoughts that begin in melancholy but end in joy:

A fir-tree without candles – a symbol of our empty Christmas . . .
The 'theatre of war': Rommel in his coloured scarf – touring the
Sollum outposts; Montgomery in his hats . . . Both sides advancing

---

8. Hamish did, however, play a major role in a series of battles that resulted in Guenther's death (at the hands of an Emilian partisan).

to unite in the great proletariat of death . . . Hitler's Germany: a nation of 70 million masochists who have let a few thousand sadists get into the saddle . . . Back at my HQ, take pleasure in the great heaped log fire they've made for me, and look around with satisfaction at my little world.

He was growing tired of war, wanted home and the peace to write poetry – as is made clear this letter to Dry Dayton:

When will I read the lesson next? And what to choose when I read it? I should think something particularly bloody about the fate of the enemy – or else, if the rectory disapproves, I might offer the public a quieter line, such as the entry into the Promised Land, or the Prodigal Son . . . [but] for the War Office's consideration 'the undersigned Capt H. Henderson gives notice of the following facts 1) there is a chair (vacant for the use of) at D.D. Rectory and 2) on 11 November 1945 he has every intention of occupying it.'

TEN

Victory and Home

Freedom, which has hitherto only become man here and there,
must pass into the mass itself, into the lowest strata of society
and become people.

HH, after Heine

From Cairo, on 1 January 1945, G.S. Fraser wrote to Hamish:

I've often enough thought of that phrase in your last letter – 'Jerry
has had it, but an army of one-eyed half-wits could hold you up in
these hills of sorrow . . .', and thought of us in our comfort here in
Cairo, our intrigues, petty quarrels, paper wars, and you out there in
the night, in the cold, in the rain and mud, and yet as always (as
Haig Gudenian wrote to me when he met you once and drank wine
with you in some mountain village) 'like the laird of the surrounding
hills'. God (or Time, or History) keep you safe this year . . . I
thought your last fragment of an Elegy strong and moving like the
others; like Whitman, the whole thing will be even more impressive
when you have it in bulk. It's like a broad river carrying a lot of
gravel along with it . . .

Hamish's days of hill-fighting were, however, almost over and he received
Fraser's letter in the relative luxury of the Hotel Lucchesi, in Florence, on
leave. After a short visit to Rome to see Liana, he returned to the Bologna
Front but, by the end of February, he was at work in a 'permanent'
Interrogation Centre on the outskirts of Florence. He writes to Shergold:

You'll be glad to hear that things have got organised and springtime
has come to Florence. The view is delightful, the work congenial,
and I have a private source of quite drinkable Chianti. Work started
earlier than I expected as 10th Indian had captured a paratroop
officer who refused to open his mouth to Jellinck and acted like a

Trappist with everyone else. So they sent him down here, and with some misgivings I consented to tackle him, although we were still in the stage of installing ourselves. Luckily, he did not take long to break, so we've acquired a little kudos at the start (actually it was the same job I've done with dozens of paratroops up forward in the last six months – just because it's done at Army group level everyone starts flinging their hats in the air!)

Hamish delighted in the architecture of Florence: he would walk up to the Piazza Michelangelo – overlooking the Arno, Brunelleschi's dome and the great panorama of the city – and wonder at the miracle of human achievement. For the first time in three years, Hamish had 'time on his hands' and he began making serious plans for his book, *German Interrogator*. He notes that it will be important 'to be like them', and he asks himself whether the book should be 'Humorous, Ironical, or Real?' After that, half tongue-in-cheek, he set down the 'greater framework' within which he would write his book.

A) 1) Buy army gym shorts, slip, gym-shoes 2) Alarm clock
B) Assemble books and documents in room with bare light and few distractions. All reference books available – all personal paraphernalia excluded.
C) Rise 0700 hrs. PT – twenty minutes. Cold shower. Breakfast 0800 hrs. Ready to start work 0900 hrs. (In intervening period clean-up, arrange things necessary, read or write poetry, take Jeep out for a run.)
D) Consult expert on correct exercises to correct stoop. Do this in conjunction with Huxley's eye-exercises . . . Keep diary regularly every morning/evening as supplement to – not substitute for – normal notebooks . . . In reading and writing – develop a plan. Exclude all items of nonsense value. Attempt to keep down extent of sex life's interference with the above programme.

Programme for arrival in Britain. 1) locate a place where I can work without distraction. (The School House, Glen Truim). 2) Finish Elegies. 3) Keep Jeep by me (or motorbike instead). 4) Get into a Gaelic atmosphere again. 5) Visit the Outer Isles . . . (The nearer R. L. Stevenson is to Scottish life and his roots – the truer he rings.)

Conscious that his analysis of his German subjects would be shaped by his own perspectives, Hamish also jotted down a list of the ways in which his personality had been altered by five years of war.

Looking at one's own development after surveying the development
of a nation (Germany) one is forced to admit that many factors can
play equivalent roles in one's own life: that a distortion and
deflection become visible even in a short lifetime. What factors
have chiefly influenced me? In the first place my long exile has
seriously disqualified me as a Scottish poet; though I may be better
as a European poet. Secondly, my English public school education
has made a visible (permanent?) deflection in my thought processes
and way of life. Thirdly, my Army career, although it has made me
100% more worldly wise and given me rich experiences, has
seriously interrupted my reading and normal study . . .

As he prepared for his return to Scotland, it is clear his ambitions were as
much political as literary: 'Scotland is one of the finest agricultural
countries in Europe . . . The legend of Scotland's poverty is a fiction (or
should be). It was not a poor country, or a country lacking identity, that
drove out the Romans, the Angles, the Danes and the Norse – fought the
battles of Carhan, Bannockburn and Flodden, that built a first-class navy
and fine abbeys and cathedrals, castles and cities.' He explored the
problems of endemic unemployment and emigration – advocating 'Socialist solutions and a Scottish population of not less than seven million . . .'.
    In the spring, the Italian battlefront suddenly opened up and Hamish
was sent north to participate in battle-planning for the advance across the
Po valley. He also drafted propaganda leaflets to be dropped by aeroplane
on the northern cities. These incited the civilian population to rise against
the remnants of the German war machine: '*Milanesi! Chi vi parla è un
partigiano*'. However, as the Allies moved into Milan and Turin, they
acted to ensure that Liberation was not followed by a left-wing Revolution. Hamish was in a quandary: as an individual he was all for an anti-
fascist 'Red Revolution' but, as a British Army officer, he was ordered to
counter any signs of a socialist or communist takeover. The Americans
used 'fear of revolution' as a propaganda weapon: the threat was grossly
exaggerated so that any movement towards radical political change could
be stifled at birth. Hamish stood squarely against such intervention.
Consequently, as the war drew to a close, he found himself moved
sideways and given the task of 'debriefing' high-ranking German officers,
war criminals and Italian collaborators. It was a task he enjoyed and it
completed his 'education' in the politics of state-sponsored brutality in the
most remarkable way.
    Things really took off on 2 May 1945, when Hamish suddenly found
himself summoned to play a leading role in the Surrender of Italy. He later
documented his experiences with relish and good-humour:

GRAZIANI AND THE ITALIAN SURRENDER: When Marshall Rudolpho Graziani was handed over to me he seemed a broken man. Until his turn came to get out of the plane he sat hunched and sobbing. The first words I heard him speak were: '*Hanno ucciso il Duce. Tutto è ormai finito*'. (They have killed the Duce: all is ended now.) From the airport he was brought in a vehicle to a *campo di smistamento* for officers on the outskirts of Florence. With him there travelled other Axis generals captured about the same time . . . the sight of British soldiers guarding the camp raised the spirits of all of my charges . . . Graziani made no bones about his pleasure at being under the protection of his desert enemies . . . However, it was clear that he remained afraid of being summarily executed, for he asked me to give certain messages to his relations '*dopo la mia morte*' . . .

Immediately after this, in accordance with directions received from the Allied Command, I ordered Graziani to prepare a message ordering all Axis troops in Italy, including the Italian and German troops of the Armata Liguria, to lay down their arms. He complied forthwith and wrote the surrender order – of which the text is well known. I then told him to get ready – as a truck was coming in ten minutes to take him to the radio station in Florence. At once his terror of the partisans returned, and he asked me if it were possible that there might be demonstrations against him in the streets. I replied, 'Quite possible, but we will provide an armed guard.' His forehead twitched in a nervous frown . . . I saw it was no use reasoning with him, so I said 'Get ready, Marshall, for you are coming with me – that's an order.' After a moment he said, 'Very well, Capitano. *Lo responsabilita e vostra*. But in any case – it is better if I go in disguise.' Out I went, and in a minute or two came back with my own military great coat, with its captain's pips; this he put on. It fitted him perfectly, as he is almost exactly my height. I also gave him my peaked cap, and he put it on too – stuffing his grey forelock under its brim. He looked a queer sight in the British uniform, with his black jack-boots sticking out from underneath. We were just ready to go when he, suddenly, said: 'Black spectacles. I can't go without *occhiali nero*!' This was getting beyond a joke, but I took a deep breath, and ordered a Scottish sergeant to find some black spectacles. He saluted, went off, and returned in an amazingly short time – carrying a pair. Where he got them I still don't know to this day. Graziani put them on. This final touch made him look so grotesque that I had a keen desire to laugh. But there was no time to lose so, collecting the German general Pemsel, who was to accompany us, I led the way to the waiting vehicle. The Lion of Cyrenaica climbed in, and we drove off.

At the radio station in Florence, Hamish organised the broadcast of both the Surrender of Italy and the Surrender of all German forces fighting in Italy. It was a historic moment – the first surrender by a major Axis nation in the course of the Second World War. The Italian Proclamation (in English) reads as follows (and carries the impress of the hand of Hamish Henderson).

> PROCLAMATION by Marshall Graziani – 'To the Italian and German Troops of the Army of Liguria.' In this final battle of Italy you have borne yourselves with your customary discipline and valour; although you found yourself in the most heavy inferiority to the enemy. The time has arrived when any further resistance would be useless, inhuman and, as far as I your Commander is concerned, criminal. The German Higher Command in Italy has, for a few days, issued no further orders, and it is not known where it is now. In this situation I have assumed personal responsibility for signing an unconditional surrender to the Allied High Command on 29th April. This order was made known to you by airborne leaflets. Obey this order – which saves your honour as soldiers – and lay down your arms. The Commander General of Army Liguria – Graziani.[1]

Few 'surrenders' in history can claim much value as literature, but Graziani's not only functioned well but stands as prose-poetry of some merit. It was designed to put an immediate end to all Italian resistance, and brilliantly mixes unambiguous command with ambiguous rhetoric – to achieve the total and immediate cessation of all hostilities. Graziani's surrender broadcast was followed immediately by a second broadcast, in German, by his German deputy commander, Lt General Pemsel. This German surrender was also overseen by Hamish: this time the wording is short, sharp, clipped, authoritarian and very German.

> PROCLAMATION by Lt General Pemsel – Chief of Staff, Army Liguria. As German Chief of General Staff of the Ligurian Army I confirm without reserve the words of my Commander Marshall

---

1. Graziani was later tried, in Rome, for war crimes. He was found guilty of criminal collaboration with the Nazis and sentenced to 19 years' imprisonment. After serving just fourteen months, however, he was released and lived out his life in disgraced luxury in Rome.

Graziani. You must obey this order! Pemsel, Lt General and Chief of
Staff, Army Liguria.

It was a remarkable moment in the history of Europe, and Hamish was
twenty-five years old.

Early on 8 May 1945, Hamish drove south from Florence for a meeting
in Perugia. Hitler was known to be dead, Allied and Soviet forces were
meeting up all over Europe, but the actual date and time of 'the cessation
of hostilities' was still unknown. It was a beautiful summer's morning, the
Chianti hills were aglow with green and gold. Hamish was exultant: he
had come through – the war was won – soon he would be home, all was
well. Then, within sight of the city walls of Siena, the Jeep broke down;
the crankshaft had gone. Seeing a pair of white oxen ploughing in a field
below the road, Hamish walked down to ask the farmer whether he might
borrow them to tow the Jeep into Siena. A requisition order was made
and, with Hamish and his driver seated in majesty, the two oxen, led by *il
contadino*, towed the bullet-scarred Jeep, emblazoned with the words
Bandiera Rossa, towards the great medieval city. It was eleven o'clock
and, as they approached the north gate, the bells of the churches began to
ring out, one after another, all over the city: peace had been declared.
Hamish stood up in the Jeep and took off his balmoral, tears pouring
down his face – after six years of the most terrible war in history, all
Europe was at peace again. The Senesi were spilling out on to the streets
and when they saw the oxen towing the Jeep they cheered in their
hundreds. Hamish, gripping the shattered windscreen with his left hand,
raised his right fist in the Partisan salute and sang the 'Bandiera Rossa'
time and again. And as they made their way towards the Piazza Comu-
nale – with shouts of '*Pace, Pace*' bouncing off the walls of the narrow
streets – it was as if the Palio was about to begin. When they stopped in
the great square, Hamish shouted out 'The crankshaft has gone – we're
looking for a garage! And I need a drink!' Shoulder high, he was carried
from the Jeep into a cafe where peace was saluted with vino, kisses and
song: '*Avanti, popolo, alla riscossa, bandiera rossa, bandiera rossa!
Bandiera rossa la trionferà, evviva il comunismo e la libertà!*' Children
came with water for the oxen, and the oxen's collars were plaited with
flowers. It was another of Hamish's great days, and that night, having
been driven on to Perugia, his celebrations continued in the company of
the Sixth Gordons. It was a night of such uninhibited release that he was
inspired to write 'Eightsome Reel' – an extraordinary victory bacchanal,
sung to the ecstatic tune of 'Kate Dalrymple'.

After that, Hamish was ordered north to the Austrian front. The nature
of his business is unclear, but it provided his first encounter with Russian

soldiers. Hamish had an unqualified regard for the heroism of the Soviet peoples in their Great Patriotic War: with grossly inferior equipment they had beaten the most powerful and brutal military forces ever assembled, but first meetings with the Russians proved disappointing. He quickly recognised that the loss of twenty-five million people and the total devastation of vast tracts of the Soviet Union were likely to have long-term psychological effects on the Soviet peoples and the future of communism. He was shocked by the manners, lack of discipline and lack of vision displayed by many of the Soviet officers. They were exhausted and overwhelmed by the enormity of their achievement, and the seeds of their future impotence – in the face of their authoritarian masters and the Western economic stranglehold – were already apparent.

However, Hamish's disappointment in the Soviets was only equalled by his disbelief at the continuing barbarism displayed by the US Military. 'And the Americans! Nowhere in Europe, not in the backwoods of the Antipodes, such an ignorance – yet they have the idea they are a democratic state – *L'Uomo monolingue* – monopolistic products of big business! . . . I think back on the verdict of the Catania man – on the Yanks: "They eat, drink and fuck – eat and drink like children, and fuck like beasts . . ." Truman the soul and heel of America!'

So the war ended, but Hamish was to spend the whole summer debriefing and interrogating, and preparing a major study of political events in Italy during the period 1943–45. This political report, which describes the history of the relationship between the German Embassy in Italy and the Republican Fascist Government, was entitled 'La Germania ed i Repubblichini'. It required him to interrogate various senior German, Italian and Vatican diplomats – as well all the surviving SS commanders. Thus Hamish completed his 'grand tour' by becoming one of the out-standing authorities on the recent history and politics of Italy.

'La Germania ed i Repubblichini' makes dull reading – but Hamish's independent notes about his relationships with the German war criminals are extremely interesting and historically important: He begins: 'I give to our German generals to read, "The Self-betrayal: Doom of the German Generals" by Curt Riess. – To Vietinghhoff-Sheel the gala issue of Die Zeitung, "Im Felde besiegt" – To Dollmann, possible candidate for the high-jump, "For whom the Bell Tolls" . . .' Of Heinz Heinze Dollmann, a colonel in the Waffen SS, at the heart of the German presence in Italy, Hamish writes:

DOLLMANN – is the typical Prussian who sold his soul to Hitler. He told me; – at the time of the Anzio landings – the only guard on Rome was a company of soldiers with VD . . . 'Mussolini should have said, "*Mein Fuhrer, 'Sie sind leider verrückt.*"' In Dollmann one can perceive the gross sin of 'historicism' . . . He is writing his memoirs and looking for a title. He says it had better be '*Je m'accuse*'. I said 'Splendid, and don't forget to add on the fly-leaf "*Qui s'accuse, s'excuse*".' . . . Dollmann knew secrets about Hitler and did nothing. He is like a garrulous old woman who makes no bones about her profession and is full of spicy gossip. He is a spiv. He is revealed, in his own book, as a man furiously second-rate – lacking all real qualities whether as a scholar, historian or writer. In a sense his memoirs are a very good example of old fascist 'culture' which is no culture at all . . . The SS men here are the ideal subjects for interrogation. A lance corporal in the Afrika Korps gave 100% more resistance to interrogation than any one of these bastards . . .

Hamish also interrogated Gestapo-SD Commander Herbert Kappler, the man responsible for organising the reprisal killings at the Fosse Ardeatine in 1944 – one of the great crimes of the war in Italy. He notes:

KAPPLER – The glassy blue stare with which he tries to dominate even his interrogator. The *Schmisse*,[2] the heavy brute face. Conscious of his intellectual inferiority (to Dollman for example) he makes a laborious 'German Professor' study of Etruscan and Volsian civilisation . . . Kappler takes the first opportunity to mention Dollman's 'homo-sexuality' – referring to the Reichsführer's order (1941?) that any SS man convicted of homosexuality should be shot. Justifies his reports against D by saying that 'if such an order existed it should be carried out'. His spleen against D is based on envy – yet, knowing of his monstrosity (*Ungeheuerlichkeit*) I cannot rob him of the right to express his own self-justification. Speaking of the Fosse Ardeatine – which I described to him as now laid out – he professes to feel horror for the act. But in actual fact (according to Lechner, from Agostini) he gave an *Ohrfeige* [slap] to an Italian Colonel before shooting him. Kappler tells me that he wanted Abteilung III to witness the shootings at Fosse Ardeatine in order to demonstrate to them the "*Seelische Uberwindung of Abteilung IV*". He despised the "*Flucht in die Euphorie*" of the other SS men. I show Kappler the poem in the magazine *Mercino* on the Fosse Ardeatine . . .

The Ardeatine Cave massacre took place in March 1944: 335 Italian hostages were shot as a reprisal for the 'bombing' of a column of German soldiers by Italian partisans in Rome. One of the dead was Aladino

---

2. *Schmisse*: scars from fencing (a sign of honour or bravery).

Govoni, son of the poet Corrado Govoni. In the months after the slaughter, Corrado wrote two poems for his son. When Hamish read them he decided they must be translated into English. The first takes the form of a conversation that Hamish entitled 'Dialogue of the Angel and the Dead Boy': the second is a magnificent elegy that he entitled 'Lament for the Son (after Corrodo Govoni)'. Sending the second poem to John Lehmann, editor of *Penguin New Writing*, Hamish pointed out 'one wonderful line, "I am the living cross of my dead son"'. Lehmann did not publish either poem but Hamish believed Govoni's lament to be 'the finest poem to come out of Italy during the war':

> He was the most beautiful son on earth,
> braver than a hero of antiquity,
> gentler than an angel of God:
> tall and dark, his hair like a forest,
> or like that intoxicating canopy
> which spreads over the Po valley;
> and you, without pity for me, killed him
> – there, in a cave of dull-red sandstone.
>
> He was the whole treasure
> of war, of sanctuary and of crown,
> of my accepted human poverty,
> of my discounted poetry –
> You, once his hiding place was discovered
> (after which no angel could sleep) –
> You, with your thieving hands
> that were strangers to no sacrilege,
> you carried him away at the run
> into the darkness
> to destroy him without being seen –
> before I had time to cry out:
> 'Stop!
> Put him down!
> *That is my son!*' . . .
>
> He was my new son, he was the triumph
> of my betrayed boyhood;
> and you changed him in front of my praying hands
> into a heap of worms and ashes.
>   Mutilated, hurt, blinded,

> only I know the tragic weight I am carrying.
> I am the living cross of my dead son . . .[3]

Despite his opposition to capital punishment, Hamish felt Kappler merited execution – and he was disappointed that this brute of a man got only a life sentence. Post-war interrogation, however, was not all gloom and doom and Hamish describes how, 'Late one night after a piss-up, Michael Clutterbuck, Eddy Eisler and I sang loud, long and raucous outside the prison doors of SS General Wolff and SS General Harster: "*Wir fahren gegen Engelland*", "*Bomber aus Engelland*", and the "*Horst Wessel lied*".' If that was the closest Hamish came to 'emotionally abusing' his prisoners it must be counted small beer, and next morning he wrote these beautiful lines:

> Either blessings rippling out to wide beatitudes
> Or curses spiralling down to the thin point of leaves.[4]

By July, Rome had become Hamish's permanent base and he began to relax and enjoy himself. He writes: 'My Jeep "Bandiera Rossa" has been the sensation of Florence, Arezzo, Foligno, Perugia. It is now the sensation of Rome. However, for various reasons – I am re-christening it "Potente"!' He renewed contact with Liana and developed a 'literary' friendship with Amleto Micozzi – a young waiter whome he had met the previous year. In 2002 Amleto recalled his first meeting with Hamish:

> It was at the Casina Valadier, I was a boy of sixteen, a waiter. He had come in for a meal with a group of officers. I didn't know he was an intelligence officer, we spoke and became friends. He sang his songs and I read him my poems. Between 1944 and 1946 I worked very hard at many different jobs – waiter, porter, scullery-boy, and as a messenger at the Allied Control Commission with Admiral Stone. For me, in those days, Hamish was a warrior, an anti-Nazi and anti-Fascist, a poet – and a communist like me . . . I did not see a Scottish Nationalism in Hamish – for me his Scottishness, his intense and serene Scottish soul, nourished a genuine internationalism and a profoundly universal spirit. Hamish had a clear, calm and universal sense of humanity . . .[5]

---

3. 'Lament for the Son (after Corrodo Govoni)', in the *Collected Poems* (translated by HH).
4. Unpublished, from notebook.
5. Letter from Amleto Micozzi to TN, 2002.

Hamish's first reference to Micozzi appears in his diary on 15 July 1945: 'Evening – Amleto (Micozzi) gives me his book of poems. The poems are by "Miceto" and the criticism of them by "Amozzo". What incredible luck I have in finding friends – Luigi at 1 Division with his literary interests, Amleto in Rome, a poet – and waiter at the Casina Valadier. Amleto does Fred Astaire dances very well and sings a passionate blues song of his own composition, "Ophelia". Two of his poems touch on our relationship – "Al compagno capitano" and "L'anima della Valadier".' On 20 July 1945 Hamish wrote to John Speirs:

> Dear John – A year after our Roman triumph I'm back again in this unscathed, incomparable and ignoble city. The July heat is flagrant, and I dream of Ostia as in Cairo you might dream of Alexandria. The heat is actually quite Cairene, and the population only needs a liberal sprinkling of tar-brushing to look like the lost tribes of Ismailia . . . So much has happened these last months that I let my correspondence go aroving on a long lead . . . John there's twa-tree things ye might do for me – 1) Send me another copy of Ruth's Rilke, together with any new elegies translated. 2) Send me a) Forster's Alexandria, b) Goha le Simple and Le Beau Said (both Egyptian Classics). 3) C. P. Cavafy's works – any edition, translations if possible . . . The greatest attraction here at the moment is the open air season at the Royal Opera House at the baths of Caracalla. The more spectacular operas – Aida and Carmen – lend themselves to flamboyant treatment in this setting: Aida could hardly be more impressive if performed in the great hyperstile hall at Karnak. The youth and beauty and elegance of the city flocks to the opera in throngs of thousands – meanwhile the plebs is guising more openly, and in no bad cause . . . The 'Wind from the North' which blew the guts out of Il Duce is playing briskly through the streets of the capital and catching the bonzes of Fascism by their tail-coats . . .

On 26 July 1945 Hamish celebrated the news that the Labour Party had won a huge victory in the British general election: he was confident that it would commit itself not just to coherent socialist policies but to a serious review of the 'Scottish Problem' and devolved government in Scotland. Of Churchill's defeat he notes 'Let Churchill go out dignified. Only no caterwauling! – Righeto and myself celebrate the Labour Victory in style with vino galore. And fix up a cena for Martedi at the same trattoria. The Greek government resigns – and Franco must be quaking in his shoes . . .' The same day, Hamish decided to end his army career and get back to Britain as soon as possible:

I must so cunningly organise matters that I am now left alone with time to write the Elegies and *German Interrogator*. While there was operational intelligence I did it – whilst there was still information to be extracted from SS Obergruppenführers on post war plans for Nazi activity, I extracted it; while the post mortem lasted on German 'Intelligence' methods in the field – I stayed – with nose to the grindstone. But now that historical surveys on the German 'supply systems' are about to begin – the time has come to quit . . .

We understand the world only by living in it –
We understand the world only when we are able to change it.[6]

Consequently, Hamish made sure he got some pre-demob leave and organised himself a fortnight in Merano in the South Tyrol. He chose the Tyrol because his friends Fritz and Bobby both lived there, and because Rainer Maria Rilke had written some of his finest elegies there. It is not clear whether he took Liana with him but he probably did. She had asked him to stay on in Italy; she had said she would move to Scotland with him, but Hamish was deeply wary of any formal commitment. For example, from Merano, he wrote a letter to Margaret Heinemann, the former girlfriend of John Cornford, who had been killed in Spain at the age of 21, in which he copied out Cornford's beautiful lines 'Heart of the heartless world / Dear heart, the thought of you . . .' In writing those words, it seems almost certain that Hamish was speaking, indirectly, to Liana. He knew that, however strongly he felt about her, his commitment to the well-being of Scotland must override everything. He knew, with cold rationality, that if he returned to Scotland with a young bride the work he was planning would be hugely compromised. Margaret Heinemann was separated from her love by death; Hamish knew his love of Scotland must now separate him from Liana. He had to return to Scotland alone; his commitment must be to the many, not to one – nor to his own pleasure.

In Merano, Hamish completed his reading of Hugh MacDiarmid's chaotic, 'dashed-off' autobiography, *Lucky Poet*. It had arrived in a bundle of books (sent from Heffer's Bookshop in Cambridge, without expectation of payment), while Hamish was on the Anzio Beachhead. Now he read it with concentrated attention and it stimulated a range of powerful responses; within a few hours, he had the bones of a substantial poem, 'To Hugh MacDiarmid, on reading "Lucky Poet"'.

In 1947, after meeting MacDiarmid, Hamish updated and completed the poem. It mixes praise and criticism, and ruthlessly exposes the

---

6. Unpublished, from notebook.

contradictions that bedevilled both MacDiarmid's life and his poetry: the generosity of soul and soaring genius so regularly undermined by out-bursts of vindictive, Calvinistic authoritarianism. The poem is consciously iconoclastic and when Hamish, in 1947, showed it to Louis MacNeice he advised against publication, saying, 'Hamish, if you want to earn a living in Scotland I think you should keep this to yourself for a while yet.' The poem then remained unpublished until 1967, when it appeared in a special edition of Duncan Glen's magazine *Akros* – in honour of MacDiarmid's 75th birthday.

The poem challenges the hero-poet as an unfathomable genius and as an old bull in the china shop of Scotch sensitivities, and it signalled the start of what was to become a thirty-year 'flyting' between the two most original thinkers in twentieth-century Scottish culture. Hamish's criticism was that MacDiarmid, for all his fire and radicalism, was a political amateur happy to see his genius flare while Scotland and the Scottish people burned. For Hamish this was inexcusable and he had no intention of allowing himself to become a similar 'lone voice, crying in the wilderness – seeking "one immortal lyric" at what ever cost!' He would work, if necessary underground, to effect real political and cultural change – not for the sake of ideology, fame or glory but for the practical well-being, and joy, of the Scottish people.

After five years' war service, Hamish knew a good deal about the practical realisation of goals and he recognised that MacDiarmid, in his isolation, had been snared by the very values he sought to change. He raged like an Old Testament prophet but remained a victim of his Presbyterian upbringing in a nation that exalted its elite – as an elect – and remained in thrall to external authority. MacDiarmid sought change by stamping his genius on the Scots people. Hamish understood that Scotland would only change when the Scottish people changed, and that he who would 'change the people' must subordinate any genius he might have to the greater common good. He foresaw that the ideal of national solidarity must be embraced at the expense of self, ideological purity and sectional advantage, and that the only reality is the here and the now – for individuals and nations alike.

Thus, in Merano in August 1945, Hamish reaffirmed his deep belief that art must address the 'whole' and that both the poet and the politician must go back to 'the folk'. He would work not from the top down but from the bottom up: his process would be the process of evolution itself. He recognised that the genius of mankind resides in, and grows out of, the mass; that cultural development, like natural selection, works not in height or in depth or in time – but 'in breadth' and in the ever-living, ever-breathing present. On his return to Rome, Hamish summed up his thinking: 'There is no value in any personal culture not organically connected with the life of the people – Gaelic + Greek = Happiness.'

In the second week of October Hamish flew back to Britain, landing in the English East Midlands after a six-hour flight. From the back of a lorry travelling towards Cambridge, he observed 'a foreign land':

> England, totally fantastic to the stranger, makes the school of Catholic alcoholics seem matter of fact. The faces – the buses – the Sarcen's Head – the cars (minor effect) driving on the left-hand side of the road – the dull yet subtle landscape – and the people – walking – young men, the broad-bottomed land girls: these are not merely the comedy of England's war – they are the logical extension of England's peace time comedy . . . England, while it remains fantastic, is no subject for the artist – he must wait until it no longer seems fantastic to him – i.e. until he has become part of the fantasy . . . These are merely notes of the impact of reunion – the element of fantasy is present in a great deal of the world – but the community in England is surely unique. This country has always been strange to me but never more so than now . . . I see clearer into the mind of an Italian Partisan than into the mind of a London Dustman . . .

Re-adaption to civilian life, after years of war, was not easy for any returning serviceman, and Hamish was no exception. As an officer he had been supplied with a bed, food, clothes, batman, driver, mess and a public status, all of which were soon noticeable by their absence. And he was shocked to suddenly find himself part of the same self-centred society that he thought he had left for good four years earlier. Dry Drayton welcomed him like a returning hero – but few others did. Some senior officers within the Intelligence Corps had tried to persuade Hamish to stay on in the Corps (there was plenty of work for him) and between 1945 and 1950 there were occasions when, desperately frustrated by shortages of money and political setbacks, he wished he had.

The Cambridgeshire fens in November 1945 were a cold hard place to be and Hamish – despite the marvellous hospitality of the Armstrongs at Dry Drayton – felt embattled and friendless. He missed Italy profoundly and on 5 November wrote to Liana:

> Liana *mia cara*, I arrived in England after a six hour flight. How strange this country seems. It is November and I am without Italy and without sun . . . and without you. Who knows if in Scotland I'll find a more blue heaven, a more sympathetic people! It's very strange – I already feel in me a strong nostalgia for the south.

Maybe I'll come back to Italy sooner than you think! . . . Where may I ever find your elegance, your beauty unless I return to Italy? . . . The Hope for me is to return to Italy and to see you one more time! If you give a letter to Peppino – he can send it to me. Don't forget me: your Hamish.[7]

Those words 'and to see you one more time!' seem to be recognition that a gulf of circumstances has now opened between them, and the poet – in the gentlest of ways – is saying farewell. The war was over. Now, alone, he must look north and travel on, alone. The following statement, set down in his notebook a year or two later, sums up what he now knew his sacred duty to be: service of the Scottish people. He writes:

> Be the depth that awaits
> The hour that sends the wave bright
> Up to the summit of life – bright like a singing light
> From the blaze that for seven years
>   has raged on these parts,
> Spring the Salamander,
>   the spirit of fire,
>
> From the dire conflagration that has reddened the earth
>   sprang up in my heart the blood of my song;
> A song that with lofty notes will crown
>   the summits of time like a dawn.

A poetry directly connected to reality, a poetry transformed into a weapon of struggle against the exploiter, its revolutionary élan opening up large and just prospects for the future, not only remaining true to every cause espoused by the working class (from the General Strike to the Fight for Peace) but risking unpopularity by fighting continuously for a Marxist view of the National Question as it affects Scotland.

> Lie alongside me, put your ear to the ground
>   and listen: the earth rocks with fruitful adventures
> And listen: the sap rises – sweet springs of song
>   like hymns of belief to the buds that will blossom.

---

7. Translated from Italian by Amleto Micozzi.

My brother, no wails and no sterile revolt!
　　Tell the words from the depth,
　　　　tell the fragrance above us
For soon, very soon, we shall harvesters be.

A lark in the skies shall arouse us from darkness
In happy embrace we shall hear in the dawn
You sowers of dreams, the crops have now ripened.[8]

---

8. HH, unpublished, from notebook.

ELEVEN

Edinburgh, South Uist
and Hugh MacDiarmid

*History has shown everywhere that real freedom begins with
the emergence of the gifted individual – and democracy of the
whole tribe is democracy only in name, it is really the tyranny
of a gereocracy – of the old men who initiate the young men
and forcibly impose tradition on the tribe.*

HH[1]

With his army gratuity Hamish bought himself a motorbike, a 500cc
Rudge Special. He liked to joke that he'd bought it 'to go with the fleece-
lined leather jacket I wangled from an over-generous American Quartermaster, one icy day, in the Apennines'. For the next five years this
powerful amaranth motorcycle became part of the Henderson persona
– mobile, aggressive, wide-ranging. It gave him the kind of freedom his
Jeep and driver had given him in Italy and, like George Barker, he enjoyed
life 'astride the creative will'.

During October 1945 Hamish lived at the Dry Drayton rectory, and in
November he celebrated his twenty-sixth birthday in exactly the style he
had anticipated a year earlier in the Appenines. Demob regulations
guaranteed him continued access to university facilities but, after five
years of wartime camaraderie, he found East Anglia dull and effete: 'this
asexual uranism of Cambridge – I could feel it infecting me . . . , like a
thin fog drifting in off the fens' so, taking every opportunity to ride his
motorbike, he went out to Ely and Newmarket and down to London. In
December he packed a tent and set off for Scotland, 'living on the Rudge
and sleeping beside her: I was a one-man poet-band – looking for a
patron'. Crossing the Border, he made a detour to visit the grave of
Thomas the Rhymer, the medieval bard, balladeer and magician. He told
me many years later that, at the graveside, he made three wishes, each of
which had come to pass.

---

1. Unpublished, from notebook.

After that he toured Edinburgh and Glasgow before riding north to Duntruim, near Newtonmore, where he had thought he might complete his Elegies. Like many returning soldiers, Hamish felt the need for isolation, quiet and the landscape of his ancestors. But he seems to have decided that now was not the time – and he returned to Cambridge before Christmas. By Hogmanay, he was back in Glasgow to see in the New Year with his Aunt Mabel – now retired. She was proud and pleased to see her sister's son – 'so tall and handsome in his great coat and captain's cap' – but the company of an aging aunt was not the company Hamish was hungry for; he wanted to talk poetry and politics and immerse himself in the life of the people of Scotland. However, very few Glaswegians knew what to make of a leather-jacketed 'officer Marxist' overkeen to sing songs 'perhaps better left in the barracks'! Hamish was just one of millions of men returning to Britain with extraordinary stories to tell: the whole nation was impoverished and the euphoria of victory had quickly been replaced by a stoical gloom and a hand-to-mouth battle with austerity. Hamish did not want special treatment yet there can be no doubt that 'the hero of Italy' hungered for attention, recognition and some hint of praise but, beyond the walls of the Dry Drayton rectory, very little was forthcoming. In addition, the revolutionary enthusiasm that had so inspired Hamish in Italy was totally lacking in post-war Britain. Consequently Hamish probably felt more alone at this time than at any other period of his life and, in January 1946, he tried to make contact with the Scott family, his 'father's' relatives, in Glasgow. He had deliberately not made contact during the late thirties but now, as a decorated British officer, he felt bold enough to knock at the grand front doors of his distinguished 'uncles' – Isaac and Sir William Scott. Things did not go well. Hamish was unceremoniously rebuffed on the doorstep. They wanted nothing to do with James Scott Henderson – or any of the four illegitimate offspring of James Scott! It is likely that the date of these attempts at a 'family reunion' was 10 January 1946 because, beside that date in Hamish's 1946 notebook, he wrote out this poem entitled 'Shema (Hear O Israel)':

> You who live secure
> In your well-warmed houses
> You who will come back in the evening
> To hot food and welcoming faces:
> > Consider whether this is a man
> > Who labours in mud
> > Who knows no peace
> > Who fights for a crust of bread

Who dies at a yes or a no.
Consider whether this is a woman
Without hair or a name
With no more strength to remember . . .
Eyes empty, and womb cold
As a frog in winter.

Think it over: this has been.
I commend these words to you.
Engrave them on your heart
When you are at home
When you walk on your way
When you lie down to sleep
When you rise in the morning:
Repeat them to your children
   Or else – may your house crumble
   Disease undo you
   And your children turn their faces from you.[2]

This translation by Hamish of a poem by the now famous Italian poet/
scientist Primo Levi is unknown but of great quality and interest. Levi had
returned to Turin in October 1945 after two years in German concentration camps. When, or how, Hamish got hold of this poem is unclear
but his translation is the poem's first rendition in English.

In February, having moved to Edinburgh, Hamish met the Gaelic poet
Sorley MacLean. He stayed in MacLean's flat, and a friendship that was to
prove hugely rewarding to both men was quickly established. MacLean
(wounded at the battle of Alamein) was teaching English at Boroughmuir
High School in Edinburgh. Hamish sang, they read each other's poetry,
they talked about the future of Scotland. Hamish was particularly impressed by Sorley's long poem 'The Cuillin', written in 1939/40. It
addresses the history of Gaeldom, the landscape of Skye and the possibilities of a socialist future in Scotland. It owes a good deal to MacDiarmid,
but Hamish recognised it to be a highly original poem – indeed, the equal of
any poetry being created anywhere in Europe. He copied the poem out in
both Gaelic and English so that he could translate it into Italian and take it
to Italy, where he was certain it would be greatly appreciated. Hamish's
contact with MacLean also reinforced his own impulse to assert the
'valorous' in poetry and not to shy from being unremittingly 'ambitious'
as he worked on his own *Elegies for the Dead in Cyrenaica*. Following

---

2. Unpublished translation by HH of Prima Levi's poem 'Shema (Hear O Israel)',
 1946.

Sorley's marriage to Renee Cameron in July 1946, Hamish continued to use the MacLean flat. Renee liked him: 'He brought the sunshine of Italy into the winter terraces of Edinburgh. He was a bohemian. He was so proud of the bottles he brought in! Going to bed late at night – with Hamish encamped – could be a problem, you never really knew who was where, or where you were; and often I'd lie there, hoping that the man climbing into bed beside me was Sorley – but not daring to find out!'

From Edinburgh, Sorley sent Hamish out to Argyll to meet George Campbell Hay, the other outstanding modernist Gaelic poet. Hay had initially refused military call-up – for a mixture of personal, moral and political reasons – and been imprisoned before being sent to Tunisia to fight with the Eighth Army. He was anything but a natural killer and his experiences led him to write some of the most powerful and shocking poetry of the war. Hay was not a native Gaelic speaker but a brilliant scholar who had felt impelled to learn the language of his ancestors, and did so in the company of the fishermen of Loch Fyne. He had great gentleness of spirit, and by the time Hamish met him he had suffered a series of nervous breakdowns from which he was never to recover fully. Hamish felt 'here is another great man'; indeed he seems to have seen Hay as a living embodiment 'of the men of peace of the blessed glens' whom he had described in his poem 'The Mountain', at the age of fourteen.

From Argyll Hamish rode north to Morayshire, where he found himself fascinated by the Lossiemouth dialect and set down long 'theatrical' exchanges overheard in pubs: 'Fat kinn o' man wad ye ca' me, see, that wad lat ony man hale ma wife oot o' ha bed by the hair o' ha heid an no fecht him?'! They sounded, he said, 'like conversations from another age!' Riding west into Lochaber he was delighted to hear Highland English (out of Gaelic) still playing an important role in the preservation of a uniquely Highland way of life. In particular he enjoyed the savagery evident in Highland wit: 'Whisky is what makes you shoot at the landlords – and miss 'em!; – Never seen such an array of melancholy mugs; – If you go to hell, look like the deil – if you come to Argyll, look like a Campbell; – If you're Christians, you'll be grateful for it – if you're not, it's good enough for you!; – The inhabitants of Tarbert? They'd be better off in a Home! – You speak Gaelic – Ah well, you'll be a gentleman anyway.' He also listed English phrases that, he felt, expressed 'the genius of the Gaelic language in both grammar and diction':

> The bull walking like a dandy
> A stroll on the delectable mountains
> The Scotsman is a hero
> The oars of the boat are here

A bull is in the field
A disc is in the officer's hand
The ears of a cat
A lock is on the door
The lock of the door is broken
The darling of the people is here[3]

Hamish recognised Gaelic culture as still expressing the wholeness of lives lived in contact 'with nature and the wisdom of the ages – always young, always in the process of becoming'. And from Morar – where sea, white sands, islands and mountains create one of the most beautiful places on earth – he wrote a letter to his friend Geordie Hamilton: 'It is in the unsounded deeps of the great laments and in the ecstatic vortex of the dance that you will find the Scottish unity – last night we had a most attractive country-dance from over your way called "The Gay Gordons". It's a really graceful dance, but flamboyant too, with an élan. We danced it to Mauersfontein on the pipes . . . And today is a morning of splendid winter sunshine. If you could only be here now you'd see a vision of Scotland, of the Sgurr of Eigg and dark green Arisaig of the birchwoods, that would take the sting out of pre-destined damnation . . .'

By April, Hamish was in Portree, on the Isle of Skye. He had expected to pick up a letter, post restante, from the poet Maurice Lindsay but because Lindsay had addressed his letter to Hamish Hamilton (the publisher), Hamish was not given it! It was a bad start to a relationship that was to get worse over the years. He then toured his old haunts around Uig before crossing the Minch to North Uist, where he met some of his old 51st Highland Division friends. Years later John A.S. MacDonald wrote to Hamish reminding him of their meeting in the Lochmaddy Hotel in 1946: 'You were renewing war-time friendships (Rev. Norman MacDonald and Norman Robertson) – the food in the hotel was superb, and there was an atmosphere of almost joyfulness about, which I, at least, never experienced before or after . . .'

On his return to Edinburgh, Hamish introduced himself to Helen Cruickshank, a retired civil servant from the Scottish Office and Scotland's outstanding woman poet. She was the leading activist in Scottish PEN (an international association of writers), a generous patron of Hugh MacDiarmid and a self-appointed 'mother hen' to Scotland's younger poets. A middle-aged spinster, originally from Montrose, she gave her life to Scots literature and Scotland's poets with single-minded passion. She took an

3. HH, notebook jottings.

immediate liking to Hamish and, for the next thirty years, each loyally supported the other. Helen told Hamish she thought there were about thirty reputable poets in Scotland but that the number might be doubled. Hamish told her that he would see this number multiplied by not less than one hundred! Helen's list of the best writers of Scots verse included Marion Angus, William Souter, Lewis Spence, Norman McCaig (the spelling changed in the fifties), Sydney Goodsir Smith, Hugh MacDiarmid, Alexander Scott, Adam Drinan and Douglas Young. She encouraged Hamish to meet all of them as soon as possible.

So on he wandered – as he was to do for ten years – seeking poets and finding shelter wherever a sympathetic ear, pocket or friend would house him. Indeed, it was not until Hamish married, in 1959, that he got himself a genuinely permanent place of abode. Not surprisingly, Hamish's need of a bed was to become infamous! So much so that the obsolete Scots word 'to sorn' was reintroduced into the language. 'To *sorn*: to come for supper and lodge for a month' is how the writer Alastair Reid has defined it, or 'to do a Henderson' as one of the less charitable muttered.

Hamish's wandering lifestyle was partly a product of need but also a consciously didactic act: he wanted to nurture 'charity' in his fellow man, and he wanted to test the 'human will' in Scotland. Would Scots still welcome the stranger, respond to ideas, espouse poetry, demand political change, sing late into the night? Not surprisingly, the arrival of this hungry, leather-clad giant off a motorbike aroused many different responses – from the most generous hospitality and love, to contempt, anger and embittered rejection. Renee MacLean, Marian Blythman and Janey Buchan are three wives of poets who deserve Scotland's thanks for the suppers and beds they provided. The first was a true Highland host, the other two were communists – and generous to a fault. Janey Buchan did not personally, or politically, much like Hamish but many was the night she and her husband, Norman Buchan, 'saved the big fellow's bacon'. In half-anger, she told how one morning he'd turned up just as she and Norman were leaving for work. 'We didn't want him! But I said, Hamish, you know where the bed is – there's some fruit in the fruit bowl – you can help yourself! I never thought he would eat the lot! When we came back that evening, he was still fast asleep on the sofa – with everything gone! Fruit was hard to get in those days. The fireplace was full of apple-cores, orange peel, plum stones and an empty coconut shell! He'd eaten a whole coconut! He must have been starving . . .'

During the late spring of 1946 Hamish got himself involved in discussions about the cultural development of the New Towns then being planned. In typed notes he set out what he believed were the important questions that planners should address at East Kilbride: '. . . the provision you are making for the cultural life of the new community is an issue of the utmost importance . . . life in a new town should be harmonious, joyous and complete – with popular participation in activities like a Theatre Workshop conceived as an integral part of the plan . . .' He also crossed to Dublin, where he somehow made contact with an impoverished family that turned out to be full of genius – the Behans, one of the great families of modern Ireland. They lived in the North Dublin slums amidst a chaos of revolutionary, idealistic nationalism that greatly appealed to Hamish. They embraced song and poetry, socialism, armed struggle, the pleasures of the pub and a hard-come-by meal. 'The Mother of all the Behans' was Kathleen: her brother Peader O' Cearnaigh had written the Irish national anthem; her sons Brendan, Dominic, Seamus and Brian would soon win international fame. They were magnificent company and Hamish had not felt so much at home since his fireside nights with the Partisans above San Lorenzo. Hamish took pleasure with the Behans but also recognised that their abundance of vitality and nationalist commitment was something that Scotland deserved a dose of and he quickly cemented an all-singing, no-holds-barred partnership with the Behan family that was to have a long-term consequence not just for Scotland and Ireland but for England too.

Throughout this time Hamish was in regular contact with a number of his comrades in Italy. At the beginning of April, Fritz wrote from the Italian Tyrol: after discussing the linguistic, ethnic and political problems of his 'disputed homeland', Fritz asks Hamish for help in emigrating – before moving on to describe his girlfriend, who speaks Chinese and four other languages. When he does this he gives us a vivid insight into the shamanic character Hamish recurrently assumed during this period:

> Her name is Marion . . . she seems to have a special preference for you – and frequently expresses her desire to spend the night with the two of us, to be sitting in front of a glowing fireplace, between the two of us, without speaking, only listening to our talk – a big dog resting at our feet, our faces shining in the gloom – a shudder would be running down our backs . . . I love to recall you – back in the days of our companion-ship – to revive my memories of you which are extremely pleasant . . . Many thanks for all the interest you have taken in my future, my parents appreciate it very much – there are still some good and true men on this rotten earth. Your Fritz.

Luigi Castigliano was now working as an English translator in Milan but, as a Classics graduate, had applied to the University of Milan to study for a PhD. On Hamish's advice, he had decided that his subject should be 'The relationship between James Joyce's "Ulysses" and Homer's "Odyssey"' and, over the next four years, Hamish acted as Luigi's long-distance and very unofficial thesis supervisor. On 23 March 1946, Luigi writes in English:

Dear Hamish, – I have received in quick succession three parcels from you, with the books and 'Our Time' and 'Penguin New Writing' with the poem for LC: well that was a treat – I had never seen my 'ego' in print before – I really must thank you with all my heart – I am absolutely bubbling with joy . . . I listen religiously to the British Forces Station every day, and sing or whistle one of the songs you taught me every five minutes, regular as clockwork – also, the Scottish tunes: I remember them all . . . Could you send me the words of 'The Road to the Isles' and that beautiful one that goes – 'Charlie, Charlie, wha wouldnae fight for ye / King o' oor Highland hearts, Bonnie Prince Charlie . . .' and 'The wearin' o' the Green' . . . Ever since I left you I have been all for Scotland . . . In less than two months with the Argylls I was able to produce a really good imitation of a Scottish accent – I know all about Inveraray and Clan Campbell . . . I think with great sympathy of Scotland because I often think of you, and you created Scotland for me . . . It is nearly midnight – I shall go to bed now, thinking about the glorious evenings we spent in that little room upstairs in Sassonero . . .

In June, Luigi wrote again: 'I practise translating on MacDiarmid, with the help of an interesting fellow, a student of the Catholic University, born somewhere in the Highlands out of a Sicilian father and Gaelic mother, graduated in Rome as a Div. Doct.; I met him during the war, mysteriously acting as a double agent – as an Italian and British soldier: now he has graduated at the Catholic University and gone back to another mysterious job in some sort of very secretive police'. (Whether this Sicilian Scot was a genuine friend or an agent planted to watch Luigi (and Hamish) is unclear but, when Hamish returned for an eight-month stay in Italy in 1950, both Luigi and Hamish were placed under surveillance.)

By mid-April Hamish was back in Cambridge, hoping to use it as a base to advance both his literary and political careers. He was also looking for 'heroes' to join him in his crusade for Scottish self-government, and one of the first people he went to see was Lorne Maclaine Campbell VC, famed as one of the 'bravest of the brave' from the Desert War and one of the men who had helped him form his Anzio pipe band. Campbell was a Highland gentleman with considerable military and social influence and Hamish appears to have believed that Campbell might join him in 'the great adventure' that he hoped would win Scotland her freedom. Unfortunately, his imagination had run well ahead of reality and Hamish was hugely disappointed by a man he describes as 'a lag figure – talking of the "Volunteer" as opposed to the "lowest conscript"! I wish he would get down off his talking-horse, fire a round at the skyhawks of political rancour ever-wheeling around him, and stand on his own legs as an individual. This would be more characteristic of a descendant of Highlanders. . . He should be evicted from the croft of his self-complacency and forced to emigrate to the deserts of obscurity, where he belongs. . . He asserts his war experience so often that one would be forgiven for suspecting – if one didn't know personally of Campbell's war record – that he had never heard a shot fired in anger . . .' Thus, Hamish was made to realise that Campbell was so entirely a product of his English education, his British Army career and establishment success that 'Scotland' was not, and never would be, a living political issue. Hamish was chastened; he knew he had overstepped the mark and decided he must, in future, take nothing for granted: 'analyse the characteristics of everyone from hidalgo to factory hand – and use Eliot's "technique of sincerity" – his exploration of language and thought . . .'

Hamish was equally disappointed by the pseudo-communist politics of Cambridge; on 29 April 1946, he wrote an angry letter to David Holbrook (a Communist Party activist, later to become a conservative literary critic and eccentric academic) with ironic scorn:

> Dear David – Sorry I can't come to your group meeting. If I did I'd infect all your members with chicken pox – a feat of divisionism and sabotage unparalleled in the history of the C.P. in this long suffering country . . . But I think you ought to change the subject of your discussion to 'Can a Communist talk utter Clock?' It seems to me that would be bringing the thing down to brass tacks . . . You might as well ask 'Can a reactionary get lovely drunk?' Or 'Can a Russian appreciate Giorgione?' . . . Here anyway is some good poetry written by a progressive (for a change) author – a member of the Communist party and a writer in Gaelic, his native language.
>
> > Beyond poverty, consumption, fever, agony,
> > Beyond hardship, wrong, violence, distress,
> > Beyond misery, despair, hatred, treachery,
> > Beyond guilt and defilement, watchfully,
> > Heroically is seen the Cuillin,
> > Rising on the other side of sorrow.[4]
>
> Yours fraternally H + his mark

---

4. The last lines of Sorley MacLean's 'The Cuillin', in *From Wood to Ridge: Collected Poems of Sorley MacLean* (Carcanet Press 1989).

There were many 'Holbrooks' in Cambridge, and Hamish determinedly turned his back on them to explore the underbelly of the city's pubs and fairgrounds. On 'Midsummer Common' he watched a group of Irish Travellers singing 'Dance to your Shadow' and 'Bold Fenian Men' as they flew 'in flying boats, swinging in the night sky'. It was a synchronous moment; 'Bold Fenian Men' had been written by his friend Peader O' Cearnaigh (Kathleen Behan's brother) – a man with whom he had been drinking and singing just a few weeks earlier – here was the 'folk tradition' in action and it had a power:

> 'Twas down by the glen-side I met an old woman
> A-pluckin young nettles, and she ne'er saw me comin.
> I stood still to listen to the tune she was hummin
>   Glory O, glory o to the bold Fenian men . . .

> Some fell by the wayside, some died with the stranger
> And wise men have said that their cause was a failure
> They loved poor old Ireland, they never feared danger
>   Glory O, glory o to the bold Fenian men . . .

It is a song that sculpts violence into cultural and political order and Hamish saw it as a product of realities that modern societies could learn much from. Social change would not come through self-satisfied word play or empty debate; peace would not come by shoving heads in sand. Hamish saw the pyrotechnics of Holbrook's debating skills as a skin-deep facade behind which 'the safely sailing' would continue to sail – while the needy drowned in the shimmering wake. But, here, in the throats of these Irish tinkers – floating in their boats in the East Anglian sky – he saw flesh of his flesh and bone of his bone. Such singers, not Holbrooks, carried the key to the Gates. In London, he passed these 'great rebel songs' on to Hedli Anderson (Louis MacNeice's wife) and in a letter he once told me that she was the first singer to present 'Banks of Sicily' as a cabaret song.

Hamish did, however, establish several important intellectual relationships in Cambridge during his post-war year, notably with the great Italian scholar Piero Sraffa and two young communist radicals – Marian Sugden, a young English graduate, and E.P. Thompson, soon to become a distinguished social historian. A larger group gathered around them: all spoke out against the Cold War, the atomic bomb and the proliferation of nuclear weapons. They were in favour of dialogue with the new 'socialist democracies' of Eastern Europe, and campaigned in support of those New Commonwealth nations then seriously beginning to demand their national independence. The group were anti-imperialist, vigorously supported the United Nations and advocated new approaches to the maintenance of international peace. Hamish's leadership, on many of these issues, was accepted as read – and his debating skills were such that he was now offered life membership of the Cambridge Union. It was an honour he was proud to accept. Consequently, the 'Voice' that he had presumed would pass 'forever into silence' was now heard again:

No! The Western bloc is an anachronism and millions of people feel it to be so. We must build a Sane, Scientific, Egalitarian Society – embracing not only Western Europe, not only Eastern Europe – but the whole world. I ask this house to reject this motion and look with courage and understanding towards the future . . . If Bevin were wanting to help forward Fascism in Greece, he couldn't be playing his hand more adroitly. He's like Chamberlain – when he flew to Berchesgarden just at the moment when the generals were planning to bump Hitler off! Chamberlain! Chamberlain ensured that Hitler would live to fight another day! Now Bevin does his bit! . . . The tragic sight of a Labour Foreign secretary helping monarchies, even discredited monarchies, back into power, or on their feet again – is obscene . . .[5]

And as a new generation of students listened to this voice – fresh from the battlefront of Italy – Hamish may well have thought of himself as a new Spartacus. During 1946 Hamish founded the Cambridge University Italian Society and took part in a major BBC Italian-language broadcast to Italy. He was also active in the Buchenwald Association: he spoke out in support of 'the New Parliament Men' (political militants within the Armed Services) led by Bert Ramelson and Phil Piratin; and he joined the campaign requesting clemency for those Scots still imprisoned for wartime 'disobedience and mutiny'. The following letter, from an ex-Army Intelligence colleague, Jack Truten of Leeds, gives a clear idea of his reputation as a 'revolutionary' at this time. 'Dear Hamish, . . . whenever I hear of lock-outs, murder, arson, strikes, street barricades etc. in Italy – I find an answer in the presence of a member of the "Buchenwald Association", sitting atop his Jeep and striking at the heart of the Italian – with songs and words beloved of his partigiani friends . . . I'm glad you had the enthusiasm to lay the foundations of an Italian Club at Cambridge – with such a scintillating committee, I cannot doubt its success. I presume you have so far prevented yourself from being sent down.'

---

5. HH, speech notes, Henderson archive.

In fact Hamish was not 'up' to be sent down but like the 'good student', when Hamish did finally leave Cambridge, he wrote out a simple list of future aims and values: 'My fellow countrymen of the word – Voltaire, Joyce, Lenin, MacDiarmid. The hard way is the only way. The worst enemy is *acedia*. The greatest mental weakness the failure to tackle it at the roots. Stick to your guns. If you win your children will justify you. If you don't it's just too bad . . .' He also translated these lines by the French surrealist poet Denis Seurat (later to be used as the introduction to his 'Heroic Song for the runners of Cyrene'):

> Without suffering and death one learns nothing.
> We should not know the difference between the visions
> Of the intellect and the facts.
> Only those ideas are acceptable that hold through
> Suffering and death . . .
> Life is that which leaps.

In the summer of 1946, Hamish returned, permanently, to Scotland. He had been 'away' more than eighteen years. He applied to Moray House College of Education in Edinburgh, and was accepted on a special two-term teacher training course in secondary education. An Army grant was available and teaching was one of the few professions open to people regarded as communists. He had been reading James Boswell and, as he biked north, his head was full of the thoughts and exploits of one of the great figures of Scotland's Age of Enlightenment and a man with whom Hamish identified strongly.

> Boswell is not conceited although he has, as the Scots say, 'a good conceit of himself' . . . He had a vanity so huge, good-natured and universal that it seems to have gone through some extraordinary qualitative change and become humility. One gains the impression (from the memoirs) that Boswell has told absolute veracity about himself (and Johnson); I do not merely mean his rumbustious descriptions of his sexual adventures in the bedrooms, in the parks, in the streets and courts – but even on the very bridges of the metropolis – with the Thames running underneath . . . How strange that this should lie underground for nearly two hundred years and then, of a sudden, break surface and be made immortal!

Hamish embarked on his new studies with his usual seriousness and sought the philosophical foundations of the art of teaching. He began a systematic study of the philosophy of A.N. Whitehead, whose unified vision complemented many aspects of Hamish's his own thinking, and he notes:

> Everything in the universe has life – the capacity for appropriating experiences into a unity. This appropriation, which [Whitehead] terms 'prehension', implies the power of self-creation. The act of self-creation is an 'occasion of experience'; every event is such an occasion. Whitehead insists that a determining characteristic of life is self-enjoyment . . . passivity is against the nature of things. 'It is nonsense to conceive of nature as static fact – there is no nature apart from transition.' . . . The common principle by which Whitehead hopes to abolish all the contradictions and dualism implicit in most philosophy is the principle of 'life' – the capacity for the appropriation of experiences into a unity. He therefore understood that every entity contains life – a stone as well as a heart. Whitehead makes every entity alive as well as lifeless, mental as well as physical. This becomes a vision of the Universe evolving dialectically under the imminent control of God. This leads him back to idealism – truth, beauty and harmony. Whitehead is the last great bourgeois philosopher: he recognises nature to be dialectical but remains an idealist.

> Among the philosophies of escape, of evasion, none has ever attained a greater notoriety than Existentialism. Post war Paris has gone crazy over it . . . Existentialism – the philosophy of existence – is the revolt of life against thought. It springs from the wish to exult *living* (experience, acting, existing) as against *thinking* (especially about life). It wishes to replace the problem of 'death' by the problem 'I die' . . . But surely, reflective thought is itself part of *life*: it can be action, it can be passion even! . . . And, it is not new – one can recognise as existential thought much of the philosophy of the Ancient World: and literature, to be literature, must desire to be *life* not an idea of life . . .'

Hamish did not enjoy his time at Moray House: in fact his distaste for the place was so great that he expunged the place from his mind and biographical record – very much as he expunged his years in the Clapham orphanage. This was a place that was not *him*. Lectures were didactic, authoritarian and deeply Presbyterian; many advanced exactly the values he was now determined to oppose. At first his Moray House notebooks are crammed but – very soon – more and more interjections begin to litter the margins. Of a lecture by 'Maxwell', Hamish writes: 'As for those with a low IQ, he dismissed the poor devils with the grim relish of a Free Kirk minister consigning lost souls to the Inferno. The elect are those with high IQs! You could hardly believe the grim relish with which he condemned them to be hewers of wood and drawers of water – for all eternity . . . The whole lecture stank of a decayed and disqualified religion perpetuating itself . . .'

When he presented a seminar entitled 'Scotland and Calvinism', Hamish opened with a quotation from the Italian author Leo Ferrero:

'Who has put this sombre intoxication which is death into our hearts?' It may be objected that, having been brought up in the Episcopal church, I am disqualified from treating this subject. It is true I was not subjected to the full rigours of Calvinist influence, and thank Christ for that: but no one who spends the crucial years of his childhood in Scotland and suffers in his flesh the bite of the Scottish education system can fail to be marked by Calvinism for life. – How was it that the Scots, the people who had produced Dunbar – were the nation to succumb most utterly to this dreadful, life-destroying creed? . . . the famous 'dourness' of the Scots is not really a Scottish quality – but a Calvinist quality. And this dourness cannot be a product of climate for it is not among the inhabitants of the bitter, biting East Coast – but among the Highlanders of the mild, Gulf-stream watered West, where palms grow and rhododendrons run wild – that we find the glummest, direst Calvinists of them all!

In the presence of some of the Moray House staff, Hamish notes that he felt close to 'the authentic flower of evil' and his distaste erupted in a song-poem that rages against these self-elected, life-hating, censorious teachers whom he now recognised as attempting to hound him, as their betters had hounded his mother a generation earlier – for *her* sin of giving *him* life! The poem's title is 'Floret Silva Undique' and it should be sung to the refrain of a song in Hugo van Hofmannsthal's 'Jedermann'. It has not been published, although twenty years later Hamish developed it into a much longer song/poem with the same title.

> *Floret silva undique*
> For bonnie Janet my spreit is wae,
> I'm feart she's waled her anither lad:
> The thocht I've tyned her, it maks me mad.
> Aye, nou they're daffan aneath the slae:
> *Floret silva undique.*

Vere natus orbis est.
I'm thinkin tae gang your ain gait's best
Och, pox on sunshine, I love the mirk
The muirland kirk haps quick an' deid.
In seely autumn I'll hae my rest –
Vere natus orbis est.[6]

Hamish's teaching practice went well but, by the end of November, he had had enough of Moray House and, with winter approaching, he packed his bundle, got on his bike and took the road west. He had seen an advertisement for a temporary part-time lecturer with the Lochaber Workers Education Association (WEA) and, having posted his application, he set out for Fort William – via South Uist. For the first time since leaving Italy the urge to write poetry was strong upon him. He decided the time had come to go to the Hebrides to work – and await whatever call came. He landed at Lochboisdale and booked in at the Lochboisdale Hotel where, to his delight, he found himself treated not as a renegade student but as a bard. The hotel's owner, Finlay MacKenzie, was a very old man, a piper – whom Hamish later claimed embodied the heroic values of pre-literate Celtic society and an age when music and poetry were valued beyond price. Finlay offered Hamish open-ended board and lodging in exchange for his poems, his songs and his company.

Uist gave Hamish tranquillity and a sense of cultural continuity that enabled him to draw his *Elegies for the Dead in Cyrenaica* towards a conclusion – more Gaelic, less African, less German. It was here in South Lochboisdale, that Hamish wrote his 'Heroic Song to the Runners of Cyrene', the poem that locked his ten elegies into their philosophical and narrative sequence. Life in an almost purely Gaelic community also gave Hamish renewed personal, cultural and political confidence. He saw Uist as the kind of community that Karl Marx had described a century earlier when he wrote: 'there is no country in Europe that does not possess, in some remote corner, at least one remnant people, left over from an earlier population, forced back and subjugated by the nation which later became the repository of historical development'. And, to Hamish, Uist exemplified the kind of society that communism proposed – a cohesive, democratic community of equals – a form of governance responding to the particular needs of a society shaped by physical and historical circumstances – at once always changing yet more constant than 'the

6. HH, unpublished poem, from notebook, 1946, later developed into a much longer poem entitled 'Floret Silva Undique' c. 1970, published in the *Collected Poems*.

recent charge for progress supposed'. The people of Uist might be 'a remnant' but they were survivors: work might still be done with the *cas curom*, fish caught on long-lines, peat carried in creels, tweed waulked to worksongs handed down across centuries, men might still wrestle bare-chested on horseback and, in the ceilidh-houses, songs and stories thousands of years old were still being told, but to these houses came letters from every corner of the globe to be read like newspapers. This was an educated and highly adaptive community. Each morning, children would lead the cattle to the *cuidhe* before going up to their tin-roofed school to study English and hear about the battle with TB – at last being won. Hamish also knew that Hebridean losses during the two World Wars had been colossal – out of all proportion to the population – and he wanted to be with the island people and to serve them. He thought they would honour his poetry and song – and they did.

One day, in early December, Hamish heard 'a stranger, playing the pipes down the corridor! So I went out to see what was going on. It was Seamus Innes, from Ireland! He was working for the Irish Folklore Commission, and had come to join me!' Seamus was a folklorist and one of the world's great uilleann pipers – he was also a man with a nose for the pleasures of life and these two very tall men immediately got on like a croft-house on fire. The ceilidhs grew bigger and bigger. One morning, they rode north to Grimsay, 'to experience the Protestant North'. They soon found themselves being welcomed into a house where:

> There, on the table was a great open bible – the winter sun was coming in through one small window: we sat down and were offered tea and cakes. There was a beautiful gravitas in every word spoken; we seemed to inhabit a painting by Rembrandt: it was an amazing thing – we had crossed a causeway and entered another world. One could not help but be moved and impressed but – it was not what either Seamus or I wanted – at least, not at that moment, and we soon headed back to the Catholic South to forget, and not remember, our sins![7]

From Uist, Hamish crossed to the isle of Canna, to spend a long weekend with the Gaelic folklorist John Lorne Campbell and his wife, the American photographer, Margaret Fay Shaw. Climbing to the top of Canna hill, Hamish described the view of the Cuillin, seen from that low vantage point, as 'the finest of them all'. John Lorne Campbell was a cool, calm gentleman scholar: Hamish was greatly impressed by him and, before

---

7. HH, from conversation with TN.

leaving, he told him he would dedicate his Fifth Elegy (the most, geographically, Highland) to him – John Lorne Campbell of Canna.

Back in Lochboisdale, Hamish wrote a letter to the *Glasgow Herald* on the subject of 'Lallans and Plastic Scots'. It was not published, but Hamish decided it could provide him with the ideal introduction to Hugh Mac-Diarmid – whom he had fought shy of contacting for more than a year. He sent his letter, and a personal note. There is no record that MacDiarmid replied, though he was normally meticulous in his correspondence. Hamish was disappointed, but he was anything but isolated in the Hebrides: he was in regular contact with Cambridge, London, Milan and Rome. One letter came from his friend the 'Carravaggioesque raggamuffin' Silvano Beltrami; Hamish sent back a 'Romanised version' of 'The Bonnie Bonnie Banks of Loch Lomond' and a short poem entitled 'Poem for Silvano'. This poem, like his earlier letter to Liana, can be interpreted as the drawing of a line under a friendship that was now over. It was Uist that allowed Hamish to now break the emotional bands that Italy had wound so powerfully around him. For the first time since his boyhood, he was content in Scotland: South Uist was a world away from Rome, and the Hebrides would now become the launching pad for his new life.

Hamish spent Hogmanay 1946 with Finlay MacKenzie, Alastair MacLean (Sorley MacLean's brother, GP on South Uist) and their Lochboisdale friends. On 2 January 1947, he ceilidhed with Archie MacDonald and during the evening heard 'Bean Airchie', one of the great tradition bearers of South Uist, sing 'Tàladh Dhomnaill Ghuirm' ('Blue Donald'). It was another defining moment in Hamish's life: here was high poetry dating back to Druidic times, here was pure pleasure, here was a woman he would return 'to record' and applaud for years to come. Hamish translated her song:

> The sun rising
> And it without a spot on it
> Nor on the stars.
> When the son of my King
> Comes fully armed,
> The strength of the universe with you,
> The strength of the sun
> And the strength of the bull
> That leaps highest.
>
> That woman asked
> Another woman
> What ship is that

> Close to the shoreline?
> Three masts of willow on it,
> A rudder of gold on it,
> A well of wine in it,
> A well of pure water in it.[8]

Next morning Hamish set off by ferry for Mallaig; he had been offered the Lochaber job. On the evening of 4 January he signed in at the Station Hotel in Fort William but awoke next day 'to find my neck and head swollen into the single form of a mangold!' Hamish had mumps and was ordered to spend twelve days in a darkened room. On 20 January he took up lodgings at Nevis Bank, Fort William, and on the evening of 28 January gave his first WEA lecture at Fort William School. The following week he delivered a similar lecture at Inverlochy School and, thereafter, gave talks at each school on alternate weeks. His course was entitled 'An exploration of the Contemporary World' and lecture subjects included 'Italy and Current Affairs', Modern Idealism', 'Germany', 'A.N. Whitehead', 'Existentialism', 'Scientific Humanism', 'The Arab World of Spain', 'Incompatible Ideals in Rabelais' and 'The New Democracies'. One member of his class, Murdoch MacKenzie of Dornie, Kyle of Lochalsh, described Hamish's classes as 'well attended because Hamish had the gift of making a dull subject interesting and humorous – I remember him talking abut the Partisans in Italy, and I shall always be grateful to him for setting my mind on higher things . . .'

The workload was far from onerous and, with plenty of time on his hands, Hamish was soon regularly biking to Glasgow where, one weekend, he met Dominic Behan. Twenty-five years later, Dominic painted a vivid picture of their meeting.

> In February 1947, I stepped off a boat and set foot for the first time in St Mungo's mansion. I was tired, hung-over and hungry . . . there was a tall Scotsman in kilt of the Macdonlad [sic] tartan addressing me in ringing tones from the corner of Byers Road . . . 'I hope,' says I, 'that there's something more substantial than oats in that sporran of yours, Hughie.' 'Ah, a gradh,' he whispered in perfect Gaelic, 'Ta luach an deoch isteach I.' (There's the price of a jar inside it.) Taking a step for a hint we went off to a hostelry and, in no time at all, Glasgow took on a roseate hue. I sang, 'Such a parcel o' rogues in a

---

8. HH translation from the traditional Gaelic. Published in Timothy Neat and John MacInnes, *The Voice of the Bard* (Canongate 1999).

nation', abused Southern invaders, praised the Covenanters and, mellow with Uisge Beatha, agreed with the man, the 'English were an innocent enough race when their guns and things were taken from them.' . . . I went home with Hughie, woke up broke next morning, asked him for the loan of his kilt and I swear it was the loveliest article that ever adorned a pawn-office counter. Four pounds the man in the shop gave me on it . . .[9]

Across Britain, the winter of 1947 was long and cold but the Western Highlands missed most of the snow and basked for weeks in 'Arctic sunshine'. Hamish notes: 'Ben Nevis in snow is magnificent from Corpach but – Fort William can be gloomy and I decided to move out to Arisaig on the coast and to live amidst what is one of the most beautiful landscapes in the world.' On 6 February he walked to Prince Charlie's Cave at Borrodale, on the 7th he attended a dance at the Fort William Hall. On 25 March he was special guest at the 'Anniversary Dinner and Social Evening of the Highland Independence Party' in the Grand Hotel, Fort William. Hamish's address makes it clear that his nationalism was not just Scottish and socialist, but also Highland and Gaelic – and his message, delivered in the heart of the Jacobite Highlands, was well received. Extracts from his speech were published as the 'end-editorial' of the March issue of the *Voice of Scotland* and précis what must have been a ferocious attack on both the Royal family and the British political establishment:

Only a single Scottish MP (Mr William Gallagher, Communist MP for West Fife) raised his voice in protest against the African tour of the King, Queen and Princesses, and no one – least of all any of the panjandrums of the Burns Federation – quoted the lines, written by Burns in an inn in Stirling, which end:

The injured Stuart line is gone.
A race outlandish fills their throne;
An idiot race to honour lost;
Who know them best, despise them most.

Surely no lines could be more applicable at a time when we find the King speaking of South Africa as giving an example to the world in the harmonious living together of diverse peoples. The fact of the

---

9. From an article published in the *Glasgow Herald* as part of the John MacLean celebration, 1973.

matter is that there is no place on earth where the black people are worse treated; and it is an appalling commentary on the condition of public opinion that the King should be allowed to make statements so utterly at variance with the facts . . .[10]

Hamish's speech was a spear-thrust at British complicity in the development of the Apartheid system in South Africa – and shows him to have been in at the very beginnings of the Anti-Apartheid Movement. Thus when, in 1964, Hamish wrote his great Anti-Apartheid song 'Rivonia' (at the time of the trial of Nelson Mandela), he was continuing his pursuit of a cause he had outlined in 1947. This was the year in which Princess Elizabeth married Philip Mountbatten and 'the press twaddle' that the wedding engendered inspired Hamish to write a poem entitled 'Here's to the Maiden'. It too was published in the March issue of the *Voice of Scotland* and, while it documents a notorious event in Highland history, the narrative is powerfully contemporary

> *(in 1331 the heads of 50 executed 'misdoaris'*
> *decorated the castle of Eilean Donan.)*

> When Moray rade intil Wester Ross
>   tae further the rue o' law
> he was 'richt blythe' tae see the heids
>   that flooerd sae weel that waa'.

> Noo, efter Sasunn has felt the win'
>   and lowsed her grup o' wer lugs
> I wadnae mind providin' for show
>   juist twa-three elegant mugs.

> A wheen Lavals got leid i' the guts
>   or danced their wey tae the rope –
> but oor Scots Quislings hae aa been spared
>   tae gie us the same auld soap.

> Ye'll see them shinin' the Southron's buits
>   or kissin' his weel-faured seat.
> They's be mair use adornin' the waas
>   o' yon tour whaur the three lochs meet.

---

10. *Voice of Scotland* March 1947.

The heids o' a score o' Vichy Scots
wad suit these partisan days,
and mak mair sense as an ornament
than dizzens o' wild Macraes![11]

Hamish's attack is directed at Scotland's 'quislings' and it retains, even today, the power to shock. The rendition of such poems, however, did nothing to reduce Hamish's popularity with the Lochaber ladies; they saw him as a Byronic figure, whom they took pleasure in delighting. His diary records: '27 March 'Walk in the direction of Morar with Margery'; 28 March 'Larachmore, with Kate Post'; 29 March 'Mass, with Miss MacLeod'. After discussing the depopulation of the Highlands with an old lady in Arisaig, Hamish quotes her as asking him: 'Can't Hugh MacDiarmid do something about it?' Hamish was thrilled by this suggestion of 'bardic omnipotence' and noted; 'Although 5000 people in Edinburgh might see only a man talking to himself, in one Lochaber cottage MacDiarmid has had his wish granted and been greeted as – *the bard, the deliverer, dexioseiros.*'

Hamish was by now an experienced motorcyclist and the speed and swoop of the biker's art was affecting his poetry – most strikingly in 'The Ballad of Corbara'. Hamish had conceived the germ of this poem in 1944 but as he cruised through the Highlands on his two-wheeled 'harpy', the whole ballad began to surge into focus. It tells the story of a Tuscan partisan hero named Corbara who, after a series of daring motorised exploits, was ritualistically executed by the Germans in the town of Forli. Today the ballad remains almost unknown but it is, I believe, a song of historical and literary importance. First, because it has claims to be the first 'motorbike poem'. Second, because it is linguistically innovative and moves between English, Scots, Italian and German to great dramatic effect. Third, this ballad was, consciously, developed as if it were a 'neo-realist screenplay for the cinema' – and might even yet become the basis of a film.

. . . An auld wife ran out
frae the bield o her hoosie:
"May God an' his mither
an' Jesus Christ sain ye

---

11. 'Here's to the Maiden', *Voice of Scotland* March 1947, later published in the *Collected Poems*.

ye campioun o aa
partisans o the Romagna
i yer haun the Biretta
i yer cap the Reid Star.

Turn ye yer ways
tae the wynds o' Faenza –
turn ye an' flee
tae your ain yins, Corbara.

The Jerries are ragin'
through tounland and clachan.
They've hangit puir Bob
wi his taes ower a fire."

Thunner's black tawse
cracked the still o the forenicht.
Bluid o' the sun
sweeled the track o Corbara.

"And hae they killed Bob
my ain fere o the Prato?
Hae they killed him, auld Bob,
that was gleg i the tulzies!

Gif they they think I'll turn
and rin frae tedeschi –
I'm tellin ye, mither,
ye ken na Corbara!"[12]

This 50-verse ballad is many things: a modern Scots folksong, cinematic agit prop, a panegyric to a dead hero, a documentary record of a forgotten historical event. Hamish presents Corbara as a hero of the New Europe (a William Wallace for the whole continent: even down to the fact that his executed, pregnant girlfriend is called Inez, as Wallace's was called Innes). And, if the European Union is looking for a ballad that documents the war out of which it was born – it need look no further than this poem. The Italian Appenines and Highland Scotland are welded into one landscape, one 'weapon of struggle' – the people of Europe into one unified humanity. But this ballad is also a song of personal remembrance: Hamish's wartime comrades – Bob, Sangue, Lupo,

---

12. 'The Ballad of Corbara', *Voice of Scotland*, Vol. 5, No. 1, September 1948; later published in the *Collected Poems*.

Uragano and Fulmine – are named in the poem, and 'Corbara' himself seems to be an amalgam of the original Corbara, Hamish and Potente.

In the middle of March, Hamish made a quick visit to Belfast and Dublin. Coming back through Stranraer he spent a night at Castle Douglas. then biked on through the Border hills to Glasgow. Affronted, as always, by the grotesque poverty of Glasgow, he writes: 'Maryhill, Cowcaddens, Townhead, Gorbals to Eglington Toll – a razor slashed across the face of Capitalism'. On 19 March, he signed into the Highlander Hotel and two days later took 'Margery to dinner at the Citadel: Carrey's', adding 'The Righteous are Bold'. This aside may describe their developing relationship but, more probably, shows him preparing for action on the morrow – when he would attend, and speak at, the first National Assembly of the Scottish Convention. This Convention was being established to draw together all Scots committed to the idea of a Parliament in Scotland. Its aim was to publicly present the case for Scottish Home Rule to the Scottish people and to create a popular extra-parliamentary momentum for political change.

Hamish foresaw that the Scottish Convention was likely to face powerful Unionist opposition and factious infighting and, within hours of the closure of this first Assembly, he notes: 'The National Assembly convened on Saturday, gave indication of the problems to come. It is popular with neither of the two main parties – however, delegates accepted a resolution to petition the government to hold a plebiscite of the Scottish people to ascertain their views on a Scottish Parliament. But – what 'status' does such a plebiscite have; who will organise it? etc.' However, in a spirit of 'solidarity without compromise', Hamish gave the Convention his full backing – he listened, he spoke and determinedly tried to establish a network of contacts to advance the cause of self-governance. The prime force behind the new movement was John MacCormick, a charismatic figure, one-time Liberal MP and former SNP leader. He and Hamish got acquainted but were never to become close colleagues. During the day, Hamish had lunch with Douglas Young, tea with Naomi Mitchison (in the Saltire Society rooms), and in the evening 'went to a pantomime with Margery'.

Next day, Hamish stayed in his hotel to write a major article for the *Voice of Scotland*. He developed it from the contributions he had made to the Convention the previous day and entitled it 'Scotland's Alamein'. His army experience had given him a very practical understanding of the need for any campaign to have clear objectives, to be well planned and pursued with clear determination. He was not interested in demonstrating his opposition to government policy, or exercising his democratic rights: he wanted change and real results. He wanted a Scottish Parliament and he wanted Scotland to take the lead in the international pursuit of world peace. He was a socialist with strong communist leanings but he saw socialism not as a form of party government but 'the process' by which Scotland would govern herself, look after her own, and pursue peace and wellbeing in the world. In 'Scotland's Alamein', Hamish very deliberately kept military metaphors to the fore. Most of his audience had direct war experience and he knew the 'whole picture' of the New Scotland he was trying to paint must include a military dimension, if radical change was to happen. He also knew that if he was to emerge as one of the leaders of the nationalist movement, his military credentials could only do him good; and for the next ten years Hamish undoubtedly was a man with political ambitions. For various reasons he was never to acquire a party power-base but, rather like General de Gaulle, he seems to have assumed that, if he held his ground, the call would come. He writes:

> During the recent war the Highland Division became a kind of symbol of Scotland . . . Scots in the field can still function with energy, initiative and courage. One felt in fact, seeing the preparations for Alamein and Sicily, that something like the perfervid spirit of our ancestors was entering the lists against Rommel. It is all the more bitter, therefore, to contrast this picture of Scotland at war with the spectre of our countrymen in peace-time, for it scunners you to see how tame, mean-spirited and ineffectual the craturs look. They doff their spirit, their bonnet and hackle. When warfare's over, they grip the rudder with fashionless fingers.

> They had better wake up to the fact that Scotland's national situation today is fully as perilous as the Eighth Army's when it faced the defensive battle of El Alamein. During those critical months of 1942, the issue of the war was at stake. It was necessary to check the Axis army, then throw it back – nothing else would do. For Scotland, here and now, the same situation presents itself. If this nation does not forthwith rally and hurl back once and for all the forces which for two centuries have been encompassing its obliteration, it will henceforward be fighting nothing but a forlorn rearguard action. It will have had it.

> The National Assembly of the Scottish Convention, held in Glasgow on 22nd March 1947 is the first sign on a national scale that Scotland is throwing off the dreadful apathy of the interwar years, is beginning to gather its strength for decisive conflict. But – without a resolute follow-up it will be a mockery. The Scottish predicament today calls for the same ruthless and objective appraisal which a general demands from his staff before action. Any attempt to fob us

off with pious platitudes (especially religious) must be met with uncompromising hostility. The Scots had better realise that spiritual up-lift is no substitute for earthly élan . . .

The fight to maintain and develop a distinctive Scottish way of life must be invigorated and sustained by political action. Without the latter, the former is – in the last analysis – only an elaborate shadow-play, which in time must become inept and meaningless. Cultural and political movements are, in occupied states, invariably complementary. Nothing could be more pathetic, for example, than the idea that we can defend our ancient Gaelic civilisation merely by organising bigger and better Mods, or railing at the Highland people for no longer speaking their language. We shall defend it only by energetic political action which will make life livable in the glens and along the shores of the sealochs. And the indispensable preliminary to *that* is the existence of a Parliament in Scotland . . . if these facts and figures are not made the grounds for *action*, without delay, we shall find that the day and the hour have slipped from us . . . But if the convening of this National Assembly means that our country is stirring at last, if it means that, in the coming months and years, Scotland is going to leave far behind her this slough of national degradation in which she is at present lying, then the battle will be won, and I see a vision of Alba in the years before us that would take the sting out of predestined damnation! . . . [13]

On Monday 24 March, Hamish lunched with Maurice Lindsay (the young man-of-letters whose letter he had 'missed' on Skye, a year earlier). Maurice had a great deal going for him: he had served as a junior army officer on the home front, had a plethora of establishment contacts, open access to the BBC in Scotland, right-wing political credentials and the ambition to make himself a major reputation as a journalist and poet. In addition he already had an established relationship with Hugh MacDiarmid. Hamish was not a jealous man but something about Lindsay (and the silver spoon he carried) aroused his animosity. Hamish recognised Lindsay as a capable broadcaster but an irredeemably second-division poet, and he was shocked that this man should not just strut the boards of Scotland but shelter safe beneath the wings of genius. The lunch was not a success!

But during the afternoon Hamish had a meeting with William MacLellan, the major publisher of nationalist literature in Scotland, and a close friend of MacDiarmid's. MacLellan encouraged Hamish to

---

13. Hamish Henderson, 'Scotland's Alamein', *Voice of Scotland* July 1947.

go immediately to 32 Victoria Crescent Road, Dowanhill, Glasgow, and meet the great man himself. MacDiarmid was living with his wife Valda Trevlyn Grieve and their son Michael in a small basement flat, owned by two art teachers, Walter and Sadie Pritchard. Hamish arrived at tea-time, and a raucous family argument was in progress! Valda, who had nurtured MacDiarmid through poverty, alcoholism and a serious nervous break-down, was in full flow in the kitchen 'giving Chris hell'. Loyal soul-mate as she was, Valda was Cornish to the roots of her red hair, and 'never took insults for compliments'! Thus, with her voice ringing in the back-ground, it was a rather crest-fallen Christopher Murray Grieve (rather than the poet Hugh MacDiarmid) who came to greet Hamish at the door. And before Hamish had introduced himself, MacDiarmid was gesturing over his shoulder to suggest that Hamish return on a more auspicious day. MacDiarmid was suffering 'a dark night of the soul': he had no secure income, his muse seemed to have left him, and Valda had become deeply angered by the manner in which Sadie Pritchard, their landlady, kept thrusting herself at Chris 'like a whore'.

Hamish's second meeting with MacDiarmid took place three months later, at the beginning of June. It lasted not three minutes but three days. Hamish's WEA lectureship had terminated and, because John Lehmann was now contracted to publish Hamish's *Elegies for the Dead in Cyrenaica*, Hamish decide to return to Cambridge to oversee the final editing from there. Driving south from Lochaber, Hamish arrived unannounced at the Dowanhill flat to find Valda Grieve alone. Over a cup of tea, she told him that MacDiarmid was now working in Carlisle as a reporter on the *Carlisle Journal*. She spoke at length about the family's financial problems. She was more or less beside herself, so Hamish decided to re-schedule his trip to Cambridge. He gave Valda six shillings and drove south over Beattock Summit – in glorious sunshine – to Carlisle. He arrived at the *Journal*'s offices in English Street just after five o'clock: 'a small doorman then took me into a large office where I, immediately, recognised Scotland's great poet bent over his desk – hard at work.' Some time later, Hamish wrote-up his recollections of this 'first real meeting' with the Scotsman he admired above all:

Finally, he looked up from the work he was doing; his expression was that perfectly caught in R.H. Westwater's painting in the University Staff Club portrait – the wary, sideways look of a cafe owner in some dangerous dockside area – half expecting trouble and already sizing up what chance he had of coping with it . . . I gave him Valda's messages about her need of money and about Mike. He asked me if *I* had any dough. No, I said, and briefly explained my situation. He then said he could get hold of some money – if he could get back to Glasgow . . .

Next day, Hamish took MacDiarmid on the back of his bike to Glasgow where they met up with Kenny and Calum Campbell, brothers from Easter Ross, at the office of the Caledonian Press, which printed the *Voice of Scotland*. MacDiarmid asked them for money. They said they had no funds but suggested names of people who might be able to help. So, in heavy rain, the two poets got back on the bike 'to make a doleful pilgrimage around Glasgow in search of money'. All to no avail. Finally, back at the Caledonian Press, MacDiarmid turned to ask him 'Hamish, could *you*, possibly, lend me £10?'

> I'd never had money, I had no paid job, my small Army Gratuity was exhausted . . . I'd never been in debt and had a dozen good reasons for refusing the request and I kept silent for some time – wondering how to word my refusal. Then, an overwhelming thought hit me – this man, who is going through all these balls-aching contortions to try and raise money for his wife and son, is the same man who has written the most wonderful Scottish poetry for over a century – if not ever; he's the man who wrote 'Empty Vessel' and 'Wha's been here afore me, lass', and the 'Second Hymn to Lenin'. This is the man who has sacrificed everything to purge Scotland of its deadening Philistinism and who – in John Speirs' words – 'still stands for health and life and sincerity in Scotland against complacency and indifference'. So, I took out my cheque book and wrote Chris Grieve a cheque for £10. I then took all three friends into a nearby pub and bought them a pint . . .[14]

Hamish completed his reminiscences of this strange day in an article for *Cencrastus*, No. 48, entitled 'Tangling with the Langholm Byspale', published in 1994:

> During our session in the pub, Chris told Kenny Campbell about my collection of Soldiers Ballads and, after I'd sung three or four, it was Chris Grieve who suggested – because, not a few of those ballads were bawdy – that a fictitious 'club' should be formed so that the ballads could be published unbowdlerized and sold, only, to club members – thereby minimalising the likelihood of police intervention (Sydney Goodsir Smith had already established his Auk Society for similar

---

14. HH, unpublished notes.

purposes). The two Campbells liked the idea, and before the end of the year they, very cheaply, printed a limited first edition of my 'Ballads of World War II'. They were available, by mail order, through the Lili Marlene Club of Glasgow, registered at 793 Argyle Street. Not many were sold but, with their appearance, the modern Folksong Revival in Scotland began . . . and by encouraging the Campbells to publish my 'Ballads of World War II', MacDiarmid did me a real favour. In a separate outbreak of good luck, within days I met an old friend in the Cambridge Union who had a permanent post in the Army Education Corps. Being told I needed work, he enrolled me on the spot – to take part in a conference for Volkshochschullehrer (People's High School Teachers) in Bad Godesberg in August 1947 and to join a team of 'teachers' debriefing German prisoners-of-war still held in this country. In fact – within days I was touring Britain, conducting courses for prisoners in camps from East Anglia to Watten in Caithness.

Hamish's 'Scotland's Alamein' appeared in the *Voice of Scotland* in July 1947, just a month after his three-day odyssey with MacDiarmid – the magazine's editor. It was an impressive issue and contained important contributions by MacDiarmid himself, William Montgomerie, Edwin Muir, George Bruce, J.F. Hendry, J. D. Scott and J. B. Pick. MacDiarmid's editorial is also of interest: 'Carlyle was right when he declared that if Burns had been a better intellectual workman he could have altered the whole course of European literature, and the question is whether or not Burns having betrayed that major *desideratum*, the task cannot yet be accomplished, and, if so, just how. That, and nothing less, is the *gravamen* of the Scottish Renaissance Movement . . .' Highly conscious of his own genius, MacDiarmid had long dreamed of doing for Scots/European literature exactly what, Carlyle believed, Burns had failed to do. Did MacDiarmid now realise that, like Burns, he had lyric genius but did *not* possess the education, the languages, the intellectual mastery to lead Scottish literature on to the European stage with such authority that the culture of a continent might be changed, as it had been in the Age of Pericles and Michelangelo? Did MacDiarmid see, in the twenty-seven-year-old Henderson, the first man in Scotland's history capable of changing the bias of world culture by combining the classical, Germanic and Celtic genius, in a new synthesis, in our time?

MacDiarmid was fifty-five. He knew he had genius, energy and will, but he also knew his creative inspiration was waning. For Chris Grieve, the encounter with Hamish Henderson was a revelatory shock: he suddenly felt himself naked – and his financial and domestic circum-stances made any attempt to come to terms with this extraordinary situation more difficult. Who was this fully fledged monster who had suddenly arrived in the shit-splattered nest of an exhausted, post-war Scotland?

The impact Hamish had on MacDiarmid seems to have been given concrete form in the first poem MacDiarmid wrote after his three days 'on the road' with Hamish. It is a strange, bedraggled prose-poem that raises wonderful thoughts heralding a new age. Entitled 'Glasgow', it was published in the same *Voice of Scotland* in which Hamish 'Scotland's Alamein' appeared:

> . . . Glasgow
> Thinks nothing, and is content to be
> Just what it is, not caring or knowing what . . .
> . . . Everything is dead except stupidity here,
> Smelling like the dissection of bad innards
> Or like the cold stench of ashes and foul water . . .
> And a deadly grey weariness fell over my thoughts,
> Almost like reading a Glasgow Herald leader . . .
>
> . . . Ah no! I am too old,
> Too old, too old, too old, and as for Scott
> The only other 'whole and seldom man' I know here,
> The cabal of his foes gives all this insensate welter
> Of a city an expression of idiot fury . . .
>
> . . . Wherever the faintest promise, the slightest integrity,
> Dares to show in any of the arts or thought or politics,
> At once the jealous senile jabber breaks out
> Striking with sure instinct at everything with courage and sincerity.
> (There's nothing too cowardly for Glasgow's spokesmen
> To have the courage to do.)
> 'Confound it all!' If once we let these young folk in
> What is to become of us?
> . . . Who knows – in this infernal brothlike fog
> There maybe greater artists yet by far than we
> Unheard of, even by us, condemned to be invisible
> In this tarnhelm of unconscionable ignorance . . .'[15]

---

15. Hugh MacDiarmid, 'Glasgow', *Voice of Scotland* July 1947.

This poem was modified when republished in MacDiarmid's *Collected Poems* of 1962, and in the *Complete Poems* of 1978, but its thrust remains clear in all versions. The 'Scott' referred to is normally assumed to be MacDiarmid's friend, Francis George Scott, the composer and teacher, but they were not close at this time, and there was of course another Scott in Glasgow at this time – James Scott (Henderson). Thus when MacDiarmid writes of 'greater artists yet by far than we' he is, I believe, throwing out compliments of the grandest kind to the young apprentice who had recently been so helpful to him. MacDiarmid recognised that Hamish had the intellectual potential to transform Scotland, but also knew that all of Scotland's leading artists and intellectuals had previously failed to encompass the fullness of their nation's cultural and political needs. It was an issue that W.B. Yeats had already addressed, in his journal:

> the fruit of Robert Burns and Scott with their lack of ideas, their external and picturesque view of life, has been to create not a nation but a province with a sense of the picturesque. A nation can only be created in the deepest thought of the greatest minds – the literature that makes it (and this making takes a long time) – who have first made themselves fundamental and profound and then realized themselves in their art. In this way they rouse into national action the governing minds of their time – few at any one time – by an awakening of their desire towards a certain mood and thought which is unconscious to those governing minds themselves. They create national character. Goethe, Shakespeare, Dante, Homer have so created and many others in lesser degree. The external and picturesque or political writer leaves the strongest intellects of their country empty (and in the case of Scotland, England has crowded into this emptiness), and is content to fill it with kilts and bagpipes, newspapers and guidebooks, the days of the least creative.[16]

In recognising Hamish as a man who could 'make profound' the Scots nation, MacDiarmid bestowed both a blessing and a terrible responsibility. This was Whitehead in action: life and nature always in the process of transition.

---

16. W.B. Yeats, *Memoirs* (Macmillan 1973).

TWELVE

The Edinburgh Festival,
and Ewan MacColl

The great bridge did not lead to you.
I would have reached you, even at the cost of sailing
along the sewers, if at your command.
                                        Eugenio Montale[1]

The reason why MacDiarmid had worked so hard to make the July 1947 edition of the *Voice of Scotland* a bumper issue was because publication would coincide with the opening of the first Edinburgh International Festival of Music and Drama. He was opposed to it, describing it as 'the farcical forthcoming!'. Hamish's attitude was, not surprisingly, very different: he saw the Edinburgh Festival as one of the Labour government's outstanding initiatives and gave it his full support. He recognised that the Festival was likely to have an establishment bias and foresaw that Scotland's indigenous cultures were likely to be marginalised but – 'the great thing was to have the Festival and then to change it'. He responded to widespread opposition to the Festival by noting: 'It is characteristic of Scotland that when anyone in this country attempts anything large and sensational, no matter how first-rate the project is, the whole nation becomes loud in discouragement and disparagement.' Hamish applauded the Festival's commitment to internationalism and artistic quality but, from year one, worked to see that the working classes, the Celtic tradition – and youth – got a share of the limelight. In addition, he began to nurture 'the bacchanalian underbelly of the Festival' to ensure that song, dance and sensual pleasure would also have their hour in the sun.

One very important by-product of this first Edinburgh Festival was that it drew Hamish and Jimmy Millar, otherwise known as Ewan MacColl, together. MacColl, with Joan Littlewood, was the driving force behind Theatre Workshop, a left-wing travelling theatre based in England. He

---

1. 'Wind on the Crescent' (Edinburgh 1948), after a poem by Eugenio Montale, published in the *Collected Poems*.

was a communist, an actor, a budding playwright and a strong-minded populist (out of a Paul Potts but more political mould). He was also developing a magnificent, rasping voice that would soon gain him a worldwide reputation as a folksinger. MacColl was five years older than Hamish. He came from Salford in Lancashire, but his parents were Scots, and, as his recognition of cultural power of the Scots folk tradition grew (with Hamish's tutorage), he changed his name, permanently, from Jimmy Millar to Ewan MacColl.

MacColl's youthful marriage to Joan Littlewood had already broken up, but changing personal relationships did not rupture their commitment to Theatre Workshop and the 'open world' it symbolised. Joan Littlewood was a Londoner who had run away north at the age of sixteen to become a modern 'troubadour'. She, too, was a Communist Party member and the Party gave Theatre Workshop a good deal of organisational support, as well as the ideological framework within which it worked. After just a few hours with Hamish, in Edinburgh, it was obvious to both Littlewood and MacColl that Hamish had a great deal to offer their company. They were making plans for a major tour of Scandinavia and the new democracies of eastern Europe, and MacColl appears to have suggested that Hamish join them. Hamish indicated immediate interest and encouraged them to develop Theatre Workshop not just as a new kind of theatre but as a new form of entertainment in which films, slide-shows, music and folk-cultures of all kinds came together and moved apart – in a living relationship. In addition he suggested that when Theatre Workshop returned to Britain from the Continent it should make Scotland its base and tour England and Europe from there: 'Theatre Workshop can become the germ of a National Theatre in Scotland.' Hamish told them that he had already had discussions with the planners of East Kilbride and Cumbernauld and believed that a National Theatre could become an integral part of one of Scotland's New Towns – as they were constructed over the coming years. Both MacColl and Littlewood showed great interest but, when Theatre Workshop decamped to England in September, plans were shelved for a year.

Somewhat at a loose end, Hamish returned to Glasgow to join the team drafting proposals for Scottish self-government, on behalf of the Scottish Convention. He appears to have been a co-opted independent member of a committee working under the chairmanship of John MacCormick, but because his political position was so close to that taken by the Scottish Committee of the Communist Party he worked in alliance with them. Unfortunately, the very presence of communists on the Convention committee soon put the fear of God into some of the more conservative and religious representatives and they quickly created an anti-communist alliance against the 'leftist nationalists'. The committee was thus hopelessly divided and by October the high hopes of the Convention organisers were collapsing in well-orchestrated acrimony. In such circumstances Hamish was not sorry to leave Scotland for Germany – to begin a two-month educational tour. He worked under a military umbrella – as a lieutenant in the British Army Reserve – and was delighted to find himself mollycoddled in a manner he had almost forgotten. Between visits to schools, refugee camps and a variety of institutions, he made time to write two articles for the *Voice of Scotland*: published in April and July 1948, they paint a vivid picture of Germany, detumescent after years of rage and destruction. Both articles were entitled 'Germany in Defeat'.

It was an ill-wind they sowed certainly: but one has to be silent before the ghastly relics of our whirlwind . . . The 'Faustian man', the man who wants to achieve everything and suffer everything and experience everything is a German ideal, and Heinz [Vogl] embodies it better than anyone else I know. Among other things he's learning Gaelic, and has already translated some of Sorley MacLean's poems into German. As for Scots he has already thrown himself into MacDiarmid and translated a lot of Penny Wheep. In economics he is busy refuting the ideas of Sylvio Gessell, which are founded on those of Keynes. He wanted to learn Swedish, in order to read Bjork and others. Psychology has occupied much of his time, and he's well read in Freud, Adler, and Jung: Jung's excursion (complete with archetypes) into the disputed field of Germany's guilt excites his scorn. He is also an athlete, a good dancer, and an excellent shot . . .

. . . In Allied Berlin it is noticeable how the propaganda of the capitalist West has taken over every single anti-Soviet slogan in the Nazi armoury – 'The Mongol East', 'The encroachment of Asia', 'Flinging back the Tartars', even the 'Iron Curtain' is of Nazi origin – it was coined by Count Schwerin von Krosigk, Finance Minister in Doenitz's short-lived government, and given world-wide coverage by Churchill in his speech at Fulton . . . And what's far worse, these phrases tend to colour the political thinking of even slightly enlightened people . . . Anyway, millions of Germans have felt in their flesh what this devilish nonsense means in the long run to the ordinary man, and at the great memorial ceremony for the Opfer des Faschismus, 'Victims of Fascism', one could see clearly that the German proletariat is still in the forefront of the European working-class movement . . .

These articles were sent to MacDiarmid as editor of the *Voice of Scotland* and, slightly self-consciously, parade Hamish's polymathic credentials. Having been recently awarded his 'pan-European mantle' by MacDiarmid, his learning is displayed with something close to an 'ostentation' rare in Hamish's writing.

In November, Hamish travelled home via London, where he visited his wartime BBC associate Wynford Vaughan Thomas and discussed publication of the Elegies with John Lehmann. Back in Glasgow, Hamish renewed contact with a young marine biologist and literary enthusiast named James Burns Singer. Their relationship quickly became a close friendship. Singer was a half-Jewish Scot, hungry for the company of poets. During the war he had made 'adolescent' contact with MacDiarmid, and in 1946 began an extended friendship with W.S. Graham. It was, however, Hamish who was to exert the most profound moral and literary influence on Singer as a poet. Singer was frail and burdened by manic energy, personal isolation and the Holocaust. He was also a young man of heroic ambition, and in Hamish he found a father-figure in whom gentleness, wisdom and courage were combined with a political and cultural vision that provided him with answers to many of the metaphysical questions that he was asking. All Singer's mature poetry owes something significant to Hamish. For example 'The Transparent Prisoner' (his first poem signed 'Burns Singer') is about the war in North Africa, which Singer, born in August 1928, did not experience. In a long article in *PN Review*, No.114, 1997, James Keery suggests that Singer based this poem on the wartime experience of a Pole 'who made Singer's acquaintance in an Aberdeen Pub'. If this is true (which I doubt) this Pole's experience was filtered through Singer's knowledge of Hamish Henderson's much wider wartime experience, and *Elegies for the Dead in Cyrenaica*, which Singer believed to be a great poem. Another poem, 'Epilogue to Another Man's Book', was written 'for Hamish' and sent, in manuscript, to him. And, in 'The Best of It', Burns Singer pays eloquent tribute to the man who was his prime mentor.

> . . . Your words make hay of me, but I'm released
> By them from standing shivering and distant.
> The best of it is that I am at least.
>
> Knees soaked rheumatic by the promised harvest
> You razed with scythe and sickle what I meant:
> Reached by these words now, measure what's increased.

But you, like a horizon or a priest,
Past every boundary of the round land, went:
The best of it is that I am at least
Reached by these words now measuring what's increased.[2]

The reference to 'scythe and sickle' makes it likely that the poet whom Singer is addressing is Hamish, and not W.S. Graham as Keery would appear to suggest (Graham being a consciously 'non-political' poet). In 1955, Burns Singer moved to London but the two men remained creatively very close. Both sought nobility and wholeness in poetry and in their lives. Like Hamish, Singer had a druidic love of the riddle, as expressed in the poem 'Your Words, My Answers', which beautifully echoes Hamish's translation of Govoni's benediction to his murdered son:

Like the two limbs of a cross
Your words, my meanings lie
Together in the place
Where all our meanings die.[3]

Hamish's relationship with the Edinburgh poet Norman McCaig (later MacCaig) was of a very different kind. McCaig was a singular individualist, a classicist, a conscientious objector and primary school teacher. Hamish admired McCaig's pacifist stance, but the two men were never to get on well. Professor Geoff Dutton, of the University of Dundee (a scientist who always loved poetry), remembers them clashing at one of the very early Edinburgh Festivals: 'The American actor Sam Wanamaker, Hamish and several more of us ended up one night in McCaig's flat. Drink was taken. Culture and class became the subject of debate and McCaig was soon denouncing the philistine uncouthness of "the Scottish working class, with its interest in football, and beer, and nothing beyond . . ." It wasn't long before Hamish stood up to confront McCaig: "Norman – what do you *know* about the Scottish working class? What it is, what it does, what it might be?" McCaig just stood there – handsome, arrogant, supercilious – but when he added a smile, Hamish knocked him to the ground with a single blow to the jaw. Norman got slowly to his feet and, looking at Hamish, said, "Am I meant to be insulted?"' Friends then intervened to prevent further trouble. Shortly afterwards, McCaig used the incident as the source of a fine short poem entitled 'Hero':

---

2. *Burns Singer – Selected Poems* (Carcanet 1977), ed. Anne Cluysenaar.
3. *Ibid.*

Cuchulain
Or any other great legend's man
Salted white with the blue Aegean
Or ruddy on an Irish strand,
What was the simplicity that made
Time tender with you and your uncrooked shade?

No need to look
For plume, carved chessmen, golden torque.
We, more than they, are your relic.
Passion remains; and south and north
Happens to us, as to you. We seek
No other than gay Celt and subtle Greek.

Cuchulain
Fighting suffered a transformation
To still Cuchulain but more than man.
– Only once Time's repetition
Showed us in him, when, staring mad,
He died fighting the waves on a friendly strand.[4]

In December 1947, Hamish got a letter from Naomi Mitchison inviting him to stay with her at Carradale House, in Kintyre. He was still refining the Elegies and it was the third letter she had sent, so he decided this was an offer no homeless man should refuse. Her letters had commended his article 'Scotland's Alamein', praised his translations from Blok and criticised MacDiarmid's recent verse: 'Do you think the MASTER is really writing poetry at all? It struck me that "Glasgow" was even worse than his usual. At least MacGonagal did rhyme!' She also praised Hamish's poetry, complimenting him on the way it 'mounts seamlessly into song and makes poetry "live" for the masses'. Such words were manna to Hamish and he soon roared off, on the Rudge Special, 'over the Rest and Be Thankful – and down to Carradale – and there, I sorned, for six weeks, on the banks of Loch Fyne, sorned with a woman who was a chieftain's daughter. Great times we had.' Naomi Mitchison was a sister of J.B.S. Haldane, the great Cambridge biologist, and communist, who wrote regular articles on 'Science and Morality' for the *Daily Worker*. Naomi was married with adult children but lived an enviably peripatetic lifestyle, moving between Kintyre, Carradale, Edinburgh, Cambridge, London and various parts of southern Africa. She was a prolific writer, but Hamish

---

4. Norman MacCaig, *Collected Poems* (Chatto & Windus 1985).

thought her reputation ran ahead of her talents. She was, however, deeply committed to a wide range of humanitarian and political causes close to Hamish's heart and the two became lifelong, though distant, allies. Indeed, Naomi's left-wing reputation was such that George Orwell appended her name to the long list of 'dangerous cultural radicals' that he presented to MI5 at this time. MacDiarmid was also on it – but not Hamish! That Orwell should have been 'shopping' Scotland's literati, for money, when he was completing his last novel, *1984*, on the Isle of Jura is ironic. But the fact that a major intellectual socialist like George Orwell was involved in McCarthyite plotting in 1947/48, shows how quickly anti-communist attitudes had penetrated British, as well as American, society within three years of the end of the Second World War.

Hamish found Carradale House a wonderful place to write poetry: the Elegies seemed to finish themselves, and with huge satisfaction he signed them off, 'Cyrene 1942 – Carradale, Argyll, 1947'.

Early in the New Year a letter arrived from A.L. Lloyd, the English folk-singer and collector. He had bought a copy of Hamish's *Ballads of World War II* and wrote to salute his fellow collector and song-writer:

> . . . your first collection – I enjoyed especially the Farouk song . . . I enclose the following for your second collection – the German ones I got from a girl who plays drums in a three-piece band at the British Officers Club in Aachen. She was an entertainer on the Eastern Front, and was caught at Stalingrad . . . There are, of course, a number of American songs; most of them have an author-made appearance, even though some are the product of genuine modern-style ballad-makers like the Oklahoma singer, Woody Guthrie, who worked in the US merchant navy during the war. I met him once. He had a guitar hanging over his bunk with a notice on it saying: 'Handle with care: this machine killed ten fascists.' You probably know the kind of things Woody wrote; stuff like: 'I just got my army call: / I went down to the army hall, / Sally came running like a cannon ball / And I told her not to grieve after me . . .'

Lloyd's letter was immediately followed by another – from MacDiarmid – asking Hamish to come back to Glasgow, stay with him and work to support Robert Blair Wilkie, the Independent Scottish National candidate for the Camlachie by-election. Within hours Hamish was at MacDiarmid's side. For three weeks they campaigned together, speaking for Blair Wilkie as 'the radical alternative to the current sorry state of British governance in Scotland'; and throughout this period Hamish lived in MacDiarmid's flat. They ate, drank and rode the trams together, Mac-

Diarmid giving Hamish advice on how to avoid paying the fare, by getting recognised as a poet, or an impoverished radical politician fighting for the down-trodden! Robert Blair Wilkie lost the election, very badly, to the Labour Party candidate and, a year later, Wilkie was expelled from the Scottish National Party for extremism.

While staying with the Grieves, Hamish got to know the painter J.D. Fergusson and Margaret Morris, creator of the Celtic Ballet, and made regular visits to Glasgow's New Art Club. He had also established a close friendship with Morris Blythman, a brilliant young teacher who wrote poetry under the pseudonym Thurso Berwick. Both Morris and his wife, Marian, were members of the Communist Party and when Hamish left the Grieves he began staying regularly at the Blythman house in Springburn. Together they visited the Vincent van Gogh exhibition at the Kelvingrove Museum. Hamish noted van Gogh's words 'I admire the bull, the eagle and man, with such adoration that it will certainly prevent me from ever becoming an ambitious person.' Morris was a member of the cultural committee of the Scottish Section of the Communist Party and he got Hamish involved in a scheme to bring members of the Italian literary Risorgimento to Scotland as part of a British-Italian cultural exchange. Consequently, on 17 March 1948, Hamish was at Glasgow Central Station to welcome Eugenio Montale, and over the following week he acted as his guide and interpreter in Scotland, taking him to MacDiarmid, to literary discussions, formal lectures and poetry readings in Glasgow and Edinburgh. The two men quickly became close. In Edinburgh, Montale wrote the first of several 'Scottish' poems. It was entitled 'Wind on the Crescent (Edinburgh 1948)' and Hamish translated it:

> The great bridge did not lead to you.
> I would have reached you, even at the cost of sailing
> along the sewers, if at your command.
> But already my energy, like the sun on the glass
> of the verandas, was weakening.
>
> The man preaching on the Crescent
> asked me 'Do you know where God is?'
> I knew where, and told him. He shook his head.
> Then he vanished in the whirlwind that caught up men and houses
> and lifted them on high, on a colour of pitch.[5]

---

5. Published in the *Collected Poems*.

When Hamish later met up with Montale in Cambridge he took him out to Ely – where the Italian was stunned by the beauty of the 'Lantern' suspended above the aisle of the great Gothic Cathedral – and it inspired him to write a poem of farewell – and encouragement. The poem speaks for and through Hamish and is entitled 'Letting Go of a Dove – Ely Cathedral, 1948'.

> A white dove has flown from me
> among stelae, under vaults where the sky nests.
> Dawns and lights suspended; I have loved the sun,
> the colour of honey – now I crave the dark.
> I desire the broody fire, and this immobile tomb.
> And I want to see your gaze downfacing it.[6]

'Downfacing' was a favourite word of Hamish's, and Montale suggests that Hamish as a man and a poet has enjoyed his moment in the sun (of youth and Italy) but now must take up, in MacDiarmid's words, 'the burden of his people's doom', in the northern dark. Montale saw Hamish as a bard of the Scots people, committed to challenging 'the death-longing that had descended over a too Protestant people' (an idea given psychological expression in the Edinburgh poem) and winning them back to 'the sun' and their true selves (as expressed in the poem of the Cathedral lantern). Montale knew this task could have only one outcome ('death and disgrace amongst his countrymen' – as Sophocles put it in the month of Ajax) but he encourages, and knows Hamish will 'downface his enemies' come-what-may – with the vision, the courage and the mystical power resident in poetry (a white dove among stelae). Today, Montale is recognised as one of the great poets of the twentieth century (and one of the most deserving of Nobel Laureates) and it is wonderful that he should have honoured and sanctioned the genius and national commitment of his young friend so early.

On 21 March, Hamish was back at Central Station to meet Alberto Moravia and his wife Elsa Morante, and they too were taken on a tour of Scotland's literary centres. Moravia was beginning to win fame as one of Europe's new realist novelists. Elsa Morante was at that time an almost unknown poet but today her literary reputation is at least as great as Moravia's. They stayed at the North British Hotel in Edinburgh. On Sunday 28 March, Hamish led them and a party of literary enthusiasts on a Highland tour to Balmoral and Glen Urquhart. One young Scottish writer stimulated by these visits was Alex Trocchi, at the time a student in Glasgow but soon to gain fame as a Scots bohemian – in Paris, New York and London.

Flushed with cash from helping the Italian writers, Hamish moved into

---

6. HH, after Eugenio Montale, published in the *Collected Poems*.

temporary lodgings at International House in Frederick Street, Edinburgh. This was a private club, set up during the war to provide accommodation for British, Colonial and foreign servicemen. Hamish liked its atmosphere and for several years it provided him with an occasional room and a permanent poste restante address. On 12 May 1948 he found in his pigeon-hole a letter of some consequence. It was from Morris Blythman:

> Dear Hamish – There are several important developments going to take place here in Glasgow in a very short time . . . One project now afoot is to hold a quarter-century meeting in memory of the death of John MacLean. The Clyde Group (writers) was to be the sponsor of this meeting, but after discussion we came to the conclusion that the Writers Group of the Scottish/USSR Society [of which Hamish was secretary] would be the best sponsors . . . If we start straight away we can pack St Andrews Hall with one of the best meetings the Society has ever had – we have contacted Chris Grieve . . . The above is an outline of one of the developments afoot, can you come through to Glasgow?'

Hamish immediately accepted Morris' invitation and offered his full support. He had long regarded John MacLean as one of Scotland's great heroes: a man of action dedicated to peace, socialism, internationalism and Scottish nationhood. On 30 May, the first meeting of the 'John MacLean Committee' took place at 51 Kersland Street, Glasgow, and Hamish notes that he was invited 'to oversee and direct the John MacLean Anniversary Celebrations and to take "the chair" at the main event in St Andrew's Hall'. He revelled in the responsibility and began an intensive study of MacLean's life, thinking and work. He also began to compose a song in honour of him. Morris now firmly believed that Hamish was not just an outstanding poet but potentially an important political leader – in the MacLean mould. He was delighted that Hamish had decided to dedicate himself to the MacLean project, and the two 'rebel' poets spent long nights planning, talking – and singing. Marian was teaching full-time and had a young baby but she too joined in, living what she describes as the happiest and most exciting days of her life:

> I remember Hamish, being so courteous, opening doors, never eating anything without being asked, always toasting before drinking. I came down one morning to find him asleep on the sofa, covered up with half a dozen coats and jackets! He'd been freezing but had not wanted to disturb us by asking for blankets. But for its

stance on the National Question, I'm certain Hamish would have joined the Communist Party, and that of course was the prime reason why we left. Even though he wasn't a member, we got him work as a lecturer for the Young Communist League. Such work allowed Hamish to travel and it gave him access to many of Scotland's most politically active and talented young people. The YCL organised summer holiday camps for young party members and deprived urban teenagers. Hamish naturally took charge of 'Ceilidh Nights'.[7]

By 30 July, Hamish had completed the song that he now titled 'The John MacLean March' and he sent it, with a glossary of the Scots words used, to his friend Chris Lloyd, who was at that time translating the work of Pablo Neruda. In August Hamish spent a few days with Ruth Speirs in Muswell Hill, London. She was living apart from her husband, in some squalor. John Speirs was teaching at Exeter University but, despite the fact that Hamish had dedicated the Prologue of the Elegies to him, their friendship had cooled considerably. Speirs had gained a respectable academic post, but Hamish believed his critical grip had gone. For example, the previous January, Speirs had concluded a review of Sydney Goodsir Smith's *Selected Poems* (for the *Arts Review*), by savagely stating 'that the poems ran false, that they were without a Scots idiom and that there was no future for Scots as practised in this book'. Hamish wrote to inform Speirs that he was 'plain wrong' and pointed out a long list of the things 'he had missed'. This letter seems to have had a remarkable effect because when, a few months later, Speirs reviewed Goodsir Smith's next publication, 'Under the Eildon Tree', he reversed the thrust of his former arguments and acknowledged the 'genius' of a great poem.

Hamish was back in Edinburgh for the start of the second Edinburgh Festival and, on 22 August 1948, Ewan MacColl, Joan Littlewood and their Theatre Workshop returned. Unfortunately Hamish was penniless, at the very moment when he needed to entertain his friends and see Scotland's National Theatre founded. Fortunately he persuaded Naomi Mitchison to employ him as co-chair of a symposium entitled 'Literature in the West and in the USSR', which earned him £15, and his old Cambridge friend E.P. Thompson turned up and contributed another £15. On 28 August, he attended a party organised by the Saltire Society, at which MacDiarmid was presented with an oil portrait by the Dundee artist David Foggie. Albert Mackie chaired the gathering and read out this tribute from T.S. Eliot:

---

7. Marian Blythman, from a converstation with TN, 2004.

There are two reasons why I should have wished to be present on this occasion. The first is my respect for the great contribution made by the Poet to poetry – in general – in my time; the second is my respect for his contribution to Scottish Poetry – in particular . . . It will eventually be admitted that he has done more also for English poetry, by committing some of his finest verse to Scots, than if he had elected to write exclusively in English . . .

Such compliments meant a great deal to MacDiarmid, but the meeting engendered so much 'self-parading and back-thumping Scotchness' that W.S. Graham informed Hamish that he could not stand 'such unhealthiness – as the literary trumpetings of Lallanists like Douglas Young' and that he would go into permanent exile in Cornwall where 'he could turn his back on the cuboid face of Plastic Scots and look on Marazion!'. Hamish was a Scots language enthusiast (and a member of Douglas Young's 'Makars Club') but, like Graham, found the 'logic' of most synthetic Scots hard to take, 'whilst the reality of living Scots is there to be heard on every street corner and furrow end'. Thus, as Hamish and Graham forged a lasting friendship, a fissure opened in their relationships with Young and MacDiarmid. Interestingly, they were both good singers, whereas Young and MacDiarmid were not. Singing the ballads and knowing the ballad singers, Hamish and Graham knew that 'dictionary' Scots was a kind of intellectual gymnastics that Scotland did not need – while living Scots was still growing on the tongues of the people.

On 4/5 September, Hamish took part in a two-day 'Battle of Ideas Seminar' organised by the Young Communist League. On 7 September he notes 'Theatre Workshop leave'. It is a minimal and ambiguous note but, once again, Hamish had spent a great deal of time in the company of Ewan MacColl: singing, eulogising Celtic tradition and discussing his plan for a Scottish National Theatre. Again, nothing was firmly agreed but Hamish seems to have presumed that he would shortly join Theatre Workshop on their European tour – as soon as visa details were complete. Consequently, he waited and waited for a telephone call that never came. Perhaps there was a genuine misunderstanding, perhaps Littlewood and MacColl got cold feet. Whatever the facts, Hamish suddenly found himself high, dry and resentful. MacColl was an egalitarian communist but also a hard-headed and ambitious individualist who steamrollered his way through life with little sympathy for those he flattened on the way. Hamish was not a man to be flattened, but it was he, and not MacColl, who suffered as a result of this 'misunderstanding', and Hamish felt it was something close to betrayal. He had given MacColl dozens of new songs and a wealth of ideas and, in return, was left 'holding the baby'. However, perhaps this rupture was actually what Hamish wanted and needed: he and MacColl were never likely to get on for long; he knew they would clash and he knew his commitment was still – first and last – to Scotland. For two months Hamish heard nothing, and when MacColl finally wrote he simply asked Hamish to get on with the work that needed to be done in Scotland!

> East Kilbride is admirably suited from a topographical point of view . . . All we need is their support to make this a reality. That is where you come in. Please Hamish let us know, immediately, if there is any chance of doing something there. If you fail us we will calumnify you far and wide until not a soul in Christendom will let you sing obscene entertainment in their ears. Best wishes for your Irish sojourn. Cest Prace. E.M.[8]

The reference to Hamish's 'Irish sojourn' is to the fact that Hamish was by this time working in Ulster. When he realised that the likelihood of his joining Theatre Workshop on their European tour was small, he leapt sideways to resume his career with the Workers Education Association and on 1 October 1948 had taken up the post of WEA Secretary in Northern Ireland.

Events had unfolded quickly: one week after MacColl left Edinburgh, on 14 September, Hamish had heaved his Rudge aboard the Belfast ferry and 'settled-in' with Irish poet John Hewitt. After two days in Belfast, Hamish offered Hewitt a ride west into Sligo: he had come to Ireland, he said, to attend the funeral of W.B. Yeats, and wild horses wouldn't keep him away. So the two poets set off to meet the great man – coming home. All Hamish's frustration fell away in the wind as they sped 'through the green and the harvest fields of Ulster, towards Atlantis – its golden palaces stacked high in the cumulus of the evening sun!' Yeats had died in the south of France in 1939; now, after nine years, his remains were being returned to Ireland, and Hamish made sure he was there to receive them. Next day the two men joined the crowd early and awaited the coffin; and, after it had passed, Hamish wrote, in one sitting, this poem, unpublished until now.

Sligo, 17th September 1948

On the hard pavement near the red Post office
that monstrous dream of a child's money-box
we waited for the poet's funeral.

Traffic ran slower and thinner, cart and car,
like a loose tap turned off but dripping still.

---

8. Letter from Ewan MacColl to Hamish Henderson, late 1948.

The tall officious garda corre the occasion,
as though tomorrow, when he'll slip them on,
his braces would lack all resilience.
The shops put on their shutters – the crowd grew,
a class of chattering children clatter round
the corner of the square. I watch them pass
and wonder if in sixty or seventy years,
an old man or an old woman would remember
the poet coming back and tell his name –
up the long street before us the crowd thickened
along the kerbs, with faces blurred and pale
as the newspapers in their vague pale hands.

We talked and waited, listened to the crowd;
and drifted into thought a sudden face
or jigging ass-cart headed off, ripped up
with vague tatters, whisked across the slates.
I thought that statue on the marble pole,
the marble mayor, had little right to stand
above us all, to give the first salute;
if there were decency, not merely justice,
he'd slither down and take his proper place
behind the curtains of the face-glazed bank –
The crowd stirred foot and elbow, screwing up
the cat-gut of our feelings. Up the street
the newspapers were folded like a wave,
as the foam runs its tongue along the sand.
And in the silence we reached up to touch.
The distant pipes cried faintly their lament,
the drum-beats dropped their clods on coffin lid
as the town band stepped bravely into view;
slow, slow, as if to stop, yet never stopping;
then the procession, square black-coated men,
the glinting chain, the coloured Galway hords,
the straight clenched faces, then the droning motors,
the pitch-pine coffin bright in the large hearse.
So without banners into Sligotown
the poet came, impressive as his verse.[9]

---

9. HH, unpublished, from notebook.

A photograph in R.F. Foster's *W.B. Yeats: – a Life, Volume II, The Arch-Poet*, shows, almost exactly, the scene Hamish describes, but Hamish's words add a genuine documentary footnote to a great moment in Irish history and a quietly Celtic realism to Auden's famous eulogy, 'In Memorium, W.B.Yeats'. The scene conjured might have been painted by the poet's brother, Jack Yeats: it combines reportage, caricature and cosmic vision.

The following day, Hamish was back in Belfast where, after a wash and a shave, he went up to the Senate House of Queen's University, to be interviewed for the WEA job. He had presumably applied for the post before being 'let down' by Theatre Workshop: it was certainly not exactly what he wanted but he needed the money and – realistic as usual – Hamish went to the interview in good humour, and determined to succeed. He notes:

> I was one on a short-leet [shortlist] of three. One of the others was Strathdee, the Irish rugby international (and it was the year of the Irish Grand Slam!) – so we played poker in an ante-room while our fate was decided. Deliberations went on for a long time – a minority were holding out for Strathdee (who indeed, I think, would have been a better man for the job) – but there was a Highlander on the panel, and I was offered the post!

After that, buoyed by the prospect of a secure income, Hamish appears to have jumped on a flight to Gutenberg to participate in an International Conference on 'Art and Peace'. Thus, he in fact got to the Continent some days before Theatre Workshop, and he let MacColl know! Some months later he received a second, slightly more explanatory letter from MacColl about his exclusion from the US Workshop tour:

> Dear Hamish, My depression isn't the result of leaving Sweden, which I detested, but Czechoslovakia which is not only another country but another world. I cannot tell you how sorry I am that you couldn't be with us. Unfortunately both the American Zone officials and the ticket agency proved difficult about arranging visas . . . Theatre Workshop is an enormous success in Czechoslovakia . . . We were offered a permanent theatre in Prague . . . For some time I have been thinking about publishing a collection of folk songs. I have about 400 – and I was wondering if you would like to collaborate with me. The 'Folksong' movement has created a tremendous market in the States for such collections . . . It could be a pleasant way of earning money . . .

I find that most people in Europe know nothing about the Scottish Renaissance – but are amazed at the extent and magnitude of our movement . . .

This letter is interesting on several levels: 1) Hamish's assumption that he was to have joined Theatre Workshop is dismissed by MacColl as a mere hiccup over tickets and visas, 2) MacColl suggests that Hamish might like to collaborate with *him* on a 'commercial' collection of folk-songs, 3) MacColl calls the Scottish Renaissance 'our movement'! MacColl was a commendable go-getter but this letter was galling, and Hamish's hurt is still evident in a letter he wrote to MacColl in the fifties: 'my acceptance of the Northern Ireland job was certainly a turning point in my life, for I imagine things would have developed very differently if I had accompanied Theatre Workshop to Czechoslovakia. I have to admit I was sore about this for a long time.' Ireland, however, was full of compensations and Hamish moved to Belfast in high spirits – confident that 'destiny' had now brought him to a country bound to Scotland by sea, land and people, and fittingly this beautiful poem, attributed to Sir Walter Raleigh, soon appears in his Irish notebook:

> Give me my scallop-shell of quiet
> My staff of faith to walk upon;
> My scrip of joy, immortal diet,
>   My bottle of salvation
> My gown of glory, hope's true gage
> And thus I'll make my pilgrimage.

THIRTEEN

Ulster, John Maclean and the Somerset Maugham Award

We may be defeated and suppressed, but at any rate we shall have the satisfaction of knowing that we have struck a real blow for freedom in these backward regions . . .

Robin Antrim (alias HH)[1]

In Belfast, Hamish took lodgings with Mrs Jean Connor, at 43 Fitzwilliam Street, off University Road: 'wonderful hooley's there at number 43!' He started work on 1 October but two days later was back in Glasgow to chair a meeting of the John Maclean[2] Anniversary Committee and on the 7th attended a WEA meeting in London. Over lunch he encouraged two fellow delegates (Elizabeth Lutyens and Alex McCrindle) to join him at 'the great John Maclean celebrations being planned for Glasgow'. Returning to Ireland, Hamish undertook a whirlwind tour of 'the Province – for which I now assumed responsibility! The Rudge came into its own – and often enough I had a passenger, pillion – within two or three weeks I had visited Carrick Fergus, Derry, Ballymena, Warrenpoint, Newtownards, Omagh, Ballycastle, Banbridge, Ballymoney, Ballycloy and Lisburn, and been bought drinks in every town! On 1 November we opened a big Exhibition of Soviet Architecture in the Central Hall of the College of Technology in Belfast: man, for a moment, I thought Belfast was the place to be . . .'

As a decorated British army officer Hamish had immediate kudos within the Unionist community, while his reputation as a rebel, singer and

---

1. Published in *Conflict*, May 1949.
2. John Maclean (1879–1923) joined the newly formed British Socialist Party in 1911 and became a vigorous anti-war and anti-conscription campaigner. He was arrested in 1915 under the Defence of the Realm Act, and lost his job as a teacher. He then devoted himself full-time to the cause of revolutionary Marxism in Scotland, and was appointed Soviet Consul to Scotland in 1918. He was imprisoned in 1921, after which the majority of Maclean's political activity was concentrated on building up his new party, the Scottish Workers' Republican Party.

Celtic nationalist soon opened doors within the republican and Catholic community. He was to stay in Ulster for less than a year but he hugely enjoyed himself and worked hard to plant his vision of a socially just, culturally dynamic and peaceful Ireland. The late forties were a relatively benign time in Irish history but, beneath the façade, Northern Ireland was still his 'Humpy Cromm'[3] writ large.

The WEA in Northern Ireland worked closely with Queen's University, Belfast, and it had presumed it would provide Hamish with secretarial assistance and a range of university facilities (as had previously been the case). Hamish, however, decided it was best if he was not seen as being 'attached to the university' so he set up office in Jean Connor's sprawling house. It was a decision that aroused some animosity – but no opposition – and Hamish settled in to his post to noticeable effect. In 1998, Paul Nolan (Head of Continuing Education at Queen's), recorded an interview with Hamish about his Ulster days. Selected quotations from this interview (and a related conversation) are set out below.

> I was the organiser. I was a one-man band. My lecturers and students came there – to number 43 Fitzwilliam Street. I thought it better they came to the house – and it was. I travelled round giving lectures myself . . . I did my own typing. I had my bike – and could be anywhere in Northern Ireland in half a day. I went down to the Shipyards, I went out to meet the folk in the countryside. It wasn't burdensome, life was a pleasure. I had time to write. I had enough money to buy a round – I was meeting all these fine folk and my memory is of a bright and eager period. I had always enjoyed Irish music: one of my great memories of the desert was hearing Irish music coming over the sand, just where you wouldn't expect to hear it! It was thrilling music and who can say they collected much of their best Irish music in North Africa? My familiarity with Ireland went back to my childhood, my mother knew a good number of Irish songs, and I had a good store of Irish jokes when I was nine years old! And one of the important things about Northern Ireland then was this – and some people find this hard to believe – few seeds of the future conflict were evident. That is a fact – I was close to both the Orange and the Green and the two co-existed: frequently, I would be ignorant of the religious allegiance of the people, students, friends I was with. Unfortunately, one cannot say that today.

---

3. The play on Irish terrorism and English Imperialism that Hamish wrote for the Cambridge Mummers in 1940.

Looking back, I see the years 1945–1955 as a surprising, golden period in the history of Northern Ireland: if not idyllic, it was a peaceful, pleasant and human society – and full of song. A song like 'The Old Orange Flute' was not then just an anti-Catholic song; it was a song – and, to me, that song gave expression to myths and forces going back thousands of years – to Orpheus, to the world of Apollo and Marsyas . . .

The WEA was a mildly left-wing organisation but I obviously got to know people of all levels and persuasions, farmers, dons, artists, writers: there was quite a Left-bank culture in Belfast in those days – existentialism was the rage. I got to know the poets John Hewitt and W.R. Rodgers; Louis MacNeice (whom I knew from my Cambridge days) came by occasionally; Andy Boyd, a journalist – a Protestant republican, a communist trades union organiser – became a close friend. I remember us going out on the Rudge – to Glenarriff in the Glens of Antrim for the unveiling of a republican monument in the Red Bay. I spoke at CP meetings he organised. Ulster has many happy memories for me. Of course – if I'd stayed on – I'd have had to risken things up a bit more – that's what the poet's for.

David Blakely, who worked with the National Council of Labour Colleges and was committed to cross-community contact, remembers Hamish during his Ulster days:

Hamish was a role model for us in the 1940s. He had mobility across the lines – he had the courage to pick up the 'hot-potatoes' other people couldn't handle – he was a bridge-builder years before others even conceived it possible. He encouraged us, especially the young. He was an optimist, saying "there is always something we can do". He asked us to practise what he called "seeing light in the dark". We used to meet in Campbell's Cafe, opposite the City Hall. There were three floors and it was on the third floor that the literary people used to meet, and there I remember him speaking another phrase I have not forgotten, 'The truth shall make you free'.[4]

From Ulster, Hamish continued planning the John Maclean celebrations scheduled for 28 November and made regular visits to Glasgow. He contacted various people who had known Maclean and noted their

---

4. David Blakely (Minister in the power-sharing government of the early 1970s), telephone conversation with TN, 2003.

remembrances. Many knew by heart the words Maclean had spoken at his trial in 1918: 'I wish no harm to any human being, but I, as one man, am going to exercise my freedom of speech. No human being on the face of the earth, no government, is going to take from me my right to speak, my right to protest against wrong, my right to do anything – that is for the benefit of mankind. I am not here, then, as the accused: I am here as the accuser of Capitalism – dripping with blood from head to foot . . .'

Hamish's personal notes emphasise Maclean's sense of morality, and how well prepared he was for the *agents provocateurs*, and the hecklers who raise religious and sectarian issues:

> Maclean never allowed himself to be drawn. He would move forward saying – 'What we are concerned with is this . . .' And he spoke about 'War with America, in the now coming time.' He was humble and unpretentious. His death? In essence it was a police murder – hushed up . . . A crowd of between twenty and thirty thousand attended his funeral – and many lay stretched across his grave as they wept, having to be pulled away from it by force. Only to very great men are such tributes paid . . . Maclean is a legend: it is only the 'mass' of ordinary people who can create a legend – this they have done.'

The Great Day was planned with military precision: Hamish's minutes record 'Chris Grieve to approach Glasgow Corporation for cooperation with flowers; H. Henderson to prepare pamphlets and organise publicity; George Hamilton to collect items for an exhibition of Maclean relics.' The main event began at 5.30p.m. on St Andrews Day, Sunday 28 November 1948, with an open-air meeting in George Square. George Hamilton took the chair, and speeches were delivered by John Kincaid and Morris Blythman. After that a 'Grand Parade to St. Andrew's Hall was led by the MacNeil Pipe Band, with banners marshalled and appropriate slogans shouted.' Entrance was free and over 2000 people were in the Hall when, at eight o'clock sharp, the formal celebrations began with Hamish presiding – and leading the singing of 'Scots Wha Hae'. He then introduced members of John Maclean's family to the platform, to thunderous applause. A massed choir sang a medley of Russian songs, then there were two short speeches: one on 'Scottish–Soviet Relations' by Joseph MacLeod, one on 'The Heritage of John Maclean' by Hugh MacDiarmid. After a selection of traditional Scottish songs came poems, especially written in honour of John Maclean, by Sydney Goodsir Smith, Thurso Berwick, John Kincaid, Sorley MacLean and Hugh MacDiarmid.

During the intermission a collection was taken and the T. Murray Pipe Band continued the entertainment.

The second half of the celebrations began with the performance of a short play by John Kincaid and a series of 'two minute tributes' by people who had known John Maclean, personally: D. Kirkwood MP, John Allan, John Clinton, Helen Crawford Anderson, Kate M. Callen MP, and Willie Gallagher MP, who, as leader of the Communist Party, was given twenty minutes. The evening then moved towards closure with 'intimations' from George Hamilton, 'conclusions' by Hamish and the first public rendition of 'The John Maclean March', sung by William Noble. It had an electrifying effect – and the whole hall rose in acclamation. For Hamish it was one of the great moments of his life, as he witnessed *his* song, for *his* hero, pass in one singing into the musical consciousness of his nation. The cheering, footstamping and applause long delayed the final singing of 'Auld Lang Syne'.

Thus, a thrilling and historic day ended. And, in retrospect, one can see that this was the day when Hamish's Scottish Folk Revival joined MacDiarmid's Scottish Renaissance as an equal partner, in the process by which the twentieth-century culture of Scotland was to be transformed. In one night, the John Maclean Celebrations did for Glasgow what the Edinburgh Festival (and its 'Fringe') was to do for Edinburgh over many years. Hamish and Morris Blythman had decided that Glasgow's tribute would be essentially artistic and poetical, and it was perhaps the greatest 'first night' in the history of Glasgow! They had brought together an array of poets, singers, actors and musicians to present a thrilling theatrical evening of revolutionary power. For example Hugh MacDiarmid's poem 'John Maclean' includes four spine-chilling lines: '. . . already it is clear, / Of all Maclean's foes not one was his peer . . . / As Pilate and the Roman soldiers to Christ / Were Law and Order to the finest Scots of his day . . .'; Sydney Goodsir Smith's 'The Ballant o' John Maclean' was gentler but hugely inspiring:

> . . . Och, tods have holes, the birds nests,
> But whaur's the Son o Man tae rest?
> On prison stanes they laid his heid
> An prison brose was aa his breid . . .

> . . . But they couldna dim his words o flame
> Nor dousit his memorie,
> – Turn ower in yir sleep, Maclean,
> Scotland has need o ye!

> . . . Muir an Wallace his prison mates,
> Lenin an Connolly,
> Nane ither ever was his maik
> Bit ithers there will be . . .[5]

Sorley MacLean read his now famous poem 'The Clan MacLean', in Gaelic, and in English, and in a few short lines he presents John Maclean's heroic struggle as the greatest achievement of Clan MacLean across the generations:

> Not they who died
> in the hauteur of Inverkeithing
> in spite of valour and pride
> the high head of our story;
> but he who was in Glasgow
> the battlepost of the poor,
> great John MacLean,
> the top and hem of our story.[6]

Thurso Berwick's poem, 'Til the Citie o John Maclean',[7] is more overtly revolutionary, and half-way through the reading of the poem, at the end of the line 'A Maclean is at yuir banquet!', spontaneous applause broke out across the whole auditorium. His poem raises the spectre of Balthazzar at his feast (and Macbeth in his madness), the idea being that 'the writing is on the wall' – that the old order must fall – that a new leader (a new Malcolm) must come. Thurso Berwick (Morris Blythman) had written his poem in the knowledge that Hamish would be presiding on the platform behind him – alongside the Maclean family – as he spoke his poem: and it seems clear that he wanted to suggest that Hamish should now assume the mantle of the great man they were celebrating. Blythman also knew that Hamish's new song, 'The John Maclean March' – full of revolutionary energy – would shortly conclude their celebrations. And, when it came, the song let no one down:

> Hey, Mac, did ye see him as ye cam' doon by Gorgie,
>   Awa ower the Lammerlaw or north o' the Tay?
> *Yon* man is comin' and the haill toon is turnin' oot:
>   We're a' shair he'll win back tae Glasgie the day.

---

5. Sydney Goodsir Smith, *Collected Poems 1941–1975* (John Calder 1975).
6. Sorley MacLean, *Spring Tide and Neap Tide – Selected Poems 1932–72* (Canongate 1977).
7. *Fowrsome Reel* (Caledonian Press for the Clyde Group 1948).

The jiners and hauders-on are mairchin' frae Clydebank;
    Come on noo an' hear him, he'll be ower thrang tae bide.
Turn oot, Jock and Jimmie: leave your crans and your muckle
                                   gantries, –
    Great John Maclean's comin' back tae the Clyde!
    Great John Maclean's comin' back tae the Clyde!

Argyle Street and London Road's the route that we're mairchin' –
    The lads frae the Broomielaw are here – tae a man!
Hi, Neil, whaur's your hadarums, ye big Hielan teuchter?
    Get your pipes, mate, an' march at the heid o' the clan.
Hullo Pat Malone, sure I knew ye'd be here son:
    The red and the green, lad, we'll wear side by side.
Gorbals is his the day, an' Glasgie belongs tae him:
    Ay, great John Maclean's comin' hame tae the Clyde.
    Great John Maclean's comin' hame tae the Clyde.

Forward tae Glasgie Green we'll march in good order:
    Wull grips his banner weel (that boy isnae blate).
Ay there, man, that's Johnnie noo – that's him there, the bonnie
                                     fechter,
    Lenin's his fiere, lad, an' Liebknecht's his mate.
Tak' tent when he's speakin', for they'll mind what he said here
    In Glasgie, oor city – and the haill warld beside.
Och hey, lad, the scarlet's bonnie: here's tae ye, Hielan Shonny!
    Oor John Maclean has come hame tae the Clyde!
    Oor John Maclean has come hame tae the Clyde.

Aweel, noo it's feenished I'm awa back tae Springburn,
    (Come hame tae your tea, John, we'll sune hae ye fed).
It's hard work the speakin': och, I'm shair he'll be tired the nicht,
    I'll sleep on the flair, Mac, and gie John the bed.
The haill city's quiet noo: it kens that he's restin'
    At hame wi' his Glasgie freens, their fame and their pride!
The red will be worn, my lads, an' Scotland will march again
    Noo great John Maclean has come hame tae the Clyde,
    Noo great John Maclean has come hame tae the Clyde.[8]

---

8. 'The John Maclean March', published in the *Collected Poems*.

The first verse should then be repeated, in Hamish's words 'starting very softly and working up to a crescendo'. The song is at once traditional in form and contemporary in content. It is intellectually complex but full of concrete imagery and Clydeside humour, carried forward by a thumping melody that ignites not just Scottish but worldwide responses. The song's 'linguistic difficulties' have a function, in that they nurture the interaction between the lead singer and the audience, and, when Hamish heard his song described as a Scots-Irish 'Come-All-Ye!' cross-dressed with the 'Bandiera Rossa', he was more than content.[9]

On 12 December Hamish was back in Glasgow attending a meeting of the 'Clyde Group'. This was a group of left-wing Lallans poets centred round Thurso Berwick, John Kincaid, Freddie Anderson and George Todd. Shortly afterwards *Fowrsome Reel*, a notable collection of poems, was published. The next day, Hamish joined a meeting in support of Highland crofters, fighting for land rights on the Knoydart Peninsula. The problem in Knoydart centred round Lord Brocket, an absentee landlord whose pig-headed self-centredness had brought all the old issues of the nineteenth-century Clearances back into focus. After five years of war service, seven crofters from Knoydart had returned home to find themselves unemployed and landless – while tens of thousands of acres lay vacant and untended all around them. Hamish encouraged the crofters to stand and fight and on the night ferry to Ulster composed his 'Ballad of the Men of Knoydart' in support of the dispossessed men. It was complete before he came out on deck 'to hail Ireland and the dawn!', and should be sung to the tune 'Johnstone's Motor Car'. Lord Brocket had been openly pro-Nazi in the thirties and Hamish went for him with impassioned ferocity, writing a modern 'rabble-rouser' designed to rally the whole Scots people in the just cause of their Highland kinsmen:

> 'Twas down by the farm of Scottas,
> Lord Brocket walked one day,
> And he saw a sight that worried him
> Far more than he could say,
> For the 'Seven Men of Knoydart'

---

9. Despite the song's immediate 'oral' success it was not published or broadcast for many years. The Communist Party found the song too nationalistic, the Labour and Scottish National Parties found it far too socialist – and for the BBC, it was completely beyond the pale. But, in the free world of the folk tradition, the song was carried irresistibly forward and quickly embedded itself on the tongues of dozens of good singers and in the consciousness of Scotland's working classes, beyond all party allegiance.

Were doing what they'd planned –
They had staked their claims and were digging their drains
On Brocket's Private Land.

'You bloody Reds,' Lord Brocket yelled,
'Wot's this you're doing 'ere?
It doesn't pay, as you'll find today,
To insult an English peer.
You're only Scottish half-wits,
But I'll make you understand
You Highland swine, these hills are mine!
This is all Lord Brocket's Land.'
. . .

Then up spoke the men of Knoydart:
'Away and shut your trap,
For threats from a Saxon brewer's boy,
We just won't give a rap.
O we are all ex-servicemen,
We fought against the Hun.
We can tell our enemies by now,
And Brocket, you are one!'
. . .

When Brocket heard these fightin' words,
He fell down in a swoon,
But they splashed his jowl with uisge,
And he woke up mighty soon,
And he moaned, 'These Dukes of Sutherland
Were right about the Scot.
If I had my way I'd start today
And clear the whole dam lot!'

Then up spoke the men of Knoydart:
'You have no earthly right,
For this is the land of Scotland,
And not the Isle of Wight.
When Scotland's proud Fianna,
With ten thousand lads is manned,
We will show the world that Highlanders
Have a right to Scottish Land' . . .[10]

---

10. 'Ballad of the Men of Knoydart', published in the *Collected Poems*.

The ballad caused a stir: the case went to courts and Lord Brocket won the day. Several of the crofters ended up in prison but, when Scotland's Parliament was re-established in 1999, one of its first actions was to enshrine in Scots Law land rights of exactly the kind that the men of Knoydart had demanded in 1948.

By March 1949, Hamish was in personal contact with the great black singer Paul Robeson, then touring the world – singing and speaking for black people's rights and advocating socialist solutions to international problems. At Robeson's major Belfast concert Hamish introduced him with these words: 'When I was last in Scotland, my visit coincided with that of Paul Robeson. I met him speaking to the Edinburgh students about "The Artist and the Citizen". One is never justified in trying to draw a line between the one and the other – but there are times when the role of the writer (or artist) must be subordinated to that of the citizen . . . My task in introducing Paul Robeson to Belfast is to commend the way in which he is exploiting his magnificent voice to the full – for the good of the citizens of this city and working people of the world . . .' Robeson's post-war tours of Britain tend to be remembered as Welsh affairs but he also made a huge impact in Scotland and Northern Ireland. For example, the students of Aberdeen University tried hard to make him their rector and only 'university rules' prevented his election.

The May 1949 issue of *Conflict* carried an article about Robeson's visit to Glasgow, and an article by Robin Antrim (a name that Andy Boyd[11] has confirmed as a Henderson alias), entitled 'Student Democracy in the Orange Unfree State'. It documents a visit by Tom Murray (from the Scottish-USSR Society in Glasgow) to Queen's University Socialist Society. The planned meeting was 'broken-up' by the Queen's University authorities before it began. Outraged, Robin Antrim, writing 'on behalf of the Student Socialist Society', ruthlessly exposes the underhand manner in which Ulster Unionists were dominating university life at Queen's:

> The government of Northern Ireland is a bare-faced boss-class tyranny which keeps itself in power by means of the shameless exploitation of sectarian prejudice and bitterness . . . The University authorities have no inhibitions about interfering in the affairs of our society – but they reckon without the will and resolve of the Socialist Society to stand its ground . . . Our membership is curtailed by the fear, already too common in many parts of Northern Ireland . . . that a dossier is kept on every Socialist student in the University is an open secret . . . Our president was called before the University authorities. He was told that

---

11. Andy Boyd, journalist friend of Hamish's.

invitations to Communists and "crypto-Communists" would have to stop (I hesitate to print the threats that were made . . .) We intend, in brief, to fight on this issue. We may be defeated and suppressed, but at any rate we shall have the satisfaction of knowing that we have struck a real blow for freedom in these backward regions . . . suppression will not lay the force of democracy low: it will call them into action . . .

It was probably fortunate for Hamish that his *Elegies for the Dead in Cyrenaica* had recently been published and, in March 1949, won the first Somerset Maugham Award for Poetry. Northern Ireland was greatly impressed, and the 'hunt' for Robin Antrim was less strenuous than it might have been. Hamish's first letter of congratulation came from his friend Neil Campbell:

> Frabjous joy. Excellent. Excellent . . . Cutting from the *Scotsman* enclosed . . . The British Council will soon be laying out the 'red' carpet for you. It would be rather neat if they feted you from the top, after refusing you, as it were, from the bottom . . . It really is splendid news. But – hold on to your conceit of yourself till you have read the notice in the '*Scots Review*' . . .

A second letter from Campbell continues with similar dizzy enthusiasm: 'Dear Hamish . . . Greece! Greece! – I am interested in the dialectical expenditure of the capitalists' prize money. Are you spending your money where it will best counter Marshall Aid? . . . I hear that there is to be no Gaelic Concert at this year's Edinburgh Festival . . . I think Gaelic Culture has to be sold afresh to the Festival Committee, and it needs a first-rate maestro to present it . . . Hamish you must do it . . .' In a third letter, Campbell draws Hamish's attention to the name Wilfred Taylor (a distinguished journalist who wrote 'Scotsman's Log', a diary column in the *Scotsman* newspaper), and who, for the next thirty years, was to play a strange, 'shadowy' role in Hamish's life.[12]

When news of the Somerset Maugham Award first came through, Hamish celebrated with an outburst of bacchanalian joy: 'We had a

---

12. The reasons for this only came to light after Hamish's death when I was told by David Fletcher, an ex-Army officer and former editor of *Blackwoods* magazine, that Wilfred Taylor was a British Intelligence agent with special responsibility for recruiting graduates from Edinburgh University. In addition Taylor kept a minder's eye on Hamish's public profile and appears to have used his 'Scotsman's Log' to subtly muffle the Henderson voice.

party! We went to a pub. Then to another. We were singing – then I was arrested! I spent the night in the Police cells! Why they arrested me I can't imagine. I was having a good time, yes, but they had no business to be arresting me – having just won this great award – it was a party to celebrate life and joy – why should I take my first bardic payment in dour gloom and silence!'

The Somerset Maugham judges in 1949 were C.V. Wedgewood and C. Day Lewis, with V.S. Pritchett as Chairman. The award was worth £310, the equivalent of a year's salary for a working man. For the first time in his life, Hamish had money and, within hours, quite a number of his friends were advising him what he should do with it. One of these was a betting-man in Jean Connor's boarding house – who had a red-hot tip for the Aintree Grand National: Russian Hero! And so it was, on the best of Irish advice and in the name of Russia's 25 million dead, that Hamish decided to splash out in style. Russian Hero was a rank outsider running at 66-1:

> The suggestion was – that I put the whole £310 on this horse! But, of course, I was young – and foolish – and I limited myself to £10! What a fool! We listened on the wireless – and Russian Hero came romping home. I was most disappointed! I returned to Fitzwilliam street with just £670 in my pocket! I shouted up the stairs – "There is a God !" But they knew already and came tumbling down the stairs – they were ahead of the game! They'd all been drinking – so, we went out and had a dram! I can't remember whether the police took me in a second time – but soon enough I was on the train to Dublin. To see the Behans. And I joined them in the Easter Parade.

Hamish's Dublin diary for Easter 1949 records extended meetings with the Behan family, a visit to the theatre to see *The Plough and the Stars* with Peeder O'Donnell, and a night with Brendan Behan in Macnamara's pub at which Hamish announced 'the Scottish Republic Proclaimed', which presumably means that in Dublin, on 17 April 1949, Hamish publicly declared Scotland an independent nation.

On 18 April Hamish returned to Belfast before travelling to Paris, as a delegate to the International Peace Congress. On the 25th he returned to Edinburgh and, flushed with his recent winnings, began planning a second edition of his *Ballads of World War II* and an entirely new collection of 'Traditional Ballads, Modern Ballads and Bawdy Songs'. His

Lt Hamish Henderson in a sergeant's great coat, January 1942

Hamish interrogating Italian officers in the desert, 1942

Hamish watching a great dust storm outside Tobruk, c. 15 November 1942

Hamish interrogating the German paratrooper commander (Captain Guenther) whom he had captured (in civilian clothes) in Sicily, July 1943

The Anzio Beachhead, May 1944: Hamish's pipe band performs for wounded American troops at Nettuno

The Beachhead band marches past the Capitol, Rome, 6 June 1944

Hamish and the pipe band, St Peter's Square, Rome, mid June 1944

Hamish relaxing on the Isle of Capri, late June 1944

Capri, late June 1944: Hamish with his friend Raphaele (a brilliant dancer of the Tarantella)

Hamish outside the Uffizi Art Gallery, Florence, following the disbandment of the Tuscan partisan battalions, September 1944. His jeep is named Potente in honour of his friend the partisan commander, Aligi Barducci, killed in the battle to liberate the city. Luigi Castiglione is on the left of Hamish

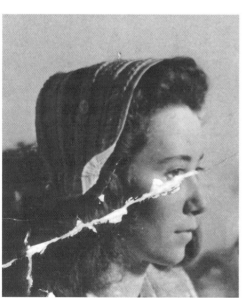

Liana Silva, the artist, journalist and broadcaster who worked closely with Hamish to nurture the post-war Risorgimento that began with the liberation of Rome in June 1944

Aligi Barducci, 'Potente', killed in the fight for the freedom of Italy

Capitano Hamish Henderson, partisan commander, giving the communist salute, summer 1945, in the Jeep now named 'Bandiera Rossa'. Beside him are Luigi Castiglione and his driver Ivan

Hamish (centre, front) with a group of victorious communist partisans, summer 1945

Hamish with a fellow intelligence officer and three Axis prisoners before the 'well of truth', Italy 1945

Hamish aged twenty-five, ready to return to civilian life after five years of war, October 1945

Hamish in a Cambridge park, 1945, the winter sun marking the cross of St Andrew on his face –
as it had lit the night sky above Alamein in 1942

Hugh MacDiarmid and Sorley MacLean, the two Scottish poets whom Hamish
most admired (Shetland 1935)

Scottish celebrations at Cambridge 1945/46. The woman on Hamish's lap is Marian Sugden (co-producer of the *Poetry Broadsheets*, Cambridge, 1951–2)

Hamish with cultural/political associates in Cambridge, 1946 (third from the left is E.P. Thompson, the distinguished English social historian)

Hamish visiting a refugee nursery in Germany, autumn 1947

Hamish with his nationalist/communist friends (from the left): Callum MacDonald (publisher), Marian Blythman, Morris Blythman (Thurso Berwick), Christopher M. Grieve (Hugh MacDiarmid) and Michael Grieve (youngest son of CMG), 1949

Nan Milton and her father John MacLean, the Scottish socialist republican hero for whom Hamish wrote his 'John MacLean March' in 1948

Jeannie Robertson, the great ballad singer and tradition bearer whom Hamish 'discovered' in Aberdeen in 1953

Alan Lomax, Tom Scott (poet) and Hamish Henderson recording the student revels in the quad of the Old College, University of Edinburgh, 1951

Antonio Gramsci, the great communist philosopher, killed by Italian fascism in 1936. This painting is by Renzo Galeotti. Hamish's translation of Gramsci's prison letters is today regarded as a major work of literature

Cover of 'The Rebels Ceilidh Songbook', published by the Bo'ness Literary Society, 1953. This lino-cut, by Jimmy Dewar, documents in symbolic form some of the dramatic 'events' that marked the campaign for self-government in Scotland 1950–53. The man labelled MOI with a divining rod, and the Scottie dog with 'HH' teeth, may refer to Hamish Henderson.

Hamish recording the singer, farm-servant and folklorist Willie Matheson in Aberdeenshire, 1951

Hamish's friend Arthur Argo recording 'King of the Cornkisters', Jimmy MacBeath, c. 1957

Hamish in the Braes of Glenlivet, c. 1954

attendance at the Peace Conference appears to have renewed police interest in Hamish's activities and on 22 May he wrote to his communist friend Phil Stein, in Glasgow: 'Dear Phil, . . . Willison sent me a bundle of French papers on Tuesday, 12th May – they arrived today, exactly a week later. It's obvious the censors aren't linguists! I've started a Prologue to my new *Book of Ballads*:

> A braw new song, a bonnie new song
>   My freans I randilie sing ye.
> – An' manger chiel, ye can listen tae,
>   For bonnilie doon we'll ding ye!
>
> Aye, these are the words o' the raucle tune
>   We'll sing like lads o' spirit –
> We want nae truck wi' Heaven or Hell
>   Wha this bra earth inherit . . .'[13]

Meantime Hamish was not neglecting his WEA duties, and his notebooks show him lecturing and stimulating cultural activities all over Ulster. One lecture was entitled 'The Role of the Artist in Society'; he delivered it in various locations and his notes suggest that it was, for him, a kind of 'art manifesto'.

Art depends on the society. In primitive societies the poet or bard was an honoured person. Integrally part of the community. His songs or hymns were a part of reality for the people (the poet's 'illusion' of the harvest field was part of the reality) . . . In all class societies the completeness of the artist's perception of reality is to a certain extent crippled . . . Even in the period of rising imperialism – the robust self-confident capitalism of the Victorian age could still produce a Dickens – but in this anxious, despondent, febrile period of late capitalism, artists have become more and more isolated, more and more shut in on themselves. Artists have tended to become very arrogant, capricious and pretentious. – Poets, of course, realize this – realize what has been lost. The Scot MacDiarmid, and the Irishman Yeats have expressed it with poignancy . . . But others have retreated into 'contempt', into what would seem to be a contempt for life . . . What is the alternative?

---

13. HH, letter to Phil Stein, 22 May 1949.

Artists must try to reach completeness again – though, in our age, they are unlikely to achieve it. How should the attempt be made? By a patient road of study, sacrifice and understanding, by a refusal to be rattled, refusal to accept the values of external mediocrities, the clique of letters. And by a growth of understanding of the duties and problems that face us . . .

The real study of folk art – the art of the labouring classes, the work-songs of the community – how they come about, how they grow, what their energy and aesthetic force consist of – is still in its infancy; – for the very good reason that it has not suited the powers that be to further such studies. Folk art is an implicit – and in many aspects an explicit challenge to the ruling class way of looking at the world. There is a philistinism in the working class and in their organisations but these things can be taken in their stride. It is an inevitable consequence of impoverished existences – but the issue is – how are we going to counteract it? By study, sacrifice and understanding. We have more to learn from them than they from us. Gradually the poet and the community must be threaded together again – and we must start here, where we stand – we can do no other.

That the country towns of Ulster should have been offered such original, revolutionary thought – specifically tailored to each community and its historical situation – is an indication of the valuable work that the WEA was doing in the post-war period. And if some students were not up to the intellectual demands that Hamish's lectures placed on them, everyone was invited – after classes – to continue the discussion over tea and biscuits, or at a local hostelry, where songs and drams would punctuate debates that went on late into the night. A high proportion of Hamish's lecture subjects might be considered male in emphasis but at least one of Hamish's zones of enquiry aroused considerable interest among the women of County Tyrone – as is made clear in this letter from Mrs Maude Smith of Coalisland: 'The subject you have chosen for our second lecture, "Ideas of Love in the Middle Ages", is most appropriate. Confidentially, I have often wondered how primitive men did woo their lady loves, or what their ideas of love, really were: – or were they conscious of such an emotion?. . .'

Hamish also spoke out boldly in favour of Ulster Scots and tried to boost the folk-song and musical traditions of Ulster. Andy Boyd reports that Hamish 'loosened a number of the firmest of Ulster jaws – but his greater task, here, was not going to be easy, not in practice, not in theory'. Hamish knew this himself: 'Between me and the people who share my ideas – and ideals – there is still a barrier and it is important to understand that – to understand everything, is not only, as the French say, to forgive everything, but also to overcome everything, and start again. Not ignoring the past, but reclaiming it – prizing it and cherishing it – and looking forward to the life and song which is to come . . .'. He believed that there is a 'Marxist lock' to mankind's cultural evolution and that the 'folk-spirit key' is the means of unlocking it – at least in the Celtic world, where the folk-continuum remains a living reality. He writes of there being 'a Marxist folk goddess' (a modern 'folk-spirit') that concentrates and develops the collective joy of social groups and who can, even in educated societies, overwhelm with her benevolent goodness. He believed that human societies must keep in contact with the best of the old – as they developed the new – and he gives an example of the negative clash of contrary forces by recalling an incident from his own 'broken' childhood.

> I remember, as a romantic and studious country boy – lodging in London – my behaviour (reading history) invoking the acid scorn of a Paddington landlady. 'Hamish, have you nothing better to do than moon around all day imbibing that old nonsense!' In taking a ticket from rural Scotland to London I had crossed without realizing it, a chasm – between an area where folk-spirit still stubbornly and joyously resisted, and an area where the particularly brutal industrialisation of the C19th had killed it stone-dead.

During his year in Ulster, Hamish met the novelist Sam Hanna Bell on several occasions and recognised that he was a man addressing similar ideas and problems. Hanna Bell was fascinated by the historical and cultural links between past and present and between Ulster and Scotland. He was strongly left-wing but, since the thirties, had worked as a BBC programme maker. Hanna Bell had been brought up within a deeply Presbyterian community on the shores of Strangford Loch, noting 'it would have been possible for an eighteenth century countryman to recognise all the furniture we used and some of the clothes we wore . . .' Like Hamish he was a country boy but also a well-educated man who knew industrial Belfast and the west of Scotland well, and, as a writer, became 'the poetical voice' of one of the most austere and thrawn communities in Europe. Hamish liked him and was one of the first people to describe Bell's novels as 'outcrops of the Scottish novel': he saw their blend of folk tradition and modern forms – a very

Scottish characteristic – paralleling the work of Charles Rennie Mackintosh in architecture.

Hamish's very presence in Ulster seems to have encouraged Bell to be bolder in his writing and, two years after Hamish left Ulster, Sam Hanna Bell published his most controversial and ambitious novel, *December Bride*. It is a work that draws together the inhibitions, the stoical heroism, the pedantry, the beauties and boldness of generations of life in Ulster. Bell's narrative economy and emotive power can also be seen as akin to the Scots ballad tradition that Hamish was championing. Today, *December Bride* is recognised as a classic Irish novel and, in 1989, it was made into a memorable feature film.

Once Hamish had the Somerset Maugham Award in his pocket, he began to make plans to relinquish his post and leave Ulster. His prize stipulated that the recipient must travel abroad. This did not greatly please Hamish; he had been travelling non-stop for ten years! He asked whether he could 'travel' to Limerick but was told 'Not far enough!' Thus, Hamish decided to return to Italy. About a year earlier, Amleto Micozzi had sent him the recently published *Antonio Gramsci: Lettere dal Carcere (Prison Letters of Antonio Gramsci)*; the more Hamish read them, the more important he saw them to be and he now decided that it was his duty to translate them. Consequently, during May and June he began winding down his Irish commitments but rarely slackened his creative pace. Having gained a level of literary fame he began to be asked to review books. One was *The Scots* by Moray MacLaren, and Hamish jumped at the chance of addressing the Scottish public:

> Although few people properly understand what has been happening in Scotland in the last couple of decades, an increasing number want to find out something about it. Hence the present spate of articles and books about one or other aspects of the Scottish national revival . . . Scottish history and the modern Scottish situation have been so effectively bedevilled by official distortionists and sentimental misrepresenters that the writer of a short book like this has a formidable task. In a sense he has to embark on a voyage of personal discovery before he can begin to survey his country's heritage. And if, like MacLaren, he has succeeded in getting one of his eyes open, he may think himself lucky if he is not simultaneously attacked as a yes man and an iconoclast. In Scotland, as in the country of the blind, the one-eyed man stands an excellent chance of being thrown out on his neck . . .

He also sought to make a public statement about the political problems simmering in the Province of Ulster and wrote a major article for the *New*

Statesman and Nation. It was not published. No copy of this article appears to exist but in 1970, as Catholic and Nationalist resentments began to run out of control in Northern Ireland, Hamish jotted down the following notes – which outline the position he had taken in 1949.

> When I was working in Northern Ireland as District Secretary of the WEA I was appalled at what seemed to me the imbecile complacency of the British Press in their comments on the Government of Ireland Act, passed by Atlee's government in 1949 ... It was obvious to me that Lord Brookeborough's apartheid-sodden ghettoes could not last, and I wrote to 'The New Statesman and Nation' saying so; I added that unless the Westminster politicians took the trouble to learn a bit about the reality of life in the six counties, there would be an explosion in ten or twenty years time which could make the 'Troubles' of the twenties seem like a kindergarten.

Before saying farewell to Ireland, Hamish advertised a 'Private Lecture' to be delivered in the Kensington Hotel, Great Victoria Street, Belfast, with this announcement: 'Mr. Hamish Henderson, the distinguished Scottish writer and critic, author of "Elegies for the Dead in Cyrenaica" etc. will speak on "Writers and the Fight for Peace" ... The audience will be asked whether some sort of committee should be set up in Belfast to initiate resistance to the present and growing tendency to regard a Third World War as inevitable, or even desirable . . .' This meeting took place at 8.00p.m. on 14 June 1949 and after Hamish's talk Tommy Cusack was elected chairman of the first Belfast Peace Committee; members dedicated themselves 'to work for Peace and against the poisonous propaganda being peddled in favour of Cold War and Nuclear Deterrence'.

Thus, Hamish left Ireland having laid the basis of the Irish Peace Movement. It was a gift of long-term consequence. Hamish gave an equally remarkable present to his landlady, Jean Connor: a large tin of white distemper and a six-inch paint brush. Andy Boyd commented later: 'She was surprised and nonplussed! Neither she nor anyone else knew how the gift should be taken. Was this a measured insult to a woman with a dirty house? Was it a Dadaist gesture towards a woman who owed money? Was it a gesture of comradely solidarity? Was it practical help?' It was in fact a 'Marxian key' for Jean Connor's 'folk-lock', and the 'goodness' of Hamish's gesture is revealed in the last verse of his great song, 'The Freedom Come a' Ye', written ten years later.

So come all ye at hame wi' Freedom
    Never heed whit the hoodies croak for doom.
In your hoose a' the bairns o' Adam
    Can find breid, barley-bree and painted room.

When MacLean meets wi's freens in Springburn
    A' the roses and geans will turn tae bloom,
And a black boy frae yont Nyanga
    Dings the fell gallows o' the burghers doon.[14]

Hamish returned to Britain with his Republicanism and pan-Celtic enthusiasm much enhanced but, as a poet and a folklorist, he had also been
vitally stimulated by his contact with Ireland's Protestant tradition. All his
life he would refer to the Ulster Scots as 'the salt of the earth'; he delighted
in their generosity, their humanity and 'their poetry of soul – which sang
out even in the teeth of "blotched bigotry"'. Hamish's Cambridge friend
Marian Sugden remembers him, in the autumn of 1949, 'waxing lyrical
about "solid silk banners bellying the wind" and interfaith picnickers
enjoying the 12th July. At the dinner table he'd deliberately taunt the guests
by suddenly singing the "Auld Orange Flute" or some other Protestant
song! I remember him describing the Ulster people as a threesome –
strapped together, inside one Janus head! "What Northern Ireland needs,"
he said "is a Paul Robeson! What they've got is Craigavon!"'[15]

During August, as he prepared himself for his work on the Gramsci
letters, Hamish wangled himself a visit to Venice – with Helen Cruickshank and Hugh MacDiarmid – as one of Scotland's representatives at the
1949 PEN International Peace Conference. And while he was there he met
up with his old friend the painter Angelo Savelli, and together they visited
the Arena Chapel in Padua to view the Giotto frescoes. The atmosphere at
the conference, however, was depressing: 'Weaving, reeling, winding,
warping, beaming and gassing – Rosencrantz and Guildenstern's
everywhere . . .' Hamish acted as MacDiarmid's translator and soon
found himself having to put everyone in their place: 'MacDiarmid has
never feared to quarrel or test his steel against the intellectual paladins of
this world – Existentialists, Constructive-Sadists, Logical Positivists – all
have known what it was to cross swords with a bonnie fechter!' He made
prose translations of two of MacDiarmid's best Scots lyrics, 'The Eamis

---

14. 'The Freedom Come a' Ye', first published in 1961 in a leaflet of 'Anti-polaris
    songs', later published in the *Collected Poems*.
15. Lord Craigavon, Secretary of State for Northern Island.

Stane' and 'Milk-Wort and Bog-Cotton', so that he could better render them 'live' to their Italian (and English-speaking) audiences: he read his own poems, sang his songs – and took great pride in presenting Italian translations of Sorley MacLean's 'The Cuillin' – after informing his audience that 'Scotland's Gaelic poet was now the leader of Europe's literary avant garde'.

Before he left Venice, Savelli presented Hamish with the sketch discussed in Appendix 2 and it adds substance to Hamish's claim that Scottish poetry was now 'the toast of Italy!' What European nation could trump the combined poetic power of MacLean, MacDiarmid and Hamish Henderson, as the mid century dawned? And what Italian could claim a greater role in the Risorgimento than 'il Capitano Hamish Henderson'?

FOURTEEN

The Disciple of Gramsci

It is necessary, with bold spirit and good conscience, to save civilisation. We must halt the dissolution which corrodes and corrupts the roots of human society. The bare and barren tree can be made green again. Are we not ready?

Antonio Gramsci, 15 May 1919

Genuinely original artists and thinkers create the taste by which later generations recognise and judge what they have done. This may well be the case with Hamish's great intellectual hero, Antonio Gramsci. Hamish knew something of Gramsci during the 1930s but it was in the mountains of Italy in 1944 – in the company of communist partisans – that he became aware of his greatness as a man: '*un grande pensatore*'. By that time Gramsci had been dead for eight years and it was only after the war that his writings began to be published to acclaim, first in Italy, then worldwide. From 1947 onwards, Amleto Micozzi sent Hamish copies of everything being published on or by Gramsci, and Hamish's enthusiasm quickly developed into a determination to make Gramsci's uniquely humanitarian vision available to the English-speaking public. Consequently, for three years, from 1948 to 1951, Hamish made the translation of Gramsci's prison letters his prime literary and intellectual concern. Some critics have suggested that it was a tragedy that he allowed himself to be sidetracked from poetry – at the very moment when his reputation as a major poet was there to be claimed. Hamish, however, was always a deeply political animal and he never saw life as compartmentalised. His work on Gramsci was not a burden but a gift: it was something he had to do. He identified closely with Gramsci and when he translates Antonio Gobetti's description of Gramsci the sense of identification becomes palpable: 'More than a tactician and a fighter, Gramsci is a prophet. The only way it is possible to be one now-a-days is to be unheard of – except by fate. The eloquence of Gramsci will not overturn any governments. His catastrophic polemics, his deprecating satire do not admit facile consolations the while for humanity. He demands justice from an implacable future avenger.'[1] Hamish was proud to be such an avenger.

Gobetti's perception of Gramsci as a prophet is important but his statement that any genuine prophet, in our time, must be 'unheard of – except by fate' is even more important. Shortly after writing those words, Gobetti was dead (at the age of twenty-four) and Gramsci arrested, imprisoned and finally 'judicially murdered' in 1936. Consequently Hamish felt duty-bound to take up the baton laid down by Gobetti, and after he had completed his Elegies he was determined that his next big project would be 'Gramsci'. His decision was at once poetical, political and a recognition of the 'folk process' he believed both he and Gramsci were part of.

Antonio Gramsci (1891–1937) was born on the island of Sardinia, the fourth of seven children. His body was small, his head unusually large. As an infant he was injured in a fall which gradually turned him hump-backed, but he had tremendous strength of character and an exceptional intellect. The family's genetic inheritance was mixed – Italian, Albanian, Spanish and Sardinian, and Gramsci was to describe himself as being 'without race'. He was, however, brought up in a deeply traditional environment, in an isolated township proud of its Neolithic Mediterranean heritage. In 1910 he left home to study at the University of Turin. In 1915 he joined the Italian Socialist Party and helped found the newspaper *Oudine Nuove* – the New Order. Later, with Bordiga and Togliatti, he founded the Italian Communist Party (PCI). By 1922 he was working in Moscow, where he married Julia Schucht, a young Russian of German ancestry. During 1924 he was in charge of the Comintern Information Bureau in Vienna but returned to Italy when he was elected to represent the Veneto in the Italian Parliament. As leader of the PCI, he became a noted and fearless spokesman for the anti-fascist cause. He was arrested in 1926 and sentenced to twenty years, four months and five days imprisonment. Mussolini asked the prosecutor 'to prevent this brain functioning for twenty years': Gramsci was declared 'guilty of conspiracy, and of agitation, provoking class war, insurrection and alteration of the Constitution and the form of the state through violence'.

In prison, Gramsci was initially treated with cold brutality but, over the years, he gained access to books and began to write political and philosophical tracts, keep notebooks and write the letters which are today the basis of his intellectual and cultural reputation. It was the notebooks and most of all the letters that appealed to Hamish. They display magnanimous humanity, an almost complete lack of personal

---

1. *La Rivoluzione Liberale*, 1924.

bitterness and a wonderfully casual cultural range. With a magical
lightness of touch Gramsci discusses history, folklore, psychoanalysis,
literature, Christianity, Judaism, sociology – St Francis, Chesterton,
Conan Doyle, Dante, popular theatre, etc. These *Lettere dal Carcere*
were first published by Einaudi, in Milan, in May 1947 and, in the spring
of 1948, Hamish wrote to John Lehmann informing him that his Gramsci
translations would 'follow the Elegies, within a year'. In fact, as he had
accepted the WEA post in Ulster, the whole project had to be postponed.
On 4 October 1949, Lehmann wrote to Hamish in some irritation:

> I feel this business of the translation of the Gramsci letters is getting
> rather urgent. I'd like you to do it, but may I put it quite brutally to
> you – what is in my mind? Simply this: what proof do I have that
> you are equipped for the job? What proof or evidence can you show
> me? Let me have your answer as soon as you can, will you?
> P.S. Cecil Day Lewis wants to read your first and tenth elegies at the
> Cheltenham Festival this month. Do we give him permission?

Hamish was pleased to give Day Lewis permission to use his Elegies, and
Lehmann's questioning of his 'Gramsci credentials' stimulated him to
write a long unanswerable case as to why he *should* translate the prison
letters:

> Gramsci was a socialist who found fruitful difference in the un-
> differentiated mass – he learned from the manual workers of Turin
> and from the peasants and fishers of Southern Italy. He made a
> special study of Italian popular culture, and if there are three words
> which epitomise what Gramsci was not – they are 'by invitation
> only' . . . He was very fond of Roman Rolland's phrase – 'a
> pessimist of the intellect, and optimist of the will', but it was
> Gramsci's intellect that strengthened his will. Psychologically he
> had a sinewy toughness of character: like Danton, 'no weakness'.
> His fanaticism was 'a disciplined controlled fanaticism' that one
> associates with all the great revolutionaries.

> Gramsci is a hero absolutely without heroics, anti-Romantic and
> anti-Rhetorical. The modern communist has left behind the old kind
> of heroism . . .

> He stood against the 'soul-destroying' littleness and monotony
> against which his spirit asserted itself with such triumphant élan.
> He had energy – 'an omnivorous and all-embracing zest for life'. He

wrote with difficulty. He was without vanity and absolutely fearless. In conversation his technique was that of the Socratic dialogue – he kindled good sense in others then took the subplots set in motion and located them within the grandeur of his own perceptions.

. . . And he knows he must travel his chosen road to the end. Entering prison he knows an important part of his job is still to do. The letters are 'tragic' in the most real sense. He has chosen his way and that cannot be separated from suffering. He wishes to live, to work and to love, but his chosen ineluctable path brings him to suffering and death. His letters are full of love: never disfigured or debased by futile regrets and recriminations. All the notes are the deep, steady, strong notes of the lament. '*Cha till, cha till mi Anilleadh*'. He looked for a new aristocracy – coming from below.

pietas and irony
culture and curiosity
civil courage
physical courage – in spite of his weakly body and
his hump[2] – he kept human dignity erect and upright.

Hamish believed Gramsci's writings on art to be the most brilliant Marxist contribution to aesthetics since Plekhanov's *Art and Social Life*, and he describes him as

a confirmed theatre goer, the first 'critic' to quote and honour Pirandello and his 'barn-stormers': Gramsci applauds Ibsen and Andreieff, he anticipated George Orwell by a decade, he recognised the mythological force in Boys' Stories, Westerns and Serial Romances. He saw Folk Art as the natural bedrock of all cultural developments. He planned a book on popular taste and studied popular 'bad art' because of what all art tells of the human and social reality. He exemplifies a 'quality of civic courage': the quality above all, perhaps, that modern man needs . . . Gramsci was a great

---

2. This reference to Gramsci's 'hump' is interesting because Hamish had been exploring the symbolism and poetic power of 'the hump' for at least ten years. In his Tenth Elegy he writes of 'the humped epigoni, outliving the fians' (the hump-backed poets, outliving the early Irish warriors). His IRA play is entitled 'The Humpy Cromm' and embodies the idea of the poet (and humanity) being both burdened and inspired. (John Bunyon had his bundle, Gramsci his hump, Hamish his scholar's stoop: all stand for 'human dignity erect and upright'.)

man. Possibly one of the few very great men to have lived in this sorry
century, he has a strange (Scottish) mixture of hardness and softness. . . .
Sardinian is not really a dialect at all but a language, like Provencal and
Lallans (no word can so well translate the Italian expletive 'Beh' as the
vigorous Scots and Irish 'och'). There is a Celtic aspect to Gramscian
culture – oral – casual – deep – he was the islander, '*l'isolano*'.[3]

Hamish also listed various world figures whom he believed shared 'aspects'
of Gramsci's genius: 'the English seventeenth-century diarist John Evelyn
(particularly his concern for his children), John Maclean (political activity
leading to imprisonment, towering intellect and rich humanity), Norman
Douglas (the Scottish pagan – for his omnivorous, Rabelaisian qualities),
Thomas Carlyle (for his critique of an age), Walt Whitman (the prophet of
democracy), Cavafy (the perverse and amoral Alexandrian), Croce (as a
great Italian thinker), Oscar Wilde (the poet broken by imprisonment),
Tomaso Campanella, 1568–1639 (27 years in a Naples prison, unbroken),
Vincent van Gogh, and Hugh MacDiarmid.' Finally, Hamish appended his
own 'poetic vignette' of Gramsci as 'a man of iron' who, through hard
work, inspired thought and creative genius, had constructed the frames
within which the good communist of the future might imagine himself:

> Unremitting, relentless
> Organised to the last degree –
> Though Lenin's politics is bairn's play
> To what a communist must be.

Gramsci's letters provide us with a marvellous self-portrait – constructed over time – and painted against a vivid background showing
the culture of his time and his love. The letters are reminiscent of
Montaigne's essays – and the fact that political discussion was
forbidden means that he dwells on the personal, on language, literature and folklore – observations of his fellow prisoners set forth
musings that then embrace the ends of the earth. Some people have
read these letters as constituting a martyrology of a secular society . . .
Gramsci's humanist vision was beyond party, law or imposed power
– and he would not compromise the union he had constructed
between his inner vision and external human need . . . Thus amongst
the last sentences uttered by Gramsci some are very like those uttered
by Christ on the cross: 'I have destroyed my own existence!'[4]

---

3. HH, letter to John Lehmann, late 1949.
4. *Ibid.*

John Lehmann was well persuaded and agreed to pay Hamish an advance of £50 (later increased to £100). Subsequently, on 9 March 1950, Hamish set off for Italy via the 'Second National Assizes' of the French Peace Movement in Paris. On 20 March he left the Gare de Lyon for Turin in a happy and poetical state of mind:

> after Virieu-le-Grand the country becomes a wee bit Glen Finnan. Mist in the mottled hills. Primroses and cowslips. Hauteville – tenements with spike rail balconies – washing out – the river below – grey-green. Culoz – buffet truck with Tobler chocolate – vineyards almost vertical on the hillsides. Chambery – 400 dead from American raid during the war. Most of the bombs fell on the town. Savoy – looking wintery. Bonnie conical shaped mountain – snow down to the track. After crossing the frontier – darkness. Young Italians with skis and winter-sports paraphenalia returning to Turin after their weekend in the mountains. The French married couple talks in whispers while the Italians talk louder and louder . . . Meet (and lodge with) Natalia Ginsberg (distinguished poet, nee Levi) and her prospective husband, Baldini.

Hamish does not mention meeting Primo Levi when staying with the Ginsbergs but it is likely that he did. He certainly quickly renewed his friendship with Eugenio Montale, who immediately presented him with a new poem. It was entitled, 'Il rosso e il negro', and he inscribed a hand-written copy of the poem to Hamish. The poem's subject is the atrocities committed in the Ardeatine caves exactly seven years earlier, and Montale was keen to honour the man who had translated Govoni's poems about the massacre, done so much to overthrow Nazi-fascism and set in motion the now burgeoning Risorgimento.

In Milan, Hamish was introduced to Einaudi and numerous leading literary figures including Sereni, Aldovrandi, Rossi, Calvino and Pavese. He found he shared much with Calvino: both were multi-lingual, communists, both had fought with the partisans, both, increasingly, sought a literary lightness of touch. For example, when Calvino writes 'I tried to identify myself with the ruthless energies propelling the events of our century . . . Soon I became aware that between the facts of life, and the quick lightness of touch I wanted for my writing, there was a gulf that cost me increasing effort to cross,'[5] Hamish might have written the same words. In 'The Literary Machine', Calvino continues: 'What we ask of

---

5. Italo Calvino, 'Six Memos for the Next Millennium', lectures at Harvard 1985: 'The Literary Machine'.

writers is that they guarantee the survival of what we call human, in a world where everything appears inhuman . . . The big secret is to hide, escape, cover your tracks . . . I reject the role of the person chasing events. I prefer the person who continues his discourse, waiting for it to become topical again, like all things that have a sound basis' – once more Hamish's philosophy and life come to mind.

Cesare Pavese also shared experiential bonds with Hamish. He was brought up without a father in a rural community, studied philosophy with Benedetto Croce and became one of the early followers of Gramsci. He suffered internment under the fascist regime but was 'taken up' by Einaudi and quickly established a major literary reputation in the post-war period. Pavese's *Dialoghi con Leuco*, published in 1947, explores the relationship between classical myths and modern studies in anthropology, ethnology and psychoanalysis (almost exactly the field of study Hamish advised Luigi Castiglione to pursue for his doctorate in 1946). In 1950 Pavese published a collection of stories, *La Luna e i Falo*, based on the human need 'to return to one's native place', the longing 'for shared roots', and the folklore research of Ernesto de Martino (whose work greatly interested Hamish). At the time Pavese met Hamish, he was preparing an article for the avant-garde magazine *Cultura e Realta* on American literature. In this article he commends Hamish's favourite American authors, Faulkner and Steinbeck (in particular *The Grapes of Wrath*, Hamish's favourite film). Pavese's interest in the United States, however, had been primarily stimulated by his affair with an American actress called Constance Dowling (and her sister) and, following a series of what Amleto Micozzi has described as 'sexual fiascos', on 27 August 1950, Pavese committed suicide. He was fifty-two. Shortly afterwards, Hamish wrote to Micozzi, 'Cesare Pavese was a valient man – what you write of his death is right. I very much admire his poem "Don't speak too much of me".' Hamish saw Cesare Pavese as a classic example of 'the artist as martyr' and, eight months before Pavese's death, he had given noble expression to this permanent creative reality in his poem 'Into the Future':

The theme of lyric perfection in exchange for the sacrifice of the
　　creator
Recur here once again denuded of myth and addressed
In direct and clear words to those who seek to enclose
The struggle of life in the crystal of the verse flames.[6]

---

6. HH, unpublished notebook jottings.

In Italy, Hamish 'sorned' with his usual abandon and was welcomed into homes all over the country. In Bologna he stayed with 'Montanari', in Padova with 'Beppi', in Sienna with the distinguished philosopher Leone Vivante. Here he stayed for almost two months at the villa Solaja Malafrasca and repaid Leone's kindness by translating a selection of his conference papers into English. Hamish also earned himself money by writing a series of articles for *L'Unita*, the Italian Communist Party daily newspaper; his subjects included Marshall Graziani, Gramsci, Sorley MacLean and the Partisan War. Throughout the summer of 1950, there were numerous celebrations to mark the fifth anniversary of peace, and el Capitano Henderson was in great in demand. He was fêted as a Partisan hero, as a great Scottish poet, and as a leader of the International Peace Movement.

Wherever Hamish went he would sing and – more importantly – announce the Scottish Renaissance and Italian Risorgimento as the twin piers of Europe's cultural renewal. He spoke against the Cold War and the institutionalisation of 'false enmities across Europe'.

At literary gatherings Hamish's ability to move effortlessly between English and Italian, Scots and Gaelic, German and French was hugely impressive. He delivered MacDiarmid in Scots, MacLean in Gaelic and both in Italian. In particular he used Gaelic culture and Sorley MacLean as a kind of 'secret weapon' with which he could beguile his audiences: here was the voice of a new great poet from an area largely forgotten since the age of Columba (when Ireland and Scotland held the torch of European humanism in the face of post-Roman barbarism). His lecture notes stated: 'MacLean was the first to break away from the pastoral and religious traditions in Gaelic poetry and to show a visionary awareness of the political and economic situation in Modern Scotland . . . He is central to the present revival of the Gaelic language and his use of Gaelic as a "living language" has stimulated others like Douglas Young and George Campbell Hay. What he has done others can do – here in Italy, with the many languages, dialects and songs you have . . .'

One young Italian who was hugely impressed was Pier Paolo Pasolini (at that time an aspiring poet, now recognised as one of the world's great film-makers). Hamish's advocacy of a poetry – of civic duty and bawdy delight – rising irresistibly into song, appealed greatly to the young libertarian, communist and ex-partisan (Pasolini's brother had been killed in the partisan war). Hamish's championship of regional dialects and minority languages, of vernacular poetry and Gramscian vision, also spoke to Pasolini as a Friulian radical. Across northern Italy Hamish was saluted as a new Byron: here was a man carrying the torch of Shelley, Keats and Burns; here was a thick-lipped Bacchus who was honoured amongst the Tuscan partisans as 'the bravest of the brave'. How could the young Pasolini not love him?

Pasolini's masterpiece, 'The Ashes of Gramsci' (published in 1954), with its conversational verse forms, hermetic difficulties and awkward thumping rhythms, shares many of the qualities Hamish had pioneered in his Elegies (and perfected in his 'Poem for the Partisans of Peace', 1949). Pasolini's three-line verses also echo a continuing Celtic tradition, used by Hamish. Both men shared an artistic delight in the confrontation between instinct and reason, personal desire and moral vocation, imaginative creativity and political duty. Neither could see the world, or their art, as divided. Shocking honesty made them both targets for virulent enemies.

To what extent the artistic relationship between Hamish and Pasolini was direct – through Pasolini's attendance at Hamish's lectures, poetry readings; at demonstrations and gatherings – or indirect, via newspaper articles, books and cultural/political activities, is unclear, but Hamish's influence on Pasolini's poetry appears to be strong and lasting. 'The Ashes of Gramsci' was quickly followed by 'The Apennines', a literary tour de force that, in many ways, parallels MacLean's mountain epic 'The Cuillin'. Ten years later, in his third great poem, 'Plan of Future Works', Pasolini again uses the three-line verse form, explores 'Celtic' cultural issues and utters a series of visionary cries that address the issues that were Hamish's central concerns in 1950.

On 1 May 1950 Hamish was a special guest at the Memorial Celebrations to mark the end of the war in Italy, at Dongo – the small sub-Alpine town where Mussolini had been captured and killed. A photograph documents Hamish at the microphone in the piazza, standing in strong sunshine beneath a shuttered window, speaking for the men of the 52nd Garibaldi Brigade – and in remembrance of Antonio Gramsci. The photographer has captured a historic moment, and if one wants to understand what Hamish meant to the Italian Risorgimento this image repays study.

By 1950 the Italian neo-realist film movement was in full swing and influencing the cinema worldwide. Most of the leading film directors had either fought with the partisans or espoused their values, and after the war they had gone out into the villages, the streets, the factories where they used their art to address murder, betrayal and love; they confronted poverty and corruption, they trumpeted human values and a democratic, more socialist future. The outstanding directors include Roberto Rossellini, Vittorio de Sica, Visconti, Michelangelo Antonio, Federico Fellini (and, a few years later, Pier Paolo Pasolini). Most of these directors were writers, all moved among writers whom Hamish knew well, and all were part of the new cultural climate that Gramsci and military defeat had triggered as the alternative to fascism. The new cinema used folk-culture as the bedrock out of which a new multi-faceted, modern Italy might emerge – urban but rural in spirit. Hamish had been advocating a new Risorgimento in Rome before Roberto Rossellini launched his seminal exploration of the 'Open City'. While staying with Leone Vivante in Siena, Hamish wrote in a notebook: 'Perhaps the moment between not knowing at all and knowing by heart is just two singings and a listener away.'

It was Leone Vivante's son, Cesare, who introduced Hamish to Adriano Olivetti, one of the giants of the Italy's post-war economic miracle. He was also a man of high culture and saw good design and business success as integral necessities and part of the blossoming Risorgimento. Hamish was invited out to the Olivetti villa near Avrea where he enjoyed the hospitality of one of Italy's grand modern families. Olivetti was an industrialist in the William Morris mould but also a technological innovator who addressed industrial manufacturing – with socialist zeal. He cared passionately about the wellbeing of his workforce, and proudly offered patronage to many of Italy's leading artists and intellectuals. And it was in Olivetti's hilltop villa that Hamish recognised the possibilities of Olivetti's new portable tape-recorder: 'That tape-recorder struck me with the force of a revelation! Here was a tool with which I could record, document and revitalise the song and musical tradition of Scotland. It was a windfall – like Newton's apple – out of the pure Alpine air!'

In September 1950 Hamish wrote to Amleto Micozzi from Milan: 'I've found a place in Tuscany where I'll go and where I'll remain until I've finished the translation of Gramsci . . .' He then moved to the Colle Val d'Elsa near Poggibonsi, where he had partisan friends, but in mid-October, in Siena, Hamish was woken at two in the morning by five Carabinieri hammering at his door. They delivered papers ordering him to leave the country. The precise reasons for his expulsion remain unclear. On 24 October, back in Cambridge, Hamish wrote to Micozzi: 'I don't know if you've heard the news of my expulsion from Italy by order of the Christian-Democrat government. When I was still in Siena I received, by the Questura, an order to leave Italy in three days. It was not an unexpected thing because I had been involved in intense political activity in Italy – I think you know about my speech in Modena . . .'[7] On 20 November, Luigi Castigliano wrote from Milan.

---

7. Hamish's Modena speech was made at a reunion of the Partisans of Emilia and Lombardia, a notably radical group.

... You must have under-estimated the suspiciousness of the L'Unita people towards you – my reception, when I went to give them your letter, was rather worse than cool – in fact, they just showed me the door (they kept the letter, however, with a covering letter of mine) ... *No flatfoot bothers us any more* – however, my passport has expired meantime and they seem to have decided not to let me have it again – I'm going to kick up a fuss through the university ...

In many ways, Hamish was more than content to be back in Scotland but his expulsion ruptured many friendships and cultural and political connections. He was put on an Italian government blacklist, his closest Italian contacts were placed under surveillance and his correspondence was regularly opened; it was to be twenty-nine years before Hamish returned to Italy. Only on his honeymoon did he attempt to break the exclusion order. In 1959, having got married in southern Germany, he decided to take his young bride south 'into Italy, where I knew we would never be short of a bed, good food – and the flow of endless vino!' At the Italian border they were both ordered off the train, rigorously inter-rogated and ignominiously sent back into Austria.

It is possible that Hamish precipitated his expulsion from Italy – knowing well that he must return some time to Scotland, and that to return as a victim of political injustice might do his revolutionary reputation no harm. His going, however, was genuinely lamented in Italy, as the following letter from Amleto Micozzi, written in 2004, makes clear.

For sure – many works and relationships were interrupted forever by Hamish's expulsion from Italy. For example Einaudi was waiting here in Rome to meet him – to sign the contract for me to publish his *Elegies* in Italian. It put an end to many relationships that Hamish intended to cultivate further – like that with my friend Mario Motto, director of the philosophical magazine *Cultura e Realta*. And I had shown Hamish the poems of an unknown girl, Alda Merini: I found her poems striking and Hamish thought them beautiful – so I charged Hamish to find her address, through his literary friends in Milano. He found it. She was in a madhouse! And Hamish was planning to visit her – when his expulsion order came! Today, she is one of the most famous and honoured poets in Italy and she is talked about as a potential winner of the Nobel Prize for Literature ... Two of Hamish's Italian colleagues, Montale and Quasimodo, went on to win the Nobel Prize, and he knew Ungaretti well but all these contacts ended with his expulsion. Despite that, the influence of Hamish on Italy has been greater than most people think . . . I worked closely with Cesare Zavatinni, the great film-writer, for many years. Many times I discussed Hamish with Zavatinni. The expulsion of Hamish was a shocking and saucy act by the Italian/ American government but, from another point of view, it was providential – looking at the good his repatriation produced for the sake and glory of Celtic culture in Scotland and over the world.

Hamish completed his translation of the Gramsci Letters in Cambridge at the beginning of February 1951. On 12 February, John Lehmann acknowledged receipt of the completed manuscript: 'Dear Hamish, I think you have done your work on Gramsci very well indeed . . . I agree with you about cutting. The best of the letters – the most human, the most revealing are wonderful, and some of those about Italian history are very illuminating, too. It is when he goes into long, dry, dialectical discussion that I quail – and fear most of the readers will quail too . . .' On 2 March, he wrote to agree that Hamish should receive a total advance of £100. After that, however, things quickly fell apart, and by May Lehmann writes to say 'You are an obstinate fellow, Hamish, but I can play the mule too; particularly when it comes to my "hunch" about persuading the British public to be interested in an author they don't know . . . And in my view it is nonsense to talk of the letters as being a "seamless garment", and they will have to be cut. I suggested about 20%, and you have cut about 4% . . . I shall have to go through them myself . . .' Relations continued to deteriorate and at the end of 1951 Lehmann had decided to cancel publication. He blamed his company's financial position, the post-war lack of paper, the need for further editing, the public's lack of interest, etc.

Hamish was astounded at Lehmann's refusal to publish, and the decision still raises questions. Were Lehmann's reasons for declaring the Gramsci letters 'unpublishable' genuine, or was Hamish's expulsion from Italy followed by a plot to silence him at home?

Between 1951 and 1974, Hamish submitted his Gramsci manuscripts to more than two dozen publishers; all refused them. A few selected letters were published by E.P. Thompson in the late 1950s, but it was not until 1974 that the letters appeared in two sequential issues of the *New Edinburgh Review* (a quarterly paperback published by the Edinburgh University Student Union, under the guidance of a student admirer of Hamish, Gordon Brown). And it was to be thirty-seven years before the letters were published in full, in hardback, by Zwan of London: *Gramsci's Prison Letters: A Selection*, translated and introduced by

Hamish Henderson. By this time, Hamish was old and tired, and the moment when Gramsci's words might have made a major philosophical impact on European thought had long passed. Alan Brien, however, writing in the *Guardian*, greeted the book with wonderful praise: 'This, the fullest English language edition, though still only a selection, is revealed as one of the great works of modern literature, fit to stand beside the best of Kafka or Rilke in this century, Dostoievsky or Herzen in the last . . .'

The following extracts from the prison letters give a flavour of Gramsci's thinking and Hamish's skill as a translator:

Turi Prison, 10/03/30 (55). Dearest Tania . . . I didn't understand the observation you made about the little flowers of St Francis . . . Artistically they are lovely, fresh, immediate; they express sincere faith and an infinite love of Francis, whom many held to be a reincarnation of God, a second appearance of Christ. That is why they are more popular in Protestant countries than Catholic countries . . . Francis came forward as the founder of a new Christianity, of a new religion, and raised enormous enthusiasm on all sides as in the first centuries of Christianity. The church did not prosecute him officially, because this would have anticipated the Reformation by two centuries; but it neutralised him, disbanded his disciples and reduced the new religion to a simple monastic order at its service. If you are reading the 'Little Flowers' with the idea of making them a guide through life, you have no understanding of them whatever . . . Francis did not go in for theological speculation; he tried to realise in practice the principles of the gospel . . .

Turi Prison, 27/06/32 (136). Dear Julca . . . And so the man remained in the ditch – until he looked around him, saw exactly where he had fallen, started wriggling a bit, arched his body, and then, using his legs and arms as levers, pushed himself upright and so got out of the ditch by his own unaided efforts . . . We must hurl all that's past into the flames and build new lives from the ground up. Why should we let ourselves be crushed by the lives we've led up till now? There's no sense in preserving anything at all but what was constructive and what was beautiful. We must get out of the ditch, and throw off that silly toad sitting on our hearts.

(214) Dear Delio . . . Tolstoy was a 'world' writer, one of the very few writers from any country to attain the highest perfection in his art. He is the font from which torrents of emotion have sprung all over the world – torrents which spring to this day, even in men and

women who have been blunted and coarsened by daily toil, and whose culture is rudimentary . . . Tolstoy really was a champion of civilisation and beauty, and in the world of today there is no one who can equal him: to find company for him we must go back to Homer, Aeschylus, Dante, Shakespeare, Goethe, Cervantes . . .

Gramsci died on 27 April 1937 at the age of forty-six. Hamish regarded him as a martyr and was never to think of Gramsci other than as an inspiration to anyone 'interested in everything concerning people'. He saw Gramsci's thinking as an evolutionary force and, quoting from the Prison Notebooks (Volume 1 page 3), writes:

If we think about it, we shall see that in asking the question – What is Man? – we want to ask – what can man become? Which means: can he master his own destiny, can he make himself, can he give form to his own life? Let us say then that man is a process, and precisely, the process of his own acts . . .[8]

This idea of 'life as an eternal process of becoming' thrilled Hamish and, having completed his translation, he knew the time had come for him to assume, once again, the habit of *action*.

8. *Gramsci's Prison Letters: A Selection,* translated and introduced by Hamish Henderson (Zwan 1988).

FIFTEEN

Socialism, Nationalism and the Politics of Peace

Dear Hamish, I recall that many, many years ago, you spoke to me about the Eleusinian mysteries: saying that after an adept had progressed to the very summit of his craft, to them was revealed the ultimate mystery – and they were shown an ear of corn . . .

Karl Dallas, letter to HH, 28 November 1997

For Hamish the pursuit of socialism, Scottish nationhood and international peace were inseparable interlinked realities. As a romantic, his vision of politics was part of his commitment to 'the poetry of life': G.S. Fraser recognised this very early on and found it difficult to comprehend. On 15 August 1942, for example, he wrote to Hamish (shortly after they first met, in Cairo) in an attempt to clarify what 'his grand political vision' was, and how *they* were going to realize it:

Hamish – can you weave into one pattern – modern large-scale industrialism, romantic nationalism, and the revival of a culture which was based on a monarchy, feudalism, and the idea of the unity of Christendom? You can try, I dare say you *will*, and I will be ready to help; but what sort of chemical compound will result from the fusion of such different elements it is hard to see. One difficulty is that for such an effort we can expect no support at all from existing parties of either left or Right . . . Our anti-calvinism is going to set all the churches in Scotland against us, and in towns like Glasgow and Edinburgh (where there is hostility to the Irish) the town mobs . . .

Hamish knew the task he had set himself would never be easy; if enthusiasts like Fraser bridled at the starting gate – how would the man in the street fare? Ratinoally, he knew Jacobitism was an anachronism but he could not deny its crucial role in Scottish history. And he would argue that it was Jacobitism rather than Whig materialism that initiated the dramatic changes in Scotland in the eighteenth century, which consequently played such an important part in the European Enlightenment. Hamish liked to quote Walter Scott's coda to his novel *Waverley*: 'There is no European nation which, within the course of half a century has undergone so complete a change as the Kingdom of Scotland . . .' And he asked: why should modern Scotland not, once more, become a light to the world and usher in a new Enlightenment? He acknowledged that the Union of 1707 had stimulated many beneficial changes in Scotland but, in the twentieth century, he believed the Union had become an albatross around Scotland's neck. Growing up in the 1920s, he had found himself part of a deeply demoralised nation – exhausted by war, commercial exploitation, religious repression and a political system that had reduced 'proper pride – to servile self-servitude. After 1918, emigration, once again, became the Hope of the Scots People!'

In the post-war period Hamish had tested the political waters in Scotland – while trying to establish a literary and political name for himself. After the success of the John Maclean celebrations and the prestige of the Somerset Maugham Award he began to raise his political profile, and the framework of his political thinking in the late forties is set out, quite clearly, in lectures he gave to students of the YCL. He would begin with a quotation from the Communist Manifesto, for example 'The free development of each is the condition for the free development of all', then tailor his subject according to whatever group he might be addressing. His notes suggest that these lectures were delivered like platform speeches rather than seminar introductions, and his rhetorical passion is obvious:

. . . Downfall within the framework of capitalism – or advance to radical transformation? That is the choice – and we must reach out on all fronts, industrial, political, social. It is very important that we give every worker the standards of a fairly prosperous middle class person . . . But – it would be a most frightful thing if a comfortable life was allowed to produce a comfortable philistinism, a smug self-satisfaction. It is certainly possible to increase the comfort, multiply the gadgets and, at the same time, debase the human being – as wide stretches of America show. Therefore while we attack those who refuse to see that culture must have a material basis, it is a simplification to suggest that all we have to do is improve material conditions and culture will flower. And it would be grotesque to pretend that the dangers come chiefly from abroad – our most deadly enemies can be found here, within the gates . . .

Look at the hostility of the great protestant reformers to Scots culture. On balance the Reformation in Scotland was a progressive event – it brought the people onto the political stage, it asserted the right to over-throw unpopular governments, it fought to increase educational opportunities. Some of the Scots radical tradition comes from this source and the stamp of that great event is on Scotsmen, for good – and evil, down to this day. It attacked our cultural heritage – as of the devil! It created great difficulties for the arts: it created a void – to be filled with what filtered or was imported from south of the border. We need not accept the Romantic, Catholic, Jacobite thesis in order to accept this. The Protestant elite defended the national Kirk with their lives but – the national culture they despised and neglected . . .

. . . If we make a beginning, if progressive people can see that what we are doing helps the cause of national independence, helps the movement towards the classless, socialist society – they will rally in increasing numbers. *It is the beginning that counts . . .*

I have deliberately dwelt on political economy and philosophy because I want to confound the notion that culture is what used to be called 'the fine arts' . . . And we must master the best of our national heritage in order to be able to advance and create a wide variety of works – poems, novels, plays which reflect, clarify and nurture the progressive struggle of the present day . . .

And History – we all ought to be conscious that there is, at this time, no worthwhile, popular history of Scotland . . . We must not forever wait for such to appear before we do anything at all – we must act. There has been a falsification of our national history, a falsification of the history of working class oppression . . . We are at a moment when the pressure on intellectuals is greater than ever. They have been forced onto the sidelines and into silence. There is cynicism, there are witch-hunts, there is a powerful wish to protect those who serve the institution and the status quo . . . What we need is a 'House of Freedom', the idea that we are the 'Feudal Slaves of Scotland' will be no more . . .

Hamish's position was that of an ancient *filidh* – he was a remem-brancer and a catalyst of continual tribal renewal. In his time the great need was for socialist change, and most of Scotland's poets took similar political positions, as is made clear in a document Phil Stein presented to the Cultural Committee of the Communist Party (CP) in Scotland in 1948. 'Those of our poets who are sincerely trying to produce work "national in form, proletarian in content" are giving expression to national sentiment most strongly of all. Hugh MacDiarmid, Sorley MacLean, Sydney Goodsir Smith, Hamish Henderson, John Kincaid, and Maurice Blythman (Thurso Berwick) are all carrying on the fight . . . With the exception of the last two names, who are members of the party, the others are divided from us only because of their determined stand on the national question . . .' Stein was by this time a close personal confidante of Hamish's, and for a period of about five years Hamish worked hard to persuade Stein – and the Communist Party in Scotland – that the National Question and the pursuit of international peace were interactive realities, and that 'peace, socialism and Scotland' were the triple pillars of national wellbeing. 1948 was the year in which the Cold War and the nuclear arms race began to gather unstoppable momentum, and Western governments began to ruthlessly negate all opposition to their policies. Many artists, however, refused to be intimidated or to cut the ties with the Soviet Union and the Eastern Bloc countries. Hamish believed good relations with the communist countries of Eastern Europe were crucial if peace was to be maintained and the trans-European economy restructured. Culture, he believed, had a fundamental role to play in the political solutions to be effected and in October 1949 Hamish wrote the first 'Manifesto of the Scottish Peace Committee'. It was entitled 'Scotland and Peace':

There are two camps in the world today; on one side the camp of reaction – on the other the camp of progress, cooperation and peace. The boundary dividing the two camps is nowhere a national boundary. It runs through city, town, village and countryside wherever the forces of progress and reaction clash. But in every country the fight for peace takes on its own peculiar complexion because no two territories have identical histories, traditions or economic build-up. No nation has suffered more in the last two centuries from futile and criminal wars than the Scottish nation. The adventure of British imperialism in the four quarters of the globe has meant a heavy drain on our manpower and wealth . . . The two great wars of the C20th have carried the process very nearly to completion . . . A third World War on a similar scale would mean the death, not only of countless Scotsmen and Scotswomen but of the nation itself. But Scotland has a proud record of resistance to imperialists and war-mongers . . . Today, the Scottish people must recreate and revive its great traditions – and work to put a stop to the plan of the war-mongers . . .

The Scottish Peace Committee calls on all Scotsmen and Scotswomen to defend Peace, and thereby defend the vital interests of their own country. We pledge ourselves to support the Partisans of Peace and to combat the instigators of war wherever they may be found – and to create a Scottish Peace Movement that will be an effective part of the world Peace Movement as a whole.

Hamish's mention of the 'Partisans of Peace' affirms his support for the non-institutional peace-activists then trying to organise resistance to governmental war-mongering across Europe but also refers to his own poem 'For the Partisans of Peace', written in the spring of 1948. It was later retitled 'Brosnachadh' ('The Call to Rise').

> Break the iron man. Forsake
> The arrogant robot's rule. Take
> Peace down from the wall. Make
> Waste the fenced citadel.
>
> Tell of the rebellious truth. Foretell
> At street corners an awakening. Swell
> The insurgent armies of knowledge.
> Foregather on field and fell.
>
> Face the imperative choice. Base
> On huge rock your building. Trace
> With arched bodies a new legend,
> Our human house greatly to grace.
>
> Hold to an unyielding faith. Mould
> Gently to the mind's unreason. Shield
> From desperate illusions our children,
> And guide them back to bell, flower and field.
>
> Know how the country lies. Throw
> Your shadow across valleys. Blow
> A summons down from the whaup's mountain
> To claw the gorging eagle low.

Above all be quick. Love
Never outlasts its movement. Prove
With us is no 'villainy of hatred',
and history will uphold us –
                    justify and forgive.[1]

This highly original poem sets out a framework for active agitation for peace – across Europe – from Italy and Greece, to Scotland and Ireland. And, from this time on, Hamish was in regular contact with like-minded activists across Europe, notably in Paris and Milan. In London he worked closely with two folk-singing communist trade unionists, Dougie and Queenie Moncreiff, and cultural-activists like Margaret Gardiner and Desmond Bernal. Because many such people suffered regular MI5 surveillance, Hamish's diaries and notebooks from this time on become increasingly circumspect. But, rather wonderfully – as if to remedy this gap in his biographical record – Hamish now began a discursive correspondence with Phil Stein that gives us invaluable information about his work for the Peace Movement and the Communist Party during this period. By 1953 Hamish and Stein had fallen out – personally and politically – but Stein kept all of Hamish's letters.

Phil Stein was a Jewish school teacher who had been brought up in the Gorbals and after the war became a CPGB branch secretary in Glasgow. He first met Hamish at a YCL camp in Kintyre. Stein presumed that Hamish would help advance his career as a political journalist, and Hamish believed that Stein might provide him with a God-given chance to dramatically influence the Communist Party in Scotland. He believed he would be able to 'educate' Stein, Gallagher and the Communist hierarchy in Scotland (with the help of friends like the Blythmans and the Buchans) to a point at which it would become Scottish, libertarian and Gramscian – then he would join it, perhaps even lead it! It was a fantastic concept! And, although his grand plan ended in failure, Stein's ambition – to become a journalist and a worldly success – was triumphantly achieved.[2]

The kind of struggle Hamish had is made clear in the following letter, from Stein to Hamish, written in autumn 1949. Morris Blythman had raised critical points (at the Cultural Committee of the CPGB, in

---

1. 'Brosnachadh', published in the *Collected Poems*.
2. In the early fifties Stein left teaching to become first a *Daily Worker* journalist, then a television reporter. In the sixties his career took off: he left the Communist Party and moved to London where he became a highly successful copywriter for Volkswagen, later a columnist on the *Daily Telegraph* before moving, in the 1980s, to the *Independent on Sunday*, where his column – to Hamish's delight – was entitled 'My Biggest Mistake'! Stein died in 1996.

Glasgow) about the Soviet Union's decision to follow the US/British nuclear defence policy, and the increasingly propagandist nature of Soviet art.

> Dear Hamish . . . Blythman has suggested – 1) Scientific achievement is not enough – it is the use to which it is put that is important; 2) Soviet propaganda has changed – it now primarily emphasizes the cleavage between East and West; 3) That whilst Soviet ballet remains great – Soviet cinema has declined and that Soviet literature now embraces a dull uniformity that could not be compared with the vital literature being created in Scotland by the likes of Thurso Berwick, John Kincaid, Hugh MacDiarmid, Sorley MacLean and Hamish Henderson! . . . He thinks that these poets are making a cultural contribution greater than that of the whole Soviet Union! Goodness knows we are tolerant with our people . . . But Morris's conduct cannot be tolerated indefinitely, and the time has come for a showdown . . .

In the face of such threats it is surprising that Blythman remained in the Party for as long as he did, and very surprising that Hamish believed that he could transform such a Party – but he did, as the following letter suggests. On 1 January 1950, Hamish wrote to Stein from Marian Sugden's house in Cambridge, and his letter has the force of a New Year's resolution.

> Dear Phil – seeing that the whole position on the national question is being transformed I am joining the Party – to celebrate Hogmanay. So here's hoping that in spite of Red Guards, Blue Nebs, Black Shirts and Yellow Bellies you had a braw red Hogmanay yourself . . . I have just completed some 'Notes on the National Question in Scotland' which I'm offering to Bill Lachlan . . . I'll set about writing a book which is forming like crystals in my head during this Hogmanay hangover.

On 5 January, Hamish wrote again. 'Dear Phil . . . Did you notice a para. in Wednesday's "Worker's Notebook" headed Parson for Peace. The bloke concerned is an old friend, Allan Armstrong, the Red Rector of Dry Drayton – a seventy year old Irishman of Scottish extraction who has years of battle against injustice behind him . . . Like MacDiarmid he has the old Border rebel spirit! As soon as he heard of the Peace Campaign he threw himself into it and says he intends to devote the rest of his life to carrying it through to victory . . .' On 17 January, attempting to get his poetry promoted in a Communist Party leaflet advertising Peace Literature, Hamish continues:

> Dear Phil, MacColl's plays 'Uranium 235', 'Operation Olive Branch' and 'The Other Animals' (his best play) are all part of the Peace Movement's work – so there's no reason why you shouldn't submit my Elegies too – after all they set out to 'Sing them who amnestied / escaped from the conflict.' Which means, among other things, that although the Elegies are about war, they try to win through to the meaning of peace . . . Have you seen my notes on the National Question yet? One thing's certain anyway – the national problem can never again be left to vegetate in the miasmal mist. For better or worse it's come to stay as a reality in the Scottish literary (and political) scene.

Despite Hamish's New Year 'resolution', there is no documentary evidence that he ever actually joined the Communist Party of Great Britain. During the early fifties, however, he did work very closely with the Party's Cultural Committee in Scotland: for example, it commissioned him to edit a new selection of poems by MacDiarmid, which he entitled *Hugh MacDiarmid: the Hymns to Lenin*. While preparing this book, Hamish read Lenin's essay on 'Party Organization and Party Literature' and notes 'Literature must become Party Literature . . . Down with un-partisan litterateurs! Down with the Supermen of Literature! Literature must become part of the general cause of the proletariat.'

In March 1950 Hamish attended the 'Second National Assizes' of the French Peace Movement. He was en route for Italy (to translate Gramsci) but his contribution to the conference was far from a 'passing' one. He took the stage as leader of the Scottish Communist Party delegation and refused to be seen as a 'northern representative' of the English delegation. He lobbied hard to be allowed to address the Assizes on behalf of an autonomous Peace Movement from Scotland. He writes to Phil Stein:

> Phil – If the Scottish Committee has any funds at all – get some stationery printed with your name, address and 'Scottish Committee, Partisans of Peace' on it. The French, like some other continental peoples, take the outward show seriously . . . The general impression here is that the existence of a properly autonomous peace movement in Scotland would be an excellent thing. Everyone feels that the 'British' movement needs to be put on its mettle, and a lively independent Scottish movement might help to do just that. One of the people I talked to was Dr Georges Fournier of the Paris

Committee – I offered to speak at the opening session of the Assizes, but the programme was too full. This was a pity because I had prepared a 'smashing' little speech, concluding with a Neruda quote – 'peace to all lands, and all waters'. Crowther [leader of the English delegation] told me afterwards: 'we had hoped to hear your dulcet Gaelic tones, but it wasn't possible to fit them in'! Between ourselves Phil, I rather think the last thing he wanted to fit in was a Scottish contribution to the Assizes . . . I enclose a couple of souvenirs – and one item to show that my feelings about the Peace Movement are not just platonic; I estimate that between April 1949 and March 1950 I have spent over £60 of my Maugham Award on the Peace Movement . . .

By declaiming his 'Poem for the Partisans of Peace', narrating McGrath's 'Warrant for Pablo Neruda' and singing his songs, Hamish made a significant impression on the conference even though the British delegation determinedly refused to allow him the 'national platform' he wanted. However, he made common cause with other representatives and journeyed on to Italy in high spirits. By 7 April, he was lodging with his old friend Luigi Castigliano in Milan and writing to Stein. 'A few nights ago I addressed a peace meeting organised by the Milanese Partisans of Peace – it was grand: ticket enclosed for the record. Next Tuesday I repeat the talk at the Porta Venezia.' On 15 May, he wrote to give his support to a 'Petition for Peace', which the Communist Party of Great Britain (CPGB) was circulating in an attempt to raise popular opposition, in Britain, against the threat of nuclear war. This threat had, quite suddenly, become very real: a group of right-wing US generals supported by McCarthyite politicians were advocating pre-emptive nuclear strikes against the Soviet Union, China and Korea. 'Dear Phil . . . I enclose my signature, as one more on the way to your million. You should aim at as many signatures as adorn the Covenant . . . I was reminded just the other day by a friend who attended the 2nd Scottish National Assembly in Glasgow in the Spring of 1948 that the central point in my speech to that gathering was that the fight for Peace and the fight for national Independence in Scotland were and are indivisible. Events are now moving fast to justify this line right up to the hilt . . .'

On 25 May 1950, Hamish sent Stein a package of 'Peace Proclamations from Italy' to be read out at a great rally being organised by the Scottish Peace Movement in Glasgow:

To the Rally of the Scottish Partisans of Peace – from the Provisional Committee of the Partisans of Peace, Milano, May 1950 [written by Dr Salvatore di Benedetto]

In this hour when the forces of Peace in Scotland are uniting in a great Rally, in order to express their indomitable will to stand beside the peoples of the world struggling to halt the advance of another criminal war, we – the Partisans of Peace of Milan – send you our warmest greetings. Our workers and our men of science are with you in the great battle of humanity. The instigators of a new war are moving forward rapidly towards the greatest crime ever committed against humanity, the hour through which the nations are passing is perilous indeed; but united and erect, the forces of peace – among which are numbered hundreds of millions of men and women – will overcome the criminal savagery of the warmongers who wish to destroy the nations, or reduce them to slavery. Your rally will show all Scotsmen the real roads forward to Peace and progress: to the mothers of Scotland it will give the force to defend their sons from mutilation and massacre. And, to the possibilities of Scottish culture – it will make it clear that knowledge and science find nobility and love only in the service of life and human progress.

A second message was sent on behalf of the 'ANPI of Modena' [written by Adelmo Babbelli]:

On the occasion of your great Peace Demonstration, the Partisans of the National Association of Italian ex-partisans send you warm greetings. From a lecture given at Modena by Captain Hamish Henderson they learnt much of the Scottish people's desire for Peace, and of its intrepid spirit. They wish to express their fraternal solidarity with you, a solidarity already tried and tested in the struggle waged side by side with your compatriots against Fascism and Nazism and for the liberty of all nations. Long live Peace!

A third message came from Carlo Gramsci, brother to Antonio Gramsci: 'I, Carlo Gramsci, send my warm greetings to the rally of the Scottish Partisans of Peace, confident that they will play a decisive role in defeating the plans of the war-mongers. The ideals for which you are fighting are those for which my brother laid down his life. Together our peoples can make them a reality. Long live the fraternal solidarity of the Scottish and Italian nations! Long live Peace, the burning desire of all nations!' Hamish also sent a personal message, to be read out to what he hoped would be a crowd of tens of thousands of people:

Statement for the Peace Rally – 4th June 1950 . . . Now that the threat of a new war hangs like a black and glowering cloud over the

world's millions, the Peace Movement in Scotland has become a key
point in this whole struggle. Scotland's manpower, industrial wealth
and strategic importance make it indispensable to the Anglo-Amer-
ican imperialists – therefore, the forces for Peace in Scotland must
see to it that our nation becomes the weak link in their chain of
aggressive designs . . . Throughout the world the eyes of the
Partisans of Peace turn today to Scotland. We must not betray
their trust. I am sure that the Scottish nation can build a movement
for Peace comparable with the great movements in France and Italy,
because for us the fight for Peace and national independence are two
aspects of one indivisible struggle for a new and free life – in
Scotland, and throughout the world . . .

On 20 July, Hamish tried to twist Stein's arm by drawing Stalin (Stein's
hero), into their on-going argument about the need for Scottish devolution. 'Stalin's intervention in the linguistic controversy is a piece of
extraordinary good fortune for us in Scotland. He has cleared away in
a few sentences all the dead wood that years of . . . philistinism had left
untouched (especially in Scotland), and has opened the way, at least for a
fruitful cultural discussion – from past experience with the "National and
Colonial Question" I know that people are willing enough in Scotland to
pay lip-service to Stalin's technical brilliance – but a damn-sight less ready
to read him . . . My articles in *L'Unita* have created quite a sensation in
Italy. Graziani replied to them in the Roman court room on Wednesday,
but he wasn't able to deny any important fact mentioned by me . . .'
Hamish's inclusion of the word 'philistinism' in this letter to Phil Stein
was not accidental – he was beginning to lose patience with his hard-
minded student; however, it was with a stroke of genius that Hamish
drew Picasso into his on-going debate with the Communist Party. In a
letter to the *Daily Worker*, Hamish writes:

> . . . As one who has seen the 'Picasso in Provence' Exhibition, I
> would like to support John Bridger's attitude as strongly and
> warmly as I can . . . Picasso has left behind him the mood of a
> 'savage indignation' which made his wartime paintings so terrible –
> and so merciless a satire on coward and collaborator. In these later
> paintings, lithographs and ceramics at Vallauris he expresses the
> meaning of 'liberation' – Liberation from the dead weight of
> ignorance and prejudice in a dying order, and prophetic greetings
> to a new world of cooperation and happiness . . . This affirmation is
> expressed in colours of pure joy, and the whole effect is one of an
> almost breathtaking radiance. Picasso's fauns and centaurs have the

same artistic function as Shakespeare's clowns. In both, 'the ancient wisdom, disguised as laughter, dances with the light of a great summer sea'. I am sure the Soviet people will learn to love Picasso, not only for his courageous stand in defence of Peace but for his great-spirited art as well.

Hamish's enthusiasm for Picasso had been restimulated the previous November when he had attended the 'infamous' International Peace Conference in Sheffield when Picasso was ignominiously expelled from Britain as a dangerous and undesirable alien. Hamish was working as an interpreter for the Italian and German delegates, his friend Nan Green as Picasso's personal interpreter, until police action saw the greatest artist of the twentieth century frog-marched to the Channel!

On 29 January 1951, having been invited to speak at a Peace Rally in Aberdeen, Hamish wrote to Stein from Cambridge:

I'd like to speak at such a rally . . . I am sure that the Communist Party will realize that up till now it has under-estimated the strength of the national movement; and revaluate its policy accordingly. If it does not it will be swamped in the great wave of rising national feeling in Scotland, and will lose the chance for many a long day of leading it . . . The issue on which everyone can unite is the fight against war. If the bigots of the Covenant Movement and the bigots in the Communist Party could forget their bleeding bigotry for long enough to unite on this issue we might get somewhere in Scotland . . . If the Communist Party (GB) saw to it that at International Congresses like Warsaw, Scotland was ranked as a nation, as she has every right to be, its claim to have analysed the national problem correctly could be taken more seriously . . . I doubt if there is another CP in the world which has made so many infantile and unimaginative errors on this issue as the CPGB . . . !

Stein replied with a fascinating letter:

. . . We had a meeting of the Scottish Peace Committee today . . . Truman's statement last week about MacArthur and the Atom bomb has filled the overwhelming majority with such horror that many people have at last realised that they are going to have to stir themselves – if they are to prevent another war . . . Hamish, don't forget the Party was in at the birth of the Covenant and in fact was responsible for a whole number of proposals – including pleading it before the House of Commons . . . But the reactionary leadership expelled our members from the Covenant committee (which has more than its share of fascist-minded gentry sitting on it) . . . While it's true there has been a growth of national consciousness and while it's true nearly every Scotsman was hugely pleased at the Stone being whipped – don't kid yourself that Scotland is in a ferment about self-government or Independence . . . It is the national independence of the whole of Great Britain that is at stake at the moment – and it is America holding this country in thrall, not England . . . You say that the issue is the fight against war . . . But, for Christ's sake don't write off the C.P.G.B. as some kind of imperialist body in which the Scottish comrades play only a subject part! . . . Your accusations against the Communist Party are extremely difficult to swallow, and are, of course, objectionable to swallow. You know, Hamish, I do get the feeling you are putting yourself further and further out on a limb . . .

By 10 February the correspondence was on the verge of becoming a genuine flyting:

Dear Phil, . . . The essence of the thing is that you have never succeeded in overcoming your tendency to view the national question as a 'factor' instead of an integral part of the whole. Thus you deny that there is a ferment over self-government in Scotland (in spite of the signing of the Covenant) but assert a 'ferment is beginning to show itself' against rearmament. This seems to me a very slack and loose formulation. Isn't it possible that the strong feeling which undoubtedly exists on both issues is part of one whole – i.e. the working class struggle in Scotland in the period of the decline of British imperialism! . . . The national struggle must not be regarded as an adjunct . . . It must be integrated with the working class struggle as it presents itself in any given country (see Lenin's controversy with Rosa Luxemburg). You may of course deny that Scotland is a nation. But if you do that, you must logically reject Stalin's definition of a nation – for Scotland undoubtedly fulfils the conditions that Stalin lays down (much more fully than Italy does for example). You say that it's the national independence of Great Britain that's at stake, not just Scotland's. Now I agree that England's independence is threatened by America, in the same way that the national independence of every other Western European nation is. But I can't agree that nations open out of each other like boxes in a Chinese puzzle. If Scotland is a nation, then Great Britain might be either – 1) a union or federation of nations – equal partners, or 2) a 'prison-house of nations (like pre-1917 Russia, i.e. a state in which one nation oppresses others). In official 'government' mythology, Great Britain is (1) but it is actually more like (2) because in the present system of parliamentary government from Westminster, England has an absolute majority, and thus exercises an effective dictatorship over Scotland and Wales (Northern Ireland is a special case) . . .

Hamish's political position was now so far from Stein's that their personal friendship began to suffer and by 1953 Hamish had begun to realise that his dream of 'nationalising' the Communist Party in Scotland was never going to become any kind of reality, as he outlines in another letter to Stein:

> . . . On the bigger issue of the Scottish National movement, I fail to see how anyone as closely in touch with developments as you have been can possibly deny that my position has been confirmed by facts over and over again. From the Maclean meeting of 1948 to the People's Festival of 1952, and from the Scottish National Assembly of 1947 (at which, two years before Paris, I spoke on the theme 'Scotland and Peace') to the mass signing of the Covenant, a wide section of the Scottish people supported – and support – the old Cunningham Graham – Keir Hardie – John MacLean line on Scotland and Socialism. The fact that a bold and constructive lead on this issue was never given to the people will certainly draw down upon Bill Lachlan and others the grave censure of future Marxist historians. As for me, you can wait till my translation of Gramsci appears before you assert (even tentatively) that I am 'out on a limb'. As far as I am concerned the battle continues . . .

With that (to all intents and purposes) Hamish turned his back on the Communist Party and indeed on all 'conventional politics'. He now turned to forms of 'direct action' and 'cultural renewal' as the prime means of effecting radical change in Scotland. If the front door was banged shut he would knock on the back door – and if that too remained closed, he would play in the garden with the children of a new generation. For Hamish, young people and old traditions were the keys to the future of culture in Scotland, and the hinge to the door was music and language. Throughout his life he was an avid proponent of both the Gaelic language and Lallans Scots in all its forms. Hamish's first public intervention in the language debate goes back to 1946 when he wrote this letter, from South Uist, to the *Glasgow Herald*.

The heavy-handed sarcasm of your Editorial Diarist at the expense of writers who experiment with Scots deserves an answer, despite its cheapness. For it is clear that the Diarist is unfamiliar with all the more important facts about the making of a poem and the nature of language. He is unaware for example that the linguistic problems which he parodies have existed for a good proportion of writers in every country and in every age . . . In spite of the sneers of linguistic quislings, who find it convenient to side with the big battalions of London press lords and Glasgow Englishmen, Scottish poets will find more and more support now in erecting a dam against the '*morshruth na Beurla*' (the big flood of English). Most of them realize this, and realize too that it is not enough merely to use 'the language of the outlaw'. Like their compeers of former ages, they must also re-create and reshape it . . .

In March 1949, Hamish's thoughts were further developed in an article for *Conflict* entitled 'Lallans and all That', and in which he openly aims a blow or two at Douglas Young (who had so recently belittled his Elegies).

The correspondence columns of *The Scotsman* have recently been resounding with shrill cries and muffled grunts on the subject of Lallans. What is it the screivers ask – language or dialect, Celtic or Anglian, speech of our ancestors or linguistic aberration? The tug-of-war went on for weeks. But in most of the letters the argumentative bitterness of the writers was only equalled by their dingy ignorance concerning the one point that really matters: namely, has our generation produced in Braid Scots any poetry worthy of the name? . . . For, after all, no one who walks through Scotland with his ears washed can doubt that the speech of the people is still a helluva lot nearer to the language of Burns than to the stringy metropolitan argot of the BBC announcer. Which means that there is still a living foundation for poetry in 'the raucle tongue'. And if that's conceded, what the devil does it matter whether the Jutes were the first speakers of it, or the Friesiens? . . . So I propose to cut out all the literary cross-talk so beloved of Mr Douglas Young, which in the main I regard as so much non-sense value. What we might ask ourselves is this: can evidence be found of a vital, contemporary and popular literature in the Scottish tongue?

To his surprise, this letter stimulated a testy but positive reply from Douglas Young.

Dear Hamish . . . I have managed to get a copy of the March 'Conflict' and read your article on 'Lallans and all That'. It is correct on most of its points, but it would have been better had it been correct on all . . . Violet Jacob really did the same thing as Mac-Diarmid. Those who knew her stuff, as I did, before we knew MacDiarmid's, realised how 'revolutionary, traditionalist and creative' she was in her day, which was a decade before his . . . However, the article is a good one, and well written. One thing you might one day consider is this, the apparent total absence of women in the new crop of Lallans writers. A generation ago we had Violet Jacob, Marian Angus, Helen Cruickshank . . .

Hamish, MacDiarmid and Young all had different ideas about the literary use of Lallans and in some ways it brought out the worst in them. They all regularly turned on each other but never with the public ferocity with which MacDiarmid turned on Maurice Lindsay in the *National Weekly*, 26 June 1952: 'It has become increasingly obvious over a long period of time that sooner or later Mr Maurice Lindsay (the genius who discourses so confidently over the Scottish Home Service on "How to remove the fishy taste from bacon", "Brighter wear for men", and similar topics) would have to be thoroughly squashed . . . I remember well when Mr Lindsay first climbed on the band-wagon of the Scottish Renaissance Movement. He came to see me about it . . . His bosom warming with the glowing ecstasy of a dog sighting a new and hitherto undreamed of lamp-post . . . He acquired for a time a virtual monopoly on the Scottish BBC (and much more) and he touched nothing that he did not cheapen . . . He has signally failed to establish himself as a poet, a music critic, a literary critic, or an authority on Scottish art and affairs . . . He may have made money but his policy of promiscuous and wholesale grab has won him nothing worth having . . .' The article was accompanied by an anonymous song entitled 'Lease me, Lindsay', probably written by Hamish:

> Chorus: *Will ye tak to the Lallans, Maurice Lindsay?*
> *Will ye tak tae the Lallans wi me?*
> *Will ye tak tae the Lallans, Maurice Lindsay?*
> *The pride o' Scots makars to be?*

> Och, Braidcasting Hoose kens nae Lallans,
> A leid that's but gude for the byre;
> Forby i'm nou ane o' their callans
> That scrieve anent concert and choir.

There's jobs on the press o' this city,
There's jobs on the BBC
Nou I haud them aa – mair's the pity –
Your Lallans is nae uise to me.

But when siller's there to be gotten
Yon Maurice sall never be missed;
As lang as there's job that's rank rotten,
As langas there's an arse to be kissed.[3]

It was Hamish's interest in the vernacular that drew him to the young poet and artist Ian Hamilton Finlay. After doing military service in Germany, Finlay had returned to Scotland in 1947 to work as a shepherd at Comrie in Perthshire. He admired Hamish's work and made contact with him. They were two very different characters but they shared a rare largeness of vision and ambition. And, in retrospect, parallels can now be drawn between Hamish's desire to use poetry to intellectually and politically transform the Scottish nation and Finlay's wish to use poetry to question and transform all assumptions about making art in Scotland. Finlay is a Modern classicist, who has re-stimulated a significant strand of European art by insisting that 'poetry' is the fulcrum on which all the arts stand – and Hamish's precept that 'Poetry becomes People' is wonderfully exemplified in Finlay's work. These two poets were to remain recurrent ideological collaborators over the next sixty years.

Hamish's championship of the Scots language was only equalled by his championship of Gaelic. He saw Gaelic culture as the cornerstone of Scots culture and a crucial component of the wider National Question. Hamish loved the Gaelic language and felt at the deepest levels of his being that it was in the Gaedhealtacht that the soul of Scotland now resided. In Glenshee, in the 51st Highland Division, in the company of Gaels, Hamish delighted in the magic of a language that exulted song and he would proudly declaim Alasdair MacMhai of Mull's description of Gaelic: 'A strong flowing speech, unhesitating in its sound. Sensible, prolific – and pungent, whether quick-spoken or slow. A musical language, rich in idiom and of splendid resonance, spoken by the noble race of Scots, and by young Gaels.'

In Sorley MacLean, Hamish knew Scotland had produced a modern poet fit to stand with the best in Europe: in Sorley's brother, Calum, Hamish knew Gaelic had a folklorist to be ranked with the best in the world. And he saw the MacLean family's pride in the Gaedhealtacht as an example of the kind of 'wholeness' he was seeking to give Scotland. In

---

3. Published in *National Weekly* 26 June 1952.

a notebook he compares Sorley's enthusiasm for Gaelic with Pushkin's love of Russian: 'A man not only may but should take pride in the glory of his forefathers. Not to revere it is shameless cowardice . . . Pushkin was the first to train literature to the dignity of a national cause in his country . . . True nationalism consists in describing not the outer dress but the very spirit of the people. A poet may be national when he is describing quite another world from his own . . .' Douglas Young was another early proponent of Sorley but it was Hamish who took him out onto an international stage and Hamish who wrote the first major article in the British national press about him. It appeared in the *Daily Worker* on 24 November 1949, under the heading 'There's a Fine Poet in Gaelic'.

> . . . When Sorley started writing he was in the familiar state of disorientation induced by an orthodox Anglo Scottish education. However, he mustered up the courage to look twentieth century Scotland in the face, and the sight daunted him. In the Highlands, depopulation and decay: in the cities unemployment, overcrowding and disease. No cultural focal point for the nation, no political focal point either. Worst of all, the old culture of which he was a rightful inheritor seemed likely to be eroded and blown away, like soil from the dust-bowl. Luckily for him he soon came on the writings of a Marxist poet who was to have an incalculable effect on his development – Hugh MacDiarmid . . . Another turning point was the outbreak of the Spanish Civil War, which aroused in the young Gael a passionate hatred of Fascism . . .

> MacLean steeped himself in [these] traditions and gave eloquent tongue to them in his greatest poem 'The Cuillin'. Readers who have seen translations of Pablo Neruda may remember his tremendous evocation of Andean scenery in a cycle of poems. MacLean does much the same thing in his 'Cuillin', which not only evokes with splendid verve the heroic landscape of the Hebrides, but also makes it a symbol of man's achievement in shaping his own history . . . The indomitable spirit of the great revolutionaries Lenin, Liebknecht, Dimitrov and John Maclean is found in 'heights beyond thought on the mountains'

> > The lyric Cuillin of the free,
> > The ardent Cuillin of the heroic.

> This poem, which ensures MacLean's place in European literature, ends in an affirmation of the 'courage of the many' – and a vision of their ultimate triumph.

The special status that Hamish bestowed on Sorley is made clear in a 'visionary review' he wrote, following publication of Derick Thomson's first book of Gaelic poems, in 1952.

> . . . Now, with this book, [Ruaraidh MacThomas] emerges as the most promising Gaelic poet since the great day when Sorley MacLean's first glorious lyrics burst in on the Scottish literary scene and to whom Ruaraidh owes a manifest debt. There are obvious temperamental differences between the two poets. Sorley let loose a wild 'cavalry of bards' with bridles jangling, now [Ruaraidh] comes trotting along behind, mounted on his own well-mannered sheltie. However, I think it has to be admitted that he has had a shot for the summit for all that.
>
> As one would expect, a Gaelic poet these days is bound to be pre-occupied with the fate of the noble culture of which he is a living part. Can the language survive, hard-pressed as it is, by the flooding ocean of English? And what place is the language question to have in the political and social struggle? (. . . I saw a rose growing in the rock face of history, sucking sap from the rock of the ages of men, and its bloom fragrant in the memory of men, and I wondered that this much of beauty should survive under the salt-licking of the sea and the cut of its sword.) Like many other Scots poets Ruaraidh sees the defence of Gaelic culture as an integral part of the Scottish national struggle. But his verse lacks the 'savage indignation' which informs so much of Sorley's fresh writing, the note is rather one of endurance and self-knowledge, cool and objective: he has no time for illusory hopes and easy solutions . . . Ruaraidh's art is pre-eminently that of the accomplished minor poet whose forces are a bit thin on the ground and whose objectives are strictly limited; even so, the intensity of the writer's feelings are discernable in spite of the restrained measures. It was this that sent me back to look again at the work of MacLean, who is probably now the best poet writing in a Celtic language . . .

This perceptive, boldly egotistic, criticism holds as true today as it did then. Hamish's ferocious honesty – as a critic and as a friend – could make him a very difficult man to get on with. He had something of the 'terribilita' for which Michelangelo was famed: exuded passion of the kind Jack Yeats describes as being 'the diffidence of the spear-point'. But he was also gentle, loving and keen to nurture, not to destroy, artistic endeavour.

SIXTEEN

Folk-song and Photography, Alan Lomax and Paul Strand

The mortal sin of antinomian Scots Calvinism
Is the monstrous conspiracy of the old against the young.
HH

By November 1950, hugely stimulated by his immersion in Gramsci and the dynamic realities of Italian culture, Hamish determined to make folk-culture the keystone of his 'proper study' – mankind. He foresaw that, as in Ireland, the folk tradition should be recognised not just as the bedrock of Scotland's multifaceted cultural renaissance but potentially as a power-ful engine of political change. Before the end of the year he had made contact with Sidney Newman, Reid Professor of Music at Edinburgh University, 'to discuss the kind of work that might, and must, be done!' And over the next two years Newman became the prime force behind the establishment of the School of Scottish Studies, the university research department within which Hamish would make his professional career. Hamish also made contact with the BBC, boldly demanding that it should address the realities and potentialities of working-class and traditional culture in Scotland – but to no avail.

Aware that all folk studies – whether traditional or revolutionary – had to function within academic and internationally acceptable frameworks, Hamish now asked himself what science, what art, what new thinking he could bring to the study of folklore in Scotland. It was not a new subject. Scotland's folk-music and song had been collected and studied for at least three hundred years – but not within a university framework, not out in 'the field', and not with good-quality portable tape-recorders. And, rather as Hamish had, in 1942, instigated field interrogation in the frontline, he now determined to centre his researches at the frontline of folklore – the fields and workplaces where the actual words, music and timings of genuinely traditional singers could be recorded and preserved. Like the neo-realist film-makers, he would address the realities behind the facade of contemporary propriety: he was a poet–folklorist going out to meet people in whom, he assumed, poetry resided, and any kind of censorship was anathema to him. He believed that Scotland's relatively unbroken genealogical, social and cultural history linked it with an un-propertied, prehistoric past that gives Scots music and song an indelible stamp unique to Scotland but accessible to Everyman. He saw living traditions that were part of an oral continuum stretching back to the beginnings of language and the foundations of human culture. He would be a 'folk revolutionary', following in the footsteps of Europe's great modern artists and – just as Picasso, in his Cubist revolution, had transformed European art by looking back to Romanesque, Iberian and African sculpture – he would transform modern music by delving the secret springs of Scotland's preliterate tradition. He knew his vision might be judged uncouth – even mad – like the beauty Jean François Millet and van Gogh had seen in the striding peasants of Barbizon and Provence. He exulted in Salvador Dali's remark: 'there is only one difference between me and a mad man. I am not mad!' He was confident his singers would come up to the mark.

Hamish believed that music and song can, with almost magical force, connect past and present: like water, they find their level and make their way. This idea of there being a cultural continuum within race memory is evident in a telling aside Hamish noted from a Scots Traveller in the fifties. He was talking about an egocentric Irish tramp: 'Charlie Doyles's not one o' us, Charlie Doyle jist lives frae day tae day but we – we live entirely in the past.' A similar sense of there being 'a folk continuum' is apparent in an epigram stated, as though it was an obvious truth, by the bard Donald MacDonald of South Lochboisdale: 'the beginning and the end of life is herding'. In an increasingly institutional and commercialised society Hamish believed it hugely important to keep alive these timeless 'other values' – the values of a people who speak of life as 'the Cave of Gold' and know death as 'the Day of the Mountain'.

By chance, Hamish's return to Cambridge in the autumn of 1950 coincided with the start of celebrations in honour of the centenary of the birth of Jane Ellen Harrison, a classical scholar who had played a crucial role in the evolution of modern archaeology. Hamish recognised that her 'antiquarian methodology' could be very useful to his own ethnographical career. Harrison had been a controversial Cambridge 'personality', a handsome linguist who had travelled alone, by mule, from Athens to Sparta and fallen in love with her subject with Byronic abandon. Hamish was captivated by her and noted:

> Jane Ellen recognised early on that Greek civilisation must be studied in its *origins*, that Greek philosophy, science and poetry were part and parcel of the life of the people who produced them –

and that they had a common origin in religion . . . Consequently she was attracted by the two new sciences that were 'arousing the Classics from their long sleep. Two great lights', she said 'had risen upon them – archaeology and anthropology' . . .[1]

Hamish points out how Harrison pioneered the idea that Greek drama, one of the great civilised art forms, arose and developed out of 'primitive ritual'. And he recognised that Scotland, by addressing its own 'barbaric and pagan past', might similarly 'civilise' itself and set in train new creative possibilities. He applauded the cultural dynamic implicit in Darwin's theories and believed that the Auld Religion[2] had much to teach modern Scotland – especially its artists. The extent to which Harrison's thinking influenced Hamish in the early fifties is clear in the following synopsis for a proposed series of radio programmes, which he presented to the Scottish BBC in 1952:

'How a Ballad Grows' will show how folk music and the ballad have their genesis, how they grow, develop, proliferate – and how they give, as nothing else can, *a conception of community* in its constant process of change and development. The ballad will no longer appear 'static' – the pinned butterfly in the collection – but 'dynamic': moving, expanding, being added to, mobile as the winds and the seasons. Such scholarship as there will be in the programmes will be in the best sense of the word imaginative – scholarship which hovers on the confines of creative art. This is the only kind of approach which can illuminate folk art, the most allusive, the most fleeting, and at the same time the most integral and faithful manifestation of the human spirit . . . Programmes will be cast as far as possible in dramatic form, taking a number of representative ballads and following them through various stages of their development. The question, 'Is folksong dead and gone – or a living thing?' will be posed and examined by the Eng. Lit. Pundit, the arm-chair folklorist, the collector in the field – and the ballad singer . . . The series would end by re-asserting the right and duty of the Scots people to preserve their folk-song as part of their incomparable heritage . . .

---

1. HH, unpublished, from notebook.
2. The Auld Religion: the pre-Christian pagan wisdom (of ancient peoples), which Hamish had recently evoked (in a letter to the *Daily Worker* 1950) as 'the ancient wisdom, disguised as laughter, dances with the light of a great summer sea'.

This proposal, like dozens of others submitted over the years, was rejected, but as one door closed others opened and shortly before Christmas 1950 Hamish met two Americans with whom he was to establish important creative partnerships. One, with the documentary photographer Paul Strand, was short-lived; the other, with the radical folklorist Alan Lomax, was to be lifelong.

Paul Strand was a middle-aged, hard-line New York communist who had played a significant role in the evolution of modern art in America. During the late 1940s, as McCarthyite pressures grew, he was 'forced' like many left-wing Americans to seek work outside the 'Land of the Free'. As a photographer, Strand's style was uncluttered, monumental and 'Soviet' in the great tradition of Eisenstein. Strand had been impressed by the Grierson/Robert Flaherty film *Industrial Britain* (1947) and decided to create a book of photographs portraying life in the British coalfields – with Lanarkshire his starting point. After meeting Hamish, however, he changed his mind and decided to document a different community altogether – the islanders of the Outer Hebrides. Hamish argued that industrial Scotland had already been well documented by film-makers, photographers and journalists but that the traditional life of the Hebrides had not been recorded by any major visual artist. He told Strand that it was perhaps the last 'heroic society' in Europe; that it was a society under threat of extinction, and he compared the struggle of the Gaels to the struggle of the Jews. He sang Gaelic songs, recited his 'Heroic Song for the Runners of Cyrene' and told Strand that South Uist was the place to go. He offered contact with Dr Alastair MacLean, and gave Strand the phone number of the Lochboisdale hotel. He even tried to excite Strand's sense of rivalry by telling him that John Lorne Campbell's American wife, Margaret Fay Shaw, had, in the thirties, taken photographs in the Hebrides but that she was not a great photographer. Thus, Paul Strand dropped his plan to work in the coalfields and went out to Uist to create *Tir a' Mhurain*, a book that is now regarded as a major work of art. Hamish's role in setting this book in motion has not, until now, been acknowledged.

When Strand had completed his photographs, an accompanying text had to be written. Various writers were considered, including Hamish, but according to documents in the Strand archive in the USA,[3] Strand was warned off Hamish by the actor Alex McCrindle (famous for his role as Dick Barton: Special Agent). McCrindle, a close friend of MacDiarmid's,

---

3. I am grateful to Dr Fraser MacDonald for supplying this information. His thesis 'The nature of vision: A history of things seen in the Scottish Highlands' was submitted to the University of Oxford in 2002.

suggested that Hamish would use Strand's book to peddle his 'folkloristical obsessions' and sully the purity of Strand's vision. He may have been right. Strand gave the commission to Basil Davidson, an English communist, a prolific author and one of the world's first post-colonial theorists. It was not a bad choice, and from the moment *Tir a' Mhurain* was published it was recognised as a triumph. Hamish's influence on Strand did not end in the Hebrides, however: Strand's next big project (*Un Paese*, 1953) was realised in rural Italy in close collaboration with the author and screen-writer Cesare Zavattini, the man for whom Hamish's dear friend Amleto Micozzi worked as personal secretary throughout this period.

If Hamish's influence on Strand is surprising, his meeting with Lomax had something of the inevitable about it. During the American Depression, Alan's father, John Lomax, had gained an international reputation as field collector in the southern States and, since his teens, Alan had worked as his father's recording assistant. He had come to Britain to work on a major contract with Columbia Records of New York – to record the world's folk and primitive music. According to Hamish, 'Lomax was looking for an assistant to research his recording trip to Scotland and I was the man he found. The Scottish album was number VI in the Columbia Series and Lomax, who had Scottish ancestry, was keen to do Scotland proud.' In return, Hamish received some much needed cash and a degree of acceptable public exposure that helped launch his career as a professional folklorist.[4] Ewan MacColl also joined Lomax's team and, on 16 February 1951, MacColl wrote to put Hamish in the picture (although Hamish was in fact already in the picture).

> Dear Hamish . . . a brief note – there is a character wandering around this sceptred isle at the moment yclept [called] Alan Lomax . . . He is over here with a super recording unit and a girl, Robin Roberts, who sings like an angel . . . The idea is that he will record the folk-singers of a group of countries (he has already covered Africa – America – the West Indies – the Central European countries). And Columbia will produce an album of discs – an hour for each country. He is not interested in trained singers or refined versions of the folksongs. He wants to record traditional-style singers doing ballads, work songs, political satires etc. It occurred to me that you could help him in two ways. 1) Record some of your

---

4. Hamish later commented that Scottish academia was more willing to be per-suaded by the arguments of a well-funded American than an impoverished Scots poet. Alan Lomax's trip to Scotland helped launch the School of Scottish Studies.

soldier songs and any other songs you know. You sang some to me in the little cafe opposite the Epworth Hall. 2) Introduce him to other Scots folk-singers. You know the kind of thing he wants: bothy songs, street songs, soldier songs, mouth music, the big Gaelic stuff, weavers' and miners' songs etc. This is important, Hamish. It is vital that Scotland is well represented in this collection. It would be fatal if the 'folksy' boys were to cash in.

All three men worked together with a mixture of enthusiasm and committed self-interest. Hamish worked only on the Scottish collection, MacColl worked on both the English and the Scottish collections. And his hint that the 'folksy boys' might cause trouble proved all too accurate. Both John Lorne Campbell of Canna (the Gaelic scholar) and Francis Collinson (a musicologist and ballad specialist) refused to cooperate with Lomax in any way. Collinson's attitude was made clear in this letter to Hamish in December 1957: 'I took great exception, on Lomax's arrival in this country – in 1950 I think, to his patronising and critical attitude to my own work in folksong and also at some of his methods in obtaining the names of informants both of my own and later John Campbell's. My own feelings are that I (still) do not want anything to do with him, though I know that you have a high opinion of him as a folksong collector.'

This resistance from established scholars, however, gave Hamish carte blanche – and he set about planning Lomax's Scottish programme exactly as he wanted. He enlisted William Montgomerie (poet, teacher and collector) to help him deal with Scots tradition, and arranged that Calum MacLean would take charge of Lomax's programme in the Gaedhealtacht. Calum then integrated his brothers Sorley and Alastair into what became an exceptional team.

To prime Lomax for his visit, Hamish sent him a typed copy of the anthology of MacDiarmid's communist poems that he had recently prepared for publication – while Hamish himself dived into the theory and practice of folklore. He read papers on the bothy ballads, cattle calls, children's songs, street cries and got particularly interested in the work of the Danish folklorist, Vagn Holmboe. Returning to Copenhagen after a year-long collecting tour in south-eastern Europe, Holmboe realised that he *now* heard the cries of the street hawkers differently, and Hamish notes:

This made Holmboe contemplate *what* the street cry actually was, *how* this musical form had arisen, and *why* one could find types of Gregorian plainsong flourishing in the streets of Copenhagen . . . The hawkers 'sing' for three reasons; if you spend the whole day shouting, you lose your voice; singing produces a fuller tone that carries further; the rhythmic and melodic configuration of the cry allows the vowels that 'carry' to be accentuated . . . One hawker speaks about learning to 'draw out the tone' which relates to the chant-like rendition of Yeats: these cries are the stuff of 'heightened speech' – of poetry . . .

In March 1951, Hamish travelled to London to formalise his contract with Lomax. He stayed with his communist friends the Moncrieffs and had 'a wonderful singing time'. His contract with Lomax, on behalf of Columbia Records, was signed at the Hotel Maurice, 36 Lancaster Gate, on 5 March. Hamish would be paid a fee, plus expenses, and be Lomax's guide, researcher, adviser and collaborator in Scotland. In a separate clause, at Hamish's insistence, it was agreed that the Scottish people (represented either by the BBC and/or the University of Edinburgh) would receive tape copies and permanent access to all the songs and music Lomax collected in Scotland.

Hamish then travelled north to Aberdeenshire to start planning Lomax's summer itinerary – making use of some earlier research carried out by Morris and Marian Blythman (on behalf of the Mass Observation Survey). On 17 March, he documents a happy afternoon spent with Jean Lennox in Aberdeen. The Lennox family were singers, tradition bearers and communist radicals whom Hamish had got to know through the Young Communist League (YCL). Later, Hamish was to dandle her baby daughter, Annie, on his knee. She was to blossom into one of Britain's top popular singers, as lead singer of the Eurythmics. After that Hamish moved out into the Aberdeenshire countryside to make contact with an old bothy singer named Willie Matheson – an 'unschooled farm-labourer who, for sixty years, had collected and sung the ballads and bothy songs of North East Scotland'. Willie was an exceptional find, and Hamish notes: 'I decided that the first man to hear about my great discovery would be Sir Hugh Roberton, conductor of the Orpheus Choir . . . then we spent the evening discussing the dangers of radioactivity and its effect on the environment.'

In early June, Hamish attended the Annual Congress of the Scottish Miners in Aberdeen. He organised a major ceilidh for delegates and was widely complimented on his rendition of the 'John Maclean March'. The Scottish USSR Friendship Society had recently asked him to write a similar song on the theme of international brotherhood and, inspired by the atmosphere of this Miners' Congress, he composed 'Song of the Gillie More' as a message of solidarity 'From the Blacksmiths of Leith to the Blacksmiths of Kiev'. By 12 June Hamish was back in Edinburgh writing to MacDiarmid:

I'm coming down to Biggar to see you one of these fine June days,
because there are a lot of things I want to talk over with you, and get
your ideas on . . . First of all 'The Hymns to Lenin', which are now
being typed for me, in three fair copies, by Mrs Ashton of Aberdeen.
I'll have them out by the end of the year; second Gramsci . . . ;
thirdly to fifty-sixthly, the present political set-up in Scotland, which
I've been reappraising since I returned from Italy . . .

This letter seems to be the earliest prose evidence of Hamish's initiating
some form of 'direct political action' with regard to the increasingly
moribund state of the 'National Question'. On 23 June 1951, he spoke at
the Annual Assembly of the Scottish Covenant, stating that he believed
the time had come for delegates to declare their willingness to *act* in
accordance with the ideas they held. Unfortunately, the Covenant movement was now in a mess – like the Convention before it. A combination of
torpor, conservatism and fear of informers was reducing the Home Rule
movement to a fractious talking shop. Delegates wallowed in reflected
glory from Ian Hamilton's great exploit with the Stone of Destiny (see
Chapter 19) while factionalism, opportunism and bloody-mindedness
won the day. An outburst of anti-Catholic bigotry stimulated Hamish to
write a ferocious letter to the *Edinburgh Evening Dispatch*. Published on
7 July it caused a stir close to outrage.

It was into this mêlée that Alan Lomax arrived to begin his collecting
tour – and Hamish was perhaps glad to leave Edinburgh for the open
country of the North-east. Lomax was the driver, and Hamish was soon
back in his wartime role – acting on 'intelligence', responding to reports
from 'informants', knocking on the doors of run-down croft-houses and
farm steadings in high expectation. Today, the North-east may seem the
obvious place to begin recording the folk and primitive music of Scotland
but, in 1951, it was not so. The Border counties (home to the Scots ballad
tradition), Ayrshire (centre of the Burns cult), the Western Isles (heartland
of Gaelic) or the BBC's archives (in Glasgow) might have been understood
to be better starting points – but Hamish believed Aberdeenshire was the
place. He had ancestors there; the Greig/Duncan Collection was there;
Willie Matheson and John Strachan were there. And Hamish told Alan
Lomax that this 'old, civilised part of Scotland is still clad, here and there,
in the raiment of the Old Religion and still resistant to unnecessary
change', explaining how, when the Vikings arrived at the port of
Gammie: 'the women made them drink whisky – then split their skulls
with steens! Here we will find song of timeless virtue! Remember, those
Vikings had killed the men folk!' Looking back in the mid fifties Hamish
noted:

I wanted to show Lomax and show Scotland that the tradition lived
– and driving north to meet old Willie Matheson I knew I had an ace
up my sleeve. He embodied the genius of 'the humble lowly' and
from the start I was fascinated by the contrast in the characters and
methods of these two folklorists – Alan Lomax and Willie Matheson
– the unbounded American go-getter and old Willie Matheson the
loyal farm-servant. Because, like it or lump it Willie was a folklorist
– he had gathered a matchless collection of ballads from the bothies
and farmtouns. Folklorists are well worth a psychological
examination! . . . Some of them began as bairns, writing down
ballads and proverbs in school note-books. Old Willie Matheson
didn't let either his father or his school teacher know that he was
doing it – for fear of getting a thrashing with the tawse (it is not for
nothing that the Scots proudly boast the most literate peasantry in
Europe) . . . With the tape-recorder I felt we could similarly subvert
the purists and hardliners of our day. They could not possibly know
what we would bring in. Ballad and tune are captured together on
the tape recorder – whereas the literature boys have denatured
both . . . To save Scottish folk-song from the professional
beautifiers . . . that was our task . . .

Hamish decided they would make the Commercial Hotel, in the ancient
market town of Turriff, their headquarters. It proved an excellent choice
and they had hardly unpacked their bags when one of Hamish's 'scouts'
came in with news that a travelling corn-kister was staying at a lodging
house in Elgin. Lomax then drove off to bring in this fellow, who turned
out to be Jimmy MacBeath – one of the great early finds of the Scottish
Folk Revival. Hamish describes him as:

> the pre-literate embodiment of an almost purely 'oral' tradition – a
> sporty little character, with the gravel voice and urbane assurance
> that would make him right at home on skid-row anywhere in the
> world: as sharp as a tack, dapper, tweed-suit, quick blue eyes, fast
> on his feet as a boxer. He's been everywhere and nowhere for fifty
> years running – and he has a song about it. He's the man who put
> the bawdy back in the bothy. He claims descent from the MacBeth
> 'who stabbed Duncan through the mattress', and – given encour-
> agement by the three witches – is still one of the Wandering Kings of
> Scotland. Born at Portsoy, he has lived as a farm-servant and
> wandering bard: – his 'Come a' ye Tramps and Hawkers', com-
> posed by Besom Jimmy Henderson of Angus, in the C19th, has been
> described by Dominic Behan as a masterpiece.

When Lomax began recording Willie Matheson he too recognised that here was another remarkable singer. Willie had left school at the age of eleven in 1891, to start work as a farm servant. It was a hard wandering life, and Willie was to work on over thirty farms in Banff and Aberdeenshire. The peripatetic lifestyle, however, gave him the opportunity of hearing, singing and collecting a vast repertoire of songs, all of which he both noted down and kept in his head. In a letter to Edwin Muir, Hamish lavishes praise on the old man who was now his close friend: 'Old Willie's collection . . . provides evidence not only of the tremendous vitality of the ballad tradition in Aberdeenshire but also of the quality of folk poetry. I'm inclined to think that the folk poetry of Scotland is superior to most 'art' poetry. I am sure now that nothing should be said about the language problem facing Scottish writers until an exhaustive study has been made of the language of the old anonymous folk poetry . . .'

Willie Matheson's artistry encouraged Hamish to 'look again at the merits and demerits of the "literary use" of the Scots language' and it reinforced his belief that the bulk of contemporary English 'art poetry' was not only decadent but running fast towards a self-serving dead end. It also confirmed his belief that neither the 'synthetic Scots' developed by MacDiarmid, nor the 'self-conscious Lallans' advocated by Douglas Young were a match for the living Scots still in use in the Doric North-east. And he offered Willie's 'The Trooper Laddie' to Muir as a living example of the kind of folk-song that was a source of good folk speech and rich literary potential:

> She made the bed baith saft an' braid
> She shaped it like a lady
> She spread it roon wi' her twa hands
> Says, trooper, are you ready.
>
> O fan will you come back again?
> O fan will you come and see me?
> When apples trees grow in the seas
> O then I'll come and see ye.

One of Willie Matheson's most dramatic ballads was his version of 'The Smith's a Gallant Fireman', a 'collective panegyric' praising all those blacksmiths and farrowers who, over hundreds of years, have played their part in the life of Scotland – rural, martial and industrial. Their lore of metals, and of horses, goes back to prehistoric times, and even in the 1950s the smiths remained men worthy of a mythic respect. The best singers deliver this song with a mixture of bacchanalian pleasure and commanding authority:

Oh wha's the King o oor toon-an, an keeps the lads an' a' man,
Wha has lasses nine or ten, whaur some ha' nane at a' man,
Oh wha can mak us dafly dance till we be like to fa' man,
Where'er the music o' his pipes are heard i' cot an ha' man?
Oh wha but Rab the village smith, I wonner that ye speir man
Whaur ha' ye been a' yer days that caused ye na to hear man?
He's knight o' war an' Lord o' Love and King o' a' that shines man
At feast or fray by nicht or day the Smith's a gallant fire-man . . .

O who wad be a lordlings slave, a thing without a name man,
Wha wad beg fae ither folk what he micht hae at hame man,
Wha wad squander a' his gear, an syne gie fate the blame man
The growin' grass abune his grave micht turn red in shame man.
Let Fowk devide an' ca' it pride – be't mine tae still inspire man,
He that winnae wale the road deserves to dree the mice man,
Let moral dignity and worth your heart and soul inspire man
Let honour pay whaur honour's due – the smith's a gallant fire-man.[5]

Hamish recorded this song at a time when 'The Movement' was the dominant new force in British poetry: a movement that Hamish describes as 'the most impoverished *avant garde* ever to dominate English literature' and, bolstered by the self-evident power of Willie's ballads, Hamish asserted that 'the time has come for contemporary art-poets to renew their energies – not in debate in university seminar rooms, not in the pages of small magazines, but in direct contact with the folk poets. Intellectual enquiry is one thing, art something else'.

Once Lomax had begun to record Willie he realised that Willie had so many good songs that if he was to get even half of them down he would have to develop a new recording strategy. According to Hamish, 'He wanted the title, the gist and the tune . . . he was an American – he knew time was money.' Thus, instead of allowing Willie to present each song in its entirety – with a breathing space in-between – Lomax began demanding just a verse from each ballad. After a while this procedure began to physically and spiritually disorientate the old man, who felt a sacred trust had been placed in him to preserve and carry these songs, and he now began to feel he was prostituting them. After a day or two, Willie told

---

5. Henderson archive.

Hamish what was going on. Hamish was genuinely shocked, and it led to a temporary fall-out between him and Lomax. He recalled the event in an interview with the folklorist Sheila Douglas in 1985:

> I said 'if you think you've had enough, Willie, you must say so.' . . . When Lomax returned, Willie said 'I'm sorry Mr Lomax, A'm awfu' tired . . .' And with a certain bad grace Lomax accepted this – but there was tension in the air and later, as Lomax drove me back towards Turriff, he said 'Hamish, never tell a singer he's tired . . .' I said 'You bloody man! These are friends of mine – don't you tell me! You've had the privilege of coming to record these singers . . .' Well, an argument began and I said 'Stop this bloody car!' . . . There were plenty of lifts on the road in those days – and wherever I was going it was not down that Lomax road . . .

In fact, Hamish and Lomax did continue working together and on 25 July Lomax wrote from the BBC in Glasgow to say 'I think it would be best if we forget all of the very slight differences we had, and just say "too bad". No point in discussing it. It's a matter of personality and nobody gains from it. We'll work together fine at a distance, admiring and assisting, but at a distance. We're two very strong egoists, and difficulties always come along there . . .' Both men were professionals, and this Lomax tour – of the North-east, the Hebrides, Glasgow and Edinburgh – is now regarded as a major folk-recording exploit, and Columbia's Scottish album a landmark production.

Lomax's introduction to the Columbia record, *The World Library of Folk and Primitive Music – SCOTLAND*, pays generous tribute to 'the MacLeans of Raasay, Hamish Henderson and William Montgomerie':

> What most impressed me on my collecting trip to Scotland in the Summer of 1951 was the vigour of the Scots folk song tradition, on the one hand, and its close connection to literary sources on the other . . . The Scots have the liveliest folk tradition in the British isles, but paradoxically, it is the most bookish. Everywhere in Scotland I collected songs of written or bookish origin from country singers, and, on the other hand, I constantly met bookish Scotsmen who had good traditional versions of the finest folksongs. For this reason I have published songs which show every degree and kind of literary influence . . .

On 20 September Lomax wrote a formal letter of thanks to Hamish:

Dear Hamish Henderson, I've been travelling the roads of the world, hitting the high places and low places, the rough and the smooth, for about twenty years, recording folksongs and ballads from all sorts of people, but I have never had such kind and warm-hearted treatment from anywhere as from the people of Scotland, and I just wanted to write this letter and tell you how much I appreciated this . . . What you have done, however, is to help the folksongs of your country to be better known. Thank you for your songs, which will be listened to by scholars and just ordinary people with the greatest interest and pleasure . . . No use will be made of the recordings by me without first obtaining *your* written permission. 'Tail Toddle' and 'Wap and Row' of the folklore you recorded for me are being incorporated in the album of Scots folksongs I am preparing for publication by Columbia Recording Company in the States this year . . . I hope you will be as generous with the next collector as you have been with me.[6]

Unfortunately, the Scottish BBC were less appreciative, and on 22 October 1951, Lomax wrote to say that the Glasgow authorities were being very uncooperative about any future projects that might involve Hamish Henderson: 'I did my best in two rather uncomfortable conversations with Gordon Gildard and Hugh McPhee to get your excellent ceilidh on the air, but in tune with the sometimes timorous policy of Glasgow, they turned it down. I made quite a fuss about it – but that's it . . .' Subsequently, in a letter to Marian Sugden, Hamish writes: 'The Scottish BBC is doing a series of talks and features . . . but they're unwilling to sign me on in any permanent capacity. The finger still hovers it seems . . .' Indeed this 'BBC finger' continued to hover over Hamish throughout his life, and his natural skills as a broadcaster were to remain essentially unused.

---

6. Hamish and Lomax maintained a lively correspondence for fifty years, which was part of a partnership that engendered a productive transatlantic exchange of ideas, folksingers, collectors and scholars of great benefit to Scotland and North America. In Lomax's last letter to Hamish, written in the late 1990s, a deep sense of brotherhood and shared values is apparent: 'Dear Hamish, Thank you for all the fine pieces you sent me – and twelve besides for the many kind words you have written me. Few others have been able to give credit so generously. It shows you have the true soul of a poet – the soul that flashes and laughs in the process you share with me. I'm listening to the lovely tape you sent me, reminding me of the wonderful home-coming that this long-strayed son of Scotland had in encountering you all – great singers, fiery democrats – when I came into your greenhills so long ago . . . Yours aye, Alan Lomax'

The most important by-product of Lomax's Scottish tour was the establishment of the School of Scottish Studies at the University of Edinburgh in January 1952. His recordings justified the claims that Hamish and others had been making of the need for a national research department. The School's first researchers were Hamish, Calum MacLean and Francis Collinson, with Stewart Sanderson employed as 'secretary archivist'. For Hamish, the School came as a heaven-sent opportunity and he grasped it with both hands. He was employed on short-term contracts and subject to 'continual assessment' until 1959, but for the first time he now had a niche in the infrastructure of Scotland's national life. For the next fifty years he used it as 'the hut' from which, like a medieval masterbuilder, he would set out each morning to build his cathedral.

Hamish's work at the School of Scottish Studies will be dealt with in detail in Volume 2 of the biography – but one of the first things Hamish did was to present old Willie Matheson as a major folksinging 'discovery'. Although Willie was never to gain fame or fortune, Hamish was deter-mined that the old farm servant should know that Scotland was in his debt and would honour him. In the summer of 1953 Hamish arranged for Willie to travel to Edinburgh – his first-ever trip south of Aberdeen – to oversee his three ledgers (with their 700 songs) being transferred by microfiche to the university archives. At the School, Hamish proudly watched Willie 'feted by three professors, and by Burl Ives the American singer and film-star, who was thrilled to play his guitar and sing duets with this waif-thin plooman from the hills'. Willie wrote to Hamish throughout the fifties and his letters show the kind of love Hamish generated among the singers and informants he brought on to the stage of Scotland.

> Dear Hamish . . . Sometimes I hear the Scottish Delight on the wireless – Seamus Innes, Jimmy MacBeath, John Strachan – but nae me – ha ha! I'm not worth putting on the wireless . . . Man I'm thinking lang tae see you again man though it were only for a crack . . .'

> Dear Hamish, I was all the month of December [1958] in Chalmers Hospital, Banff – then – since I came home I had another blackout . . . They say 'You could have killed yourself'. 'Min', I says, 'that's what I was trying to do but I'll make a better job next time' . . . I was roon by Grantown-on-Spey last year on a pensioners trip – man it was great – but what a place! Miles upon miles, not a house, not a farm – until we came to two Standing Stones and on

one was written 'Jesus Saves'! We were joking among ourselves . . . Hamish – May God Bless and keep you in the wish of your auld freen Willie.'

Such letters reflect the realities of rural life in Scotland across many centuries and they contain echoes of the values of that 'auld religion' that so interested Hamish and which, he believed, retains its psychological and sociological relevance.

SEVENTEEN

The Cambridge *Broadsheets* and *Lines Review*

I am the fallen leave,
Becoming beautiful as the wind moves me.

Arthur James Arthur

Hamish's work with Lomax was exciting and productive but the financial rewards were minimal, and throughout 1951 Hamish lived close to the breadline. He continued his occasional lectures for the Young Communist League, and made a rewarding new contact in Edwin Muir, principal of Newbattle Abbey College at Dalkeith. Muir was a distinguished author, and his wife, Willa, a ballad enthusiast ever keen to swap songs and ideas: indeed they offered Hamish 'sanctuary' at Newbattle, should his future needs become acute. Newbattle College was a charitable institution set up to meet the needs of mature and 'unqualified' students, and the Muirs saw no reason why it should not support poet–lecturers as well as student–poets (W.S. Graham and George Mackay Brown were Newbattle students). In the spring of 1951 Hamish gave a short series of lectures on 'Highlands and Lowlands' and enjoyed several weekends at the College. With its shabby gentility, its fine paintings, its beautiful grounds and rare mix of people, Newbattle reminded Hamish of Dry Drayton – and he repaid the Muirs' generosity with a lifetime's support for a College that he believed was an exemplary Scottish institution.

While still engrossed in the final editing of his Gramsci letters, Hamish suddenly decided to try his own hand as an editor. Perhaps there was money in it! He had completed his collection of MacDiarmid's political poetry, 'Hugh MacDiarmid: The Hymns of Lenin'; now he planned a major collection of Sorley MacLean's poetry (based around 'The Cuillin'); and he began work on an annotated collection of dialect poems by the radical eighteenth-century Ulster poet, James Orr of Ballycary. The Scottish Cultural Committee of the British Communist Party (CPGB) offered encouragement for all three projects, but no funds were forthcoming. Hamish then began touting a more commercial idea – that he be commissioned to write a series of popular books aimed at 'the discerning traveller'. The first three were to be: 'Italy as the Germans See her', 'The Alpine Folksongs of Italy' and 'Italy, Seen and Unseen'. When these proposals also aroused no publishers' interest, Hamish began to feel that his work was being officially 'black-balled' – that there was an institutional campaign to silence his 'voice'. Thus, in February 1951, with his Cambridge Communist friend Marian Sugden, Hamish launched *Poetry Broadsheets (Cambridge)* – a publication that they alone controlled.

These *Poetry Broadsheets* were humble in form but artistically and ideologically ambitious. They were typed and cyclo-styled by Marian Sugden who, as Hamish's secretary and co-editor, also saw the *Broadsheets* out onto the streets. Eleven issues were produced. They cost threepence each, usually consisted of a single sheet of four folded pages, and were designed to be folded, stamped and posted without an envelope. The aim was to circulate poetry 'unavailable in the market place' and, for a year, these *Broadsheets* gave Hamish and his friends a literary platform when the normal channels of publication were denied to them. Contributions came from a wide range of 'working people and students' and some of the giants of modern European literature. Each *Broadsheet* usually carried at least one poem or song by Hamish (often published under a pseudonym) and he saw every issue as an act of 'witness' at a time when any left-wing voice was liable to be denounced as Stalinist treachery. Around the world radical poets and communist activists were disappearing, being imprisoned and murdered, and Hamish recognised that he himself might be 'snuffed out'. Thus the *Broadsheets* were a means by which, if the worst happened, he might leave something behind: – something like 'the blinterin' o'/ a snail trail on their closet wa'!' of which MacDiarmid had written.

Surprisingly, no overt institutional attempt appears to have been made to curtail or stop publication of the *Broadsheets* – but it is highly likely that there was some 'official' satisfaction to see that Hamish Henderson – war-hero, Somerset Maugham Award winner, translator of Gramsci and over-weening Scots patriot – was now reduced to peddling 'penny-dreadfuls' in halls and pubs for thruppence a go! Certainly the *Broadsheets* were small, insignificant, 'underground' publications, but 'rebel broadsheets' have a long and honourable history, and the *Cambridge Broadsheets* helped resurrect an essentially moribund tradition. In the second half of the twentieth century, dissident literary publications similar to Hamish's *Broadsheets* had a profound influence on the national politics of many nations, particularly in Eastern Europe. Today the *Cambridge Broadsheets* may be 'unknown footnotes to unwritten history' but they are evidence of Britain's McCarthyite past and Hamish's lifelong belief in the power of art.

The centrepiece of *Broadsheet* No. 1 is a savagely satirical anti-American anti-war poem by Hamish's friend E.P. Thompson, entitled 'On the Liberation of Seoul'. Hamish himself contributed two songs, both under his real name. The first, entitled 'Honest Geordie', lambasts the recent behaviour of his old Cairo buddy, G.S. Fraser. During the war Fraser had given Hamish the impression that he could hardly wait to join him in his revolutionary campaign for Scottish self-governance but, returning to London and discovering the pleasures of success as a literary critic and British Council lecturer, Fraser had quickly deserted the cause. Thus, in song, Hamish denounces 'wee Geordie' as another Scots go-getter 'bought and sold for English gold':

> When honest Geordie said Goodbye
> Tae truth, an a' the diddle o't –
> The cherry tree? Some other guy . . .
>   Och deil take the riddle o't/
>
> Ye couldna hear frae awfy near
> Ye couldna hear the piddle o't
> When auld Mahoun poured oot his beer
>   Och deil tak the riddle o't . . . (tune, 'Monymusk')

The second song, entitled 'Strathspey', is about Hamish himself and with Highland braggadocio he, very consciously, presents himself as the opposite of the appeasing Fraser: he is the 'youthful hero' who stands his ground, fulfils his destiny and, despite pain and sorrow, will enjoy himself as others enjoy him; he embraces the egotistical sublime.

> There's nae lass can haud the laddie
> Nae lass but's up an' ready
> Nae lass cuid let him pass
>   When Johnnie gaes doon the High Street.
>
> Frae Brighton tae Clachnaharry
> He's left horns for a' tae carry
> There's ae loon will wear 'em soon
>   When Johnnie gangs doon the High Street . . .
>   (tune 'Highland Whisky')[1]

---

1. Original composed 1940–1: see page 66, notes on Keidrych Rhys, Cairo, 1942.

Broadsheet No. 2 contains two powerful poems by Thomas McGrath,[2] a young left-wing American who, in 1947, had escaped the McCarthyite yoke by taking up a Rhodes scholarship at New College, Oxford. He made contact with Hamish and, in December 1948, *Voice of Scotland* published a bitterly elegiac poem by McGrath, entitled 'A Warrant for Pablo Neruda'. Three years later McGrath became a regular contributor to Hamish's *Broadsheet*. The first of his poems in *Broadsheet* No. 2 is 'John's Soft-hearted Song for Counting Croup', and it appears to be an attack on John Lehmann (for not publishing Hamish's Gramsci Letters); the second, 'Incident in the life of a Prophet', can be read as a roar of encouragement to a poet-friend suffering like some modern Job for his beliefs and ideals:

And a voice like a voice in dreams cried in the stone wilderness,
Calling out of the whirlwind, sounding its gongs and thunders,
Saying: death to the four kings of indifference,
To all despoilers of sweat and virtue and
Death to the defamers of the sacrament of wheat:
Destroy the temples of these pious sinners . . .

Broadsheet No. 4 is important because it presents translations of two fine poems by the Greek modernist Odysseus Elytis – winner of the Nobel Prize for Literature in 1979.[3] Elytis had come to London in December 1950 and stayed for six months. During this time he wrote what many believe to be his finest poem, 'Axion Esti' (It is Worthwhile). Hamish and Elytis made contact and found they shared many literary and political interests and similar partisan experiences. They sang, and talked – particularly about Cadafy, MacDiarmid and MacLean. And, it seems likely Hamish's passionate advocacy of MacLean's 'The Cuillin' may have inspired Elytis (as it inspired Pasolini) to make mountains one of the prime subjects of his 'Axion Esti': 'My foundations on mountains / and

---

2. Thomas McGrath (1916–90) was born in North Dakota of Irish, Gaelic-speaking parents. He laboured on the waterfront in New York and did four years' military service before taking up a place at Oxford in 1947. He later held a faculty position at Los Angeles State University. In 1953 he was called 'as an unfriendly witness before the House Committee on Un-American Activities' and his lectureship was terminated. In 1960 he resumed his academic career in New York and during the sixties his status as a major revolutionary poet slowly gathered momentum. By 1986, when Studs Terkel hosted Thomas McGrath's Seventieth Birthday Ceilidh, he was widely regarded as one of America's outstanding socialist writers.

3. When Elytis was awarded the Nobel Prize in 1979 the Hellenic Society of Edinburgh and the Greek Students of the University of Edinburgh (with inspired propriety) invited Hamish to preside as guest of honour at the formal celebrations.

the people carry the mountains on their shoulders / and on these mountains memory burns . . .' Elytis left London in May and the two poems he offered Hamish for publication in the *Broadsheet* No. 4 are resonant with comradely encouragement.

> . . . Yet one day the vision awakes flesh
> And where but naked solitude glittered before
> Now smiles a city, beautiful as you wished her;
> You almost see her, she waits for you.
>
> Give me your hand, let us go down before the dawn
> Pours down on her with cries of triumph.
> Give me your hand, before birds gather
> On the shoulders of men and sing this;
> That she appeared at last coming from afar,
> Across the sea, the virgin Hope.
>
> Let us together, though they may lynch us
> Though they may call us head-in-air,
> My friend, those who have never guessed
> With what metal, what stones, what blood, what fire,
> We build, we dream, we sing.[4]

Broadsheet No. 5 published 'Words from the Cross of Korea' by James Constance, and a poem by a ship's carpenter, Thomas Johnston. *Broadsheet* No. 6 presents a fine poem by Robert Garioch entitled 'Now in Late Autumn', three translations of poems by the Greek poet C. Gianari and two poems by Arthur James Arthur – an unknown poet. Future research may reveal who Arthur was, but his poetry shares qualities with Hamish's and only appears to have been published in magazines controlled by Hamish or his friend Alan Riddell, so it may be that Arthur James Arthur is another alias for Hamish Henderson. The second of these poems, entitled 'Timor Mortis', appears to give expression to 'a dark night of the soul' but is also redolent with hope:

> Under the midnight stars and measured stones,
> The wind of death, and on the wind a bell,
> Some whisper from the ruins of cathedrals:
> 'Life will break you; death will take you;
>   all is well!'

---

4. From 'Sun the First' by Odysseus Elytis.

So must the wind blow silently on bones
To harden, but, quicken the living – yet
With slow death-winding, lest they should
                              forget
The silence that enfolds their cheering
                         zones.
Move, ancient wind, though half time's
                         iron bells
Were rung, and lost upon your carrying.
New passing flowers will spring; your
                              breath compells
Children to pain, and sacred blossoming.

In *Broadsheet* No. 7 a long poem by Joseph Chiara, entitled 'Procession', explores the 'journey' of Christ and the Christian message through the world as generation succeeds generation and the suffering of mankind continues. Chiara was a Corsican who emigrated to Britain in 1939, and later joined the Free French forces. After the war he helped set up the French Institute in Scotland. He was a close associate of MacDiarmid, knew Hamish well, and became a notable and prolific English-language Scots poet.

Broadsheet No. 8 was a special Hugh MacDiarmid issue designed to salute MacDiarmid's 'Gaelic persona'. First comes a quatrain giving expression to the permanent clash between the poet and authoritarian power:

A' men's institutions and maist men's thochts
Are tryin' for aye to bring tae an end
The insatiable thocht, the beautiful violent will,
The restless spirit of man, the theme of my song.[5]

After that comes 'The Mavis of Pabal', a poem in which MacDiarmid (echoing a poem by the Gaelic bard John MacCodrun) describes a thrush (the poet) – singing 'on the tap o' the hill'. Despite the ecstasy of its song, the bird laments that it is 'a pool cut aff from the sea, / a tree without roots – for poetry's not made in a life time . . .' By choosing this poem, Hamish appears to be seeking to remind MacDiarmid not to cut himself off from 'the sea' of the common people, or the fellowship of his artist friends.

---

5. *Complete Poems of Hugh MacDiarmid* (Martin Brian and O'Keeffe 1978); now republished in two volumes by Penguin Classics.

  – O its fine to be back in the sun
  And the shoots are tender and green,
  But I'm lanely, an' flute as I will
  There's nae sign o' a mate tae be seen.[6]

Publication of this MacDiarmid issue was timed to coincide with the opening of the first Edinburgh Labour People's Festival (see Chapter 18), which took place in August 1951 and concluded with the now-famous Ceilidh (organised by Hamish and recorded by Lomax) in honour of MacDiarmid. It was at this Ceilidh that Hamish presented for the first time on a public platform 'untrained, traditional folk singers and musicians in the company of Scotland's leading art-poets . . .' Hamish consciously planned the event as a revelatory and revolutionary cultural statement. He wanted Scotland's leading art poets to be reminded that they shared a common heritage with the genius of the folk tradition that gives them a permanent 'leg-up' in Eurpoe's cultural stakes.

 Broadsheet No. 9 contains a poem by the Bulgarian author Nicola Vaptsarov; 'Vision of Eden' by E.P. Thompson; and three poems by Connie Rivers. *Broadsheet* No. 10 was a special edition of 'Poems from the Greek Resistance Movement' with contributions from Assimakis Panselinous, Rita Boumi and two fine poems by G. Kodzioulas.

 The final *Broadsheet*, No. 11, appeared in January 1952 (it was the last because Hamish was now working 'full-time' for the School of Scottish Studies). It presents two anti-nuclear poems by James Constant; short poems by Robin Rolland and Arthur James Arthur; two poems by Alan Riddell; and a poem translated from the Ancient Greek by R.F. Willets. Entitled 'Paean of Peace: Bacchylides', this poem allowed Hamish to sign off on a very Hendersonian note: 'Great Peace brings wealth to birth for all mankind . . . The very streets are pregnant with joy of the banquet / And the children's hymns blaze high.'

 It was, however, Hamish's decision to publish the work of Alan Riddell that makes this last *Broadsheet* historically important. Hamish had met Riddell at International House during the Edinburgh Festival of 1949, when he described him as 'a rather worried-looking thin-faced young chap – who came up and introduced himself – as from Australia and Greenock'. Riddell was twenty-two, a student hungry for contact with the Scots literary scene. He had been brought up in Australia but educated at Merchiston Castle School in Edinburgh. After service as a radar mechanic in the Royal Navy, he had done a science degree at the University of

---

6. *Complete Poems of Hugh MacDiarmid* (Martin Brian and O'Keeffe 1978).

Edinburgh but his great enthusiasm was for the arts, and it was Hamish who helped him blossom as a writer, publisher and artist who would play a seminal role in the literary life of Scotland.

In 1950 Hamish encouraged Riddell to go to Paris. In August 1951, Riddell distributed Hamish's *Poetry Broadsheets* at the Edinburgh People's Festival, and six months later Hamish gave Riddell a page in his final January 1952 *Broadsheet*. Both of the poems published are, in my opinion, about Hamish. The first is entitled 'Free One':

> All joys are his
> > Wind-free to hover
> Still over mountain
> > And snarling sea.
>
> Hump-backed clouds
> > Under him are beautiful
> As he rises, only
> > Perfect one, eagle.
>
> Day and night
> > He spans the world;
> Wings wonderful
> > Lift him swimming,
>
> Fill falling from him,
> > Falling, the earth
> Grows small as he
> > Shoulders the sun.

The second poem is entitled 'The Shower' and describes a shared moment: 'The rain was rainbow / falling, a golden halo / circling your hair / the sun was.'

The two men had already discussed using the *Cambridge Broadsheet* as the template for a new Scottish poetry magazine, to be edited by Riddell. The only poetry magazine then being published in Scotland was Maurice Lindsay's *Poetry Scotland* and Hamish was keen that Riddell's magazine should mount a clear challenge to it. The idea was that the new magazine should be fresh, anti-establishment and aligned with folk developments. Consequently Hamish helped Riddell become part of a circle of radical poets in Glasgow (including Edwin Morgan and Alexander Trocchi) and Paris, where Brendan Behan was beginning to feature in avant-garde magazines such as *Merlin* and *Points*. By the summer of 1952 Riddell was back in Edinburgh and ready to launch his own magazine. He entitled it *Lines* and it quickly evolved into a powerful cultural force that was to outlast the century. Hamish describes Riddell's achievement as 'a small miracle, from nowhere – he just went ahead regardless and created a genuinely new poetry magazine'. Twenty years later, Alexander Scott was to write unequivocally: 'there is not a single contemporary [Scots] poet of any worth who does not owe Riddell a debt of gratitude'.

Lines No. 1 cost one shilling. It had a cover and three times as many pages as Hamish's *Broadsheet*, but the two publications shared remarkable similarities. The first issue was launched at the Second Edinburgh People's Festival in August 1952 (in honour of the sixtieth birthday of Hugh MacDiarmid), exactly one year after Hamish had produced his *Broadsheet* No. 8 (in honour of MacDiarmid) for the first People's Festival. It contained two poems by Norman McCaig, one by George Kay, two by Sydney Goodsir Smith, one by Hamish Henderson, two by Alan Riddell – and it was an immediate sell-out.

One of the people impressed by it was the Edinburgh publisher–poet Callum MacDonald, whom Hamish was later to describe rather dismissively as an 'enterprising Lewisman with literary interests'. MacDonald quickly established a friendship with Riddell and volunteered to oversee the printing of *Lines* No. 2. This offer was gratefully accepted, and during the following year MacDonald also published the first collection of Riddell's poems, 'Beneath the Summer'. MacDonald's patronage, however, came 'with strings' and, by the time *Lines* No. 3 appeared, Riddell was no longer editor but 'managing editor' – and the broadsheet had become a handsomely designed literary magazine entitled *Lines Review*. It was a rare mid-twentieth-century Scottish publishing success story. In less than a year, Riddell's 'broadsheet' had evolved into a prestigious literary magazine, distributed internationally. MacDonald, however, had little interest in the folk angle peddled by Hamish, and largely accepted by Riddell; he championed Scotland's serious art poets – MacDiarmid, McCaig, Sydney Goodsir Smith and Sorley MacLean.

Lines Review No. 6, which came out in September 1954, was Riddell's last issue. After that Goodsir Smith became the first of a series of 'guest editors' and in *Lines Review* No. 7 he presented long extracts from Sorley MacLean's 'The Cuillin' and the revelatory new poem, 'Hallaig'. Hamish was thrilled to see Sorley at last being publicly honoured in Scotland: he proclaimed 'Hallaig' a great poem and immediately learned it by heart in both Gaelic and English. However, disturbed by Riddell's treatment, Hamish now stood back and published nothing in *Lines Review* until 1962, when Riddell was invited back to the editor's chair (to save the magazine from foundering).

Retrospectively, 1954 can be seen as the moment at which a decisive gap opened between the so-called literary poets and the so-called folk poets in Scotland. The rift had various consequences, one being that, after this date, MacDiarmid's literary circle tended to drink in the New Town – at the Cafe Royal, the Abbotsford and Milne's Bar – while Hamish and the folksingers drank at Sandy Bell's Bar and in the Old Town. The breach sprang from clashes of personalities but was also a genuinely ideological phenomenon that both stimulated and narrowed cultural debate in Scotland.

The privatisation of philosophical debate, however, was anathema to Hamish, and over the next twenty years he would use this 'unprofitable' split between Scotland's so-called 'high arts' and 'low arts' as the rationale for a series of impassioned flytings – engineered to unify and heal by the grasping of irons. For the moment, however, he was appalled that Edinburgh's *radical* literati should have succumbed to the temptation of becoming what he described as the 'Scottish renaissance *establishment*' and he was content to 'move out with the rebels'. He wanted unity, he delighted in diversity, but he would not sabotage his vision or ideals for any kind of couthy friendship or easy life. Sensing that a confrontation with MacDiarmid and the Rose Street Gang was probably imminent, he noted down a telling statement: 'Death or the bed of contention – MacDiarmid or me?' He saw important issues looming and gave form to the storm gathering, in an unpublished quatrain that clearly shows that, if forced to fight, he would fight to win.

> Wheesht, wheesht, Grieve I dinnae care
> Whether you're richt and I'm wrang –
> Gin dark is the price o' licht
> And silence the price o' sang

EIGHTEEN

Founding the Edinburgh Fringe – the People's Festival (1951–54)

The Modern Prince – cannot be a real person, an actual individual; but only an organism, a concrete element of a society in which there has begun the actual formation of a collective will that is acknowledged to some degree to have acquired strength in action.

Antonio Gramsci[1]

In a BBC radio programme entitled *Damn, Damn, Damn, the Communist Party Man* (broadcast in 1992), Hamish pointed out that not only did the Communist Party play a role in establishing the Edinburgh International Festival in 1947 but it played the prime role in organising the Edinburgh People's Festivals, which subsequently blossomed into the Edinburgh Fringe. In recent years cultural commentators have tended to ignore this People's Festival, but it was one of the catalysts that transformed the nature of contemporary culture in Scotland. This 'lost festival' was originally labelled 'The Edinburgh Labour People's Festival' but neither the dullness of that title nor any attempt to rewrite history can alter the fact that this 'fringe before the Fringe' released new ideas and bacchanalian energies of international consequence. And the key person stimulating developments was Hamish Henderson.

The first People's Festival took place during the last week of August in 1951. The lead organisation was the Scottish Section of the British Communist Party, but from the beginning the Labour Party, the trade unions and a variety of Edinburgh cultural organisations were also deeply involved. When Hamish spoke on *Damn, Damn, Damn, the Communist Party Man*, however, it was to the great internationalist Antonio Gramsci that he gave the laurels:

---

1. Translated from Antonio Gramsci's *The New Prince*, Vol. 5: a book that Hamish Henderson describes as 'a magnificent work on the forces that go to make a political movement'.

Gramsci was the force that engendered the People's Festival: Antonio Gramsci was a man who put communism into action . . . It was obvious that Rudolf Bing's International Festival was going to be a one-dimensional, high class affair – totally neglecting the native, domestic culture – so, we decided to remedy this in no uncertain fashion. The Cultural Committee of the Communist Party began organising the first People's Festival and did wonderful work. I have said before that the greatest event in Scottish History, after the battle of El Alamein, was the Edinburgh International Festival (and it goes on in perpetual, peaceful, international glory), but the real breakthrough was the People's Festival – which became the Fringe. What is now the largest and greatest Arts Festival in the world was kicked into being by the Edinburgh People's Festival – by Antonio Gramsci, a dead man – and by the Communist Party . . . The aim was to present a more democratic art – for the people by the people – a new art that would reveal itself capable of great things: the kind of things that Neruda, Picasso, Bertold Brecht were doing elsewhere in the world.

During 1950, Hamish had hugely enjoyed several of the festivals organised, all over Italy, by *L'Unita*, the PCI daily newspaper. Known as La Festa de L'Unita, these festivals were local events where intellectual debate jostled with horse and gondola races, puppetry and fun-fair rides, theatre, dancing, poetry, song and outdoor film-shows. Hamish believed Scotland would greatly profit from similar celebrations and he decided to use La Festa de L'Unita as a template for a new kind of Scottish festival that would mix entertainment, art and politics. Years later he notes: 'we wanted to prick the pretension of the Edinbourgeoisie, the city's arty elite and effete middle class – they organised the party – it was they who drew up the invitations – they who closed the doors! And they remain firmly in charge to this day, self-elected critics and guardians of taste and morality . . . We wanted to give ordinary people a look in. We wanted to show them what, so-called, ordinary people could do.'

Hamish believed that, at the time, in the Western world, only the Communist Parties took working-class culture and folk-culture seriously. He was not a member of the Communist Party (CPGB) but he certainly worked closely with members of the Party's Scottish Cultural Committee in establishing the framework of the Festival. Martin Milligan, a blind, Oxford-trained philosopher, was the prime 'organiser', and Hamish was genuinely delighted to see him take the Chair at the first People's Festival committee meeting – which took place at the Scottish Miners' Headquarters, Rothesay Place, Edinburgh, in December 1950. Subsequent events are described in an article Hamish wrote for *A Weapon in the Struggle*, edited by Andy Croft (Pluto Press, 1998).

> The body set up to plan and run the People's Festival was the 'Edinburgh Labour Festival Committee'.[2] . . . Our slogan was 'By Working people for Working people'. We aimed to attract people who felt excluded from the International Festival by offering radically different kinds of entertainment, by keeping admission prices low and including children . . . Far from opposing the 'big' festival, it was agreed the Left should welcome its existence, take advantage of so many five star foreign actors and singers on Scottish soil, and try to present an Edinburgh People's Festival which would complement its senior brother, and in some selected zones of cultural enterprise actually outdo it . . . The committee deliberately set its sights high. The festival ran for a full week, from 26th August to 1st September. We began with a one day Conference entitled 'Towards a People's Culture' which argued that 'all forms of cultural activity, at their best, depend on ordinary working people . . . and that the happiness of the people depends on the condition of science and the arts . . .'

That last sentence carries a powerful idea – and conference speakers asserted the need for Scotland's artists, technologists and academics to take *responsibility* for the work they were doing. Britain had secretly now joined the nuclear arms race, the United States was openly discussing pre-emptive nuclear strikes against North Korea, China and the Soviet Union – and many people on the left believed it imperative that scientists, artists and citizens should take responsibility for their work and its consequences – and *act* accordingly. With such topics being openly addressed, it is not surprising that the Edinburgh establishment and British Intelligence moved to negate the People's Festival – even before it opened. On 8 August, for example, Wilfred Taylor in his *Scotsman* 'Log' sneered at the proposed festival's use of the word 'People' and warned the organisers that their hopes of future financial support from the trade unions would 'probably' be in vain. Eighteen months later, this proved to be the case. (Wilfred Taylor knew what he was talking about in matters concerning British Intelligence activity.)

---

2. It soon comprised 40 people, representing 17 trade union branches, five Labour Party organisations, the Workers Music Association, the local Labour League of Youth, the Edinburgh Trades Council and many poets and artists belonging to the Cultural Committee of the Scottish District of the Communist Party. Activists included Norman and Janey Buchan, Hugh Paterson, Simon and Ella Ward, Bill MacLellan and one or two unattached individuals like John MacDonald, a Highland psychologist from Sutherland who spoke for the Gaelic component.

On 26 August 1951, however, the first Edinburgh Labour People's Festival got off to a splendid start with Glasgow Unity Theatre performing Joe Corrie's *In Time of Strife*. This was followed by a Theatre Workshop production of Ewan MacColl's *Uranium 235*. It was advertised as a morality play for the atomic era, and Hamish described it as 'a brilliant historical gallimaufry'. Later in the week there were amateur theatrical performances by the Barrhead Co-op Junior Choir, the Lesmahagow Male Voice Choir; the Tranent Fa'side Players and the Ferranti Drama Group. A series of lectures was presented by Ralph Bond, Tom Driberg, Ewan MacColl, Helen Cruickshank, Hugh MacDiarmid and Hamish himself. The last night was given over to a grand concert by the Scottish miners and their families, but the most innovative and seminal event of the week was the People's Festival Ceilidh. It had been planned in some secrecy by Hamish and took place on the penultimate night in the Oddfellows Hall, across the road from Sandy Bell's Bar in Forrest Road. This hall was a stunning venue for a ceilidh that Hamish rhetorically described as being 'scarcely less important that James VI's decampment to London!' The whole event was tape-recorded by Alan Lomax (as the grand finale to his Scottish tour) and his recordings remain a monument to an evening that *The Times* reported as being 'the most interesting musical event in the whole Festival'. A packed house cheered performer after performer, and in *A Weapon in the Struggle* Hamish paints a thrilling vignette:

The singing started at 7.30 pm, and finished, hilariously, at about 2.00 in the morning. It was an event of incalculable importance, because from it sprang a hundred other fruitful cultural enterprises in subsequent years. Instead of 'Muckin' the Byre' in white tie and tails and Kelvinside accents there was the glorious singing of Flora MacNeil and Calum Johnston from Barra, John Strachan singing the classic ballads 'Clyde's Water' and 'Johnnie of Breadislea', the expert piping of John Burgess and, above all the unparalleled artistry of Jessie Murray, whose 'Skippin barfut throw the Heather' enjoyed its city debut at the same ceilidh . . . And after the official ceilidh had finished we carried on in St Columba's Church hall in Johnstone Terrace, where Jimmy MacBeath installed himself – and Ewan MacColl and Isla Cameron joined us . . . The pipes sounded again and the dancing started. MacDiarmid was there, and I recited long sections of 'The Drunk Man'. After that John Strachan sang 'Goodnight and joy be wi ye all'. MacDiarmid was overcome and embraced the old farmer with tears in his eyes . . . Later that night – or was it in the morning – Jimmy MacBeath shook himself free of the friends who were supporting him home and, lifting his mottled face to the moon sang the 'The Bleacher-lass of Kelvinhaugh' . . . All over Auld Reekie the ceilidh was continuing. In a sense it's continuing still.

A month or two later, Martin Milligan announced that the Festival had made a financial loss of £50, but by modern standards this was small, and the organisers were soon planning a second bigger and better Festival to publicly celebrate Hugh MacDiarmid's sixtieth birthday. Subsequently, MacDiarmid agreed to become the Festival's Honorary Chairman, and Ewan MacColl led a campaign to make the 1952 People's Festival a major three-week event – like the official International Festival. Without large-scale funding or institutional support – and amid McCarthyite threats – it was a decision that bordered on 'hubris', but, far from being cowed, the organisers became doubly determined to give Scotland a vernacular alternative to the elite grandeur of the official Festival. Thus battle was joined, and the following article in *Reynolds News* on 16 March 1952 gives an indication of the storm to come.

'Edinburgh Festival Idea to be Wary Of' . . . The Edinburgh Labour Festival Committee last year organised a People's Festival week . . . demonstrating the cultural achievements of working people as a contribution to the capital's world-famous Festival of Music and Drama . . . "Unfortunately" said a member of the Edinburgh Trades Council "the programme presented, proved to include a considerable amount of Communist propaganda directed chiefly against America, in which we do not want to participate." To the general public the venture would appear to have the official backing of the Labour movement. "This is not the case", said Trades Council Secretary, George Lawson . . .

Such reports were the tip of an iceberg of orchestrated opposition to the People's Festival, but by the beginning of August a 16-page Guide to Events, priced 9 pence, was advertising a full 21-day programme. The Guide begins with Hamish's words: 'That the People's voice may be heard and the needs of the People met', and the Festival was opened by Councillor Jack Kane, introducing an alternative Film Festival.[3] This

---

3. Films shown were *David* (the Welsh contribution to the 1951 Festival of Britain), *Wake up and Dance* (produced by the English Folksong and Dance Society); *The Gorbals* (an amateur film made by a Glasgow worker, *cont'd over/*

was followed by a mini Music Festival with Beethoven as the featured composer – on the 125th anniversary of his death. A series of recitals took place in George Heriot's School, featuring Alan Loveday (a violinist from New Zealand) and two rising young pianists, Leonard Cassini and James Gibb. In addition, Alan Bush, a professor at the Royal College of Music in London and President of the Worker's Music Association, gave a lecture. Works of art were presented in the Upper Oddfellows Hall and included a Scottish photography exhibition, a Hungarian photography exhibition, a selection of 'People's Prints', a selection of reproductions entitled 'People's Artists from Italy', and an 'open section' displaying 'pictures by working class and professional artists from Scotland and the North of England'. Everything was for sale.

The theme of the Literary Festival was 'Contemporary Writing' and it featured the work of MacDiarmid and his Scottish Renaissance associates. In the Guide, Alan Riddell commends the way in which MacDiarmid's genius had thrust a new generation of poets into being. Each afternoon, readings by 'The Younger Scottish Poets' took place in the Oddfellows Hall: Sydney Goodsir Smith was twinned with Alexander Scott; George Kat read with Alexander Trocchi and Alan Liddell; Norman McCaig with Sorley MacLean. There was also a one-day conference entitled 'Our Cultural Traditions and their Advancement Today', plus a ten-day series of lectures entitled 'Our Traditions'. Hugh MacDiarmid examined the life and work of 'Sir David Lindsay'. Sam Pollock gave two lectures, one entitled 'From Thomas Muir to Robert Owen', the other 'From Keir Hardy to John MacLean'. Desmond Greaves lectured on 'James Connolly – Socialist and Nationalist', and on 'The Celtic Renascence and the Irish National Movement'. Hamish spoke on 'The Folk Song of Scotland'; Ewan MacColl on 'The Work of Hugh MacDairmid'. There were also lectures on 'Auld Reekie's Rabble' and 'Robert Burns', and MacDiarmid concluded events with a lecture on the 'Radical Tradition in Scottish Culture'. In retrospect, these remarkable events can be seen to have laid the foundations of what is now the Edinburgh International Book Festival.

Theatrical performances took place either in the Oddfellows Hall or in the Cygnet Theatre in St Leonard's Street, where three very different plays

3. *cont'd*   Charles Bucellis); and *Their Great Adventure* (made by the Film Department of the Co-operative Wholesale Society). A series of foreign films included *That Others May Live*, the Polish winner of the Golden Lion at Venice in 1948; *The Village Teacher* (a post-war Soviet film presenting the life of the nation through the eyes of a school-teacher); and *Daughters of China* (the first full-length film produced within Communist China) and two of Hamish's favourite films: *The Grapes of Wrath* and the Italian neo-realist classic, *Bicycle Thieves*.

were performed. The first was *The Travellers*, written by Ewan MacColl and directed by Joan Littlewood. It celebrated the humanism of the New Democracies struggling into existence in Eastern Europe (in the face of Western sanctions and Soviet military control) in contrast to the dehumanising Americanised capitalism of post-war West Germany. The second play, *Out of Bondage*, written and directed by James R. Gregson, a playwright and broadcaster from Yorkshire, dealt with the struggle for women's rights but adapted to Scottish circumstances by members of the South Lanarkshire Labour Party. The third play, *Flatter no Flesh*, by Kenneth MacAlbyne (who was he?), was a new work: the product of a competition organised by the Edinburgh Labour Festival Committee. Hamish describes the play as exploring 'some of the most turbulent and decisive years in Scotland's annals – the early, fierce years of the Scottish Reformation . . . Protagonists included John Knox, the Queen Regent, Mary Queen of Scots, five beggars and a cast of well over forty.'

Thus the second People's Festival bristled with high cultural purpose, but pleasure and conviviality were also nurtured across the whole of the city – beginning with a Ball at the Eldorado Ballroom in Leith and ending with a grand end-of-Festival concert entitled 'The Voice of the People' at the Cygnet Theatre. The theme of this concert was 'song and poetry from Scotland and beyond' with special honour given to community groups from the Scottish Coal Field. The Festival Club in the Oddfellows Hall was open all hours and, across the road, Sandy Bell's Bar offered music and song – free of charge – day and night. But once again the seminal event was the People's Ceilidh at which Hamish presided and Hugh MacDiarmid was guest of honour.

The evening began at 7.30 with the great Hebridean piper, Calum Johnston, leading MacDiarmid onto the platform, playing 'Blue Bonnets over the Border': the capacity audience rose, as one, to cheer the poet – who embodied Scotland and the living relationship of our art and our politics – to the echo. The Oddfellows Hall is a strange gladatorial space: the atmosphere was electric. And I, once again, introduced an array of singers unknown to normal concert goers . . . once this ceilidh had taken place, the dust and rubble of poverty and war were finally behind us and the sunlit uplands opening – my aim was to present the finest flower of our folk song tradition and celebrate the young singers who were carrying that splendid tradition in its integrity and I knew they would not let Scotland down. During the run up – even the Glasgow Herald got into the spirit. It carried an article that set the scene and brought in punters we'd never seen before![4]

Hamish's foreword in the Festival programme is also worth quoting because it is, in essence, his 'Folk Manifesto' and interestingly presents – in nascent form – many of the images and ideas that he represents in his last poem 'Under the Earth I Go', completed forty years later.

> Although Scotland's heritage of folk-song is justly famed for its richness and variety, very few Scots ever have a chance of hearing the old songs given in the authentic manner. This is a great pity, because on the lips of concert hall performers most folk-songs completely lose their character – what was robust becomes insipid, and what was simple becomes artful in the worst sense . . . This year's Ceilidh will again bring together singers from parts of Scotland as far apart as Barra and Buchan. Its aim will be to present the finest flower of our folk-song tradition – Gaelic, north-east and Lowland. *The emphasis will be on young singers who are carrying the tradition.*
>
> If the Ceilidh succeeds in its purpose, it will perform something of tremendous cultural significance in Scotland. In our cities the folk tradition has never completely disappeared, in spite of all the inroads made upon it, and it is still possible to graft these flowering branches from the North and West upon a living tree. *We are convinced that it is possible to restore Scottish folksong to the ordinary people of Scotland, not merely as a bobby-soxer vogue, but deeply and integrally . . .*
>
> The Ceilidh has another aim, no less ambitious. Throughout Scottish history there has been a constant interplay between the folk tradition and the learned literary tradition – an interplay more constant and more fruitful with us than in the literatures of most other European countries. Burns is the pre-eminent example of a poet who understood and recreated in his own work the folk tradition of his people. *If the renaissance in Scottish arts and letters is to be carried a stage further, our poets and writers could maybe do worse than to go to school with the folksingers . . .*

---

4. HH, unpublished, from Henderson archive.

As the Ceilidh drew to a close, Hamish paid his own personal tribute to MacDiarmid, who in turn rose to give an impromptu and powerful vote-of-thanks:

> It would be wrong of me, and remiss, if in proposing this vote of thanks I didn't point out that our treasury of folksong in Scotland – whether in Lallans or Gaelic – is a treasure that has been occluded, very largely for political reasons, from the knowledge of the majority of the people. This Edinburgh People's Festival and the movement with which my friends on this platform, and others in this audience, are concerned, is a reassertion of that tradition – against the tide of all things – all the cultural enemies besetting us at this time. We've got a tradition in Scotland as magnificent as any in the world and we must reassert it in its full unity. In precisely the same way the Lallans tradition, and the Bothy Stamp from the North East corner, and the Gaelic tradition in all its magnificence are able to go together – and form a perfect programme – so we in our lives and all our interests must have regard for all the variety in Scots tradition – and we must not allow ourselves to be divided into Highlands and Lowlands. One thing must have struck you . . . all the items in the programme have a direct correlation to the lives of the common people, the daily darg of the common people. We are not going to be taken away from them . . . However, magnificent as our tradition is, wonderful as all these songs are, they were all written, or made then written down, a long time ago . . . Why today, with all our advantages, are we not able to construct songs in our labour, and sing as splendidly as our ancestors did?[5]

The self-evident success of the second People's Festival unfortunately ensured its destruction, and during the winter of 1952–53 the British Labour Party and the Scottish Trades Union Congress placed the Edinburgh People's Festival on a long list of proscribed organisations. Indeed they declared that any kind of 'association' by a member of the Labour Party with any representatives of the Edinburgh Labour People's Festival was 'incompatible with membership of the Labour Party'. In the following months a number of people opposed to the Festival got themselves appointed to the Festival committee – Hamish noted that 'Scots Lowland society is contra the non-conformist by nature; it transforms its natural otherness into a visible grotesqueness'. Once the Labour Party and STUC had withdrawn their support, it became easy to present the

---

5. HH, unpublished, from Henderson archive.

People's Festival as a Communist Front. Thus at Easter 1953, with little money and savagely reduced institutional support, it was decided that the 1953 Festival must be scaled down again to a one-week event.

In league with Norman Buchan[6] and a small band of loyal supporters, Hamish tried to keep things going – by making a direct appeal to the mineworkers union, by speaking to the University Student Unions and at factory gates. He also became a regular speaker at the Mound – Edinburgh's Speakers' Corner – where he propounded the virtues of Scottish Socialist Republicanism, but raised none of the funds necessary to mount a People's Festival.

It had been decided that the Festival's theme in 1953 would be 'Scotland and Ireland' – a controversial theme in the year of a Coronation – but Hamish was delighted. He wrote to the Behans inviting them to come over from Ireland, but they were suffering hard times and delayed answering his letters. However, on 14 August, Dominic wrote: 'Dear Hamish, As you can see (from the enclosed cuttings) we are on the verge "as it were" of reclining for a while in "Lord Mountjoy's Palace of Culture" and it will take us all our time to beat the rap. In the present situation my mother feels going to Edinburgh would not be possible. However, if you were to write to her again asking her I would be very pleased . . . Am rushing off to address a meeting in O'Connell Street. Regards to Chris, F.S., E.H. and company . . .'

In fact both Dominic and Brendan Behan did manage to get over to enjoy the tail-end of the 1953 Festival, but the participation of such revolutionary characters did little to rehabilitate the People's Festival, or Hamish, in the estimation of the Edinburgh establishment; indeed their wild genius might be said to have put the final nail in its coffin.

After the Armstrongs of Dry Drayton, the Behans were the one family that really took Hamish to its heart – without qualification: they recognised him as one of themselves, as a Celtic bard: a *filidh* of rare greatness. Kathleen Behan loved him as if he were another son, and saw in him a Scots Michael Collins – as is beautifully expressed in *Brendan Behan's Ireland* (Hutchinson 1962). Hamish, in turn, honoured and loved the Behans. He collected their songs and triggered in them a cultural *raison d'être* that enabled them to marry their oral fecundity with the formalities of literary achievement in the twentieth century. He recognised the Behans as exemplifying the process by which a family, a clan, a nation lives, grows and maintains itself. He saw them as embodying the identity of the Irish nation and demonstrating how – through centuries of cultural and political suppression – a nation can renew itself at the well of its deep

---

6. Norman and Janey Buchan had played central organising roles throughout the Festival's existence.

musical being. 'The sang's the thing!': music – preserved and nurtured across the generations – can defy both time and despoliation. Hamish knew that Ireland, in the first half of the twentieth century, had recreated itself politically on foundations laid by its poets, artists and singers; likewise, he believed that Scotland, in the second half of the century, could become herself again through the poetry and song of her people. Ireland demonstrated 'Gramscian philosophy in action'.

Hamish's contact with Brendan Behan was less regular than with Dominic and Kathleen, but it see-sawed productively across fifteen years. At the time of their last meeting in 1961, Brendan was an international celebrity and the most famous man in Ireland, but when they first met in 1946 the cultural and experiential gap between the two men was huge. Brendan was a singer, an IRA man who had spent six years in prison; Hamish was a noted European intellectual with a World War behind him, and the surrender of Italy in his pocket. And it is not surprising that during the following decade, as Brendan transformed himself from being an 'anarchic tough-guy' into a highly original writer, Hamish provided the rebellious Irishman with a powerful literary model. He influenced Brendan's view of the Irish national struggle, he introduced Brendan to Joan Littlewood; Brendan sent samples of his early writings to Hamish and it was after Hamish had introduced Brendan to Edward Halliburton (the libidinous, eccentric son of the Countess of Mayo and owner of the notorious Porch Club in Edinburgh) that Brendan used Halliburton as the model for the character 'Monsewer' in his first play, *The Quare Fellow*.

On one of Brendan's visits to Edinburgh, Hamish began making a collection of 'Brendan's Oscar Wildeish epigrams': on Edinburgh: 'The midnight court in permanent session'; on romantic love: 'Give me the man who knows on which side his bride is bartered'; on homosexuality: 'Put it this way, given the choice between Whistler's mother and the boy David – I'd go for the young fellow every time'; on Presbyterians: 'They think there are only two people of importance in the world, one is the De'il and the other is himself.' This stimulated Hamish to write a flurry of his own. On Edinburgh: 'there's a fallacy in this town that if you oblige people you're their inferior'. On the atmosphere in Edinburgh: 'it builds up in one like radium in a deer's antlers'. On the Scottish industrial belt: 'Jock-straps in mortal combat' or 'a whole lot of people who'd be happier apart'.

The melancholy in these aphorisms reflects the fact that the summer of 1953 was a difficult time for Hamish. He recognised that the People's Festival was in terminal decline; four of his friends were awaiting trial, charged with 'conspiracy' and membership of the SRA (see Chapter 19), while he himself was under surveillance. But, as had happened so often in his life, just as he seemed to be 'out for the count' he had a stroke of luck.

Funded by the School of Scottish Studies, he had, in July, gone up to Aberdeen on a collecting trip – and hit the jackpot! His diary entry for 9 August calmly documents him spending hospitality money on about a dozen 'Travelling People', including 'Jeannie Higgins' – the woman who would, very soon, be recognised as the greatest ballad-singer of the English-speaking world: the great Jeannie Robertson.

The details of Hamish's relationship with Jeannie Robertson will be dealt in Volume 2 of this biography but, having heard her sing, and knowing something of the huge song repertoire she carried, Hamish returned to Edinburgh in a state of scarcely restrained euphoria, full of wonderful plans for the future. He told MacDiarmid, he sent tapes to Ewan MacColl and Alan Lomax, he wrote to the Behans. In Jeannie he believed he had found Scotland personified: here was the 'voice' he had been looking for, here was Scotland's Gypsy Queen, here was an immortal singer – an Earth Mother – whom 'the whole world could take in hand'. She whom Hamish had long dreamed of existed: he had found 'the inglorious mountain-track that is the Way!' He had found her – and there was nothing that the police, the *Daily Telegraph*, the Labour Party, the STUC, or Wilfred Taylor could do about it!

Hamish's role in the third People's Festival in August 1953 was relatively small. The Festival opened with a public discussion entitled 'Working Class Culture and the aims of the People's Festival'. Leading speakers were Peter Ness, Norman Buchan, Alex McCrindle and Hugh MacDiarmid. Theatre Workshop performed as usual and Ewan MacColl gave what Hamish described as 'an amazing three-hour unaccompanied folk-song recital'. Hamish's end-of-festival Ceilidh was advertised as 'Scotland and Ireland in Song and Music' and featured 'two great artists whom Edinburgh had never heard – the renowned Tennessee diva, Jean Ritchie – and the recently discovered Jeannie Robertson'. Hamish rightly felt their contribution made an appropriate end to what had been a wonderful three-year experiment in the teeth of received opinion and powerfully antagonistic forces. The following year a number of events 'in the name of the People's Festival' took place across the city, but in essence that was that: the People's Festival passed into history and was wilfully forgotten. The Fringe replaced it but has shown no interest in acknowledging its forerunner. For example, a 2005 BBC Radio 4 programme about the history of the Fringe made absolutely no mention of the People's Festival.

Certainly the 'political framework' that was so important to the People's Festivals is not part of the contemporary Fringe – but the historical and creative links between the two festivals are undeniable. Both the cultivation of controversy and sense of carnival that follow the contemporary Fringe were there in the People's Festival. The sexuality, eroticism and humour, so important to the modern Fringe, have roots in the bacchanalian music unleashed at the People's Festival Ceilidhs. Indeed, even today, few Fringe events match the eroticism and raw-knuckled savagery aroused by Hamish rolling out 'King Faruk and Queen Farida' and Ewan McColl responding with 'The Ball of Kirriemuir'.

Like the Fringe, the influence of the People's Festivals was felt far beyond Edinburgh: the idea that festivals themselves can be works of art, and the fact that folk festivals are now a worldwide phenomenon, owe a good deal to Edinburgh's pioneering efforts – with the impact on America being particularly strong. When Lomax took his Scottish recordings – in particular his recordings of the 1951 Festival Ceilidh – back to the United States he set in train events of huge impact, still unfolding.

Another unforeseen consequence of the People's Festivals was that they helped transform Hamish from being a one-man-band into a public conduit of Scottish consciousness. The Festival Ceilidhs affirmed Hamish's long-felt instinct that his 'calling was outwards and not inwards'. He saw that any lingering ambitions he had of great achievement as an individual artist – or as any kind of conventional political leader – must be renounced. It was with the people and for the people he would live and work.

Finally, the People's Festival encouraged Hamish to establish Sandy Bell's Bar as his secret and most unusual 'weapon' in the struggle he would continue to wage. Strategically sited close to Edinburgh University, the Royal Infirmary, the High Street and the National Library, 'Sandy's' now became *the* gathering place for folksingers, musicians and a fair proportion of Edinburgh's more radical thinkers. By the summer of 1953, Hamish had consciously decided that Sandy's would be the 'fulcrum' of his work, his Ossianic cave, his Columban cell. Hamish began to believe that what Socrates had done for Greece in the market-place of Ancient Athens he might be able to do for Scotland, from within the confines of Sandy Bell's Bar. It was a ridiculous, fantastic and glorious idea – with alcoholism only one of a long list of dangers – and, very sensibly, for a long time he kept very quiet about it.[7] He just went ahead and, against the odds, for the next fifty years, Sandy Bell's Bar, in Forrest Road, Edinburgh, was to become the most entertaining, creative and seminal tutorial room in Scotland.

---

7. Hamish never publicly discussed his 'plans' for Sandy Bell's Bar but private jottings made after a day's drinking in McDaid's, the famous literary pub in Harry Street, Dublin, on 28 January 1965 reveal his thoughts: 'IDEA: Sandy Bell's Bar. The folk revival in Scotland exists within a particular milieu. It is a unique mixture of poetry, folksong and politics. Because of Sandy's? When I returned from the war, Scots philistinism was the most solidly entrenched in Europe. What to do? And how to do it? Through a pub . . .'

By the mid 1950s Sandy's was widely recognised as the hub of the Scottish Folk Revival. Any visiting scholar, artist, poet, musician or sociological thinker seriously interested in Scottish popular culture, radical politics and the Scottish psyche was advised to visit Sandy's or meet Hamish. Here, it can be claimed, modern Scotland was conceived and sung into being: here came the Americans Alan Lomax, Pete Seeger, Serge Hovey; here came the Glaswegians Alexander Trocchi, Billy Connolly, Alasdair Gray, Liz Lochhead; here came the Liverpool poets – and folksingers in their thousands; here came students from all over the world; and here came Bruce Chatwin shortly before setting out for the Black Hill, Patagonia and the 'Song Lines' of Australia; here came Gordon Brown, Iain Banks, Ian Rankin.

Sandy Bell's also provided Hamish with a domestic conviviality that he lacked before his marriage in 1959, and it gave him basic personal security. He knew that most organised radical groups in Scotland had been systematically infiltrated with informers, but the informality of Sandy's provided him with a cocoon of comradeship. With friends around him, he would listen, speak, sing and encourage people – to become themselves, address their lives and the future of Scotland.[8] Sandy Bell's became the vantage point from which he could survey and 'order' his vision of Scotland into being. Like Brunelleschi, he created a single viewing point from which a new perspective of the world could be drawn. He imagined a renaissance that was here, waiting to be constructed, and enjoyed, by the people of Scotland.

---

8. After Hamish, the most significant 'Sandy Bell's man' of the early period was Stuart MacGregor: variously a medical student, folksinger, nationalist rebel, poet, novelist, army officer, doctor and university lecturer. His fame as one of Scotland's angry young men endures, as does his song 'The Sandy Bell's Man' and his novels *The Myrtle and the Ivy* (Macdonald 1967) and *The Sinner* (Calder Boyar 1973). Hamish and MacGregor were close friends for more than fifteen years. In his novels MacGregor paints a vivid picture of Sandy Bell's Bar, the Edinburgh folk-scene of the fifties, and indeed the personality of Hamish. In *The Myrtle and the Ivy*, the key figure of Hector Gunn, a radical university lecturer and folk-entrepreneuer, is based on Hamish and is described as 'the saviour of Scotland'.

NINETEEN

A Touch of Treason

Nicol's actors and singers are all dispersed to the winds, poor loyal souls. Roll up your sleeves, maybe we can give them some greater ammunition some day.[1]

Following Hamish's expulsion from Italy, in October 1950, factual information about his political activities becomes increasingly difficult to find. For example, the wonderfully fulsome diaries of the war period and the late forties were now discontinued. Hamish knew he was being 'watched' and began *'tae ca' canny'*, not just in his own interest but in the interest of his friends. He recognised that Scotland was enmeshed in a 'crisis' of exactly the kind described by Gramsci; 'when the old is dead – and the new cannot be born'. By early 1952, with the Scottish Convention and Scottish Covenant confined to the dustbins of history, he appears to have decided that the time for 'direct action' had come. The boldness of Hamish's thinking is outlined in a poem that his friend Peter Duval Smith arranged to be published in the *Spectator* on 28 March 1953. Its title is 'Jokers Abounding':

> I'll acclaim the accomplished
> who wield two-edged history.
>
> . . . Ay, brought to the ring
> they'll dance a galliard . . .[2]

The reference here is to Wallace's address to the Scots army before the Battle of Stirling Bridge: 'I have brought you to the ring, now you must dance.' Hamish clearly suggests that a similar determination and fortitude

---

1. From Stuart MacGregor, *The Sinner* (J. Calder 1973), in which the character of Nicol Ross is based on the character of Hamish Henderson.
2. Published in the *Collected Poems*.

is necessary in 'our day'. At much the same time Hamish noted down the philosopher A.N. Whitehead's statement: 'Times come when it is essential to defend one's ideals by force': on 6 May 1953 he adds 'with them in spirit and song'. What these writings actually mean, or add up to, is unclear, but we get general clues in a letter Hamish wrote to his old wartime Intelligence comrade, Jack Truten of Leeds, in 1983, in which he summarises his view of the nationalist direct action that developed in the early 1950s.

Dear Jack – in the aftermath of the Covenant (signed by over a million Scots, 1949–51), several young blokes turned to direct action of one sort or another. The pinching of the Stone of Destiny was the first 'coup' in a series: – it was 'terrorism without terror'. Nobody was hurt but the British Establishment was distinctly shaken (as subsequently released Cabinet papers show), and the escapade made worldwide headlines. After the 'Stone' was 're-turned' in April 1951, and nothing more happened, the young militant Scottish nationalists felt that something more should be done to indicate the strength of what they felt was – 'countrywide feeling'. The Coronation of the Queen as ERII gave them a much appreciated chance. A pillar box was blown up at the Inch in Edinburgh, and the people who blew it up began to toy with the idea of blowing up St Andrew's House – or part of it at least – to make even bigger international headlines.

One of these youthful idealists was Bobby Watt, from Fort William, who was at that time (1953) a vet student at the Dick Vet. Hospital . . . He was expecting much more of a 'Scottish resurgence' than ever actually came about, and could talk of little else. He was also a singer and, in mid 1951, when I returned from my recording tours in the North East he latched on to the Jimmy MacBeath version of 'The Barnyards of Delgaty' and, in no time, he and his friends had 'workshopped' a nationalist version of their own. Not long after the present Queen was proclaimed Queen Elizabeth the Second – a chorus began to circulate

ERII was ne'er my fancy
ERII is no for me . . .

. . . One night at a party in Fettes Row, Bobby asked me to do a 'D Day Dodgers' with the various verses and produce a finished 'singing' version – that could be printed as a leaflet. With the versifiers consent I then turned 'Fettes Row' into the Aberdeenshire 'Mains o' Rhynie' and Bobby, himself, into Lang John Scott. The result was the leaflet I send you now. There can't be more than two or three of them left . . .

This leaflet, 'The Mains o' Rhynie', was subtitled 'A Modern Folksong now going the rounds in various parts of Scotland, collected in Aberdeenshire by Seumas Mor'. The collector, Seumas Mor, is Hamish Henderson, and his 'unknown ballad' is a footnote to a history of Scotland that – as yet – 'dare not speak its name':

> As I cam in by Mains o' Rhynie
>   Early on a summer's day,
> I met in with Lang Jock Scott
>   Wha speir'd gin I'd join the SRA.
>
> *Liltin adie tootin adie*
>   *Liltin adie toorin ee*
> *Liltin adie toorin adie*
>   *ERII is not for me.*
>
> Says I, man Jock, I wish ye weel.
>   Although your numbers are but sma'.
> The maist that talk o' Scotland's wrangs
>   They havnae got a clue at ava.
>
> Says he, my lad, we'll try wer strength.
>   A guid strong blow 'ull ring the bell!
> I need twa chaps tae do a job –
>   Come on and gie's a hand yersel'.
>
> A hundred men was a' were portion –
>   Noo we hae a puckle mair.
> When we fight for Scotland's honour,
>   Ilka Scot will dae his share.
>
> Will ye join your home battalion?
>   Will ye fight in Scotland's wars?
> Or will ye crawl on your bended knees
>   Tae lick auld England's EIIRs?

EIIR was ne'er my fancy,
EIIR is nae for me.
I had aye a better notion –
SRA, an Scotland free . . .

The ballad continues with another four increasingly seditious verses in support of the 'Scottish Republican Army' (SRA) and, if one links the song with Hamish's statement (to Truten) that the name Lang Johnnie Scott is a pseudonym for his young friend Bobby Watt, Hamish's closeness to the SRA is quite clear. The ballad presents the aspirations of the SRA as part of a noble tradition of resistance going back to the Declaration of Arbroath and Bannockburn. On one level the ballad is little more than a bar-room rabble-rouser (of some historical interest) but, in 1952, it could easily be interpreted as a recruiting song, summoning Scots to rebellion against the Crown. At a time when Hamish was still a serving officer in the British Army Reserve to write and sing such a song was clearly treasonable and dangerous. Marian Blythman, for example, reports that her husband was 'beaten-up more than once' for singing similar songs. This being so, why did Hamish arrange that his ballad be professionally printed – and why did he openly state that it had been 'collected in Aberdeenshire by Seumas Mor'? Was he inviting his own arrest? Did he hope to use a public trial as the forum for a great national debate? At a time when it was a court-martial offence for a British soldier to sing the far less seditious army ballad 'McCafferty', Hamish's actions must be adjudged hubris or courage and ambition of a very high order.

The issue of treason brings us back to Ian Hamilton and 'the rieving' of the Stone of Destiny. Today, Hamilton's act tends to be looked back on as an 'escapade' but, at the time, it was regarded by the British establishment as a despicable act of treachery. Indeed, King George VI believed that its non-return would presage the end of the Hanoverian dynasty, and it was with good reason that Hamilton later entitled his memoirs *A Touch of Treason* (Neil Wilson Publishing, 1990). In 1950 Ian Hamilton was only twenty-four but he had long been involved in nationalist politics – particularly the Scottish Convention and the Scottish Covenant – and the question arises: were the various 'nationalist spectaculars' of the early 1950s coordinated? In his letter to Jack Truten, Hamish states that 'the pinching of the Stone of Destiny was the first "coup" in a series', although of course such a series was not necessarily planned from the beginning.

When Hamilton removed the Stone of Destiny, Hamish recognised his achievement as 'a poetical act', noting that national poets are usually 'the antithetical selves of their people, revealing truths they had forgotten, bringing up from the depths knowledge they would deny. They are the subconscious breaking the surface of being.' And, knowing Hamilton to be a singer and writer, Hamish recognised that the young lawyer – having created a drama of enduring national interest – had, with one blow, made himself 'a national poet'.

As a student in Glasgow, Hamilton had been very aware of Hamish's dynamic presence in the nationalist debate. He knew Hamish's songs, greatly admired his Elegies and on reading Hamish's 'Brosnachadh – the Call to Rise' (published in Norman Buchan's *Conflict,* in June 1948) felt himself personally addressed. He was also a regular reader of the *Voice of Scotland*, which had in 1947 published a remarkable poem entitled 'The Ballad o' Stane Jock'. Hamish, working as MacDiarmid's assistant editor on the magazine, noted the poem as 'attributed to W.H. Burt, an officer in the Highland Recce Regiment – HH'. No other poems by Burt are currently known so it seems possible that this poem was either written by HH (Hamish Henderson) or conceived by Burt and 'workshopped' into finished form by Hamish. It uses cosmic imagery similar to that in MacDiarmid's 'The Bonnie Broukit Bairn' and 'The Eemis Stane' but crucially brings the idea of 'the Stone of Destiny' into a human and contemporary focus. The poem's subject is the advance of the 51st Highland Division at El Alamein on the night of 22/23 October 1942:

. . .

> But this nicht stane Jock
> Walks i' the sand.
> This nicht I hear the pipes
> I' the wasteland.
>
> There's nane deid but his deid een
> Glower at the west.
> There's nane livin' but steppin' hard
> Towards the west.
>
> For the stane faan in France
> He rises a livin' stane –
> For the mindin' o' men killed
> Here rises a killin stane!
>
> Yon, pink eyed craw, the mune
> Sees a field o' strange plants –
> Fire and sand fused glessily
> Intil floors on a waa;

> An the waa is o' stane'
> An the waa walks
> Covered wi reid floors
> A stane stridin tae destiny!
>
> Gallas laddies a'
> Gallas laddies a'!
> Stanes o' Destiny!
> Stane Jock i' the man-trap field
> Walkin saftly.[3]

The march of the Highlanders – into the minefields – is described as if seen from the Moon. The soldiers become stones in a wall that moves forward: occasionally, the wall flares with red flowers as pieces of mines or shrapnel strike, or as light catches a hackle. The men march towards their deaths and towards a victory in which the poet proclaims the survivors 'Stanes o' Destiny'. The poem evokes the sacrifices of the First World War and the loss of the first 51st Highland Division in France in 1940, but resurrection is here – as Scotland's mythic Stone of Destiny becomes flesh in the bodies of Scotland's youth, 'stridin tae destiny'. When the poem was published it spoke straight to the heart of many young Scots, including Ian Hamilton, and some accepted the fact that it was they – and not the Stone of Destiny – who must shape their nation's future.

Once the Stone of Destiny was back in Scotland, disinformation, myths and legends began spreading like wildfire, and Hamish leapt at the chance to choreograph a heaven-sent opportunity to advance Scotland's cause. In particular he encouraged the making and singing of ballads about the event and its consequences. Thurso Berwick, Norman Buchan, Tom Law and Norman McCaig made notable contributions – but the song that caught the public's attention was by Hamish's close friend, John McEvoy, a young Rolls-Royce machine-tool maker from Springburn. This song, 'The Wee Magic Stane' or 'The Reivin' o' the Stane', is sung either to the tune 'The Ould Orange Flute' or 'Villikens and his Dinah'.

> O the Dean of Westminster was a powerful man
> He held all the strings of the State in his hand
> But with all this great business it flustered him nane
> Till some rogues ran away wi his wee ragged stane.

---

3. Hamish appears to have met W.H. Burt in Eygpt in 1942. Burt came from north-east Scotland and became a lieutenant in the Highland Light infantry; he was killed in Germany on 10 April 1945. The poem 'The Ballad o' Stane Jock' was published in *Voice of Scotland* in 1947, but was originally published in Cairo in 1943.

Wi a too ra li oor ra li oor a li ay

> Noo the Stane had great pow'rs that could dae such a thing,
> And withoot it, it seemed, we'd be wantin a King,
> Noo he called in the Polis and gave this decree –
> 'Go hunt oot the Stane and return it to me.' . . .

The popularity of this ballad set in train all kinds of developments, and academics now use it as an example of the dictum, attributed to Fletcher of Saltoun, in 1707, that 'if a man were permitted to make all the ballads, he need not care who should make the laws of a nation . . .' John McAvoy's fame rests on this single song but he wrote quite a number, and for some years became 'one of the handsome faces' on the Scots folk scene. He accompanied Hamish to Aberdeen on at least one of his folk tours – working as a machine-tool fitter to fund Hamish's collecting. 'The Wee Magic Stane' was published in 1953 in 'The Rebels' Ceilidh Song Book', by the Bo'ness Literary Society, which met in the Lea-Rig Bar, a hostelry conveniently on the line halfway between Glasgow and Edinburgh, and a hotbed of nationalist enthusiasm. This songbook was to have a powerful influence on the Folk Revival worldwide. It contains thirty-five songs, including six by Hamish, and another six 'collected' by him. The cover of 'The Rebels' Ceilidh Song Book' is also of historical interest. Based on a lino-cut by Jimmy Dewar, it presents a collection of images that symbolically encode a mini-history of nationalist activism during 1950–53 (see second plate section).

Thirteen months after the removal of the Stone of Destiny from Westminster, in February 1952, George VI died. Subsequently the Prime Minister, Winston Churchill, announced that the new Queen would be known as Elizabeth II – throughout Britain and the Commonwealth. As far as Scotland was concerned this was historically inaccurate, and many people believed that the fact that this decision had not even been discussed raised important constitutional questions. When the General Post Office then announced that all its post-boxes would in future carry the logo – EIIR – Hamish was in the van of the protest that erupted. He realised that here was another symbolic issue that could be used to highlight the need for Scotland to have more control over its affairs. Consequently, in the late spring of 1952, he convened a meeting at Sorley MacLean's flat, at 8 St Ninian's Terrace, Edinburgh, to discuss 'new approaches to the Scottish Question in the light of the EIIR scandal'. His notes for this meeting read:

> Two million people signed the Covenant, it was a clear democratic expression of popular feeling in Scotland; by flouting it – the

Westminster Parliament has dealt a blow at democracy and democratic institutions . . . We are not fascists – or Nazis – we are not
against democracy – we believe in democracy – but we think true
democracy is being denied to Scotland . . . Something else is called
for (Chris Grieve's critique). Must set out to do what H. had failed
to do . . .

It is not clear whom the 'H' mentioned here refers to – possibly to Ian
Hamilton, whose exploit had created a media sensation but no serious
political repercussions. Hamish believed that new pressures needed to be
applied if the continuing erosion of Scottish identity was to be reversed
and the British establishment made to realise the reality of Scotland's
demand for a Scottish Parliament. By mid-1952 the popular movement
for constitutional change (via the Convention and Covenant) had self-
evidently lost its momentum: a photogenic young Queen was on the
throne, a new proudly Unionist Tory Government in power at Westminster and the end of rationing in sight. Hamish believed that some kind of
'direct action' was necessary if Scotland was not to sleep-walk into
permanent subordination to English governance.

The St Ninian's Terrace meeting appears to have resulted in a loose-
knit but tightly controlled organisation, committed to stop the planta-
tion of any EIIR letter-boxes in Scotland. The group's larger objective
was to inflame public opinion against the British state's heavy hand-
ling of constitutional affairs in Scotland. Questions would be asked:
Who governs Scotland – who makes and implements our laws?' The
question the police were soon asking was – who controls this organisation now declaring itself the SRA? Because such a title immediately
brought to mind the Irish Republican Army (IRA) the British government felt intimidated and bound to respond. This was what the group
wanted.

That any Scots should consider active resistance to state power was
anathema to most of the Scottish population, but disaffection was such
that for the first time since the eighteenth century the 'threat' of armed
resistance became, once again, briefly, part of the political equation in
Scotland. However, from the beginning, the Scottish Republican Army (at
least the SRA with which Bobby Watt and Hamish were associated) was
conceived not as an 'army' but as a shocking and provocative idea – 'a
shadow of a shade' – designed to ginger Scotland into confronting what it
was, and where it was going.

Towards the end of 1952, Bobby Watt appears to have assembled a small
group of trained ex-servicemen with a variety of skills and backgrounds.
Numbers were kept very small and in separate cells; all volunteers took an

oath, accepted discipline and offered themselves as potential 'martyrs' to the national cause. The SRA's first objective was to achieve a propaganda blow that would impress its name and policy objectives on the Scottish public.[4] Describing themselves as 'the three letter men'[5] they declared that any and all GPO letter-boxes carrying the English EIIR cipher in Scotland would be removed. Consequently when, on 22 November 1952, the GPO unveiled (from beneath a large Union Jack) its first Scottish post-box displaying the insignia EIIR, the SRA took up the challenge. On 3 January 1953, the *Scotsman* reported what was already a long-running story:

> GELIGNITE IN EIIR LETTER-BOX
> Postman Finds Bomb That Could Have Blown Up Building.
> A postman found an explosive charge of gelignite in Edinburgh's newest letter-box yesterday. The box that stands on the corner of Walter Scott Avenue and Gilmerton Road in the Inch housing estate, bears the new Royal cypher EIIR. The postman was making a routine inspection at nine o'clock in the morning. When he opened the box he saw the explosive and immediately sent a message to officials at the General Post Office who, in turn, notified the police. When the charge was examined it was found to consist of a stick of gelignite cut into two four and a half inch lengths with a blue safety fuse and detonator. The fuse had been lit but gone out after two inches had been consumed. One letter in the box was slightly charred . . . This is not the first attempt to destroy or damage this post-box – the only one in Scotland to bear the new cypher . . .

The attack engendered real shock across Britain. It was described as an attack upon the Queen herself, but at the same time another thrill, very like that associated with the return of the Stone of Destiny, passed into the Scottish psyche. The establishment, however, quickly rallied 'to the defence of the ordinary people of the Inch', and the Edinburgh GPO announced that it would be sticking to its guns, that it would not give in to terrorism, that the post-box would be repainted and opened for letters long before St Valentine's Day. And so it was but, on 13 February 1953, the bombers struck again and the *Scotsman* ran a new headline:

---

4. As was made clear at the Conspiracy Trial at the High Court in Edinburgh in November 1953.

5. This poetical 'covername' for SRA men appears in Stuart MacGregor's first novel *The Myrtle and Ivy* (M. MacDonald, Edinburgh 1967). The book is dedicated to the 'Brotherhood of Sandy Bell's' and is set in the Edinburgh of the mid fifties. It deals with love, medicine, the folk-scene and SRA activity.

EIIR Post-Box Blown-Up: Explosion Heard Half-Mile Away.
At 10 pm last night the EIIR Pillar-Box at Liberton was blown-up by
a bomb . . . the front of the box was blown 30 yards across the main
road. Two passers-by saw an elderly man place something in the
box, and shortly afterwards saw smoke coming from it, followed by
a loud explosion . . .

Next day, the story continued: 'POST-BOX CULPRIT USED GELIGNITE –
"Had Good Experience of Explosives" – Police Hunt Goes On. The Police
have issued a description of a man they wish to interview in connection
with the explosion: – "Young, about 5 feet 9 inches in height; dark, curly
hair, wears a long dark overcoat; he runs in a crouching position . . ."
During lunchtime yesterday a small Lion Rampant flag was found on a
pile of bricks and rubble where the box had stood.'

Over the following days, much of the Scottish press reported events
with something close to tongue-in-cheek glee, and the GPO soon
announced that its plans for EIIR letter boxes in Scotland were being
'temporarily abandoned'. Thus the SRA won a 'bloodless skirmish'
and the letter-box bomber was soon a legendary figure – now young,
now old, now dark, now fair! Thurso Berwick named him 'Sky-High
Joe'[6] and wrote a splendid mock-heroic ballad about him. And, following the
removal of the offending box a second ballad appeared, entitled 'The Ballad
of the Inch', which reads very much like an 'unofficial' history of an event:

> Ah'll tell tae ye a story,
>   An' I'll swear tae ye it's true,
> Aboot the Pillar Box –
>   The ane wi' ERII.

> *Chorus* –   *Singing,*
>   *Fa'll blaw it this time?*
>   *Fa'll blaw it noo?*
>   *The anes that blew it last time,*
>   *Canna blaw it noo.*

> They took this mickle Pillar-Box,
>   And stuck it in the groon,
> Wi' Edinburgh C.I.D.
>   An' Polis a'aroon.

---

6. That Blythman should name the letter-box bomber 'Sky-High Joe' suggests that
the bomber was a tall fellow with 'Stalinist' leanings.

A noble lady in the Sooth
    Said, 'Let it weel be seen
By a' thae traitrous Scots up North
    That I'm their English Queen.

'Sae watch it weel ma merry men,
    An' keep it in your care,
For England's nearly bankrupt
    An' we havnae ony mair.'

They guarded it richt faithfully,
    They guarded it fell weel;
But in ahint their backs there nipped
    A big black-coated chiel.

Ye read it in the papers,
    Ye saw it in the news –
How he stuck his "Coupon" in,
    Wi' a yard-lang fizzin fuse.

As he hirpled back across the road,
    Tae the cops he bade 'Goodnight!'
Ah wadna stand sae near the box,
    For yon wis gelignite!

A minute later aff it went,
    Wi' a flash an'wi' a thump
An' noo they've taen awa' the bits
    Tae the Corporation Dump.

The bottom bit they left there,
    A' ragged-edged and shairp;
But the lid was in St Peter's hands,
    Bein played on like a hairp.

It's said that on the next day –
    Pit there tae get thir rag –
Upon the mound o' rubble
    Wis a wee bit yella flag.[7]

---

7. 'The Ballad of the Inch' gathers another layer of historical interest because it is
one of the songs that inspired Roy Williamson to write his now world-famous
'Flower of Scotland'.

Not surprisingly the author of this 'rebel song' remains anonymous but it carries echoes of both the 'Ballad of the Men of Knoydart' and the 'Mains o' Rhynie', which we know to have been composed by Hamish. Unconfirmed rumours about the authorship of this ballad have circulated for half a century but a little known article by Morris Blythman, published in *Chapbook* Vol. 4, No. 6 in 1966, appears to suggest that the letter-box bomber was also the writer of 'The Ballad of the Inch':

> Every culture has its heroes . . . in the Scotland of the fifties, there was Sky-High Joe . . . When the new pillar-boxes were erected with their EIIR insignia, he was the man with his 'yards o' fizzing fuze' blowing them up and dispatching their contents 'by airmail'. He himself wrote 'The Ballad of the Inch' and I wrote 'Sky-High Joe'.

Reverberations from the letter-box bombings spread wide. Fears that Scotland was descending into ungovernable chaos began to circulate and, on Monday 16 February 1953, the *Scotsman* reported a lecture delivered by the philosopher Dr W.A. Sinclair to the Carlyle Society. 'Dr Sinclair concentrated his analysis on neurotics in politics . . . Whatever the proportion of neurotics in the population, compared to what it used to be, their political importance has increased enormously . . . Today, many of them become communists, or, in our own country, Scottish Nationalists, as twenty years ago they might have become fascists . . . Our society today is now so intricately organised that a few men of such types could cause something approaching a breakdown . . .'.[8]

In England, MPs and newspaper editors began a concerted attempt to pour scorn on the 'dangerous tom-foolery associated with Royal insignia'. With the Coronation imminent and Britain's military forces overstretched – in Korea, Kenya, Malaya, Cyprus and Germany – unrest in Scotland was the last thing the British government wanted. Consequently the police appear to have been given *carte blanche* to nip any threat of a 'Scottish Rising' in the bud. Levels of surveillance were stepped up and a host of informers and *agents provocateurs* recruited.

Throughout March the hunt for the letter-box bomber continued while

---

8. In the same issue of the *Scotsman*, Wilfred Taylor in his 'Scotsman's Log', explored the problems likely to have been generated 'If that tiresome but wholly admirable fellow Socrates had been a Scot, alive today'. He suggests that such a man would 'be constantly in trouble with the authorities. He would be looked upon as a dangerous mountebank, corrupting the minds of the young men and being politically disrespectful of those occupying high office . . . Socrates would be put down as a national nuisance . . .'

disparate groups of 'SRA rebels' began deploying diversionary tactics. In Glasgow, William Oliver Brown (leader of the Scottish National Congress) took a Gandhian pride in becoming the *Sunday Mail*'s prime bomb suspect. The SRA then announced that any commercial property in Scotland displaying EIIR insignia was 'liable to have its windows smashed and all items displaying the EIIR cipher removed'. In Sauchiehall Street, posters offering a '£2000 Reward for identification of Queen Elizabeth II of Scotland!' kept appearing and being torn down. In Edinburgh, a young Aircraftsman, Derek Sharp Neilson – described as an 'SRA worker' – was fined five pounds for throwing a 'tyre-lever through the plate-glass window of the Scout Shop in Forrest Hill Road' (close to Sandy Bell's Bar). In Gourock, Francis Farrell was charged with threatening to blow-up Glasgow Central Police Station.

When Churchill was questioned in Parliament about the threat of a Scottish insurrection, he responded magisterially 'When I think of the greatness and splendour of Scotland, and her wonderful part not only in the history of this island but of the world – I really think they should keep their silliest people in order . . . [But] it is no part of my duty as Prime Minister to work up into all these ferret holes.' Hamish's response was a parody of one of Churchill's most famous wartime speeches and he delivered it from beneath the arch of Sandy Bell's:

> We will fight them on the Lochside
> And in the sheiling –
> We will fight them in the corrie
> And in the glen.
> We will fight them in the gloaming
> And in the moonlight
> And we will never give in.

On 17 June 1953, six days before the start of Queen's Elizabeth's first State Visit to Scotland (for her Scottish Coronation), two of Hamish's close friends, Malcolm MacAlister and Bobby Watt, were arrested and charged with 'contravening the Firearms Act of 1937'. Their arrest coincided with a series of police swoops on nationalist sympathisers across Scotland. By 30 June two more of Hamish's associates, Owen Gillan and Raymond Forbes, had also been arrested and charged under the 'Explosives Act', whilst the charges against MacAlister and Watt were upgraded to 'having explosives with intent to injure or destroy'. Hamish himself was not arrested or charged with any offence but he moved immediately to support his friends and help them organise their defence for what soon became known as the Conspiracy Trial.

Bobby Watt came from Fort William. Hamish had known the Watt family since the 1930s and Bobby himself since his stay in Lochaber in 1947. Hamish's friendship with Callum (Malcolm) MacAlister went back about a year, but his relationships with Owen Gillan and Raymond Forbes appear to have been short-term. Bobby Watt and Callum MacAlister shared lodgings in a top flat at 18 Fettes Row (where Hamish was a regular visitor). Callum's parents were school teachers and, after being released on bail, he wrote from the School House, Kilconquhar, Fife, to keep Hamish aware of developments:

> I was in no mood to drag my '*duine uasail*' [surveillance police-man] around behind me so I jouked him at the Old Quad and caught the train home . . . What are Gillan and Forbes saying? I would greatly like to be in Edinburgh to see them and yourself and to try and straighten the whole mess out . . . The peelers seem to have taken everything that takes their fancy – passport, driving licence, motor-cycle documents, family snapshots, type-writer and paper etc. and, greatest drawback of all – most of my working clothes . . . Try your hardest to help Gillan and Forbes – I know you would do it for Bob and I – if our parents weren't taking the stand they are.

Hamish persuaded Lionel Daiches, a young Edinburgh lawyer and former-soldier, to join the defence team, without payment. He also helped organise the defence case and the hunt for character witnesses.[9]

The SRA 'Conspiracy Trial' began on 17 November 1953. It lasted seven days and excited a debate that filled the Scottish newspapers for almost a fortnight. On one level it was a dreadful time for Hamish and the four conspirators – but it was also exactly the kind of spectacular public

---

9. On 31 July, the nationalist cause was given a fillip by the conclusion of an important 'Constitutional Case' – brought before the Court of Session in Edinburgh by 'John MacCormick and another (Ian Robertson Hamilton) against the Lord Advocate'. As leader of the Scottish Covenant movement MacCormick had decided to test the legality of 'the constitutional inequalities and illegalities' exposed by the EIIR controversy. He argued that the nature and status of the Act of Union of 1707 had been brought into question. MacCormick's action was lost but Lord Cooper gave an opinion on the Constitutional position of Scotland that stands to this day. 'The principle of the unlimited Sovereignty of Parliament is a distinctively English principle which has no counterpart in Scottish Constitu-tional law . . . I have difficulty in seeing why it should have been supposed that the New Parliament of Great Britain must inherit all the peculiar characteristics of the English Parliament . . .'

event that the poets who had gathered at St Ninian's Terrace had hoped to engender – and the four accused men were never to complain about the predicament they had got themselves into. And Hamish had long foreseen the consequences of any stance against 'the juggernaut of established power' – as his Third Elegy makes clear:

> Do not regret
> that we have still in history to suffer
> or comrade that we are the agents
> of a dialectic that can destroy us
> but *like a man prepared, like a brave man*
> *bid farewell to the city . . .*[10]

Government and police records related to the Conspiracy Trial remain classified Top Secret and unavailable to the public for one hundred years, but a great deal of information about the case is in the public domain, and the trial itself was well documented. The *Scotsman* began its 'full-page' coverage on 18 November 1953 with these words:

> Sensational Evidence concerning an alleged plot to blow up St Andrews House, communications, and railway and road bridges – was given in the High Court at Edinburgh yesterday . . . The Trial [will take place] before Lord Justice-Clerk (Lord Thomson) and a jury, of four men on charges alleging conspiracy 'to coerce her Majesty's Government into setting up a separate Government in Scotland' or alternatively that they 'conspired to overthrow the government of Scotland'.

The first witness for the Crown was John Cullen, a Special Constable in the Edinburgh Police. Cullen told the court:

> On the evening of the 31st of May I was listening to public speakers on the Mound in Edinburgh where there was a fellow in kilts[11] complaining about the Corporation of Edinburgh spending £80,000 on decorations for the Royal Visit and Coronation . . . When the

---

10. *Elegies for the Dead in Cyrenaica* (John Lehmann 1948).
11. This 'fellow in kilts' was not identified at the trial. Cullen described him as having a fine speaking voice, commanding his audience, enjoying repartee. Hamish often wore a kilt at this time and is documented as speaking at the Mound, so this 'fellow' may have been Hamish, although William Oliver Brown is another candidate.

speaker asked for questions, I said *he* should do something about it. There was no point in shouting about using the Coronation money to clear the slums of Edinburgh if he wasn't prepared to do something about it . . . Afterwards I felt my elbow being bumped as I boarded a tram and a gentleman said he wanted to speak to me – this was Raymond Glen Sturrock Forbes . . . He asked me to come into an organisation . . . He said there was a little danger involved – there were big risks to run. He said it may involve even a long term of imprisonment. It may also involve a commission of murder . . . This is an organisation that intends to separate the border of England from Scotland. Our intention is to terrorise the nation to such an extent that martial law will be declared . . . Then we shall know how much of the army is for us and against us. I asked – is this the SRA I've been reading about? Forbes answered, perhaps it is, perhaps it is not – let's call it for the moment – the organisation . . .

Thus began a cloak-and-dagger game of deceit, misinformation, bluff and counter-bluff between the nationalist conspirators, the Edinburgh Police and some of Scotland's most distinguished law officers. During the trial it emerged that John Cullen was not just an excavator driver and Special Constable but an *agent provocateur* working for British Intelligence who, by the end of the trial (despite being the prosecution's key witness), was recognised by both the Crown prosecutors and the Lord Advocate as an untrustworthy informant with 'an unsavoury past'. However, Cullen was the prosecution's main witness and his role raises crucial questions. For example, did Cullen, on police orders, legally and properly infiltrate an illegal and dangerous organisation in order to expose crimes of high seriousness? Or did he falsely and knowingly entrap the accused men into the crime of which they were accused? But, as the trial developed, an even more important question was raised: did the entrapment, in fact, work the other way round? Did the four accused men 'pretend' to be planning violent actions in Scotland so that Cullen and the corrupt activities of the Scottish Police Force could be exposed in open court and before the Scottish people? This is what the leading defendant, Bobby Watt, was to argue.

Hamish was in the public gallery throughout the seven days of the trial. Bobby Watt was the first of the accused men to enter the witness box. He spoke with remarkable youthful authority and began by stating that the so-called 'plot' was actually a 'hoax' – with a serious purpose behind it. 'Our object', he said, 'was to expose the attempts being made to incite Scottish nationalists to violence and to expose the methods used to sabotage Scottish interests.' Some idea of the quality of Watt's defence can be gauged from the following, consciously theatrical, exchange with the Lord Advocate:

> LA: Did it never occur to you that after the Coronation and before the Queen's visit was not the most suitable of times to play a hoax?
> Watt: We could not have chosen a better time.
> LA: There was a political motive behind all this?
> Watt: As a Scotsman – yes . . .
> LA: When did it first occur to you to represent all that you have been doing as a hoax?
> Watt: It was a hoax all along from start to finish. Our principles were deadly serious, our method to express them through the medium of a hoax . . . We wished to impress upon the authorities the fact that if we had intended violence and intended to go through with the thing, we could have done it. We had the means at our disposal . . . We were endeavouring to show that in Scotland today there is a very strong feeling about the Scottish Home Rule Question. How could we bring this fact to the notice of the authorities? We had two courses of action – violence or words. We chose words. We could easily have resorted to violence but we did not.
> LA: If you are saying the whole thing was a hoax why didn't you say it to anyone?
> Watt: I say it to you now.
> LA: You are not saying, are you, that you have not had opportunities on which you could have said this before?
> Watt: Not such a splendid opportunity as this!

When Watt then stated 'I am proud to be standing here in this court' a loud stamping of feet in the public galleries broke out and only ended when the Lord Justice Clerk threatened to clear all the galleries. The trial had now become drama of a high order and when Watt was asked where he met his friend MacAlister he replied: 'I first met him on the summit of Ben Nevis, in June 1952, wearing a swim-suit and skiing boots but now we are both members of Edinburgh University Scottish Nationalist Party.' When asked about his introduction to John Cullen, Watt stated that he had told Forbes, 'he is "a madman!" But – as such – the ideal person to whom to pass vital information about the SRA. An organisation which, as far as I know, does not exist!'

When MacAlister came to the dock, he confirmed Watt's testimony: 'We realized that whatever control the authorities for the enforcement of law had over these matters – the law of Scotland had control over them . . . We planned to lead Cullen on, and then expose him.' When

Gillan was sworn into the witness box, he agreed that he was author of the following statement: '. . . We do not consider Queen Elizabeth as having been crowned Queen of Scotland and furthermore condemn the appellation Elizabeth II of Great Britain as being unlawful and historically inaccurate.' From the dock Raymond Forbes stated: 'We got together to do something for Scotland. We were able to expose the methods used to incite Nationalists. When the other three had been arrested and I was still free – I thought the other three might think I had let them down if I was not arrested. So, I made sure I was arrested.' He also admitted his involvement in the 'fly-posting of posters advertising a £2000 reward to anyone who could reveal the identity of Queen Elizabeth II of Scotland'.

Each of the four accused was intelligent, likeable and idealistic. They came from Highlands and Lowlands; they were mountaineers, dancers, singers, good-humoured poor students (Daiches describing them as living on oats and salt-herring), but also military men representing the three Services. The Lord Justice Clerk concluded the trial: '. . . Whatever was plotted was plotted fairly hurriedly among men of no particular resources, and as far as we can see they were acting on their own . . .' All four men were acquitted on the charge of Conspiracy but, by a majority verdict, all four were convicted of 'the unlawful and malicious possession of explosives etc . . .' The Lord Justice Clerk (Lord Thomson) then passed sentences of one year on each man, saying 'Let this trial be a warning – any – who, in future, intend or think of using violence – will not be able to rely on being treated with leniency . . .'

Thus the SRA played the only strong card it was prepared to play – and lost. The Scottish people showed great interest in the trial but absolutely no inclination to take on their government – constitutionally, intellectually, or in the streets: they were content with things as they were. However, establishment *fears* of a popular rebellion lingered for some weeks. The *Scotsman* editorial of 26 November asked: 'Was it wise to inflate this thing into a conspiracy against HM's Government in Scotland? . . . Are these men now to be regarded as martyrs in the cause of Scottish Nationalism? . . . The striking disparity between the ends alleged and the means at the disposal of the accused is obvious to all, though that again, is not an exculpation; but to use a steam-hammer to crack this nut was probably politically unwise.' And 'Log', in his diary, caught the public mood exactly – describing the trial with a typical mixture of salacious excitement and complacent largesse: 'it was an almost universal talking point far beyond the boundaries of Parliament House . . . throughout the proceedings the privileged benches were packed . . . over the crowded press benches we could see the heads of the four accused . . . the number of policemen in attendance seemed unusually large . . . The Judge delivered sentence, and one of the most widely argued cases of modern times was over. All that was left was for the nation to discuss the verdict which, we have no doubt, it will be doing.'

However, the Lord Justice Clerk's verdict was not received with equal equanimity in the public gallery, which erupted in consternation and, by the time the court had been cleared, three hundred protesters had gathered in the High Street outside. When police had the audacity to bring the Crown's chief witness, John Cullen, out before them – cries of 'imprison the bastard!', 'lynch him!' resulted in him being rushed back inside. John MacInnes, a Gaelic scholar and friend of Hamish's, recalled the moment fifty years later:

> it was one of the few occasions in my life when I felt my head leave, I felt myself becoming one of the Edinburgh mob – a group psychology had taken a grip – and, if the police had not got Cullen away quickly, we would have become a mob – no better and no worse than our forefathers two or three hundred years ago – we would have torn that man apart with our hands – even though it was with the law, and not him, that the deeper wickedness lay.

Collection boxes were passed to help defray the defence costs, leaflets entitled 'England's Gestapo Exposed' were distributed, Hamish led the crowd in singing 'Scots Wha Hae' and the anger of the crowd dissipated as it dispersed into the narrow streets of the Old Town. During the evening the Scottish National Congress issued a statement demanding that 'the traitor Cullen' be removed from Scotland. In the following weeks Jo Grimond, Leader of the Liberal Party, demanded in Parliament that the use of *agents provocateurs* in Scotland should be ended.

The activities of the Edinburgh Four were far from a total failure but no great success, and the sentences imposed came as big shocks to men on the threshold of their careers. Sent off to Saughton Prison, all but Callum MacAlister began a hunger strike in protest at 'the failure of the authorities to investigate the police methods used against them' but, with Bobby Watt's parents, and Hamish, pleading that the strike be ended, it was called off after just two days. Always resolutely opposed to self-destructive action, Hamish asked that the prisoners be sent letters and songs and supported not just in prison but in their future lives. Hamish's deep empathy with the suffering of his comrades inspired him to complete a key section of the long Gramscian poem he had been struggling to write since 1949. It was entitled 'The Cell' and in short, slow lines Hamish conjures the psychic claustrophobia of imprisonment as he salutes the millions of political prisoners incarcerated and murdered across the twentieth century. The poem's orginal title was 'Christus':

> Evening is the worst
> years as long as hours
>
> Night's better
> the heart's rebellious
> arguing the toss
>
> whether at a given point
> forestalling counter-measures
> but allowing for come-backs
>
> One should have
>
> could have . . .
>
> Think, and think long
> on all that horror, history's saturnalia;
> the tortuous power-webs,
> the boxes, the alcoves,
> the souped-up ideologies,
> the lying memoranda,
> the body count,
> the tenders for crematoria,
> the wire, the ramp,
> the unspeakable experiments
>
> White earth   not earth
>
> Evening
> the fall
> and despair gathers
> like a stain on the white loin of the wall.[12]

---

12. Published in the *Collected Poems*.

As 1953 drew to its close, Hamish was both melancholy and defiant, and his notebook jottings reflect his mood: 'the reality is a thing which has to be reinvented continually'. 'In Scotland: the Caliban, the Satanic, the Calormist Face: The people of Edinburgh – as flat as the fens / if only they would lift their eyes / to the spires of the kirks they go to on Sunday.'

During 1954 some sporadic, small-scale SRA activity (bill-posting etc.) continued, but as an organisation the SRA now ceased to exist. Police surveillance of nationalist suspects, however, was maintained for years. About twenty of Hamish's 'activist' friends appear to have had their lives and careers ruined. Some were imprisoned, some accused of sexual deviance, some certified 'insane', some committed suicide (Bobby Watt was one of them), quite a number made (or had to make) new lives for themselves in faraway countries. In this light, the first verse of Hamish's great anthem 'The Freedom Come a' Ye', written in 1959/60, can be seen to be (among other things) a noble salute to comrades, broken, exiled and – as yet – unhonoured.

> Roch the wind in the clear day's dawin
>   Blaws the cloods heelster-gowdie ow'r the bay,
> But there's mair nor a roch wind blawin
>   Through the great glen o' the warld the day.
> It's a thocht will gar oor rottans
>   – A' they rogues that gang gallus, fresh and gay –
> Tak the road, and seek ither loanins
>   For their ill ploys, tae sport and play . . .[13]

On 26 July 1954, a grand reception and dinner was organised by the Edinburgh University Nationalist Club to welcome Malcolm MacAlister, Owen Gillan, Robert Watt and Raymond Forbes on their release from Saughton Prison. It took place in the Adam Rooms in George Street, Edinburgh. Piper was Pipe-Major Donald MacLean. The young Edinburgh student nationalist Douglas Henderson took the Chair. Prayers were said by the Rev. J.C. Gunn. The meal started with Powsowdie (sheep's heid broth) and concluded with a Celebration Cake. Speeches were made by Dr J.M. MacCormick, Sir Compton Mackenzie, James Glendinning and three of the four conspirators – Raymond Forbes, Owen Gillan and Malcolm MacAlister. Hamish was *fear an tigh* of what was billed as 'The Unjust Incarceration Ceilidh'. It was a grand and emotional evening but more of

---

13. Published in the *Collected Poems*.

a wake than a renewed call-to-arms – and this dinner can be seen to have marked the beginning of the end of this period of the Scottish national struggle. During the mid fifties only a small minority of Scots were psychologically and politically capable of embracing the idea of a national Parliament, and Hamish recognised that the nationalist movement, having tried every kind of political methodology and the threat of violence, should now 'scatter, for a generation, into the heather'.[14]

Within a day or two of the George Street dinner, Hamish himself organised a second celebration: a 'Public Rally in Honour of the Four Conspirators – in the Edinburgh Meadows'. It was a gesture of defiance and a statement of future intent. It drew only a small crowd but when the newspapers chose to ignore it or ridicule it, Hamish felt real anger and penned the following letter to the *Scotsman*:

> Dear Sir, I have lived in various countries and seen a number of hostile Press accounts of popular demonstrations but I doubt if, anywhere, you could find one more spiteful and misleading than your paragraphs today about Saturday's Nationalist rally. With restricted space at his disposal, your reporter found room to mention 'half a dozen small boys perched on a Jeep' at the Rally in the Meadows. He does not, however, mention the singer at the Rally was Jeannie Robertson, whom the American folklorist Alan Lomax has described as 'one of the finest folksingers in Western Europe' and 'a monumental figure in the world's folksong'. This rather odd omission is characteristic of your report and very revealing. As the Scotsman is a paper that usually reports what is actually said at public meetings, allow me to quote from the speeches of two of the ex-prisoners: 'I have nothing against the English people: my battle is with those people in Westminster who are subjecting us to her will. We are at present members of a subject race . . . – and I am prepared to die for Scotland . . .'

Those dramatic words suggest that this 'forgotten' rally in the Meadows was something unusual, and there is little doubt that Hamish's aim was to present 'his' four young men to the Scottish public as heroes – worthy of

---

14. On 20 July 1954 William Oliver Brown of Glasgow (the pacifist leader of the Scottish National Congress) had lost a major case at the Court of Session in which he had claimed £3000 against the *Scottish Daily Mail* re the publication of an article that 'falsely, calumniously and maliciously' had linked him to the unsuccessful attempt to blow up the EIIR letter box at the Inch at New Year 1953.

their nation's honour. They had harmed no one, they had suffered greatly, he knew they were likely to suffer further, and he planned the rally so that it would have ceremonial force and symbolic resonance. He wanted Scotland to know that the actions of these men would, in future years, seed the rebirth of Scotland as a self-governing nation.

The 'heroes' of this rally were the four conspirators but the central figure was Hamish: he controlled events from the back of the Jeep – which Bobby Watt's father had driven down from Fort William – and, rising to speak, he was in his element, as he had been with the partisans in Italy. The fact that a Second World War Jeep was the speaker's platform was no accident: Hamish used it as his mound, his pulpit, his chariot. Here was theatre, here was youth – at the altar of 'the early days of a better nation' – and the presence of Jeannie Robertson beside Hamish was equally important. That the cultural leader of the socialist and nationalist causes in Scotland should speak with a tinker ballad-singer beside him was a revolutionary statement. Here was a new cultural totality: Hamish and Scotland's 'prisoners of conscience' would speak; Jeannie would sing, and those gathered around would sing with them. This was a new Scotland gathering; this was a new Scotland singing.

By every external measurement – a police head-count, an aerial photograph, an analysis of column-inches – this rally in the Meadows was a complete and dismal failure, but as an act of witness it was timeless and sublime. Hamish was showing the people of Edinburgh that neither he nor the youth of Scotland would be cowed, and that the cause of self-government was part of a historical continuum, a democratic right that they would not give up.[15]

By one of those strange synchronicities that shaped so much of his life, 'The Unjust Incarceration Celebratory Dinner' also put Hamish in contact with a man who would help swing the compass of his life's future direction. This man was Maurice Fleming, a young journalist from Blairgowrie who had been taught by the same Miss Peterkin who had taught Hamish and who lived just a few doors from 'Ramleh', the house in which Hamish had been born. Maurice was a small, elfin, pale-skinned, blue-eyed Picto-Celt with a missionary zeal for Scots history and tradition. As the ceilidh in the Assembly Rooms ended, Maurice went

---

15. Thirty-eight years later, the great Devolution Rally of 1992 took place in the same Meadows where the conspirators had been dismissed. (This was the rally, attended by 40,000 people, that finally set in train the campaign that led to the establishment of the new Scottish Parliament in 1999.) And it was appropriate that Hamish's singing of 'The Freedom Come a' Ye' became the pivotal, emotional moment of that truly historic event.

up to Hamish and told him how much he'd enjoyed the 'rebel songs' but that he liked the 'auld sangs' best. He mentioned a recent series of BBC Home Service radio programmes about traditional English folk-music and lamented that the fact that there was no *living tradition* like that left in Scotland. To this, Hamish responded with a small explosion: 'But Maurice – there is! And you live at the very heart of it!' Within a few days the two men were out in the field, recording *living tradition* of the most wonderful kind:

In the fable
God is murdered, but is born again too.[16]

---

16. HH, 1941, 'Dark Streets to Go Through', published in the *Collected Poems*.

TWENTY

The Man for whom Gaeldom is Waiting

Scotland has never had a Shakespeare but she has the Ballads . . .

HH

Hamish's meeting with Maurice Fleming in August 1954 produced a great upsurge of home-longing – for the hills of Perthshire and the streets of Blairgowrie. Maurice reports their conversation:

> Hamish waxed lyrical about the singing of Jeannie Robertson. He told me she'd been to school in Blair. He spoke about the bothy tradition, about the great ballads he'd heard sung in Glen Shee as a boy – and he said to me, 'Maurice, at this moment, Blair will be full of singers of every description! Why don't you go out into the berryfields and see what you find? I have no money – and no time to get up there just now – but you could go out. Why don't you introduce yourself to the Travellers – and when you find something good – I'll be straight up with a tape-recorder . . . there's one thing in particular I'd like you to look out for – the author of a marvellous new song I've heard going the rounds – it's called 'The Berryfields o' Blair'.[1]

Two days later Maurice wrote: 'Hamish a cara . . . I took your advice and went out into the berryfields of Blair. I'm delighted to tell you that tonight I found two good singers. They sing like angels and include in their repertoire 'The Berryfields o' Blair' . . . When can I have the machine?' Over the next forty years, Maurice Fleming became Hamish's 'unpaid folk assistant' in east Perthshire, Angus and Dundee, and their collaboration was to become one of the key relationships of the Scottish Folk Revival. Within days, Hamish was on the train to Blairgowrie,

---

1. Maurice Fleming, conversation with TN, 2003.

and he and Maurice went out to the berryfields to meet the women 'who sang like angels' – Belle Stewart and her daughter Sheila. They were two members of a large family who would gain fame as 'the Stewarts of Blair' and were part of a huge Traveller clan – with septs in Aberdeenshire and Sutherland – that Hamish was soon describing as 'one of great musical dynasties of Europe'. So, shaking the mould of Saughton from his shoes and putting the muddy waters of the 'conspiracy' behind him, Hamish re-entered the land of his boyhood, where he found himself welcomed and fêted: 'the berryfields in those days were an Eldorado of song, ancient lore, stories, riddles and vibrant, joyous life. Going out into those fields, I felt I was coming home.'

In 1954, many Scots considered the Tinkers and Traveller People a separate race. In some areas they were treated as 'untouchables': none of Scotland's earlier folklorists had entered their society or in any significant sense documented their culture. Consequently, Hamish discovered 'amidst what was considered the detritus of the Scottish population, a concentration of musical artistry probably unmatched in the whole world of folk culture' and it was with a feeling of euphoria that he put up his small 'two-man ridge-tent' and settled in with the Travellers in the Standing Stones berryfield. Very soon he was writing a triumphant letter to Sydney Goodsir Smith describing 'life, once again, in the field'. On 29 August 1954, Goodsir Smith replied:

Dear Hamish, I had your letter here yesterday, and I hope this may reach you before you come south for your Festival sojourn. I have been all over your country and in fact all over Scotland these last two days (in my imagination) with Montrose as recounted by Buchan. Every time I return to James Graham I am more over-whelmed with amazement, admiration and emotion. He made the whole *land* alive and doubly alive . . . Your news is as good as I know your songs to be and as welcome as all the undying singers who sing them. Yes, you shall go out for much longer yet – but first gather in this harvest and thresh it before the rickyard is bursting. Then we'll be buried in our own steadings and others will be tempted to pillage us . . .

It is a wonderful, many-layered letter. Goodsir Smith, one of the outstanding Scottish poets of the twentieth century, conflates Hamish, Montrose and the Travellers into a single image of 'Scotland'. Goodsir Smith knew that Hamish had loved Montrose since boyhood, and that his grandmother's recitations of Ayton's description of Montrose's execution for treason, exactly three hundred years previously, were one of Hamish's abiding childhood memories. The letter came as a poet's blessing, and Hamish took it as one of the great compliments of his life. The world was as he imagined. Here were 'contemporary ancestors', here was a palaeolithic society – recumbent in the sunshine and largesse of Strathmore: as far as he could see, bending in the drills, singers were picking berries, rehearsing songs and 'enjoying life'. Singers who needed no stage, no permissions, no subsidies and thought nothing of copyright: each night they queued to offer him their songs, their stories – music as old as Alba and fresh as the day. In the Egyptian Desert, having read the poems of G. S. Fraser, Hamish had asked rhetorically 'where is the Niagara underneath?' and heard nothing. Now, amidst a sun-splashed spate of a cappella song – expressing the *coinneach*, the *duende* of Traveller pain and ecstasy – he heard the thunderous roar of 'the cataract of day'. As he was to later comment: 'Attempting to record the super-abundance of folksong and music amongst the Perthshire Travellers was like holding a tin-can under the Niagra Falls!'

Travellers began coming in from all over the east Highlands to meet him – asking 'where is the *Beinn Coul* (the great gentleman) – the *gadgie* with the speaking machine? *Shamus Mor*'. And now, instead of lugging a great tape-recorder for Alan Lomax, he found himself surrounded by children and young men, ever eager to help him. Scene after scene opened and folded before him: smoke, shafting light, great fires burning on the Essendy Ridge, Marlee Loch black in the moonlight, distant pipes, the thunder of hooves, the silent dismount of bareback riders. Hamish wandered from fireside to fireside where garrulous crones and girls – shying behind hands – awaited their turn: 'Tell us a story, sing us a sang – show us your bum, or oot ye gang!' Here was a community outside the loop of 'Church, State and Property', here was a conviviality where the fireside still meant 'life', where men fished for pearls, and dogs took down deer, as on the Pictish Stones. Here were youngsters who beat grouse for the lairds by day and gaffed 'the king o' fish' at night. Here were drums, bare feet, rebel songs, old men with Arthurian tales: 'hen-wives' with jokes to blue the bluest fringe of Edinburgh – the Prince of Cities. Here were ex-soldiers who, having fought to rid Europe of Nazi tyranny, were handed beer in enamelled buckets at back doors of pubs. Here was a woman who accepted childbirth on the floor of a doctor's garage as 'a big step-forward'. Here was a bedrock of the human condition, here the wind fanned the lyre of Orpheus: here the poet no longer needed to be a poet.

Eleven years had passed since Ruth Spiers, in Egypt, had wondered, 'Hamish, you're only twenty three – and you do so much!' Now he was almost thirty-five and, as his career as a folklorist opened before him, he paused to look back. For fifteen years Hamish had been engaged in ceaseless work. Small wonder then that he felt something akin to artistic exhaustion. He seems to have recognised that a turning point in his life had come and that his real 'powers' were public, communal and theatrical. He began to foresee that his future responsibility should be not to his own talents or to 'literature' but to the neglected oral tradition and the greater, national culture of Scotland.

In September 1954 an ambitious new poem entitled 'The Human Spring' was published in the last issue of Alan Riddell's *Lines Review* (No. 6). Its subject is a Blakean embrace of Man's lot in a geological universe – and a poet's farewell to his muse. It was attributed to Arthur James Arthur (the once and future king) but evidence suggests that this was Hamish writing under another alias.

> These visions of dying poets win
> From his true, early task of growing
> The young thinker with seductive song
> Other than of the garden's glory.
>
> Never in evasion desperate
> Choose for its own stony sake
> The inglorious mountain-track that is the Way! –
> Or on its loaf-white boulders die
> Too early, to the outraged world's attack![2]
>
> Sooner, as a coin, you may grasp,
> The sovereign golden sun than wear
> Perfections inhuman, separate mask,
> Yet every child born on earth
> Carries from birth such a coin
> Of gold imaging the sun.

---

2. The imagery of this verse shares similarities with the opening of James Leslie Mitchell's great novel *Spartacus*, 1933.

Where on a forest sign-post, shaping
Opposites, impossibly into one,
The owl of worldly wisdom sits,
The truth essentially is vagueness
That man, at whatsoever cost,
Through trees must follow like the sun.

Through such times travelling, few escape
Anything in their own living span
Of the eternal human fate.
Why doubt, then, certainty like rays
Vertically from the sun will concentrate
As one the earth's inchoate images?

It is a difficult, philosophical poem but also highly personal. The 'mountain-track' across 'white-loaf boulders' is the ridge-track to the summit of Schiehallion, the magnificent lion-mountain that acts as a visual fulcrum to the entire west Perthshire landscape, the mountain that Hamish – brought up in Glenshee – had long seen as a sacred symbol of his life's quest. 'The Human Spring' attempts to distil 'the million years' of humanity's cultural development in a vision of evolutionary progress that man 'through trees must follow like the sun': it is cultural, Rosicrucian vision and worthy of serious study.

As Hamish's thirty-fifth birthday came and went, he saw that he had arrived on a plateau of cultural and political achievement, and that the time had come for him to dig in. For the first time, he began to feel that the cultural burden he had borne so long 'alone' was beginning to be shared by the Scots people as a whole. With his 'Marxist folk-key' firmly in the lock of the School of Scottish Studies, he began to believe that all he needed to do was hold course and his boyhood vision of a new Scotland would be realised.

Perhaps just one major issue might be said to have remained unresolved at this time. This concerns the nature of Hamish's relationship with MacDiarmid. Were they friends and allies, or personal and intellectual enemies bound to make a desert of their incompatible lives? The settled opinion of the academic and media communities in Scotland is that their relationship was personally antagonistic and culturally destructive. Even sympathetic commentators tend to see MacDiarmid as a crusty literary elitist – totally opposed to the folksie concerns of the dissolute Henderson; while Hamish is travestied as an advocate of a folk tradition that MacDiarmid despised as 'the illiterate bawling of peasants!' In reality, the Hamish/MacDiarmid relationship was one of the great cultural partnerships in the history of Scotland. As this biography has already documented, for at least ten years, Hamish and MacDiarmid enjoyed a wonderfully symbiotic creative friendship, and the fact that, during the 1960s, the two men got involved in a series of ferocious arguments was just part of what was a dynamic, bardic and very Scottish relationship.

Hamish's lifelong admiration for MacDiarmid is well known; Mac-Diarmid's admiration for Hamish is less widely recognised. That Hamish's work shows echoes of MacDiarmid's is also well known but it is now clear that the influence was not one-way: some of MacDiarmid's poems written between 1947 and 1957 bear the 'impress' of Hamish Henderson: poems such as 'Glasgow', 'The Universal Man' (To Lady Astor), 'Old Woman in High Spirits', 'Faugh-a-Ballagh' (to the SRA) and 'In Memoriam: James Joyce'.[3] None are written in 'the style' of Hamish but all are coloured by new perceptions and forces introduced to MacDiarmid by Hamish during this period.

To MacDiarmid, however, Hamish's personality was even more interesting than his ideas or experience. He was the Prodigal Son returned from the war. MacDiarmid was fascinated and 'overwhelmed' and, during the early 1950s, he wrote three poems that can be read as discursive evaluations of Hamish's art, persona and ideas. The first, 'A New Scots Poet' (1952), reads as though it were the 'critical review' of Hamish's *Elegies for the Dead in Cyrenaica* that MacDiarmid had signally failed to write in 1949:

> It was difficult for his work at first
> To secure the reception it required
> Among such sentimentalists as the Scots.
>
> They did not realise he had
> Already put such emotion and feeling
> Into it that all *they* had to do
> Was to accept it straightforwardly,
> Directly and simply, and that the emotion
> Would liberate itself like a volatile vapour
> Of its own accord,
> Without any efforts on their part . . .

---

3. This poem is now notorious for its extensive use of unacknowledged quotations.

Though simple in the sense of single,
Of unified in aspiration,
His work of course is not 'simple' in any way.

Bringing Scotland alive in people's blood again
Rather than in their minds at first,
Through their instinctive actions and sense perceptions,
Through their sight, touch, smell and hearing,
Making them vividly aware
Of every element in the Scottish scene.[4]

The second of these 'portrait poems' is 'The Poet as Prophet – The Man for whom Gaeldom is waiting'. Written in 1953, the year during which SRA activity in Scotland was at its height, the poem applauds the politics of direct action and salutes a poet of European importance but uniquely Celtic genius. The poet described is evidentially not MacDiarmid, nor is it Sorley MacLean, the pre-eminent Gaelic poet. It is just possible that MacDiarmid has conjured a composite, metaphorical 'bard' into being, but the combination of skills, qualities and experience this poet has are very much those that his prodigal friend – the prophet-*filidh* – Hamish Henderson embodied.

Au fait with the whole range of European arts and letters
As few have ever been, he proudly proclaimed himself
A barbarian, in the sense that the art
Of the Celtic lands and Scandinavia
Were both on the edge of the world

                    . . . I am in favour of all
That remains remote from centralisation – preserving
Its spiritual vigour and independence; not falling like Rome to the
     barbarians,
But inviolable, preferring death to any barbarian's or infidel's
     yoke,
Accepting nothing forced on them from without, nothing not
     issuing
From the innermost recesses of their spiritual life,
Independence, peace, and goodwill . . .

---

4. Hugh MacDiarmid, *Complete Poems* (Martin Brian and O'Keeffe 1978).

In a distinct world altogether,
The separate and sovereign world of Gaeldom . . .

The reason was that he rose
Out of the category of men
And entered the category of the elements.
He was the wind, the sea, the tempest, the hurricane.
He was the marvellous embodiment
Of the complete identification
Of the Celtic mind with all nature and all life . . .

For the real Gael has something which the old Greeks had . . .
– He has an ideal, a plan of life,
Transcending the mere means and apparatus of living.
Feverish immersion in secondary and ancillary matters
Leaves him unsatisfied.
He has a craving for essentials.
The miracle of literature,
Of culture, in racial history
Is that it is at once the bow and the mark,
The inspiration and the aim.

. . . Suddenly, splitting the sky
Was heard a great voice
Which echoed round the firmament.
'Stand fast for Scotland!'

The whole nation felt itself shaken
As by an electric shock
Into one great sob which burst forth
In a flood of jubilation over the miracle.
An indomitable ardour blazed in all hearts
Until each man had the strength of four.

In him were incarnate at that moment
The liberties and rights of man asserted in the face of power,
The independence of the spirit which demands
That conscience be satisfied
Even against one who ranks himself higher than its claims.
Scotland felt at that moment
That no man ever personified her,
Ever would represent her,

As he did,
And she grew in glory
And was transfigured with pride.
It was not a Scottish moment;
It was a universal moment.[5]

This paeon of praise to an 'unknown warrior poet' stands equal to
a great portrait by Titian, Rembrandt or Goya, and MacDiarmid's
portrayal, like theirs, is great because it effortlessly combines the
universal with the uniquely personal. For example, the cry he
hears, 'Stand fast for Scotland', was a favourite of Hamish's, ever
since it had been 'offered him' by an old Highland woman named
Catherine MacDonald Grant in 1935. For Hamish, Catherine
embodied 'that feisty auld Scotland' he loved, and he undoubtedly
told MacDiarmid a good deal about her. She figures prominently
in Hamish's 'Journey to a Kingdom' and enters the poem with self-
dramatising style:

. . . By Babylon, I knew
That you'd be late tonight – and knew you'd climb
The painful stairs out of damned Highland pride!
Welcome then
The high hidalgo nose and humorous eyes
And welcome the indomitable heart.
You gallant, graceless, grey-haired old Diana,
I greet you. Catherine MacDonald Grant
How well we understand each other. When
I joked, you'd laugh and tell me I was Highland
In every flicker of my wicked tongue.
And when we talked, you asked where was
Our Boswell?
To scribble us down and put us in a book.
Your speech had dignity, wit and easy knowledge
Quoting Eliot and expounding Swedenborg –
But you were best on your neighbour's characters
And your sly tod neighbours in Newtonmore – that loathly broth
Of Highland cauld and hunger . . .[6]

---

5. Hugh MacDiarmid, *Complete Poems* (Martin Brian and O'Keeffe 1978).
6. Extract from 'Journey to a Kingdom', published in *Aberdeen University Review*,
   no.178, Autumn 1987, in an article by Andrew R. Hunter, 'Hamish Henderson:
   Odyssey of a Wandering King'.

MacDiarmid's poem 'King Over Himself' was written in 1955, shortly after Hamish had returned from Sutherland with his historic recordings of the Ossianic, Tinker patriarch Ailidh Dall (Blind Alec Stewart of Lairg). Hamish went out to Biggar, in Lanarkshire, to tell MacDiarmid about his latest 'amazing discovery'. It was a breakthrough in European folk-collecting that would prove of great importance to cultural developments in the Celtic world; and 'King Over Himself' can be interpreted as a panegyric to both Hamish and the Ancient Scotland that his work was unearthing. The poem presents a man who – above all others in his time – personifies the very being of the Scots nation: as it was, is and will be. The man MacDiarmid describes loves to sing, and sing into being. This man makes Scotland's poorest citizens feel like kings: he is a man who is in thrall to passion and human frailties, and yet lives free as a bird. If this man is substantially Hamish, MacDiarmid pays his fellow poet one of the noblest literary salutations in Scotland's history.

> How he loved to survey the lands of Scotland
> From some nest of eagles in a cloud of stone
> – To let his soul pasture in her valleys
> And frolic on her mountains,
> Roam from her Northmost to her Southmost point,
> Watch her skies, drink her waters,
> And breathe her forests and her fields!
> And all the flowers of Scotland grew in his soul,
> And he felt that savour of his own soul rise to his head.
> All the people of Scotland once more
> Were timeless, aflame and virile.
> Their speech rang like steel.
> They talked in poems and their words
> Held echoes of miracle.
> Miracle followed the man like a domestic animal . . .
>
> And instantly, summing up in himself
> The whole range of Gaelic wisdom,
>
> . . . to every man in Scotland he cried:
>
> 'Remember that thou art a man,
> And there is nothing like him
> Who is King over himself.'[7]

---

7. Hugh MacDiarmid, *Complete Poems* (Martin Brian and O'Keeffe 1978).

The fact that MacDiarmid and Hamish would soon be quarrelling, over 'art poetry' and 'folk poetry', should not obscure the greater reality that these two men rejoiced in each other – rather like father and son. Hamish was always in awe of MacDiarmid's unfathomable genius, and Mac-Diarmid recognised Hamish as a political revolutionary: perhaps the only man in Scotland with the vision to heal 'the disastrous split between Highlander and Lowlander', and the will to see 'a united Scotland arise in the world'.[8]

Although proud that his own Scottish literary renaissance had shifted some rocks on the mountainside of Scotland's twentieth-century renewal, MacDiarmid, by the mid fifties, was only too aware that – for him – the time had gone. He also knew that it was only the Scottish people – whom Hamish so strangely embodied – who could precipitate the avalanche that would engender the second Enlightenment and the New Scotland he dreamed of. Hamish was more than ready to accept such responsibilities; indeed, he had anticipated them since boyhood:

> Spring quickens. In the Shee water I'm fishing.
> High on whaup's mountain time heaps stone on stone.
> The speech and silence of Christ's world is Gaelic,
> And youth on age, the tree climbs from the bone.[9]

'Youth and Age on the face of Corravine.' Hamish knew years of hard work and huge difficulties lay ahead but, based in his 'cell' in the attic of the School of Scottish Studies, he became increasingly confident that the promise he had made to the seer, Kenneth Begh, in *The Ingleton Raconteur* in 1936, would be fulfilled:

> . . . with reverent steps the cavern I approached
> And whispered: 'Holy seer: thy wait is over!
> The gods have willed a pilgrim youth to come
> To beg thy magic aid to make anew
> The glory of the Kingdom Angus ruled' . . .

Thus it was in good heart that Hamish Henderson embarked on the second half of his life's long journey – as a folklorist – and who but Hugh MacDiarmid would have had the courage to say of him: 'Miracle followed the man like a domestic animal'?

---

6. From Hugh MacDiarmid's 'The Poet as Prophet – the Man for whom Gaeldom is Waiting'.

7. 'Ballad of the Twelve Stations of My Youth', in the *Collected Poems*.

Other Claims about
Hamish Henderson's Paternity

With regard to the other claims about Hamish's paternity, the first point to make clear is that Hamish was a great believer in the oral tradition: thus if people wanted to say he was the son of this man or that Duke – why should he gainsay them? Also, as an anarchic Darwinian he would be the first to acknowledge that the name 'James Scott' on one of his birth certificates is absolutely no proof that James Scott was his *biological* father. Secondly, Hamish was well aware that men like James Scott had been 'bought and sold' to hide the identity of embarrassed fathers for hundreds of years – for dynastic, financial and every other kind of reason. If Hamish was the illegitimate 'heir' of such a man, the eighth Duke of Atholl is the outstanding candidate. Photographs show the two men to have shared striking physical and psychological similarities. The Queen Alexandra Nurses are known to have worked at Blair Atholl during the Great War, and the Duke certainly had personal and estate connections with Blairgowrie and Glenshee; we also know that both Hamish and his mother had meetings with him.

John Murray-Stewart (1871–1942) was the eldest son of the seventh Duke of Atholl, and was a notable member of one of Britain's pre-eminent aristocratic houses. As a child he ran wild on his father's Perthshire estates and, after schooling at Eton, as Marquis of Tullibardine (Bardie), became a favourite of Queen Victoria. He then served with Kitchener in Egypt before returning home to raise his own regiment, the Scottish Horse, to fight the Boers in South Africa. During the First World War he commanded the Scottish Horse in Gallipoli, returning with the survivors to Scotland, via Egypt. In 1917, on the death of his eccentric and tyrannical father, he became eighth Duke of Atholl. His wife, whom he had married in 1899, was Katherine Ramsay (1874–1960), a daughter of the Ramsays of Banff and Alyth. She was a fine musician, Oxford educated and strong-minded – later becoming known as 'The Red Duchess' on account of her support for the Republican cause in Spain. Katherine had no children and is presumed to have been infertile. Bardie, on the other hand, is understood to have fathered at least one illegitimate child, possibly several. The first was Eileen McCallum, daughter of the wife of a British diplomat who served many years in Ceylon. Eileen McCallum became 'a ward' of the Atholls, and the Duchess herself openly saw Eileen into society and well-married. The archives at Blair Castle contain a 'scrapbook cum photo-album' of pictures collected by Eileen documenting life at the castle during the First World War period. Many of these photos show the nurses, including the Queen Alexandra nurses, who worked at Blair Atholl at this time.

Information about a second illegitimate daughter is more speculative and comes from the descendants of Duncan Stewart, a Traveller piper, whom 'oral tradition' asserts was nine times Pipe Champion of Scotland. Duncan was a piper of such rare genius that Bardie insisted he become his personal piper at Blair Atholl. Some time later, Catherine, the most beautiful of Duncan's daughters, found herself pregnant to the young Marquis, and the Stewart family was moved out to Dunkeld, where Duncan was re-employed as piper to Bardie's friend, Lord Dudley. He also got a 'pay-off' that allowed him to buy a cine-projector and a shooting brake – and piper Stewart set up the first travelling cinema in Perthshire. The money rolled in and before long Duncan left Dunkeld to buy himself a house, with raspberry fields, near Blairgowrie. Catherine meantime had fallen victim to tuberculosis. Hearing of her plight, Bardie sent to South Africa for maggots – of a kind he had seen used to clean wounds during the Boer War – these maggots did their job, but Catherine's disease was incurable and she died at quite a young age. Her daughter, however, grew into womanhood, settled in Montrose, where she died in the 1980s. It is a story so like 'a ballad' that many will dismiss it as Traveller fantasy, but others will accord it the veracity of truth.

Was Hamish an illegitimate son of Tullibardine? The principle of 'hereditary rights' tends to shroud the lives of illegitimate sons in secrecy and subterfuge, but there are numerous facts, events and anecdotes that link Hamish to the eighth Duke of Atholl and a selection are worth relating. One story is told by Dolina MacLennan, the Gaelic singer and television actress. She first heard of Hamish's Atholl ancestry on the Edinburgh folk-circuit in the late 1950s: forty years later Hamish gave these ideas substance when he was offered a holiday in her house at Blair Atholl, in the autumn of 1999. She gathered an array of singers and musicians 'for a last ceilidh with the master' and he stayed for a week. She recalls: 'Before going up to bed on the first evening, Hamish asked if he could choose a book from the bookcase. He picked out the biography of Lady Evelyn Stewart-Murray. Lady Evelyn was Bardie's sister, a brilliant young woman who suffered a nervous breakdown and was sent away to

Belgium. As a girl she had learned Gaelic and, like her sister Lady Dorothea, collected folklore, music and song. She was also a gifted artist and whilst locked away on the continent worked hour after hour making exquisite lace embroideries; she was like a medieval princess shut up in a tower. Anyway, Hamish dipped into that book throughout his holiday and whenever I took him up his morning tea or evening dram, he would turn the conversation to Lady Evelyn and he always referred to her as, "my auntie" or "my auntie Evelyn".'

There is no doubt that in old age Hamish was sometimes disorientated and confused and could, when drunk, be maudlin and sentimental, but his powers of recall remained remarkable and one has to ask why – in his extreme old age – he should have wanted Dolina to know that he believed himself to be, or wanted her to believe him to be, a direct descendant of the Stewart-Murrays of Atholl? Was this because he believed himself to be the son of Evelyn's brother the Duke? Or might he have been making some indirect connection – via his Dishington ancestry – whose aristocratic connections were wide and went back to Robert Bruce's sister?

I, too, can relate various 'Atholl stories'. For example, in early autumn 1976 I drove to Sutherland with Hamish and his two daughters, Janet and Tina. We were working on a film about the Highland Travelling People, *The Summer Walkers*. On our return – driving from the Kyle of Tongue to Helmsdale in a howling gale – Hamish insisted we detour to visit the ancient graveyard at Braemore to search out the tombstones of his Gunn ancestors. Next day, as we approached Blair Atholl, he suggested we stop at the castle, which the girls had not visited. As we moved towards the doorway of the great hall, an elderly guard turned towards us and, 'recognising Hamish', sprang to attention and saluted. As we passed, the old man completed his salute and ushered us into the hall, with all the deference due to a duke *en famille*. He did this to none of the other visitors.

Another story concerns Hamish's dog 'Sandy', an alsatian-cross-collie rescued from the Edinburgh Dog Pound, Hamish's boon companion through the 1980s. One evening, Hamish suggested I take Sandy for a run on the Meadows (the park opposite his Edinburgh home) insisting, 'Tim, he needs a walk, he's a dog of royal blood! Look at his nose – he's the Duke of Atholl!' and he roared with laughter (Hamish's book of selected letters is entitled 'The Armstrong Nose' because it raises the idea of there being a hereditary continuum). On another occasion I remember him asking, 'Tim, could you scrub out Sandy's bowl? The Duke of Atholl doesnae sup from a dirty dish.' Such incidents can be dismissed as good-humoured banter but other incidents must be taken more seriously. For example, on several occasions Hamish described to me a memorable visit he and his mother paid to Blair Atholl, shortly before they left for England in 1928. The Duke invited them to visit, gave them a personal tour of the castle, and they ate together. Hamish was particularly impressed when the Duke spoke about his ancestor Lord George Murray (General to Charles Edward Stuart) and he never forgot the thrill when the Duke took down the breastplate of Bonnie Dundee, 'to point out the hole through which the cannon ball had passed to kill the hero of Killiecrankie'. That meeting, coming just days before Hamish left Scotland for his 'eighteen year exile in England', was felt by Hamish as 'a laying on of hands' and there can be no doubt that this meeting, with a scion of one of Scotland's great houses, affirmed in Hamish his sense that he was destined to play some major role in Scots history. Such anecdotes, of course, *prove* nothing about Hamish's paternity.

The historian Angus Calder has recently speculated that it was the eighth Duke who paid for Hamish's education at Lendrick School, Dulwich College and Cambridge University. He has not yet, however, come up with any solid evidence for this. And if the Duke helped with Hamish's education he gave him and his mother nothing else! My own understanding is that Hamish's education at Lendrick School was 'free', because the headmaster, James Maclaren, was his guardian. Certainly, Hamish, himself, always insisted (to Katzel Henderson) that it was hard work and academic scholarships that took him on to Dulwich and Cambridge. Yet, there is the possibility of a connection – James Maclaren came of an old Perthshire family and might well have been willing to help out his Lord Lieutenant and feudal chief: throughout the twenties, the Atholl Estates were in constant financial crisis – with banks and creditors demanding sequestration. Indeed, in 1921, the Duke let his name go forward as a candidate to become King of Albania – because he was told there might be money in it! However, no Dukes of Atholl are penniless and Bardie, if he was Hamish's father, must have been able to cover the cost of Hamish's school fees. And who can doubt that if James Scott had been offered a thousand guineas in 1919 to pass himself off as the father of Janet Henderson's new bairnie – he would have jumped at the offer? In addition we know both men were Free Masons.

The Savelli Sketch

The sketch shown on the endpapers of the book was made by Angelo Savelli and given to Hamish (see page 141). It was important to him and is worthy of some analysis.

The scene of the sketch is Rome on the evening of 20 June 1944 – the day on which Liana first introduced Hamish to Savelli. The sketch tells a story and has powerful symbolic force. The action takes place in the open air amidst the ruins of the ancient city of Rome: in the far distance, helmeted US soldiers fire heavy guns and mortars. Ruin and death are everywhere but renewal is at hand. Savelli records a moment of transformation, when twenty years of fascism began to be replaced by new ideas and ideals, and a renascent Italy began to reconstitute herself. The central character in the sketch is, I believe, Hamish. He stands in the left foreground, on a low stage, addressing the people of Rome in the wake of the Liberation. He leans forward, reading from a book. He is not in military uniform but cloaked in a great gown. He is seen in profile and a little from behind; his face is strongly lighted and he speaks with impish intensity and love. This man is 'the poet', the bringer of the Word: before him stands a naked, strong-bodied young man, listening intently. This man supports himself on a makeshift crutch; his left leg has been amputated above the knee and replaced with a wooden peg. His head is turned towards Hamish; his right arm is raised, his hand opened as if to 'cup' an invisible chalice. This man, I believe, represents Italy: Italy broken by war, Italy on the cusp of regeneration.

Below the dais on which Hamish and the wounded man stand, two others watch and listen. Immediately behind Hamish, a man lies dead in a pool of his own blood: this is an image of the past, the war that has gone. At the centre of Savelli's sketch, just behind the stage, is an older woman observing and listening to the poet speaking; she is full of compassion and pity. This is probably the mother of the sons of men, the Virgin, the Madonna. Behind her, to the right, two men carry a stretcher, bent under the weight of a long-haired woman being hurried off to hospital: this may represent bloodied Italian womanhood, Mary Magdalene sullied by fascist war – forgiven and about to be healed. In front of these stretcher-bearers, an 'aged carer' (St Joseph) bends forward to take the hand-brake off a wheelchair in which a disabled man sits, his face in shade, his brain 'illumined' beneath a great shock of dark hair: this man is possibly the crippled-hunch-back Antonio Gramsci, the murdered Sardinian communist whose vision, Savelli suggests, will light a way to the future. The sketch is signed at the bottom left 'Il Capt. Hamish Henderson cordialemente Roma 20.6.44.'. This is the date on which Savelli first met Hamish. Top right there is a signature 'A. Savelli '49', which I believe is the date when Savelli made the sketch and gave it to Hamish. By this time the Italian Risorgimento was well underway and my interpretation of the sketch is that Savelli believed the post-war rebirth of Italy began in Rome in June 1944 – and that the two men primarily responsible were the Scots poet, Hamish Henderson, and the Sardinian philosopher, Antonio Gramsci.

A New Scots Poet:
'Elegies for the Dead in Cyrenaica'

*In the human story, poetry has more to offer than prose,
especially the clinical prose of the professional head-shrinkers.
Poetry is one aspect of human love. As such it is hugely
valuable and sets itself against the religious and legal attitudes
to life that are, frequently, not just stupid and cruel but
practically obscene.*

HH

Hamish's long awaited collection of war poems, *Elegies for the Dead in
Cyrenaica*, was published by John Lehmann in London just before
Christmas 1948 as a high-quality hardback of 72 pages, with a handsome
dust jacket. The book consists of a Prologue, five Elegies, an Interlude,
another five Elegies and a concluding 'Heroic Song' – but Hamish saw
them as comprising one long poem. The poem's themes are universal but
its subject matter very specific: the war in the Western Desert (1942–43),
seen from a Scottish perspective. Hamish wrote as a 'remembrancer' and
in the hope that his poem would help create a better world – a Scotland
worthy of the sacrifice of tens of thousands of his countrymen – a world
worthy of the tens of millions who had died in an avoidable world war of
unconscionable brutality.

John Lehmann had paid Hamish an advance of £100, but sales were
very limited and he was never to receive any kind of royalties. Critically,
the book was generally well received but real acclaim came very slowly
and only after Hamish had received a number of savage personal blows.
The first came from Douglas Young, a man whose status as a radical
intellectual was, in Scotland, second only to MacDiarmid's. On 30
January 1949, Young wrote to Hamish from 36 Maclaren Road, Edinburgh:

Dear Hamish Henderson . . . The bookshop Browns finally got me
your 'Elegies for the Dead in Cyrenaica' which I have read with

great interest. The claim of the dust jacket is correct, that they are 'vigorous and vital expressions of the human situation as it appeared to the soldier in the field.' As such they are moving and stimulating. But the claim that they are poems, or indeed verse at all, is erroneous. They are in fact a sequence of dramatic short stories in a poetical prose akin to much contemporary journalism, e.g. the better Daily Express war reporters. If you take the quotation from your notebook on pages 55/9, and print it in irregular lines, you get just the same effect as from the bulk of your elegies. The same occurs with your notes at the start of Elegy VII, and with Seurat's on P. 51.

Many of your telling phrases are rather journalistic than poetic, e.g. the 'sleep of the dust', 'the malevolent bomb-thumped desert', etc. This is, of course, entirely in a certain fashion of decadent English bourgeois writing pretending to be poetry. But it is not going to outlive the transitional period it sprang from . . . I see these Elegies as only the raw material of poetry, worked up only a small degree beyond the notebook stage. Compare any passage of Somhairle's Ruweissal poem, which you print on page 35, and by that touchstone you can judge how far they are from poems. I say all this because I am convinced that you can and will yet make excellent poems, perhaps even in English . . . There are some misprints and errors which I subjoin in case you put out another issue. I can believe there will be a demand for this book, as it is, from the English public likely to hear about it . . . Yours sincerely Douglas Young.

It was an honest letter but meant to be damning, and Hamish wrote back: 'Sometime I shall take you by the beard on this prose–poetry question – possibly at a makar's meeting? But just now I'll only say – if you imagine that my notes and foreword, split up into irregular lines, would read like the poetry of the Elegies your ear is definitely less good than I would have thought. These poems (or rather this poem, for it is clearly one single poem, a building, an edifice, or – as John Hewitt might say – a broch of a poem entirely) are poetry . . .' It seems possible that this first critical response to the Elegies inflicted lasting damage on Hamish as an 'art poet'. Four months later, on 15 May, Hamish wrote to the *Scotsman*:

Sir, . . . The reason why the makars are so boisterously assailed by all and sundry is not primarily because they write in Lallans, but because they form an avant-garde. One hardly need point out that an avant-garde as such is traditionally suspect. Keats, for example, would consider the present correspondence merely so much matey badinage:

in his day he had to take infinitely worse slangings. In fact, Byron's celebrated line about Keats being killed off by 'by one critique' (and an Edinburgh critique at that!) had a certain degree of truth to it . . .

Hamish's Elegies had all been written at a Keatsian age and, although Hamish was remarkably self-propelled in both his art and his life, the manner in which Young had so brutally corralled his 'masterpiece' could not be shrugged off. A copy of the Elegies was also sent to Hugh Mac-Diarmid, but he appears not to have responded until 9 April 1949 when, after the announcement of the Somerset Maugham Award, he finally submitted a complimentary but brusque review to the *National Weekly*:

> . . . Edwin Muir has pointed out that the distinctive vision of Scottish poetry 'is profoundly alien to the spirit of English poetry – it is the product of a realistic imagination.' It is this vision that informs all Henderson's work. In form and substance [Elegies for the Dead in Cyrenaica] compares with most of the war poetry of Rupert Brook, Sassoon and even Wilfred Owen . . . It is in fact one of the few books – and the only volume of poems in English that have come my way – that expresses an adult attitude to the whole appalling business, and thoroughly deserves the honour of the Somerset Maugham Award.

The first positive Scottish response came from Lorne Maclaine Campbell VC (who in 1946 had so 'politically' disappointed Hamish): on 29 January 1949 Campbell wrote: 'As a litterateur my opinion is valueless and my only claim to have one at all is that I was also "in the midst of things". I find your poems give a voice to all the queer, and, to me, quite inarticulate feelings one had in the Desert, the sort of feeling I got for example on first hearing "Lili Marlene" . . .' A month later, Hamish received the first solid criticism in a wonderful letter from his Cambridge friend E.P. Thompson.

> . . . I also proffer you some heavy advice which I hope you will take as carefully considered and deeply felt – and not dismiss as marxist phrase-mongering . . . I greet you with humility, *compagno*, for you are that rare man, a poet. You have achieved poems out of our dead century. I hope you have had bad reviews from the culture boys, because their approval today is cause only for shame. But you must remain a poet. Remember always who you are writing for – the people of Glasgow, of Halifax, of Dublin – not of Edinburgh and Hampstead. I don't mean always, today, or for all of them – but for

the vanguard of the people, the thoughtful ones. You will know
Mayakovsky's reflections on the difficulties of writing 'Big Poetry –
poetry genuinely created', which can be understood by the people. I
think this is your greatest danger – you must *never* let yourself, by
the possible insensitivity or even hostility of those who should be
your greatest allies – into the arms of the culture boys who
'appreciate' pretentiousness and posturing. They would kill your
writing – because you, more than any other poet I know, are an
instrument through which thousands of others can become articu-
late. And you must not forget that your songs and ballads are not
trivialities – they are quite as important as the 'Elegies'.

Thompson's approach was the opposite of that taken by Douglas Young
and chimed with Hamish's own thinking; this letter became a lodestone
that would guide Hamish for the rest of his creative life. He notes: 'No
one can interest me in "fine" writing as such. Any fool poet can write well
if he happens to have the talent – but the poets who love have a much
larger problem, not only to write well, but to express once again – after a
lapse of several centuries, the *whole* world, and this impinges not on one
individual but on the collective.' It was as 'a whole', and in the grandest
company that Hamish wanted his Elegies to stand. Who were the artists
who embraced this 'whole world' in their creativity and philosophical
vision? Hamish named them – Homer, Dante, Rabelais, Shakespeare,
Michelangelo . . . and he knew that, however good or bad a poet he
might be, like them, he was a man propelled by love. He also knew that
'artistic love', in modern societies, must address and embrace 'the
collective'; and that the art produced by these 'collective artists' would
be different in kind from that produced for the onanistic delectation of
any educated elite, be they sensitive, artistic or privileged. This 'collective
enthusiasm' was no assumed pose; it was naturally part of Hamish's
being. His ambition to achieve 'wholeness' was part of a philosophical
vision grounded in a democratic wish to raise the bar of our understanding of what human beings are capable of. Similar ideas were also
being expressed at this time by various Marxist writers – including
Arnold Klingender, Ernst Fischer and his friend, the very young John
Berger, with whom Hamish was to work closely in his old age.

In April, a vividly compact letter arrived from the Irish playwright Sean
O'Casey. He too embraced the Elegies as a marvellous new achievement:

Good man – a grand book, thank you for sending it to me. I get in it
the brown snarly rocks, the suffocating sand, the sigh of all the
laochrais, German & English, Scots & Irish, falling for ever into the

sniffling sand, falling forever from the hills, the dales, the streets they knew, and the warm kiss from a favoured lass when the times were quiet . . . *Na laochrai Eirean agus na Laochrai Alban.* I am so glad you got the Somerset Maugham award for the work; it deserves it. And I hear in it that the desert which has buried so many dead, should now itself be buried by the living, that we might see the blossoming of the rose . . . May it be but the beginning of a great time for you.

The subtle Rosicrucian symbolism in that letter was placed there with a purpose, and shortly afterwards the English poet David Gascoyne wrote an equally affirming letter:

> . . . Since I read your Elegies last Spring, your name has been in my mind as one of the small group of contemporary poets whose work especially interests me. The Elegies made a real impact on me, and I regard them as the most significant martial poems to have come out of the war: something about them only to compare with Wilfred Owen, David Jones (maybe also Isaac Rosenberg?). The form and manipulation are enterprising and efficient enough to attract unusual attention, no doubt; but the spirit is what makes them rare and unforgettable. Not much warm-blooded, aristocratic authenticity and humanity about like yours . . . It seems to me that you may not care for the epithet 'aristocratic' as applied to the spirit of your poetry: but of course I don't mean anything 'ruling class' by the word, only in the sense that the Carpenter's Son was aristocratic.

The professional reviewers, however, were less forthcoming – respectful, not impassioned; discursive, not philosophical – and most seem to have been slightly intimidated by the sudden arrival of such a fully formed voice. In the early fifties, Hamish collected the various reviews together and divided them into three categories – A) favourable: *Times Literary Supplement, Daily Worker, New Statesman and Nation, Varsity Supplement, Tatler* (Elizabeth Bowen), *Poetry Quarterly, Observer, The National Weekly, Radio Review* (1952), B) middling: *Galliard, Irish Writing,* C) unfavourable: *Edinburgh Evening Dispatch, Scotsman* (C. Graves).[1]

1. Thus, the critical response was positive – except in Scotland, where the BBC added insult to injury by refusing the Elegies any airtime at all. Perhaps, by 1949, the Second World War was being seen as 'old hat'. Perhaps the left-wing nationalism evident in the poems was deemed unacceptable in the wake of National Socialism. Perhaps men like Wilfred Taylor used their influence to tip the scales against a man who was now being quietly tarred as a homosexual.

However, if the contemporary media response to the Elegies in Scotland was muted, today's academic 'silence' is deafening. Hamish's poetry is not part of the secondary school examination syllabus in Scotland, no Scottish university currently teaches his literary work at undergraduate level, no postgraduate students appear to be engaged in studying any aspect of his work. 'The literature' also shows a complete lack of interest. No recent critical studies of twentieth-century English and Scottish literature have paid serious attention to Hamish's work and most scholarly studies of the poetry of the Second World War now seem to exclude him. For example, Jonathan Bolton's *Personal Landscapes – British Poets in Egypt during the Second World War* (Palgrave Macmillan, 1997), Linda M. Shires' *British Poetry of the Second World War* (Macmillan, 1985) and Edna Longley's *Poetry in the Wars* make no reference to him. Similarly, while the walls and vaults of the Scottish National Portrait Gallery bulge with portraits of Scotland's great and good, it holds no painting of Hamish Henderson.

Thus the question must be asked: is the poetry of Hamish Henderson really no good? Was Douglas Young right in describing the Elegies as no more lasting that the war journalism of the *Daily Express*? Are the Elegies a relic of a now dying modernist aesthetic, nationalistic rhetoric, mere communist propaganda? Are the poems too Scottish for the English and too English for the Scots and best confined to oblivion? Was Hamish's literary output so small as to invalidate any claim that he might be a major poet? Or is it because he became the champion of Scotland's oral tradition that literary academics, paid to teach and research written literature, ignore him? In an age when 'the rules have changed', is the poetry of Hamish Henderson now an anachronism? Or are his ideas more important than ever – and publicly damned for that reason? Certainly, for sixty years attempts have been made to pigeon-hole Hamish – both as a man and as a writer – as a narrow-minded Marxist, as a drunk, as 'a folklorist seduced by the rude bawling of peasants'.

One problem for academics is that, although the Elegies are directly based on personal experience, they are also Miltonic in their ambition. When Hamish writes 'I want the whole and with the whole my hairt', he means it. Another problem for academics is that, even if they look seriously at the Elegies they shy from the fact that these poems comprise only a small part of Hamish's oeuvre as a war poet. The common judgement is that Hamish's output as a poet was small and his war poetry merely evidence of a promise that was never fulfilled. Be that as it may – the facts are that Hamish's oeuvre as a war poet was enormous: he was probably the most various and productive poet of the whole war, in any country, in any language; and he, like few poets, worked in many languages. His war poetry can be classified in various ways but I have subdivided it as follows:

1) Poems of Germany and the English Home Front (1939–40).
2) Poems of the Home Front (Scotland) (1939–41).
3) Songs and Poems of the Pioneers (1940).
4) Songs of Sabotage and Sedition (1940–45).
5) Elegies for the Dead in Cyrenaica (1942–47).
6) Desert Songs from North Africa (1942–43).
7) Songs and Poems of the Italian Campaign (1943–45).
8) Poems Translated in a Time of War (1939–46).
9) Ballads of World War II – in Five Languages (1939–46).
10) The Bawdy at Home and Abroad (1939–46).
11) Aphorisms of Heaven and Hell (1939–46).

Hamish Henderson was not therefore the author of 'one slim volume of war poetry' and he is a poet ripe for re-evaluation as the author, adapter, translator and collector of something like one thousand songs and poems written during the six years of the Second World War. That such a vast body of work could be written and collected while he was involved in continuous interrogation and frontline action is astounding. And this literary achievement was only half of his poetic achievement because, throughout the war, Hamish lived and performed his duties as a Highland bard – singing the songs and carrying the traditions of his people into the bars and out onto the battlefields of Africa and Europe. This man was the last champion of a genuinely druidic bardic tradition. He carried the learning and music of his people, so that those fighting and dying around him knew who they were, where they came from and what they doing – in the midst of the mad slaughter of the rational world.

Index

Page numbers followed by n (as in 19n) indicate information appearing only in a footnote.

This sketch was given to Hamish Henderson by the artist, Angelo Savelli, and is discussed in Appendix 2.

al Capt. Hamish Henderson
cordialmente

Roma 20.6.44